Karloff and Lugosi

Karloff and Lugosi

The Story of a
Haunting Collaboration

WITH A COMPLETE FILMOGRAPHY
OF THEIR FILMS TOGETHER

by
Gregory William Mank

McFarland & Company, Inc., Publishers
Jefferson, North Carolina, and London

British Library Cataloguing-in-Publication data available

Library of Congress Cataloguing-in-Publication Data

Mank, Gregory William, 1950–
   Karloff and Lugosi.

   [Includes index.]
   [Filmography: p.]
   1. Karloff, Boris, 1887–1969.   2. Lugosi, Bela,
1882–1956.   3. Motion picture actors and actresses —
United States — Biography.   4. Horror films — United
States — History and criticism.   I. Title.
PN2287.K25M66   1990   791.43'028'0922 [B]   90-42734

ISBN 0-89950-437-X (lib. bdg. : 50# alk. paper)

Manufactured in the United States of America

McFarland & Company, Inc., Publishers
   Box 611, Jefferson, North Carolina 28640

For my beloved parents,
Bill and Fran Mank,
who always protected me
from real-life monsters

Table of Contents

Acknowledgments

I wish to thank the following (in alphabetical order), all of whom contributed to this book: Buddy Barnett (Cinema Collectors), the late Charles T. Barton, Richard Bojarski, Carroll Borland, Eddie Brandt (Saturday Matinee), John Brunas, Michael Brunas, Mae Clarke, Robert Clarke, Rita Corday, Frances Drake, Mike Fitzgerald (MCA Video), Alex Gordon, Richard Gordon, Dan Gunderman, Valerie Hobson, Josephine Hutchinson, the late Steve Jochsberger (Horrors!), Zita Johann, Tom Johnson, the late Elsa Lanchester, the late Reginald Le Borg, the late David Lewis, Arthur Lubin, Doug McClelland, David Manners, Marian Marsh, Dick May, Julie May, Charles A. Moses, the late Alan Napier, Bill Neal, John Norris, Garydon Rhodes (president, Bela Lugosi Society), Blackie Seymour, Curt Siodmak, Sally Stark, Gloria Stuart, Jim Trocki, George Turner (*American Cinematographer*), Shirley Ulmer, Russell Wade, Malcolm Willits (Collectors Book Store), Scott Wilson, Robert Wise, Ian Wolfe.

Also thanks to the Academy of Motion Picture Arts & Sciences Library, Los Angeles, and the Lincoln Center Library for the Performing Arts, New York.

Special thanks must go to Ned Comstock, of the Archives of Performing Arts at the University of Southern California, and to the staff of the RKO Archives, Hollywood.

Special billing, too, for Gary Svehla *(Midnight Marquee)*, John E. Parnum *(Cinemacabre)*, and Tom Weaver (author of *Interviews with B Science Fiction and Horror Movie Makers*) for their contributions to the "Mythos" chapter—with an extra "thank you" to Tom for his leads, humor and encouragement.

Finally, my heartfelt appreciation to the late Lillian Lugosi Donlevy, Sara Karloff Cotten, and Bela Lugosi, Jr., for their kindness and cooperation.

And—climactically—my thanks and love to my wife Barbara, who printed these chapters from our computer, accompanied me on my interviews, encouraged me in so many ways, and, who years ago, listened raptly as I told her the plot of *The Black Cat* during a date. For saving my life from becoming a horror movie—my deep love and gratitude always.

Preface

Together, they haunt imaginations, like beloved ogres from the Brothers Grimm.

Bela Lugosi's Dracula — tall, sleek, satanic, posing with a candle on an ancient gothic staircase, listening fondly to "the children of the night" howling mournfully outside his decaying castle in Transylvania...

Boris Karloff's Frankenstein's monster — gawky, towering, eyes like an insane baby deer, his scarred hands pathetically reaching for the rays of the sun, shining through the skylight of his creator's blasphemous laboratory...

Over thirty years have passed since Bela Lugosi, poor, forgotten, but purged of drug addiction, was buried near Hollywood, wrapped in his Dracula cape. Over twenty years have passed since Boris Karloff, wealthy, celebrated, a journeyman actor to the end, died in a London hospital, almost as he had wished — "with my boots, and my greasepaint, on." Yet the names of these men loom today legendary.

Fear has always been one of mankind's strangest, favorite indulgences. For ages, little children have loved fairy tales, and their villains: the Wolf, trussed up in Grandma's nightgown, leering "The better to *eat* you with!" at the terrified Little Red Riding Hood; the bellowing Giant, roaring "Fee-Fi-Fo-Fum...!" as he pursued Jack to the Beanstalk; the cackling Witch, gleefully sticking a skeletal finger through a cage to see if Hansel and Gretel were plump enough to pop into her oven. Today, thanks to television, and its fantasy-indulging mistress, video, the old classic horror films have joined Grimm and Andersen, as Dracula, Frankenstein's monster, the Mummy, the Invisible Man and the Wolf Man have perpetuated their popularity; they have become the fairy tale characters for recent generations.

As such, Boris Karloff and Bela Lugosi, the screen's most famous bogeymen, have not become mere nostalgia. They have become folklore.

Boris Karloff struck many as a gentle British exile; gaunt, aesthetic, his face the Halloween mask of a poetic demon, his lisp an impersonator's daydream; in love with his pets and flowers and "dear old Monster"; the masterful creator of a parade of versatile horror characters.

Bela Lugosi, the proud Hungarian exile, was tall, handsome, his Slavic features and rich accent evoking a Dracula Bram Stoker never envisioned to a generation of moviegoers. Proud yet resentful of his horror fame, Lugosi dreamed of his days as Romeo and fleshed out the most flyweight scripts with his bombastic personality.

Each star a legend as both man and actor, new significance can be found in their screen unions; they teamed in seven motion pictures (aside from guest appearances in 1934 in *Gift of Gab* for Universal and *Screen Snapshots* #11 for Columbia). The films themselves were often among Hollywood's most eccentric products; the participation of Karloff and Lugosi, noteworthy then, makes even their most dreadful efforts of historical note today.

First, of course, came Universal's three celebrated "KARLOFF and Bela LUGOSI" vehicles of the mid-30s, Hollywood's "Golden Age of Horror," when that peculiar (but very telling) billing (without the "Boris") promised moviegoers the hoariest of nightmares. Vignettes from these films are unforgettable. There were the "Poe Homages": 1934's *The Black Cat,* with Karloff, in satanic hairdo and stripped to the waist, hanging on his own "embalming rack" like a snared prize wolf, Lugosi leering, "Have you ever seen an animal skinned . . . ?" and preparing to flay him alive as Liszt booms in the background; 1935's *The Raven,* with Karloff, his face hideously disfigured by his costar, madly firing his gun at full-length mocking mirrors, Lugosi sadistically laughing behind a dungeon window. And there was 1936's *The Invisible Ray,* a striking mating of assured gothic horror with the maiden genre of science fiction, with Karloff, in black cloak and slouch hat, glowing with "Radium X," preparing to kill a proud Lugosi with the words, "It'd be easiest just to shake hands. . . ."

After Hollywood had buried the horror genre alive for over two years, Universal's 1939 *Son of Frankenstein* premiered Friday, January 13, 1939. Giant, Germanic, it epically presented Lugosi's bearded, broken-necked Ygor and Karloff's melancholy monster as two of the most striking and oddly appealing misfits of screen history.

In 1940, the stars made their final tandem Universal film — *Black Friday,* a fascinating misfire that had the temerity to not feature the actors together in a single scene; *You'll Find Out,* that same year for RKO, employed Boris, Bela and Peter Lorre as stooges for Kay Kyser and his coven of musical curiosities.

Finally, their last film, RKO's 1945 *The Body Snatcher,* produced by Val Lewton, is a masterpiece — and a movingly poetic, tragic final union of the screen's Greatest Horror Stars.

The styles were unique; but together — be they bastardizing Poe, perpetuating Mary Wollstonecraft Shelley, or improving upon Robert Louis Stevenson — Karloff and Lugosi created a queer, sublime chemistry in their work together. They complemented each other dynamically; they were magical box office names, like Gable and Harlow, Laurel and Hardy, Mac-Donald and Eddy. And, as time adds an increasingly romantic aura to their work, movie disciples have argued the "rivalry" of the maestros of horror — often forgetting that no real "rivalry" ever existed during their lifetimes.

Bela Lugosi always referred to Boris Karloff as "my rival." However, from the Yuletide of 1931, when Universal released *Frankenstein,* and the world first beheld Karloff's monster — a role Lugosi had scorned and lost in the wake of *Dracula* — Karloff always surpassed Lugosi in billing, salary and box office power. In the twelve-and-a-half years that Karloff outlived Lugosi, his fame and stardom eclipsed Lugosi even more; venerable Karloff became "the King" while Lugosi (partially, no doubt, because of his pathetic demise) became known more and more by the term Boris always applied to him — "Poor Bela." Then, after Karloff's death, an insurrection of Lugosiphiles took place, emotionally arguing for Lugosi's supremacy over his famous, intimidating costar. As debates waged of "Karloff the Actor" vs. "Lugosi the Personality" (often ignoring the real powers of each man), the Video Age advented, opening floodgates of critical reappraisal which have carved their own judgments.

Strangely lost in the academic debates and the shadows of the growing legend, however, have been the real pathos and human dimension of this filmic relationship. Indeed, behind the billing "Karloff and Bela Lugosi," a sad and moving Hollywood melodrama was playing. It was a saga of ego, Machiavellian studio ploys, and jealousy, acted against the scenery of Universal's pastoral back lot and RKO's tomb-like soundstages; a drama fated to end almost as horrifically as their screen shockers.

Hence this book.

Writing this book was a true archaeological adventure. Research included analyzing the Universal records — the budgets, the salaries, the production reports — made available through the ever patient, helpful and resourceful Ned Comstock and the University of Southern California Archive of Performing Arts. Then there was the RKO warehouse in Hollywood, with that late-lamented studio's fastidiously-preserved files, now a part of the Ted Turner empire. These records have become a time machine back to the Hollywood studios of the past, and revealed — free of romantic flourish, and often in cruel honesty — just how each studio respectively regarded and valued Karloff and Lugosi.

Of course, there were the files of the Academy of Motion Picture Arts and Sciences in Los Angeles, the Lincoln Center Performing Arts Library in New York, and the American Film Institute in Washington.

As always, however, the real excitement and insight for this book came in interviews with the Hollywood survivors who participated in the Karloff and Lugosi legend: David Manners, the famous, effete hero of *Dracula, The Mummy,* and *The Black Cat;* Mae Clarke, the leading lady of *Frankenstein;* Gloria Stuart, the porcelain blonde beauty of *The Old Dark House* and *The*

Invisible Man; Zita Johann, the infamous Anck-es-en-Amon of *The Mummy;*
Carroll Borland, "Luna" of *Mark of the Vampire;* the late Elsa Lanchester, *Bride of Frankenstein;* Valerie Hobson, Elizabeth of *Bride of Frankenstein;* Ian Wolfe, "Pinky" of *The Raven;* Marian Marsh, storybook heroine of *The Black Room;* Frances Drake, moon-eyed leading lady of *The Invisible Ray;* Josephine Hutchinson, the elegant Elsa of *Son of Frankenstein;* Arthur Lubin, director of *Black Friday;* Curt Siodmak, screenplay author of *Black Friday, The Wolf Man, Frankenstein Meets the Wolf Man,* and other Universal melodramas; Robert Wise, director of *The Body Snatcher,* and his cast members Russell Wade, Rita Corday and Robert Clarke; the late Charles T. Barton, director of *Abbott and Costello Meet Frankenstein* and *Abbott and Costello Meet the Killer, Boris Karloff;* Alex Gordon and Richard Gordon, the British producers who associated with Karloff and Lugosi during the curious era of the early 1950s; and the late Reginald Le Borg, director of Lugosi's last completed feature, *The Black Sleep,* and Karloff's *Voodoo Island.*

I must thank also such people as the late Alan Napier, the veteran British character player (and close friend of Karloff); Julie May, niece of the late David Lewis (the man who had shared James Whale's life for over 20 years), and, finally, three very special individuals: Sara Jane Karloff, Boris's only child; Bela Lugosi, Jr., Bela's only child; and the late Lillian Lugosi Donlevy, Bela's fourth wife and mother of Bela, Jr.

My adventures with these people (some of which will be documented in the book) were, in some cases, sagas in themselves. I am indebted to them all, not only for their memories of Karloff and Lugosi, but for their evocations of their fascinating satellites: the arch, bitter James Whale, the forgotten Carl Laemmle, Jr., the doomed, alcoholic Colin Clive, the kinky Lionel Atwill, the insanity-fearing Edgar Ulmer, the elegant Basil Rathbone, the inelegant Lon Chaney, Jr., the lovely Evelyn Ankers, the tragic Dwight Frye, the hypersensitive Val Lewton, and the many others who became heroes, villains, and the vital supporting cast of a real-life melodrama.

This book covers the crossroads, the intersections of the careers of Karloff and Lugosi; it does not purport to be a documentation of each man's complete career, tackled in other books by authors of varying depth and perception. Also, I offer my apologies in advance to devout fans of both actors, whose sensitivities might be hurt by the remarks of some people interviewed for this book. Please realize their opinions do not necessarily reflect the feelings of the author.

Above all, however, I hope the book conveys some of the magic of two remarkable men, each beloved, each irreplaceable, and each finding his own immortality in the gothic fairy tales of the movies.

—Gregory William Mank
Delta, Pennsylvania
Spring, 1989

1
Universal City, Summer, 1931

The most heartrending aspect of the creature's life, for us, was his ultimate desertion by his creator. It was as though man, in his blundering, searching attempts to improve himself, was to find himself deserted by his God.
— Boris Karloff, on Frankenstein's monster

Anybody can moan and grunt.
— Bela Lugosi, on Frankenstein's monster

September, 1931. Universal City, California. The little movie studio nestles under the looming, moonlit purple mountains of the San Fernando Valley. Stars fill the sky; atop the studio's highest hill sits a sparkling, 500,000-gallon lake.

On the back lot, with its gingerbread Tyrolean village, the joyous German Army marched in *All Quiet on the Western Front.* There can be found Notre Dame Cathedral, from Lon Chaney's *The Hunchback of Notre Dame,* the old ruins of von Stroheim's Monte Carlo casino from *Foolish Wives,* the Wild West Town. Spanish star bungalows stand, each with its little lawn and flower garden, on lanes where palm trees are sentries, and great soundstages, silent in the dark.

Suddenly, the headlights of a wheezing Ford flash through the darkness. A lonely figure with the face of a lovesick Satan walks toward a bungalow, where solitary light streams from the windows. It is the makeup department. The actor is Boris Karloff. It is time to begin a new day on *Frankenstein.*

English exile Karloff has experienced all variety of strange situations as he scratched out a living in stock companies and Hollywood; yet his present engagement is one of the most bizarre episodes of a bizarre life. Far more frightening a film role than Galloway, the glowering convict of *The Criminal Code;* far more grotesque than Isopod, ex-divinity school pervert of *Five Star Final* — here is Mary Shelley's Frankenstein's monster itself! Karloff has to report to the studio at an unholy hour for a torturous makeup ordeal; so demanding is his role that the actor's gaunt figure is melting away under the sadistic summer sun. Such an assignment! Yet the actor counts his blessings; the role means a salary, and the monster is, in Karloff's opinion, "one of the most sympathetic characters ever created in the world of English letters. . . ."

The City of Streets
Universal Studio
Universal City, Calif.

Schettlenmyer Photo

Boris Karloff relaxes on the *Frankenstein* set as Jack Pierce (center) and an assistant refine the monster make-up.

Meanwhile in Hollywood, tall, lean, handsome Bela Lugosi extinguishes his cigar, and wraps up his habitual post-midnight addiction — reading. As is his custom, the star prepares for bed shortly before dawn. The former Romeo of the Hungarian stage, the triumphant creator of *Dracula* on Broadway and in Universal's hit movie, he is at the peak of a 30-year career — and can smile in relief that he would just now be reporting to Universal, had he signed to play that "dumb brute" in *Frankenstein*. Imagine — moaning under all that putty, without a word of dialogue! Surely Fate was kind in sparing him the dumb part, and it had gone to that sad-eyed character player, Karloff. Poor fellow! The part's nothing, but perhaps it will make him a little money . . .

Opposite: Universal City (in the 1920s): far up center is Notre Dame cathedral sans towers; far right is the Monte Carlo casino from von Stroheim's *Foolish Wives*.

Frankenstein poster, 1931.

Title card for *Frankenstein,* 1931.

*   *   *

Uncle Carl Laemmle,
has a very large faemmle.
    — Hollywood satire by Ogden Nash

By 1931, Carl Laemmle, five feet tall, a 64-year-old Bavarian immigrant and founder of Universal Studios, New York, in 1912, patriarch of Universal City, California, since 1915, producer of *Foolish Wives* and *The Hunchback of Notre Dame* and *The Phantom of the Opera,* was merrily ensconced in his own legend. He regally resided in Benedict Canyon in a palace named "Dias Dorados," complete with its own zoo; gambled lavishly Saturday nights in Tijuana; had the distinction of being the only Hollywood producer ever to try to engage the Pope for a movie, only to balk when the Pope demanded a $10,000 donation to charity ("Forget Pope," wired Laemmle); and had personally hired John Drinkwater, biographer of Lincoln, Byron, and Robert E. Lee, to pen the official Laemmle biography. Reputedly, signs on the Universal bungalow lawns read, "Keep Off the Grass — Carl Laemmle."

Still, "Uncle Carl" Laemmle was most notorious in Hollywood for his "Foreign Legion": his shameless, wholesale hiring of Bavarian relatives and friends for studio positions. It was a titanic nepotism, which climaxed Sunday, April 28, 1929 — when Carl Laemmle, Jr., received the post of general manager of Universal City as a 21st birthday present.

Like his beaming Dad, "Junior" Laemmle was barely five feet tall; his tiny size, bright eyes, and excessively toothy smile made him resemble a cousin to Snow White's Seven Dwarfs. Universal PR reverentially painted Junior (always smartly dressed, and ever with a fresh carnation in his lapel) as "such a babe" and as "a boy wonder," à la MGM's Irving Thalberg (whom Laemmle Sr. had lost years before over money) with a shy, sensitive nature, dramatically inclined toward popular novels and plays.

Junior, however, had problems. "He was very pleasant, and a nice man, but talented? No," says Gloria Stuart, Universal's beautiful blonde contract lady of the early thirties, well-remembered for *The Old Dark House* and *The Invisible Man*. "I remember once, at a Hollywood party, he asked me to dance," remembers Zita Johann, portrayer of the reincarnated Anck-es-en-Amon in *The Mummy*. "Junior was a very sensitive man, and he shyly whispered as we danced, 'We have a lot in common.'" Shirley Ulmer (widow of *The Black Cat* director Edgar G. Ulmer, and a former in-law of the Laemmle family by a previous marriage), remembers him very well:

> He was a poor soul, really. He was under the control of a very tyrannical father and family. His big love was actress Alice Day, and Uncle Carl kicked him out of it (he didn't want any boy of his to marry what he called "schitkas"), and I heard the same thing happened in Junior's romance with Constance Cummings.... As a producer, he may not have been creative within himself, but he could put a package together. He knew about casting, he knew who could direct.... But he got sicker and sicker. It was very sad....

Both spoiled and handicapped by fate, the hypochondriacal Junior was sometimes colossally ignorant in studio matters; reputedly, he once gave a director dozens of silent films to burn for a bonfire scene, never considering their historical worth. Junior's "throne room" at Universal, decorated for "the Crown Prince" in red velvet and mahogany, usually hosted knots of race track touts, all advising the compulsive little gambler while directors and actors awaited audience for hours. And Hollywood rumored that Universal's elfish Crown Prince (who never married) fancied himself a ladies man — especially in the throne room, where he invited some female contractees for "interviews."

Once, Junior summoned an unsuspecting actress from New England to his opulent lair — only (according to the lady) to look at her legs, wince, and close the door in her face. Her name was Bette Davis — who, over 50 years later, said of Junior's distaste, "Thank God!"

So it was Junior who reigned at Universal, and it was a feeble rule; in 1930, the studio lost $2.5 million Depression dollars. However, there was hope. On Wednesday night, November 5, 1930, at the Academy's $10 per plate banquet at the Ambassador Hotel, Universal's *All Quiet on the Western Front* — which Junior had produced over the figuratively dead bodies of all studio advisers — had won the Academy Award as Best Picture. It was "Uncle Carl," of course, who accepted the award smiling that this was his second greatest thrill — the first was when he became a grandfather. Junior was also producer of a St. Valentine's Day, 1931, release that had been one of the season's top hits — *Dracula*. And now, Junior was producing a new melodrama, for which Universal held high hopes. The story was Mary Shelley's *Frankenstein* — and the director was Universal's "ace," James Whale.

> There was always a touch of the macabre, the sinister, the sadistic about Jimmy, you couldn't get away from it. . . . To the English aristocracy in Hollywood, Jimmy never made it. He was simply "that funny queer who makes horror movies." After he stopped making them, he ceased to exist. . . .
> I remember the scandalous stories about Jimmy. . . . Shortly before he died, he invited me to see his pool house. I remember walking with him through a bit of his English garden, down to the pool. . . . It was a magnificent pool house, with very impressive Graeco/Roman pillars, rather dwarfing the pool. But inside was the real surprise: a luxuriously furnished chamber — couches, chaise lounges, daybeds — and, dominating all, crimson-red velvet curtains, on the pool side, from floor to ceiling — twenty feet.
> Well, I'm an open-air boy, and not impressed by "decor" — or orgies.
> — Alan Napier

May 29, 1957. A maid named Anna Ryan walked down the hill behind a lovely villa in Pacific Palisades, through a beautiful English garden, down to the Graeco/Roman studio, with the 20-foot high pillars, looming over a swimming pool. Seeking her master to announce lunch, the maid looked into the shiny water of the pool — and screamed. There, floating face-up, with an awful gash in the forehead, was the fully-clothed corpse of her master, James Whale.

Hollywood cruelly considered the mysterious death of Whale a piquantly baroque climax to the English director's long exile from the studios, and a sordid scandal followed. There were ugly rumors of Whale's affairs with young boys; tales of a wild orgy, which supposedly ended with the director's body being tossed into the pool; stories of Whale having his head bashed in by a beach boy lover whose nude portrait the victim was painting. It wasn't until 25 years later that a suicide note finally became public — a note explaining the last act of a lonely old man, terrified of old age and insanity.

In the spring of 1931, James Whale, fresh from his triumph of Tiffany's 1930 *Journey's End,* had signed a five-year Universal contract. Overnight, he reigned supreme, proudly heralded as "The Genius who made *Journey's End. . .*!" All took notice of the tall, foxy "Jimmy," handsome as Lucifer, his red hair salted with silver, a cheroot usually in hand, peacocking across the lot like a Byronic hero. High up on the mountain above Universal, the

Jimmy Whale, satanic "Ace" director at Universal in the early 1930s. Whale's insistence on casting Karloff as the monster in *Frankenstein,* despite Universal's preference for Lugosi, made him a dramatic figure in the intertwined lives of the two horror stars.

ex-cartoonist, painter and actor could overlook the panorama below — the zoo, the lakes, the edifices of all countries — all waiting to serve his dramatic imagination.

In truth, the English aristocrat who elegantly paraded about Universal City was a role James Whale had rehearsed passionately. Born in a sooty village under Dudley Castle, England, the 42-year-old Whale (who vowed he was 35) was actually one of ten children (seven of whom survived infancy) of a blast-furnaceman and a social-working nurse. His dramatic training came

Boris Karloff in the early 1930s.

at a World War I prison camp in Holzminden, Germany, where the second lieutenant staged and acted in plays presented by his fellow POWs. After the armistice, Whale abandoned his post as a cartoonist for the London *Bystander,* trained in repertory and in Shakespeare at Stratford-on-Avon and leaped into the "wicked world" of the London theatre as an actor, director, stage manager and scenic designer. His first real success was as "Gas" Jones in 1925's *A Comedy of Good and Evil,* a play about the child of the Devil. The play's star was 22-year-old, 6'5" Alan Napier — a superb actor who, after scores of plays and movies, became known to millions by playing Alfred, butler of the *Batman* teleseries.

Alan Napier died in 1988. A few years before, in his little castle with its tower, hanging on the cliffs of the Pacific Palisades, a vital Napier, silver and bronzed in his eighties, vividly remembered this major force of Universal:

> Jimmy was indeed enigmatic — with a taint of sado-masochism in his homo-sexuality, which doubtless became more dominant as success adversely affected his career....
> He had been a skinny, slightly undersized kid in a lower middle-class family in a small industrial town in the midlands. With his artistic talents and ambitions, he was a fish out of water.... He had a dream. After the war, he entered the theatre, learned to speak like a gentleman, realizing this opened doors to advancement. There is, of course, much homosexuality in the theatre, and Jimmy took to it like a duck to water, picking up the tones, the gestures, the mannerisms of his "gentlemen" lovers. (Did you know that gentlemen in England hold their cigarettes and penises differently than the working classes?)

Whale progressed, always ambitiously. In London's theatre circles, he became famous for elegantly dancing the tango, usually performed with Doris Zinkeisen, a stage designer whom Whale reportedly loved. After they separated, Whale became totally homosexual — and found other dancing partners. Alan Napier remembered:

> After a matinee on a hot day, I was removing my makeup, stripped to the waist. Jimmy came up behind me, laid delicate fingers on my shoulders, looked me in the eye in the mirror with an enigmatic smile and said, "I know someone who would be *crazy* about those shoulders." A few days later he invited me to a party to meet my prospective lover.
> "Come in pajamas," Jimmy said. "There'll be dancing."
> I went — curiosity killed the cat, and the party killed any homosexuality in my little psyche.... Jimmy was there, as much at ease as I was a fish out of water.

Whale scored as an actor, playing the lunatic son of Charles Laughton, helping his father imprison and torture a young beauty in 1928's *The Man with Red Hair*. His life changed, however, on January 21, 1929; *Journey's End*, R.C. Sherriff's World War I saga of a tormented alcoholic young captain commanding a doomed dugout, opened in London's West End. Directed by Whale, the stark drama became the town's hottest ticket — and launched three men strangely fated for Hollywood tragedy: Colin Clive, who played the alcoholic Stanhope, and who drank himself to death in 1937; George Zucco (who, according to John Carradine, had suffered a shriveled arm and lost fingers in World War I), who played the gentle officer Osborne, and whose final mysterious decade ended in a Los Angeles sanitarium in 1960; and James Whale.

Whale's success with the play on Broadway won him passage to Hollywood, to prepare the film version of *Journey's End* for Tiffany Studios.

Karloff as Frankenstein's monster.

For experience, Whale first served as "dialogue director" of Paramount's 1929 *The Love Doctor* and Howard Hughes' 1930 classic *Hell's Angels*. "Blonde Bombshell" Jean Harlow, formerly of Laurel & Hardy two-reelers, won cinema infamy in *Hell's Angels;* Whale had to provoke a performance out of the curvaceous novice, and the icy English homosexual and the breezy, nipple-icing platinum blonde detested each other. Ironically, Whale's ashes would be entombed just around the corner from Harlow's $25,000 crypt, with its stained glass window and candelabra from the Seven Hills of Rome, at the Great Mausoleum at Forest Lawn, Glendale. Such are the ways of fate in Hollywood.

Journey's End was a great cinema success, and Junior Laemmle — who had been inspired to produce *All Quiet on the Western Front* after seeing *Journey's End* on the Broadway stage — signed Whale to a deluxe contract. Whale had just completed *Waterloo Bridge*, which promised to be one of Universal's successes of the season. It was Mae Clarke, as the pathetic streetwalker Myra, who played the unforgettable climax of walking into the bombs falling upon Waterloo Bridge.

Miss Clarke, best remembered for the grapefruit she got in the face from

James Cagney in 1931's *The Public Enemy* ("How did it feel? Wet!"), lives today at the Motion Picture Country House, where she rides about the grounds on an adult tricycle, complete with an E.T. bell. She made three films for Whale. "James Whale is a giant to me, and my words are inadequate," she says emotionally. "Always he was the plu-perfect gentleman, and not only that—the *genius.*" As for her big scene in *Waterloo Bridge:*

> I remember it—a night scene on the back lot of Universal. . . . The feeling of that scene was so overpowering! Everyone felt a reality over pretense.
> By that time, we had all learned to take advantage of every second Mr. Whale could give us—because his finger and his mind were in every single facet of the production. You'd ask, "Where's Mr. Whale?" "Oh, he's up on the boom crane tower, creating the bomber effect." (He wanted to see Myra from the bomber's point of view.) You'd ask, "Where's Mr. Whale now?" "Oh, he's in checking the sound." He knew just where he wanted the shadows . . . everything. It was *his* picture: a James Whale Production!

So Universal gave *Frankenstein* to James Whale, with a $262,007 budget and a 30-day shooting schedule. The director was something of a monster himself, sewn together by bits of a dream, the emulation of those "gentlemen lovers" Alan Napier recalled, and an arrogance; in fact, in creating his "genius" self, Whale had played his own Frankenstein as well, and as such had a strange sympathy for both "grand characterizations."

Meanwhile, the studio tried to bypass the stories, already leaked to the Hollywood press, of the behind-the-scenes machinations that had gone on before shooting officially began. For James Whale had not been the original director.

And Boris Karloff had not been the original monster.

*   *   *

I was a star in my country, and will not be a scarecrow over here!
— Bela Lugosi, during his test for *Frankenstein*

Monday, September 29, 1930. Universal had begun shooting *Dracula.* For Bela Lugosi, starring in the title role of this movie, budgeted at $355,050, directed by Tod Browning, was the climax to a career of nearly 30 years; indeed, so thrilled was he to reprise his Broadway vampire in the film that he signed a contract for only $500 a week. Decades later, Universal would resurrect this contract from deep in the vaults when the studio—hell-bent on wringing the last ounce of blood from Bela Lugosi's corpse—waged a 13-year battle with the Lugosi heirs to defeat their claim to "right of likeness" compensation for Universal merchandising Lugosi's image.

During this battle, the only surviving star of *Dracula* was David Manners. In 1976, 40 years after he made his last Hollywood movie, Manners— still classically dapper—was in his house high in Pacific Palisades, pooh-poohing his legendary status as the romantic lead of *Dracula, The Mummy* and *The Black Cat.* I asked about *Dracula:*

Bela Lugosi in the early 1930s.

As for *Dracula,* Bela Lugosi was a mystery, and I have only one vivid memory of him from the picture. I can still see Lugosi, parading up and down the stage, posing in front of a full-length mirror, throwing his cape over his shoulder, and shouting, "I AM DRACULA!"

The memory caused Manners to burst out laughing. Yet, with his anecdote, he had strangely captured the ego, passion, solitude and tragedy that was Bela Lugosi.

Nobody knew Bela Lugosi more intimately nor loved him more deeply than did his fourth wife, Lillian Lugosi Donlevy, who died in 1981. The widow of actor Brian Donlevy (who died in 1972), she was a tall, handsome woman, kind, candid, a little shy, almost childlike; as she sat in her modest apartment, not far from the old MGM lot in Culver City, a cigarette holder was the only sign of distinction of a woman who had shared the lives of two famous men. She talked of moving to this apartment in the late 1950s (and which she kept throughout her marriage to Brian Donlevy, who had a house in Palm Desert) because "Bela was nearby"; I assumed she meant Bela, Jr., a prominent Los Angeles lawyer. Then I realized that the "nearby" she meant was Holy Cross Cemetery—where Bela Lugosi was buried.

Lillian recalled her first glimpse of Bela, just about the time he completed *Dracula* in 1930, when she was only a teenager:

> My father was always involved in different social events of the Hungarian Colony. They were planning a banquet for a dignitary from Hungary, and that was why Bela came over to the house.
> When I first saw Bela, I thought he looked older than my father. Oh, but he clicked his heels and kissed my hand, and I thought, "Well! This is the way it's done!" He asked me to marry him after the third time he saw me...

Bela Lugosi, born in Hungary as Bela Ferenc Dezso Blasko; 6'1" tall, blue-eyed, 48-year-old; thrice married and divorced; survivor of a tempestuous affair with Clara Bow; portrayer of such roles as Romeo and Armand Duval and Jesus Christ on the European classical stage; actor in German silent films (under the name Arisztid Olt); exile from Hungary after leading a bitter battle for actors' rights ("Love the actor—for he gives you his heart!"). In 1922, he had made his New York debut as Fernando, sexy Spanish Apache pirate, in *The Red Poppy;* he knew such little English at the time that he had learned his lines phonetically, "like the music of a song"; still, the New York critics praised him as an actor of great power. In 1927, Lugosi was a Broadway sensation as *Dracula;* it was a role he almost turned down. Yet he had triumphed in the part, and—after Universal had tested such players as Ian Keith, William Courtenay, Conrad Veidt and (by some accounts) John Carradine for the Count—Bela Lugosi had enjoyed his moment in time. He proudly escorted Lillian to the premiere, where there was little fanfare, as Lillian recalled:

It was a theatre in downtown Los Angeles—God knows what it is today, I don't think it's a theatre. It really wasn't a big deal. No ballyhoo, no nothing!

Dracula, however, became the hit of the season for Universal; the film's power was, as it is over 50 years later, its star. Bela Lugosi was the screen's new aberrant sex symbol, a morbid Valentino, serenaded with passionate fan mail. "Ah, what letters women wrote me!" boasted Bela, who announced that 97 percent of his mail came from women. "Letters of a horrible hunger. Asking me if I cared only for maiden's blood . . ."

Universal wanted a follow-up for Lugosi. The 30-year-old Frenchman Robert Florey, noted for his "experimental" films and the Marx Brothers 1929 *The Cocoanuts* (codirected with Joseph Santley), adapted Mary Shelley's *Frankenstein,* collaborating on a shooting script with Garret Fort. Florey later claimed he favored Lugosi for the role of Frankenstein; at any rate, Universal, hoping for a new Lon Chaney (who had died August 26, 1930), preferred Bela for the monster. Junior was not at his best the day that Florey met him to discuss the treatment—in the Crown Prince's "chamber" full of bookies:

> . . .Junior listened impatiently—playing with the carnation in his lapel—to my first two lines before talking to some girl for fifteen minutes on the phone— then gone out for half-an-hour, returning to say, "Well, go on . . ." and as I was saying, ". . .the monster . . . ," he interrupted me with, "What monster? Who is the monster?" before placing a bet on a race . . .

Somehow, Junior managed to approve a test—the creation scene filmed on the set of *Dracula,* and directed by Florey. Bela Lugosi received a script, and looked over his role of "the monster." The matinee idol perused the script's description of his first close-up:

INT. FLASH CU FACE OF CORPSE
It is chalkily white and expressionless—moulded so as to be just a trifle out of proportion, something just this side of human—but that narrow margin is sufficient to make it insidiously horrible . . .

There was no dialogue in this scene, nor any other; the monster did not speak—he howled. Lugosi continued pasting advance publicity about *Frankenstein* in his scrapbooks; however, his vanity bristled.

Lugosi's test—by most accounts—was a disaster.

In the makeup laboratory of Jack P. Pierce, former Chicago shortstop, Lugosi huffed as that godlike cosmetician tried to experiment with his monster getup. Some accounts state Lugosi tried to do at least part of the makeup himself. "Lugosi," said Pierce, "thought his ideas were better than everybody's!"

Dracula **poster, 1931.**

Ad for *Dracula*, 1931.

The final makeup was a monster à la Der Golem, with a broad wig and polished claylike skin; thusly did Bela Lugosi storm onto the soundstage for the *Frankenstein* test. Edward Van Sloan, Lugosi's "Van Helsing" in *Dracula* on Broadway, tour and the movie, was a coplayer in the test; so was Dwight Frye, who had played lunatic Renfield in the movie *Dracula*. Van Sloan earned a special place in cinema history with his description of Lugosi in the long-lost test.

"Lugosi looked," said Van Sloan, not long before his death in 1964, "more like something out of *Babes in Toyland!*"

"Enough is enough!" protested Lugosi, as Florey directed the other test players. "I will not be a grunting, babbling idiot for anybody!"

As Lillian remembers, Bela was aghast at the four- to six-hour ordeal, and was ready to get a doctor's certificate to get out of making *Frankenstein*. But more painful to him was the nature of the part itself. "I need a challenging part," Lillian recalls Bela lamenting. "I need a part where I can *act!*"

Shot at Universal on June 16 and 17, 1931, the test (according to all but Florey, who died in 1979) was a failure; some accounts state that Junior Laemmle laughed aloud at it, although both Florey and test cameraman Paul Ivano dismissed this as "myth" in later years. Whatever, *Frankenstein* was shelved until James Whale picked it up, and "bumped" Robert Florey off the project. (In the ensuing fracas, Whale managed to delete Florey's name from the script credit on the opening titles — a spitefully bitchy act.) And, in the controversy of the test, Bela Lugosi had offended the hierarchy at Universal.

"He's a lot like his father," Lillian Lugosi Donlevy once said to me about her son Bela, "only nicer. His father was domineering — you know, 'I am the head of my household!,' 'I'm this, I'm that. . .'" A bit uncomfortable, I suggested that perhaps stardom had done that to him.

"Oh no!" said Lillian. "That was his nature."

The Hollywood trade papers soon announced that Florey and Lugosi were officially off *Frankenstein,* and would team for Edgar Allan Poe's *Murders in the Rue Morgue* instead. There never has been an official Hollywood announcement as to whether Lugosi's ego, spite for the role, or poor test caused him to lose *Franken-stein.* All three undoubtedly played a role in what would be a cataclysmic disaster in his life.

For, as Lillian Lugosi would say, "Bela created his own monster."

And, on a hot summer's noon, the monster was in Universal's commissary, sipping a cup of tea.

> I was having lunch, and James Whale ... asked me to join him for a cup of coffee.... He asked me if I would make a test for him tomorrow. "What for?" I asked. "For a damned awful monster!" he said. Of course, I was delighted, because it meant another job if I was able to land it.... At the same time, I felt rather hurt, because at the time I had on a very good straight makeup, and my best suit — and he wanted me to test for a monster!
>
> — Boris Karloff

For many years, the true background of Boris Karloff, born William Henry Pratt, has mystified film historians. At the time of his birth on November 23, 1887, his father — Edward John Pratt, of the British Civil Service of India — was 60; his mother, Eliza Sarah Millard, was 29. The year after his birth, his father left Mrs. Pratt.

Karloff, the youngest child of a cold and frosty family of British diplomats, always intimated he was an unloved black sheep; ever since "Billy" was nine, and played the Demon King in a parish play of *Cinderella,* his love of the theatre had so shamed his family that the Pratts exiled him to Canada when he was 21.

There might have been more — much more — to the story. Alan Napier, a close friend of Karloff, recalled:

> Sometime in the fifties, Brian Aherne had lent me for a month his ranch house in the Coachella Valley where he grew, at considerable expense, Thompson's seedless grapes. I asked Boris and his wife Evie down for a weekend. It was very hot but, undeterred, I practiced my passion for sunbathing. When I asked Boris to join me, he declined, saying that his skin was dark enough as it was. He then amplified with the following confession/revelation:
>
> When his mother was returning to England one time, she, Mrs. Pratt, a pillar of middle-class virtue, fell from grace and had an affair in the Suez Canal with an Egyptian gentleman!
>
> Whether Boris stated that he was the result of this adventure, or whether my wife Gip and I surmised it, I cannot be sure. But it fits so perfectly: the split with his family's middle-class Victorian respectability to become an actor; his intellectual political liberalism combined with a yearning for the British establishment (the last time I visited him in England he proudly took me to the members viewing section of the Middlesex Cricket Club) — it all adds up to the portrait of

Lugosi as the Count (note Bela's omnipresent cigar, resting on the door bolt, far left).

one aware of being "different" by reason of "half-caste" illegitimacy; one who had trimphed over this disadvantage by turning young Mr. Pratt into Boris Karloff.

There had been years as a stock company player, barnstorming in everything from *East Lynne* to Shakespeare to *The Virginian;* scores of movies,

Publicity photo for *Dracula:* Lugosi poses with costars David Manners, Helen Chandler, Dwight Frye, and Edward Van Sloan. Frye and Van Sloan, fated to appear in *Frankenstein,* also acted with Lugosi in *Frankenstein* test footage.

including the role of the hypnotist à la Caligari in 1926's *The Bells;* many heartaches; a spell as a truck driver; and at least four wives. Now, William Henry Pratt, aka Boris Karloff, was playing the monster in *Frankenstein*. After many small roles in silents and talkies, Karloff had scored, reprising his Los Angeles stage role of the jailbird Galloway in Columbia's *The Criminal Code;* he was now a much-in-demand character player. By the time he had played in Warner's *Five Star Final* that summer, lisping the role of sex pervert T. Vernon Isopod ("I rode uptown in a taxi with him," cracks fishnet-stockinged blonde floozie Ona Munson, "and I haven't any skin left on my knees!"), Karloff's salary had risen to $350 per week.

How did the gaunt, brown-eyed Karloff land the part of the monster? Lugosi, in an account fully believed by Lillian but not even included by the authors of three separate books on him, claimed he had "scouted the agencies" and suggested Karloff in a desperate move to elude the monster role. David Lewis, the associate producer of such films as MGM's 1937 *Camille* and

Warner's 1939 *Dark Victory,* and who lived with James Whale for over 20 years, claimed he suggested Karloff to Whale after seeing the actor in *The Criminal Code.*

At any rate, on that noon at Universal's commissary, Whale saw Karloff. The ex-cartoonist was fascinated by the visage—"Your face has startling possibilities!"—and sent Karloff to makeup chief Jack P. Pierce. While tests went on for weeks, Junior Laemmle tried to convince Whale to recall Lugosi for the monster; *Murders in the Rue Morgue* wasn't ready, and Lugosi, after all, had the box office power of *Dracula.* Whale cavalierly insisted on Karloff—and hence became a major figure in the classic Karloff vs. Lugosi rivalry. Weeks later, Whale had his monster.

* * *

This was a pathetic creature, who like us all, had neither wish nor say in his creation and certainly did not wish upon itself the hideous image which automatically terrified human beings whom it tried to befriend...
— Boris Karloff, on Frankenstein's monster

Monday, August 24, 1931, was a special day in Universal's history: James Whale began filming *Frankenstein,* on the old mountain cemetery set.

"He's just resting, waiting for a *new* life to come!" avowed Frankenstein, grave robbing in the moonlight. Portrayer of "The Modern Prometheus" was Colin Clive, Whale's Stanhope of *Journey's End,* in life a tragic, Jekyll & Hyde personality whose demonic elixir was alcohol. High-strung, smoking cigarettes endlessly, the doomed Englishman "mesmerized" his leading lady, Mae Clarke, as he mastered the spectacular electrical creation in the tower laboratory—"one great and special 4th of July fireworks display—just for us!" recalls Miss Clarke—and climaxed the classic line, "It's alive!"

He was the handsomest man I ever saw—and also the saddest. Colin's sadness was elusive: the sadness you see if you contemplate many of the master painters' and sculptors' conceptions of the face of Christ—the ultimate source, in my view of all sadness.

"One man *crazy*—three very sane spectators!" cackled Clive in the great creation sequence. Filling out the trio with Miss Clarke were John Boles, all-purpose Universal leading man, as the solid Victor, and Edward Van Sloan, Van Helsing of *Dracula,* as sagacious Dr. Waldman. Scampering about the laboratory, as the hunchbacked dwarf Fritz, was Dwight Frye, former Broadway star and concert pianist; "Fritz," along with Frye's pop-eyed fly-eater Renfield of *Dracula,* would forever warp his Hollywood image—much to this little man's own horror.

Most infamous of all was Karloff's monster. There was a magic in the air that summer as Karloff played his scenes, and Mae Clarke's eyes glow as

she remembers the monster's classic discovery of sunlight, in the tower laboratory:

> I thought Karloff was magnificent. That scene with the skylight! When he looked up and up and up and waved his hands at the light, it was a spiritual lesson: Looking at God! It was like when we die, the Beatific Vision, which makes people understand the words "Eye has not seen, nor ears heard, the glories that God has prepared for those who love Him."

"Monster indeed!" Karloff originally smiled, when Whale had mentioned the role. Yet the adventure became truly monstrous: the actor was in makeup at Jack P. Pierce's lab at 4:00 a.m.; he worked in the September summer heat, in 48 pounds of makeup and costume, a prisoner of the soundstage, traveling to and from the set with a veil over his head ("Uncle Carl" had mandated the monster sport this veil after a secretary reportedly fainted at the sight of him). Come lunch, the monster, stripped naked, dined (alone) in his bungalow, escaping his perspiration-soaked underclothes; then, after a scorching afternoon's work, there came one-and-a-half to two hours of makeup removal, via assorted oils and acids. Yet Karloff never complained, nor lost insight into the plight of his bewildered creature. Mae Clarke says:

> Observing Boris, in makeup by the great Jack Pierce, taking director instructions: towering over the tall Mr. Whale, listening meekly as an obedient child, both so softly spoken I couldn't hear a word — then he'd nod his head and Whale would give him an affectionate push at his enormous hanging arms and call out "Ready for camera." Boris was unbelievable patience and endurance and, as the world now sees, he gave an incredible performance. He made that monster understandable and painfully pitiable.

For "Dear Boris," the only true pleasantries were the daily tea break, and hiking up to the Universal mountains (sans veil) like a lost shepherd, enjoying a cigarette, seeking a merciful breeze and playing with the lambs who grazed on the hills.

The most haunting episode of the *Frankenstein* saga is the flower game, by the mountain lake: Karloff's monster, tenderly holding a flower, laughing in joy, meeting "Little Maria," whom he will accidentally drown. Karloff's gentility glowed through the mortician wax makeup in this infamous scene (recently rediscovered for MCA's "restored" version of *Frankenstein*). Seven-year-old Marilyn Harris, as Little Maria, in tights and curls and with a "kitty," tossed into the lake by Karloff, sensed and responded to the monster's magic. In Richard Lamparski's tenth *Whatever Became of. . .?* book, Miss Harris (later known as Marilyn Wood), the haunted child of a sadistic stage mother, remembered the monster. She rode with him to the lake, where

Opposite: **Bela Lugosi, ca. 1931.**

Whale, dapper in beret and sunglasses, staged the drowning. The first toss didn't satisfy Whale (or Marilyn's mother, who shouted, "Throw her in again!"), so Marilyn (who had hurt her back in the splash) let Mr. Karloff "drown" her once more after Whale promised the diet-regimented child a dozen hard-boiled eggs. "Actually, he gave me two dozen," remembered Marilyn. "My mother was furious I hadn't asked for something like a bicycle." Marilyn's memory of Karloff's monster:

> He had such warmth and gentleness about him. There was little of either quality in the home I grew up in. I was very strongly drawn to him.

Marilyn appeared to recall Karloff's monster much more warmly than she did her mother, who once held Marilyn's hand over a hot gas range because she caught her biting her nails.

For all his passion in playing the monster, Karloff always kept his humor — and could use it to help a fellow player. Come the famous scene in which the monster invades Elizabeth's boudoir on her wedding day, terrifying the blonde bride, Mae Clarke feared she would truly surrender to hysterics. The lady recalls how Karloff helped:

> When we rehearsed, I said, "Boris, what are we going to do about this? When we play it, and I have all my motors running, and turn and see you, I'll fall to the floor! I won't make it to the bed!" Boris said, "Mae, I'll tell you what I'll do. When you turn around, my one arm is up-camera; focus on the little finger — I'll be wiggling it — and you'll know it's Boris in makeup." So I looked at Boris' little finger (and it was a little finger, compared to the rest of him), and I was all right —

With this bravery, sly humor, deep artistry, and many cups of tea, Boris Karloff beautifully recreated Mary Shelley's Frankenstein's monster. By the time Whale filmed the climax of *Frankenstein,* as Colin Clive, the torch-bearing villagers and the bloodhounds pursue the monster, cremating him (or so they thought!) in the old mountain windmill, Karloff's performance and professionalism already were legend. And then a strange, sick thing happened. James Whale — with both the talent and ego of a genius — revealed a vain, sadistic side of his personality. Cynthia Lindsay, a personal friend of Karloff's, wrote in her book, *Dear Boris:*

> Boris never understood why Whale insisted on his carrying Clive up the hill to the mill in the famous scene where the Monster dies. Whale shot the scene dozens of times, using primarily long shots in which a dummy could have been used . . . but Whale insisted on using Boris and Clive over and over and over. . . . Whale had the reputation of being an egomaniac, and Boris always felt, though he never said so publicly, that the Monster had caused such wild interest not only from the studio people, but from the press, that Whale was actually jealous of him and decided to punish the Monster, and inadvertently, the man who created him. Not Frankenstein, but Boris.

On Saturday, October 3, 1931, James Whale completed *Frankenstein*. The movie was shot in 35 days, 5 days over schedule; the final cost was $291,129.13, almost $30,000 over budget.

On Friday, December 4, 1931, *Frankenstein* premiered at New York's RKO Mayfair Theatre. It was, of course, a sensation; and almost 60 years later, *Frankenstein* still has magic — a strange, sad, Gothic poetry, bequeathed by the three Englishmen who made it great. The director, an arch, bitter homosexual, who had created his own public "self" that in time increasingly became a monster; a tragic, tortured actor with a Christ-like face and an addiction to alcohol as destructive as Frankenstein's addiction to blasphemy; and, ultimately, a sad-eyed, forlorn, possibly illegitimate aesthete who himself had felt the pain of rejection, loneliness and abandonment; each made *Frankenstein* timeless.

It was Boris Karloff, of course — billed only as "?" on the opening credits, his name fourth billed on the closing "A Good Cast is Worth Repeating" roster — who became Hollywood folklore.

Before Christmas, 1931, arrived, Boris Karloff had signed a Universal star contract. In the first week of 1932, the *L.A. Examiner* reported that Universal was preparing J.B. Priestley's *The Old Dark House* and H.G. Wells' *The Invisible Man* just for him. Trade papers hawked the enormous success of *Frankenstein,* which went on to reap a domestic gross of $1,000,000 — double the take of Bela Lugosi's *Dracula*.

*   *   *

> Such is Whale's amusement at the possibilities in Mary Shelley's tale that he bends Universal's monster imagery back upon itself, allows sympathy for the ghoul in his anger, bewilderment, torment. Yet he bends it once again to admire the beauty of the night sky as screaming peasants burn the Monster in a windmill. A good cast is worth not only repeating but celebrating; at the end, Universal names Boris Karloff, and a star is born.
>
> — Ethan Mordden, *The Hollywood Studios*

During the Yuletide of 1931, as visions of Santa Claus and sugarplums danced in the dreams of children, a new, classic bogeyman was invading the dreams of moviegoers — the vision of Frankenstein's monster, pieced together from churchyard corpses, terrifying, yet pleading and lonely, all the more haunting for his pitiful nature, all the more powerful as he miraculously found a soul.

With Karloff Frankenstein's monster had become one of our classic, most profound nightmares. He had also become one of the great nightmares of Bela Lugosi's life. And it was a nightmare that Lugosi would encounter in the flesh as the two men went on over the next decades to create Hollywood history.

2
The Years 1932 and 1933

> Boris, women are thrilled by Dracula, the suave one.... Why does a
> woman always tell the story of her husband's death so often and with such relish?
> Why does she go to cemeteries? Tenderness? Grief? Bah! It's because she likes
> to be hurt, tortured, terrified.... Ah, Boris, to win a woman, take her with you
> to see *Dracula,* the movie...!
> Ha! Ha! Ha! You fool, Bela.... These two hands of mine, clenched
> together above my head, could descend at any moment, in a second, ay, even
> before I finished this sentence, if I wanted them to, and they'd bash your
> distinguished head in as if it were an egg. Your brains would run out like the
> yolk of an egg, and spatter your pretty tuxedo...!
>
> —from Ted LeBerthon's "Demons of the
> Film Colony," *Weird Tales,* October, 1932

Thus did the bloody badinage flow (according to the Halloween, 1932, edition of *Weird Tales*) when Boris Karloff met Bela Lugosi on a rainy morning at Universal City, early in 1932. John Le Roy Johnstone, Universal PR chief, had arranged the rendezvous of Frankenstein's monster and Count Dracula, to be photographed for posterity by Ray Jones and documented by Mr. Le Berthon.

The stars, dapper in tuxedos, posed for a variety of publicity photographs: smiling at the camera, hoisting beer steins, standing with arms around each other's shoulders. They volleyed virulent verbiage (clearly tongue-in-cheek) to delight the PR squad. And, ultimately, they made a wager as to who could scare the other actor to death.

Of course, it was really all a hoot, and perhaps the true tone of the meeting is witnessed by the fact that Boris, despite his evening wear, is clearly sporting his cricket socks.

Yet, for all the Hollywood hoke, *Weird Tales* had hit on the classic rivalry—one destined to become less of a hoot and more of a tragedy as the years passed....

> Boris Karloff was first to arrive—and, fantastically enough, in evening clothes, worn under a rain-flecked overcoat which he tossed off with a mischievous, almost boyish fling.... He is slender, debonair, graceful, with powerful shoulders and large strong hands, smooth iron-gray hair, darkly tanned skin, and lucent, deep-set brown eyes. A witty, casual, well-bred

Bela Lugosi (left) officially meets Boris Karloff, Universal City, 1932.

fellow, with one of those strong-boned, hollow-cheeked countenances that seems carved out of hickory. . . . He joked waggishly, this Englishman from God knows where, whose name is *not* Karloff, about his coming meeting with Bela Lugosi. . .

The year 1932 began for Boris Karloff with a Universal star contract. Of all the actors dining at Universal's commissary in 1932 — Lew Ayres, Gloria Stuart, Tom Mix, Genevieve Tobin, Zasu Pitts, Slim Summerville — Karloff was the most famous, and infamous. Hollywood studios all sought the most clever ways of "selling" their stars to the public, such as Garbo, the Goddess of Mystery, or Gable, the Rugged Outdoorsman. For Boris Karloff, the attack was genuine, and ingenious: Frankenstein's monster as a gentle, poetry-loving Englishman of letters. Jim Tully, in "Alias the Monster," *The New Movie Magazine* (September 1932) waxed eloquently about the star soon to be known throughout Hollywood as "Dear Boris":

> His eyes are dreamy. . . tragic. . . . He does not seem to be in tune with the materialistic world. I would hazard the guess that he may often find it hard to keep his dreamy and poetical nature in rhythm with modern life. . . . There is a rose in his soul which the searing wind of Hollywood has never touched. . . .

Fan magazine reporter Mary Sharon had an appointment to meet Boris Karloff at Universal for an interview. ". . . I had not the slightest desire to meet the man," she wrote, having seen him in *Five Star Final* and *Frankenstein.* "I felt certain that he would be aloof and probably repellant." Still, she prepared herself for the interview, only to miss the streetcar to the studio. She called the publicity office, and, within ten minutes, a Ford pulled up to fetch her — driven by Boris Karloff! Miss Sharon was smitten by her subject:

> I have just met the most amazing man in Hollywood. I say amazing, because he can play the most abnormal, horrible characterizations without being affected by them. . . . You can easily picture him in a romantic role. He is tall, well-built and very dark-skinned . . . the sort of fellow that would cause you to turn around, even on Hollywood Boulevard. . . . He is suave, without being slick. . . . I wouldn't hesitate to call him distinguished, and there are only three other men in Hollywood who rate this adjective in my estimation. . . . He likes to sit by the fire in the evening and read Conrad's tales of high adventure. . . . I like Boris Karloff. Tremendously.

Of course, Universal was packaging vehicles for the sensation of *Frankenstein.* First, however, came *The Cohens and the Kellys in Hollywood;* the monster, now in tuxedo and mustache was glimpsed in the Coconut Grove, along with such Universal luminaries as Tom Mix, Lew Ayres, Genevieve Tobin and Sidney Fox. There followed *Night World,* a wild bootleg liquor melodrama full of chorus girl legs, gay humor and early Busby Berkeley choreography. "Lew Ayres had been in *All Quiet on the Western Front,* I had

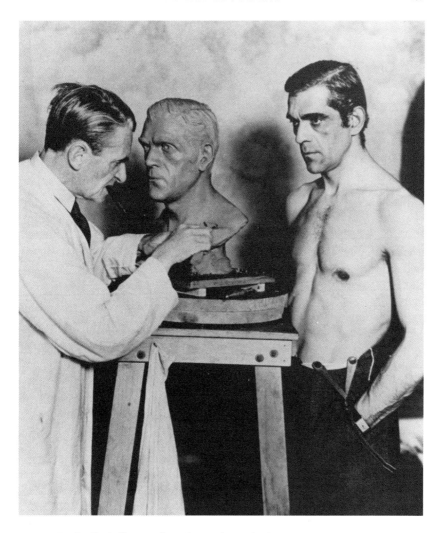

Boris Karloff poses for a bust; the artist is actor Ivan Simpson.

done *Waterloo Bridge,* and Boris had *Frankenstein,*" Mae Clarke told me, "so why did all three of us agree to be in *that* turkey?" Boris played "Happy" Macdonald, hotshot nightclub owner; in his big death scene, shot by a rival hoodlum, he expires in gaudy character — flashing one last Happy smile.

However, come the spring of 1932, Boris began work on a new horror show: *The Old Dark House.* The Byronic ghost of "Jimmy" Whale seems to be lurking in the shadow of this old house, enjoying the gallery of grotesques: Ernest Thesiger as prissy, atheistic Horace Femm, mincing lines like, "We make our own electric light here — and we're not very good at it!" Eva Moore as his deaf old hag of a sister, Rebecca, leering at Gloria Stuart's silk evening dress, "That's nice stuff—but it'll rot!" and then, at Miss Stuart's bosom, "That's finer stuff—but it'll rot too, in time!" Brember Wills as Saul Femm, a waif-like madman who loves knives and flame. A wild, irreverent black comedy, boasting Melvyn Douglas, Raymond Massey and Charles Laughton, long-lost and only available now in revival showings and boot-legged video prints, *The Old Dark House* features some of the cinema's most macabre ensemble acting and Whale's most naughty flourishes. After all, what other director would have the patriarch of the sinful Femms, Sir Roderick Femm, 102 years old, played by a woman (Elspeth Dudgeon) in falsetto and chin whiskers?

However, for the 1932 public, it was Karloff's show as the horrific, bearded butler, Morgan. The star enjoys the movie's most frightening vignette—his attempted rape of Miss Stuart, chasing her about the dining room, with Whale close-ups of the eyes and broken nose and twitchy mouth, overturning the great dining table as Miss Stuart screams and screams—as well as the film's most quirky: Finding his friend, Saul, dead after the night's climactic mayhem, Karloff's Morgan whimpers—then carries the cadaver of Saul in his arms, up the stairs, his hips swaying, metamorphosing before our eyes from bogeyman to a heartbroken, horrible nanny.

Universal released *The Old Dark House* for Halloween of 1932 with appropriate ballyhoo, and no one was ballyhooed like Karloff. The opening credits featured this teaser:

> PRODUCER'S NOTE—Karloff, the mad butler in this production, is the same Karloff who created the part of the mechanical monster in *Frankenstein*. We explain this to settle all disputes in advance, even though such disputes are a tribute to his great versatility.

Gloria Stuart, beautiful blonde leading lady of *The Old Dark House* and Universal's loveliest star, recalled Boris warmly: "...beautifully educated, very soft-spoken, and charming."

The great Metro-Goldwyn-Mayer lot beckoned, and Universal lent Karloff to MGM for *The Mask of Fu Manchu*. Boris created a leering, lisping reptile of the Yellow Peril, reveling in his torture devices: a ringing bell, which drove its victim mad; spiked walls which nearly punctured Jean Hersholt; a harrowing seesaw over a crocodile pool, which kept dipping Lewis Stone's old grey head down as a morsel for the pets. Myrna Loy, of course, was Fu's nymphomaniacal daughter, and the climax found Karloff, in robes and mask, looming over blonde heroine Karen Morley, exulting, "Conquer and breed! Kill the white man, and take his women!"

It was penny dreadful stuff, but Boris had fun at Metro. For the scene in which Fu tortured hero Charles Starrett, injecting a needle into his neck, director Charles Brabin sent to the commissary for baking potatoes, hidden behind Starret's neck to absorb the needle. The potatoes kept exploding, all over Boris and Starrett. Fu and hero surrendered to such hysterical laughter that Brabin finally sent them home for the day to recover!

Back at Universal, the studio exalted its $750 per week attraction, now proclaiming him in publicity simply as KARLOFF. Meanwhile, Boris celebrated stardom, buying a bungalow overlooking Toluca Lake in North Hollywood. There, he and Dorothy would feed the swans, and Boris could relax after a long day at the studio, reading his English poetry and Joseph Conrad tales:

> Looking around at the quiet hills and the blue, sparkling lake, I often wonder if it is really me, the same man who arrived at Halifax, penniless and friendless, whose first job was on a farm in Ontario. I wonder, too, if I really ever was one of the pick and shovel brigade!

In the fall of 1932, Boris was starring in Universal's *The Mummy.* He played the 3700-year-old Im-Ho-Tep in a masterpiece Jack P. Pierce makeup which took from 11:00 a.m. to 7:00 p.m. to apply; shedding the wrappings, he haunts the movie as shriveled Ardath Bey, an evil, lovesick hieroglyphic, seeking the reincarnation of the vestal virgin he had dared to love in ancient Thebes. It's a performance of power, poetry, and a striking melancholy; and, if Alan Napier's account of Karloff's birth is true, it was a role that must have stirred strange feelings in its star. *The Mummy* would fully establish Karloff as a major Hollywood attraction; KARLOFF THE UNCANNY, heralded the posters.

Universal City was still a bizarre place, and nobody felt it more cruelly working on *The Mummy* than Zita Johann, who so passionately portrayed the Princess Anck-es-en-Amon, soulfully acting in long, curly wig, Egyptian headdress, and filmy, hootchie-kootchie dancer costume, as Karloff prepares to embalm her. Fifty years later, in her pre–Revolutionary War mansion near the Hudson River, Johann, her eyes as magnificent as ever, told me of the true horrors she suffered on that classic: how her director, obese, Bohemian Karl "Papa" Freund (legendary cinematographer of *The Last Laugh* and *Dracula*) threatened to have her pose nude from the waist up; how he saw to it she didn't get a chair with her name on it, as did the other leading players; how he worked her so sadistically that, late on a Saturday night, as Karloff was playing a scene with her, she collapsed. "I was out for an hour — dead. They couldn't get a doctor — it was eleven o'clock at night — so the crew prayed me back to consciousness."

However, Miss Johann's most spine-tingling adventure came on a day Universal had shrewdly saved for the last day of production. The famous long-lost reincarnation episodes, which showed Johann in various reincarnations since Thebes (and cut by Junior Laemmle, according to Zita, because she wouldn't make another film for him!), featured Johann as a Christian martyr, fed to lions. Universal had saved the scene until last, in case a lion overacted. As the actress exclaimed:

Karloff and his wife Dorothy, a former librarian, at Toluca Lake.

...Monday morning, I was at Universal, on time. And there were the lions! They had this great big enormous arena outside on the back lot, and everybody was protected. Freund was in a special cage all his own; the cameraman was safe; the whole crew was safe, and there I was at the gate of the arena with the lions. My secretary ran up and said, "You're *not* going in there!" I said, "Look, I get paid, I'm going in — I don't care." I ventured among the lions, exhausted beyond fear.

Well, it proved to me one thing: the old saying, "Don't be afraid of a dog or he'll bite you" is true. Those lions saw no fear in me — just exhausted bones! And they must have figured, "Who needs them?"

Zita Johann has one happy memory of *The Mummy*: the Mummy himself:

Karloff was really, truly a great gentleman. He minded his own business and was very seclusive, very good, very kind and very nice! There was in Karloff a hidden sorrow that I sensed and respected — a deep, deep thing. Still, whatever that may have been, there was a true respect between us as actors. He was a marvelous person.

Curiously, no word leaked at this time of Karloff's quite mysterious past in regard to the past wives; in her book *Dear Boris,* Cynthia Lindsay refers to this as "The Snow Job." Perhaps Universal never had the nerve to ask the monster to document those early marriages, and certainly Boris would have been loath to discuss it. Dorothy Karloff herself told Lindsay that she only found out "inadvertently" she was wife number four (or was she five?). Cynthia Lindsay asked the former Mrs. Karloff if she ever discussed it with her famous spouse.

"No," answered Dorothy. "None of my business."

*   *   *

There stood Lugosi, filling the doorway, quiet as death, and smiling in his curiously knowing way. It is the smile of a tall, weary, haunted aristocrat, a person of perhaps fallen greatness, a secretive Lucifer. . . . He too, was in evening clothes — on a rainy morning! He advanced with a soft, springy tread. . . . Finally he said slowly:

"I think I could scare you to death."

Karloff struck a match, lit a cigarette, puffed a couple of times and retorted with an air of whimsical scorn:

"I not only think I can scare your ears right off, Mr. Dracula, I'll bet you that I can. . . ."

In February of 1932, *Murders in the Rue Morgue* opened at New York's Mayfair Theatre, where *Frankenstein* had made show business history only weeks before. Filling the screen was Bela Lugosi as Dr. Mirakle, in curly hair and one long eyebrow, looking like Hell's foremost Shakespearean, smirking at the crowd, smiling tenderly at his pet Erik the ape. Speaking to Erik in his

own language, sporting high hat and cloak, haunting the old village sets from *The Hunchback of Notre Dame,* shrieking "Bad blood!" at a syphilitic prostitute (Arlene Francis, no less) whom he had hoped to mate with Erik; all of this made for one of Bela's most passionate, colorful, radiantly demonic performances.

Yet the project that Bela Lugosi had embraced in lieu of *Frankenstein* was only a moderate success. Robert Florey originally "wrapped" *Rue Morgue,* November 13, 1931, at approximately $160,000; Bela must have realized the film was in trouble when, on December 10, following the premiere of *Frankenstein,* Laemmle put *Rue Morgue* back into production, with an estimated $21,870 for emergency action scenes — mostly night shots on the village rooftops, and process shots. Still, the production (eventually costing $190,099.45) had serious problems; at its first day's screening, New Yorkers raspberried the climactic chase, as Erik the Ape cavorted over the Paris rooftops with Sidney Fox. Florey's direction was rich in atmosphere, but stale in treatment — with its cornpone love scenes between Leon Ames and Miss Fox, and an almost comic intercutting of close-ups of a real monkey (filmed the last day of retakes, at the Selig Zoo) with shots of Charles Gemora's ape mask.

Murders in the Rue Morgue did not do a fraction of the business *Frankenstein* had enjoyed and Universal made the obvious inference in comparing Karloff to Lugosi, to the latter's disadvantage.

Boris Karloff, now on contract to Universal, had the whole studio behind him: scripts tailored for him, publicity hailing him; indeed, he was one of the great hopes of the erratic lot. Bela Lugosi, having completed his Universal obligation with *Murders on the Rue Morgue,* was independent. It was now up to him and his own business sense to advance his career in the wake of *Frankenstein,* and the sharp contrasts with Karloff's promotion, style and (perhaps most of all), luck began instantly.

Bela Lugosi's publicity rarely varied. "Dracula is Bela Lugosi. Is Bela Lugosi Dracula?" asked Gladys Hall, of *Motion Picture Magazine;* the feature was titled "True Hollywood Ghost Stories — The Case of the Man Who Dares Not Fall Asleep," and published in August, 1929 — over a year before Bela even signed to play the movie *Dracula:*

> There are stranger things in life than we have wind of. You know this, you feel it, while you are talking with Bela Lugosi. He has touched the charnel houses of the Plutonian shores. He has ripped the heart of the night from its most foul hiding place. He knows the secrets we dare not listen to. He has heard the language of the dread horned owl and listened to a green moon whispering in the cypress trees. . . .

Opposite: **A pipe-smoking Lugosi relaxes at home. The nude portrait is of Bela's former lover Clara Bow; the picture above the curtain at right shows Bela as Christ in "The Passion" for Hungary's National Theatre.**

The same reporter Hall visited Lugosi again for the January, 1931, *Motion Picture Classic* story, "The Feminine Love of Horror." Once again, Bela proved how sharply he realized his image:

> Women wrote me letters. Ah, what letters women wrote me! . . . They hoped that I was DRACULA. They hoped that my love was the love of DRACULA. They gloated over the thing they dared not understand. . . . It was the embrace of Death their subconscious was yearning for. Death, the final triumphant lover. . . .

Mary Sharon, the interviewer so agog over Karloff, noted her meeting with Bela with some disappointment: "Bela Lugosi, who played Dracula, was Dracula at heart. Meeting him under normal circumstances did not destroy that sinister something that enabled him to play his weird character so convincingly."

Clearly, Bela Lugosi had chosen to accentuate his natural aura of mystery to sustain him in interviews. Effective, true, but it also served to limit his image.

Also limiting were the roles. In spring, 1932, Bela signed with the Halperin Brothers to star in *White Zombie,* filmed at night on property leased on the Universal lot, and released by United Artists in July, 1932. Bela's Murder Legendre is a classic performance, in a cultish film, memorable for its bizarre use of sound and basket case supporting cast, fated to appeal primarily to lowbrows and scholars with degrees; many of those in between dismiss it as twaddle. It was a bravura performance in a film which made a fortune for its producers (Bela made only about $800), but did little, because of its low budget patina, to advance Lugosi's career, except in the folklore of his fans.

Bela worked steadily: on the Los Angeles stage in the play *Murdered Alive;* as the wild-eyed Roxor of Fox's *Chandu the Magician;* the hirsute Sayer of the Law of Paramount's 1932 *Island of Lost Souls,* in which his awful, hairy makeup proves Bela was not as repulsed by heavy makeup as he was in the summer of 1931. In both of the above (special favorites of Lugosi fans), Bela had to accept third billing.

Even in these palmy days, Bela's free-spending ways, giant tips at Hungarian restaurants, and almost childish generosity (especially with countrymen) brought on financial woes. On October 28, 1932, a Los Angeles newspaper noted that Bela had filed bankruptcy in the U.S. District Court — listing $2695 in debts against $600 in "possible assets." The actor of over 30 years listed those assets as $500 equity in furniture, plus four suits. The publicity hardly boosted Bela's bargaining power with the studio moguls.

While Karloff charmed his coworkers with his gentility and humor, Bela Lugosi remained a world-unto-himself on movie sets; very few people got to know the man who was Dracula. In a retrospective on *White Zombie* in the February, 1988, *American Cinematographer,* Enzo Martinelli, sole surviving member of the camera crew, told Michael Price and George Turner:

Lugosi wasn't really a friendly type. In those days, of course, most of the stars were a little aloof in order to preserve their mystique. Only a few would fraternize with the help or be chummy with the guy who fixed the coffee. I thought he looked ill, as though he was in pain. Later, I learned that he *was* ill during the whole production!

"Aloof" and "mysterious" were the adjectives habitually applied to Bela Lugosi. One actress today finds descriptions unfortunate. She is Carroll Borland, who played Lucy to Bela's Count in a road company of *Dracula* just before he signed for the movie, and, of course, later created the unforgettable Luna, slinky daughter of Lugosi's Count Mora in MGM's 1935 *Mark of the Vampire*. This charming lady vividly remembers Bela Lugosi, and told me in 1988:

> Bela had a great deal of difficulty with English. And I think the whole thing of "He was aloof," "He was mysterious," and so on was because he had a heck of a time expressing himself....
>
> When I first met him, it was about 1928; I was 14 or 15, and he was in Oakland, playing on the stage in *Dracula.* I went backstage and told him about this book I had written, *Countess Dracula.* It was an extension of the Dracula story, ahead 50 years. He liked that idea very much, and later called me and asked me to come down to the hotel and have lunch with him. But, being the European gentleman he was, he of course invited my mother — he would never have considered asking me to come down alone!
>
> Later, he would come out to our house, because I was reading him *Countess Dracula.* He was very interested in it, but I had to read it to him. He could follow spoken English, but English is a funny language — it isn't always pronounced the way it looks. So I would read to him, and he would lie back on the sofa, smoke his cigars — those never-ending cigars! — and have coffee. He liked to be read to; he liked this domestic thing. And of course, this is terrible, because it isn't appropriate for the terrible Dracula to like to lie around someone's house, enjoying coffee and donuts! But he was a very simple person that way...

In 1930, Bela sent for Carroll; he was going on the road in *Dracula* again, and asked her to play Lucy:

> Bela had sort of a childish sense of humor. Once when we were playing *Dracula,* he had a drink backstage. And in the horrible clutching scene of Lucy fainting over his arm with the cape around her, a cube of ice went down my neck!

Carroll was now Lugosi's costar, and she had changed in his eyes. Although he was still wooing Lillian (who was very much under the control of her dominating Hungarian family), Bela saw Carroll as a worldly young lady, and the relationship took on a new dimension:

> When I was 16 or 17, playing Lucy with him, that was different. I was grown up in his eyes. I called him by his first name then. We would walk up and down Hollywood Boulevard after rehearsal, hand in hand, looking in the windows. We

would go to the Roosevelt, and have supper, and dance; I was a professional
dancer, and he liked someone who could do a Viennese waltz. We would dance
together, and I always remember being close to him while he was humming,
dancing, that reverberation in his voice and chest....

Oh, we had such fun! We would play Shakespeare together—he in Hungarian, and I in English! I had gone to Berkeley on a Shakespeare scholarship,
and so, of course, we had a marvelous time. I would try it in English, and he
would try it in Hungarian, and we each knew what the other was saying!

We had a beautiful time together. We were both young, somehow....

Throughout the early thirties, and until his marriage to Lillian in
January, 1933, Bela and Carroll Borland enjoyed what she calls "this incredible
playmate relationship." She says that while they never became intimate, she
was always aware of Bela's magnetism:

Bela had an incredibly wonderful devilishness—that devilish charm! I have
never known a man who could sit still in a room, and all the women were just
drawn to him like pieces of iron to a magnet. He was incredible—the sexiest man
I ever knew!

Of course, he was domineering—oh, I should say so! I've always said I probably loved him longer and better than any other human being because I never had
to live with him! When he would come into our house, and want coffee poured for
him, he wouldn't get up from the couch—he would just snap his fingers and point!
He wasn't used to American women. I was so fond of him, but I was so glad I
never had to live with him—I would have killed him, or he would have killed me!

To me, he was a charming wonderful person—but it was rather like having
a large, tame panther around the house. A friendly panther. You can pull his
whiskers—but you had to be very careful not to upset the panther...

Always, he treated me as a friendly playmate. It was wonderful.

*   *   *

Bela, it's dark in here, but you know me.... You know it was no accident
or chance, but significant, that I—the Englishman from God knows where whose
name is *not* Karloff—was called upon to play that monstrous role! You know me,
Bela, you know me.... You know that both of us are nearly six thousand years
old! And that we've met many times before, the last time not more than two hundred years ago.... And you shouldn't have made that foolish wager. Admit it,
Bela!

—from *Weird Tales*

Karloff and Lugosi were not the only stars to score in Hollywood horror.
Paramount's Fredric March won a 1932 Best Actor Academy Award for his
performance in Rouben Mamoulian's *Dr. Jekyll and Mr. Hyde.* However, the
young, handsome March was very much a glamorous leading man; he had
no fear of typecasting, and would only return to the genre marginally—as
Death in Paramount's 1934 *Death Takes a Holiday.*

Then there was Lionel Atwill, who made Fay Wray scream in Warner's
two-strip Technicolor thrillers *Doctor X* (1932) and *Mystery of the Wax Museum*
(1933), as well as in Majestic's *The Vampire Bat* (1933). A laureled star of the
London and New York stage, plump, British Atwill was the thinking man's

horror star of the early thirties, playing with a sophisticated decadence. He told *Motion Picture:*

> Look at this side of my face—it is gentle and kind and good. Look at this other side—it is evil and predatory. . . . I shall say this much: I believe that I am a Good Man, but I break loose on Fridays, and this—THIS IS FRIDAY!

Atwill, known as "Pinky" to his friends, was a Hollywood aristocrat whose stage career made him welcome in such MGM fare as *The Secret of Madame Blanche,* with Irene Dunne, or Paramount's *The Song of Songs,* with Marlene Dietrich. At the time, he didn't have to fear typecasting, either; he was married to Louise Cromwell MacArthur (former wife of General Douglas MacArthur), heiress to a fortune of over $100,000,000.

John Barrymore, who had given his greatest screen performance as *Svengali* (1931) at Warner Bros., was now at MGM, going glamorous for movies like *Grand Hotel.* Colin Clive commuted from London to New York to Hollywood, playing in films like RKO's *Christopher Strong* (as the aristocrat who impregnates Hepburn), spending leisure time flying a plane in the Hollywood skies, and—so tragically—drinking. Claude Rains, who would prove a sensation in Whale's 1933 *The Invisible Man,* would be promptly dropped by Universal at the end of the filming, and return temporarily to his farm in the East and the New York stage. Tod Browning's *Freaks* went back to the carnivals and sideshows. And RKO's *King Kong,* after all, had only been an 18-inch doll of framework and hair and marble eyes.

So Karloff and Lugosi reigned as Hollywood's top horror stars; 1933 would be a colorful year for them both. In January, 1933, Bela and Lillian Arch eloped to Las Vegas; the groom was 50, the bride was 21. Lillian thought they had escaped the press, but told me:

> The telephone at my parents started ringing so much so my mother finally took the receiver off the hook. So the reporters started coming to the house! And one reporter saw a picture of me, taken when I was about 17, on the piano. "Is that her picture?" he asked. My mother said, "Well, you might as well have a *good* picture of her," so she let him have it—and that's the picture that made the papers—the front page yet! A big one of me, and a little one of Bela! And the caption was, "DRACULA WEDS BEAUTY."

The newlyweds returned to Hollywood, to Bela's flat at the Hollywood Athletic Club—and unpleasant publicity. "Bela Lugosi Sued for Rent" read a February, 1933, headline; the amount was $700, on an apartment he had enjoyed in 1932 at 2643 Creston Drive. The building still survives, a three-story house hanging over Beachwood Drive, in the Hollywood Hills.

In March, 1933, Boris Karloff had a joyful homecoming in England, where Universal dispatched him to star in Gaumont British's *The Ghoul.* Off went Boris, by plane to New York, by ship to Southampton, with Dorothy and at least one Bedlington terrier, the touted trip gloriously publicizing his international stardom. The journey also offered the star a reunion with his

Lugosi and his fourth wife, Lillian Arch, sporting matching suits and caps.

brothers, all distinguished members of the consular service. One of Boris's favorite lifetime stories was how he dreaded a photographer's requesting a picture of him and his brothers at a London reception. Instead of deeming such a thing beneath their dignity, the Pratt brothers ("pleased as three boys!" recalled Karloff) all posed before a fireplace, excitedly arguing as to where each should stand. "No sooner was the picture taken than all three brothers began to inquire how soon they could secure prints," said Boris, "and by this time I was in a positive glow of relief. A film actor had been received in the British diplomatic circles and had made good!"

Beside the reunion, the publicity, and the London sightseeing, *The Ghoul* offered Boris a separate advantage. He was fortunately out of town when the Panamanian government deported Polly Karloff, "singer and dancer and the former wife of Boris Karloff," back to Los Angeles on a steamship, hence sparing the actor any unpleasant inquiries into his past life.

Back in Hollywood, Karloff was very much in the trade news. In an early showcase of his business sense, he walked out of Universal City, June 1, 1933. He had been drawing $750 weekly in 1932; when the financially-troubled studio pleaded poverty in January, 1933, when Boris's salary was to hit $1000 weekly, Boris agreed to keep collecting $750 weekly — provided he get the full raise to $1250 by June 1. The Laemmles refused to keep their promise, and out walked the biggest star of Universal. By July, Karloff was back, with a new deluxe contract, and the right to work at other studios.

Boris took full advantage of this new concession, and signed with RKO to play the religious lunatic Sanders in John Ford's *The Lost Patrol*. In late summer, 1933, Ford and company, including Victor McLaglen, Alan Hale and Reginald Denny, took off for the 120° F. sand dunes near Yuma. Boris gave a wild-eyed, cackling, screaming performance as Sanders, climaxing with the madman, in rags and carrying a cross like a biblical martyr, marching up the dunes and into the Arab gunfire — all to the roaring strains of Max Steiner's Oscar-winning music. It is, perhaps, Boris's most infamous performance — endearingly hammy, admittedly manic, at times seeming the result of sunstroke; certainly it's the most entertaining thing about this stiff-upper-lip thriller today.

The Lost Patrol was fated to be one of the major films of 1934. So was *House of Rothschild*, which Karloff did on loan to 20th Century, late in 1933, playing, out of respect for George Arliss, the supporting (but juicy) role of Jew-baiting Baron Ledrantz. Both films were grand career moves; KARLOFF was Hollywood's great character star.

Bela Lugosi, meanwhile, wasn't nearly so shrewd. He was a wonderful comic heavy as General Nicholas Petronovich, marvelously holding his own with W.C. Fields, Burns and Allen and Peggy Hopkins Joyce in Paramount's delightful 1933 *International House;* but surrounding it were red herring parts in such dogs as World-Wide's *The Death Kiss* and Columbia's *Night of Terror.* He was Professor Strang in Mascot's 1933 serial, *The Whispering*

Shadow, and in July, the month that Karloff was signing his new Universal contract, audiences saw Bela unbilled as a prosecutor in Fox's 1933 *The Devil's in Love,* a role only attributable to the actor's desire to escape horror roles while lacking the business sense to do so effectively. He also appeared in a 1933 short, *Intimate Interviews,* in which a little blonde named Dorothy West called on Bela at his Hollywood home. Bela, tall, sleek, towering over Dorothy, smokes his cigar, and discusses various topics — including his study of American slang: "I know how to say 'Okay,' and 'Cat's Whiskers,' and 'Baloney,' and — 'And-How'!"

In the summer of 1933, Karloff and Lugosi had joined in a major enterprise: the founding of the Screen Actors Guild. Karloff was one of the 13 founders, and served aggressively and bravely as an officer; it added to his prestige and popularity in Hollywood. Bela, nervously recalling his troubles in Europe on behalf of the actors' revolution, kept a less noticeable profile, but still served on the Advisory Board.

By the end of the summer, as Karloff was in the desert with John Ford, Lugosi returned to New York with Lillian to play the Swami in Earl Carroll's Broadway play, *Murder at the Vanities,* which opened September 12, 1933, at the New Amsterdam Theatre.

Meanwhile, Karloff and Lugosi had their first screen union — of sorts. Walt Disney delightfully caricatured each star in his 1933 cartoon, *Mickey's Gala Premiere,* which also featured such luminaries as Garbo, the Barrymores, and Laurel and Hardy.

*   *   *

I shall never know whether it was Lugosi or Karloff who struck the match. All I do know is that when the match was struck it apparently revealed, not Lugosi and Karloff on that davenport, but two slimy, scaly monsters, dragon-like serpents, with blood-red venomous eyes. The apparitional thing flashed before me so suddenly that I became sick to my stomach and made a rush, on buckling legs, for the exit — and the cool air . . .

— from *Weird Tales*

The Scare to Death contest, according to Ted Le Berthon, had ended in a draw; he ended his *Weird Tales* story surmising that he was the victim of a practical joke, or his own hallucinating nerves, as Karloff and Lugosi seemed to transform into those "dragon-like serpents." Yet he ended the story on the proper poetical note:

Opposite: **Carl Laemmle's 66th birthday party, January, 1933. Front row: Tala Birell, Baker Paul Gross, Charlie Murray, Carl Laemmle, Carl Laemmle Jr., Rosabelle Laemmle Bergerman, Ken Maynard, Nancy Carroll, and Gloria Stuart. Top row: Edward Laemmle, Henry MacRae, Sam Jacobson, Frank Morgan, Clyde Beatty, Karl Freund, Karloff, Tom Brown, Kurt Neumann, Al Cohen, James Whale, and Robert Wyler.**

Many people, deep down, still are superstitious. And there are many things in life, we do not fully understand, such as why it is the destiny of certain human beings to portray certain roles — whether in real or "reel" life.

Karloff and Lugosi were Hollywood's greatest horror stars. Yet, in the two short years after *Frankenstein,* Karloff had surpassed Lugosi in versatility, salary, and star power. The saga of *Frankenstein* and the rise of Boris Karloff were sensitive points that Carroll Borland saw in her proud, emotional friend:

> *Frankenstein* — I cannot say anything in words, but I had the feeling that it was a great disappointment to Bela that he didn't do it. As for Karloff, Bela always spoke of him very respectfully. "Karloff is a good actor," he would say — "and, of course, he has no trouble with English!" He admired and respected him. I think there was a bitterness, but Bela would never say so; it was part of his cavalier attitude — "I am never hurt, I am above anything like this" — I never heard it expressed, I could only feel it. . . .

However, one night early in the 1930s, as Bela and Carroll took one of their strolls on Hollywood Boulevard, Bela lost his cavalier cool. It was the Christmas season, and Bela revealed an emotion which would become increasingly pronounced in the years to come:

> We were walking down Hollywood Boulevard, and in those days, the celebration for Christmas meant that every streetlight was decorated with a circle of lights, and tinsel, with a star's picture inside.
>
> It was after *Frankenstein* had been released. Lugosi looked up — and there, in a circle of lights, was a picture of Boris Karloff.
>
> And I'll never forget Lugosi, looking up at that picture of Karloff, glaring at it, taking his cigar from his mouth. I'll never forget the look on his face. And I'll never forget the sound he made . . . "Grrr . . . *arrgh!*"

3
The Black Cat of 1934

... May God shield and deliver me from the fangs of the Arch-Fiend! ... and a dozen stout arms were toiling at the wall. It fell bodily. The corpse, already greatly decayed and clotted with gore, stood erect before the eyes of the spectators. Upon its head, with red extended mouth and solitary eye of fire, sat the hideous beast whose craft had seduced me into murder, and whose informing voice had consigned me to the hangman. I had walled the monster up within the tomb!

> — from Edgar Allan Poe's *The Black Cat,* 1843

"FRANKENSTEIN" Karloff, known to showmen throughout the world as "Frankie."

"DRACULA" Lugosi, whom his exhibitor friends all call "Drac."

And the third lad, EDGAR ALLAN POE, whom everybody knows as "Eddie."

These three have made good in a tremendous way, and they are getting together for one picture to scare your patrons into fits of pleasure; to tickle them pink with goose pimples; to give them the most delightful jitters of their lives, and to make them love it!

> — from Universal's pressbook for *The Black Cat,* 1934

Poor Poe. The things we did to him when he wasn't there to defend himself!

> — Boris Karloff, 1965

*   *   *

...Announce a black cat show to be staged in your theatre with prizes going to the biggest, the most beautiful, and weirdest-looking specimens. Winners can be given prize ribbons.... In every case, the cat can be treated to a big bowl of milk and the youngster who brings him or her given a pass to see the show.... You might also get the local branch of the S.P.C.A. interested....

> — from Universal's pressbook for *The Black Cat*

One sunny day, early in 1934, a strange, pastoral spectacle took place at Universal City. There was a happy mob, mostly giggling children and excited ladies, each of the members proudly cradling a black cat. It was, as Universal proclaimed it, "the first Black Cat show on record"— celebrated to select a feline for the title role in the "Karloff and Bela Lugosi" vehicle, *The Black Cat.*

"Black Cats Parade," announced a Universal Newsreel. Of course, the

Boris (bending) and Bela merrily officiating at Universal's Black Cats Parade.

stars were there: Karloff, in his black robes and satanic hairdo, a jolly Satan,
merrily hobnobbing with the contestants, petting the cats, hugging the little
finalists; Bela Lugosi, sleek and handsome in his elegant dressing gown,
genuinely warm and kind and charming as he officiated with his costar. The
day was a bonanza of publicity for Universal, which hailed the stunt in its
pressbook for *The Black Cat* as "a tremendous success."

The happy, festive black cat show was an ingenuous gimmick for what would prove to be the darkest, most perverse movie of all Universal's classic horror shows.

And it would also prove a strangely light advent for the most celebrated union of all in the world of horror films.

*   *   *

In 1933, I married Max, "Uncle Carl" Laemmle's nephew, and worked at Universal as a script clerk (we're called "script supervisors" today!). Universal was an eccentric studio, and Uncle Carl was an eccentric, dear, crazy old man — let's face it! When we arrived at work in the morning, there was a big billboard as we entered the studio, and there would be the motif of the week — "Be Kind to Others — signed, Carl Laemmle" — or some beautiful little sentimental message. Every Monday morning, it was changed....

It was amazing! At the big Laemmle estate in Benedict Canyon, every Sunday, we all came into the dining room, maybe 24 strong — all relatives. And we were not allowed to speak or sit until Uncle Carl had made his entrance. Since he was always fussing with his son, poor Junior, and his daughter Rosabelle, I finally got the seat of honor at the table, next to Uncle Carl....

—Shirley Ulmer

On January 17, 1934, Carl Laemmle, Sr., turned 67 years old. Naturally, Universal City hosted a gala birthday party, and the resident celebrities gathered around the giant chocolate birthday cake — topped by Universal's talisman of a plane circling the globe. Photographers were there, Junior Laemmle was smiling ear to ear, and a crowd including Margaret Sullavan, Ken Maynard, Andy Devine and Vince Barnett smiled around the little patriarch. Also at the festivities, back from filming RKO's *The Lost Patrol* and 20th Century's *House of Rothschild,* was Boris Karloff. And Universal welcomed him back on this auspicious day by awarding him an honorary place at the party: in the front row of guests, and on the right hand of the founder — a blessing the star accepted with a wry grin.

Universal was desperately anxious to get a new Karloff vehicle into the works. Late in 1933, Universal had announced a lineup of Karloff projects: *The Return of Frankenstein; A Trip to Mars; The Golem.* Meanwhile, on the lot was a 30-year-old Austrian boy wonder who had worked on the original German 1920 *Der Golem.* He also had worked as art director for Murnau, assistant to Lang, von Stroheim, and DeMille, a builder on the set of *The Phantom of the Opera* (and many other Universal films), codirector (with Robert Siodmak) of Germany's 1929 *People on Sunday,* and director of 1933's *Mister Broadway* and *Damaged Lives* (a saga of syphilis that wouldn't escape the censors until 1937).

His nickname was "the aesthete from the Alps"; his name was Edgar G. Ulmer.

Today, Shirley Ulmer, who married the fabled director in 1935 and was his script supervisor and life companion until his death 37 years later, actively

helps keep his great reputation alive. In the summer of 1988, she journeyed to Kenya, to speak at an Ulmer retrospective. Her memories of meeting Ulmer, just before *The Black Cat* began production, are happy, and emotional:

> I fell in love with Edgar the first time I met him—the first time I *heard* him. I was in the kitchen of my Hollywood apartment, (trying to make a pot roast!). He had come in, with some friends; I heard this thunderous voice—and I started to shiver. I thought, "I want to meet this man!" There he was, with the moustache and the wild hair—he was everything I would never have thought I'd care for—but I thought he needed me. . . .

Fated to be best-remembered for his war years work at PRC on such stylish, six-day productions as *Bluebeard* and *Detour,* Edgar Ulmer was a complex man—an artist who, by various accounts, had a strange, unorthodox view of Christianity, a fierce Oedipus complex, and a fascination with insanity. Just as James Whale found catharsis for his homosexual bitterness via Frankenstein's monster, just as Tod Browning released his grim memories of his early carnival days in *Freaks,* so would Ulmer brew his favorite fascinations and fetishes in the bubbling caldron of *The Black Cat.*

James Whale disliked the script for *The Return of Frankenstein; A Trip to Mars* appeared very costly; the German version of *The Golem* was still fresh in audience's minds. It was now that Ulmer approached his friend Junior, to sell his concept for a horror film. As Ulmer told Peter Bogdanovich in the anthology, *Kings of the Bs,* Junior was "a very dear friend of mine"; Ulmer, along with Lewis Milestone, the Wylers, and "the so-called intellectual crew with whom Junior palled around," had convinced him to produce *All Quiet on the Western Front* against Laemmle Sr. wishes:

> . . .Junior had made, against all advice from his father, *All Quiet on the Western Front* . . . I was very much taken by a German writer of the time called Fallada, who was very much like Remarque, only younger. And I sold Junior on an idea to make his book, *Little Man What Now?* (directed by Frank Borzage; Ulmer built the sets). So Junior found himself in the intellectual picture making. So when I came to him with the idea of *The Black Cat* . . . Junior gave me free rein to write a horror picture in the style we had started in Europe with *Caligari* (1919). And he gave me my head for the first time. He was a very, very strange producer; he didn't have much education, but he had great respect for intelligence and creative spirit.

As taken by Ulmer's ideas as Junior might have been, the grim truth of the matter was that the producer saw Ulmer's project as a potentially

Opposite: **On the set for *The Black Cat,* 1934. Egon Brecher (shiny hair, center), trench-coated Lugosi, Harry Cording (uppermost), Jacqueline Wells (above Cording) and David Manners (sitting on stair rail) prepare for the scene in which they arrive at Poelzig's fortress. Director Edgar Ulmer is left center with moustache.**

tiny budget opus which could deliver KARLOFF to the awaiting public far
less expensively than the previously announced vehicles. He gave just two
dictates: call the film *The Black Cat,* so to evoke the name of Edgar Allan Poe
at the box office, and star Karloff. Ulmer threw away the 1843 Poe story, as
well as three treatments already in Universal's story department.* He recalled his work on 1920's *Der Golem;* as he told Bogdanovich in *Kings of the
Bs,*

> . . .I met at that time Gustav Meyrinck, the man who wrote *Golem* as a
> novel. Meyrinck was one of these strange Prague Jews, like Kafka, who was very
> much tied up in the mystic Talmudic background. We had a lot of discussions,
> and Meyrinck at that time was contemplating a play based upon Doumont,
> which was a French fortress the Germans had shelled to pieces during the First
> World War. There were some survivors who didn't come out for years. And the
> commander was a strange Euripides figure who went crazy three years later
> when he was brought back to Paris, because he had walked on that mountain
> of bodies. . . .

While this was grim stuff indeed, *The Black Cat* critically needed a horror
element to sell it—and Ulmer lifted it from the headlines.

*   *   *

> And I saw a beast coming up out of the sea, having seven heads and ten
> horns, and upon its horns ten diadems, and upon its heads blasphemous names.
> And the beast that I saw was like a leopard, and its feet were like the feet of a
> bear, and its mouth like the mouth of a lion. And the dragon gave it his own
> might and great authority. . . . And it opened its mouth for blasphemies against
> God, to blaspheme his name and his tabernacle, and those who dwell in
> heaven. . . .
> —from Chapter 13 of the Book of the Apocalypse

"The Wickedest Man in the World" was the press appellation enjoyed by
Aleister Crowley, a Satanist with shaved head and sharpened teeth who
proudly proclaimed himself "The Beast of the Apocalypse." Born in Leam-
ington, England, on October 12, 1875, the son of hysterically religious
parents, Crowley had dabbled in "magick" (the "k" was to distinguish occult
ritual from conjuring) since 1898; he had been the inspiration for Somerset
Maugham's 1908 story "The Magician." The wealthy heir of Crowley's Ales,
and a mountain climber, writer, poet, chess player, sex maniac, drug addict

---

*Universal's story editor Richard Schayer had originally concocted a 1932 script true to Poe's story, in
which Karloff would play hard-drinking fiend Edgar Doe, who walls up his wife and cat in a cellar;
in late 1932, Junior's brother-in-law Stanley Bergerman joined with Jack Cunningham for* The Brain
Never Dies, *to feature the House of Usher and a cat with half a human brain; and in early 1933, Tom
Kilpatrick and Dale Van Every (who together would script Paramount's 1940* Dr. Cyclops) *created
a* The Black Cat *script about a wicked Count Brandos who entraps a young couple in his cat-strewn
Carpathian castle, and tries to drive the cat-fearing girl mad with various tortures—so to mate her with
his insane son Fejos, and perpetuate his lineage.*

and high priest, Crowley professed a Rabelaisian and satanic theology: "Do what thou wilt/ shall be the whole of the Law."

Crowley "peaked" in 1920, when he founded the Abbey of Thelema in a farmhouse in Cefalu, Sicily. There, with his "scarlet women" mistresses and a coven of followers, Crowley celebrated all variety of obscene rites. One witness reported a black mass in which the "scarlet woman" performed bestially with a goat — after which the goat's throat was slashed, and the blood poured over the naked back of another woman. Finally, on February 16, 1923, an Oxford undergraduate named Raoul Loveday died, following his drinking the blood of a sacrificial cat at Crowley's temple. There was a wild public scandal, and Crowley won the distinction of being exiled from Sicily by Benito Mussolini.

Basically, Crowley was a very imaginative showman, a passionate writer (his masterwork, *A Hymn to Pan,* contains the alliterative "I rave, I rape, I rip, I rend...."), a sexual degenerate — and a charlatan. The story is told how, one night, "the Beast" decided he would prove his power to become invisible by walking about London's Cafe Royal. The British diners went on with their meal, coolly ignoring Crowley as he made the rounds in his wizard's robe and conical hat. "There you are," said Crowley, "that proves I can make myself invisible. Nobody spoke to me, therefore they couldn't see me!"

Climactically, in 1932, sculptress Nina Hammnett wrote in her memoir, *Laughing Torso,* that Crowley had performed human sacrifice at Cefalu. Relishing the attention, and having squandered most of his inheritance, Crowley sued — and a sensational trial followed. "The Beast" took the stand with such flamboyant, demonic passion that the judge publicly condemned him: "...I have never heard such dreadful, horrible, blasphemous and abominable stuff as that which has been produced by the man who has described himself as the greatest living poet." Crowley lost his case and what little remained of his fortune. He faded into obscurity, living in a sad boardinghouse in Hastings, England. "These long, lonely evenings," he lamented near the end of his life. "They are so boring..." The Beast died December 1, 1947, and his ashes were sent to his followers in America. (A few years ago, filmmaker Kenneth Anger, author of *Hollywood Babylon,* visited the Abbey of Thelema, rediscovering some of Crowley's murals, while satanic groups in California are still today under the influence of "the Beast.")

The ravings of Aleister Crowley fascinated Edgar Ulmer; critically, they became the influence which made *The Black Cat* a horror film. Taking inspiration from "the Beast" (as well as Teutonic director Fritz Lang, whom Ulmer had described as "a sadist of the worst order you can imagine"), taking the "Poelzig" from Dr. Hans Poelzig (scenic designer of 1920's *Der Golem*), taking the "Hjalmar" from *The Wild Duck* by Ibsen (whom Ulmer admired deeply), Ulmer fashioned the role of Hjalmar Poelzig — High Priest of a Carpathian Lucifer cult, betrayer, murderer, necrophile, who sacrifices virgins, kills his wife, weds his stepdaughter, poses female corpses in glass coffins in his cellar, and dies skinned alive on his own embalming rack.

Of course, Poelzig was designed for poetry- and pet-loving Karloff. Would the star accept such a role? After all, having just raved in the Yuma sand dunes in John Ford's *The Lost Patrol,* and sneered at his idol George Arliss in *House of Rothschild,* two of 1934's most prestigious releases, Boris was reportedly reluctant to jump back into shockers. However, in the late 1960s, Ulmer told an interviewer:

> . . .On *The Black Cat,* I designed the sets, that "way out" house, and, if you really want to know, Mr. Karloff's wardrobe. . . . One of the things he found most exciting in the film was the wardrobe. . . . He felt in these duds, he could employ a sort of "out-of-this-world" appearance. That, as you know, was exactly as he appeared. . .

Also, Karloff found playing so horrifically evil a role as Poelzig irresistible. In an interview with *Screen Play* magazine, "Hollywood's Forbidden Face," decorated with a portrait from *The Black Cat,* Boris spoke of his attraction to such screen ogres:

> . . .it dates right back to Mother Eve, who perhaps first revealed that evil is much more fascinating than good when she allowed the serpent to merchandize his apple. There's a little bit of evil in us all. . . . Most people—even most actors—don't get the chance that is mine to indulge this inherently bad streak. . . . I insist upon taking on not only the exterior appearance of the creature but also his psychology as completely as possible for me to do. This allows me an escape from myself. . . . When I am .through with a character, he has definitely vanished and with him all that is unsettled and restless in my being. I have done with the fellow, so to speak, and you have no idea what a contented state results!

Working along Ulmer's conceptions, Jack Pierce would make a devil out of Boris, giving him a triangular coiffure, along with a sick makeup of white greasepaint and black lipstick that transformed the actor into an effeminate Beelzebub.

With Peter Ruric, a young writer who contributed to *Black Mask* under the name of Paul Cain, who streamlined Ulmer's ideas into a screenplay, and whose $1966.65 salary surpassed Ulmer's own compensation for the film, *The Black Cat* sinuously evolved into the most perverse of Universal's horror tales, spiked with necrophilia, incest, sexual perversity and insanity.

Yet it was only now—with production imminent—that Junior Laemmle had the brainstorm which would award *The Black Cat* its major fame in Hollywood history.

FRANKENSTEIN
and
DRACULA
together in
THE BLACK CAT
— Universal PR material for *The Black Cat*

On Saturday night, February 10, 1934, Bela Lugosi was a resplendent guest of honor at the Hungarian Actors Ball at New York City's Pennsylvania Hotel. Having left the Broadway company of *Murder at the Vanities* and completed a tour of vaudeville houses in scenes from *Dracula,* Bela, dramatically lamenting his vampire typecasting, was about to begin rehearsals for the play *Pagan Fury,* in which he would star as a bohemian painter. "Seldom does a part in such a monumental and symbolic drama come to an actor!" rejoiced Bela of his new play.

Then came Universal's offer: a three-picture deal for Bela Lugosi, with roles in *The Black Cat, Dracula's Daughter,* and *The Suicide Club.* Mercurial Bela, finding the glory of Hollywood irresistible, abandoned his "monumental and symbolic" play and headed west for the sunshine of Universal City. The actor enthusiastically met with Ulmer, had a long talk in German, and convinced Edgar he could play "a romantic or at least a benign role." Ulmer began fattening the part of Dr. Vitus Werdegast, the avenging angel who would so grimly right the wrongs his "old friend" Poelzig had savored. The sympathetic role had a macabre, Caligari-like twist; Werdegast was a psychiatrist who had a dread terror of felines.

Universal City was thrilled to have paired Karloff and Lugosi. In fact, Junior Laemmle was so pleased that he blueprinted *The Black Cat* to rely almost entirely on their names—affording Ulmer an absurdly tiny budget and shooting schedule:

•The Universal Picture Corporation Production Estimate for production #677 revealed a budget of only $91,125.00—25 percent of which was studio overhead. (The budget of *Dracula* had been $355,050; the budget of *Frankenstein* had been $262,007.)

•The shooting schedule for *The Black Cat* was only 15 days—about half the time afforded a moderate "A" production. (*Dracula* had a 36-day schedule, and had taken 42 days; *Frankenstein,* a 30-day-schedule, and had run 35 days.)

•Ulmer's fee as director was only $900—about one-third what James Whale was reaping weekly at Universal.

However, the most fascinating statistics concerned the stars of *The Black Cat:*

•Universal's "Picture Talent" estimate for *The Black Cat* set Boris Karloff for the role of Poelzig at a guaranteed "flat fee" of $7500—actually four weeks' accumulation of the $1875 he was weekly earning as a Universal contract star. Also, just as MGM billed its top deity simply as GARBO, Universal would proclaim the top-billed Boris, for the first time on the screen, simply as KARLOFF.

•Bela Lugosi, as Werdegast, was guaranteed three weeks' work—at a rate of $1000 per week. It was a painfully modest salary for a star; in fact, David Manners, veteran of *Dracula* and *The Mummy,* signing for the role of romantic hero Peter Alison ("one of America's greatest authors—of

unimportant books"), originally secured a better deal than Bela: $1250 per week for two and a half weeks' work (total: $3125).

Having paired the "Twin Titans of Terror," and supplying the ever-dapper Mr. Manners, Junior Laemmle felt obliged to add little else in the way of high-priced talent:

•For the role of heroine Joan Alison, the honeymooning (presumed) virgin whom Poelzig desires to sacrifice to Satan, Universal signed Jacqueline Wells, a brunette, bee-stung-lipped *Wampas* Baby Star, late of Principal's 1933 *Tarzan the Fearless*. Miss Wells signed for *The Black Cat* for $300 per week, and a guaranteed $900.

•For the part of Karen, Poelzig's doomed stepdaughter/wife, the studio set blonde contractee Lucille Lund, one of Miss Wells' fellow 1934 *Wampas* Baby Stars, and winner of a Universal beauty contest. Miss Lund was set for one week's work at $150 to play a role of special interest to Ulmer: in his original conception, Karen had decayed morally (and supernaturally) until she looked like a Siamese cat.

•For the role of Thamal, Werdegast's mute, giant servant, Universal tagged Harry Cording, for $200 per week, and two and a half weeks' work. Over the decades, the heavy, balding, moustached Cording became a fixture at Universal, and acted in such horror films as 1939's *Son of Frankenstein*, 1941's *The Wolf Man*, and 1942's *The Ghost of Frankenstein*.

Egon Brecher, who had played such parts as Captain Hook and the Master Builder in Eva Le Gallienne's then recently-disbanded Civic Repertory Company, got a $500 per week contract to play the sinister Majordomo, set for two weeks and one day's work; Henry Armetta and Albert Conti signed on (at, respectively, $150 and $125 for one day's work) as the bickering Sergeant and Lieutenant who provide the film with its one fleeting vignette of comic relief; and Anna Duncan, stepdaughter of dancer Isadora Duncan, signed to play the Poelzig maid, set at $125 per week and two weeks' work. (Universal's wheezy Andy Devine was announced for *The Black Cat,* and his name even appeared on some of the film's early posters, but it appears nowhere in the movie's preproduction sheets.)

How did Ulmer get by with so perverse a script? "Uncle Carl" was on a vacation junket to Germany; Junior, who hated to read scripts anyway, departed for New York in mid–February, facing court charges of "salary gouging." This left the "supervising" (or lack of it) to E.M. Asher, who got a flat $2000 for *The Black Cat,* and who (as Shirley Ulmer remembers) had the strange habit of meeting Ulmer for conferences while the producer sat on his toilet.

Destined to help capture the warped vision on *The Black Cat* were two Universal compatriots: John Mescall, the gifted (but sadly alcoholic) cinematographer whose most famous credit would be Whale's 1935 *Bride of*

Opposite: Poster for *The Black Cat,* 1934.

Frankenstein, and Heinz Roemheld, who had just dynamically scored *The In visible Man.* The 32-year-old, Berlin-trained composer had been head of Universal's Music Department, composing music for the studio's release of G.W. Pabst's *The White Hell of Pitz Palu* and supervising the music of *Dracula;* the studio had laid him off in 1931, and Roemheld had spent two almost destitute years in Washington, D.C., playing piano in the lobby of the Shoreham Hotel and giving piano lessons. Now back in Hollywood, Roemheld (fated to win an Academy Award for Warner's 1942 *Yankee Doodle Dandy*) would embrace Ulmer's idea to score *The Black Cat* with classical motifs, and their major inspiration would be none other than Franz Liszt — who himself had a fascination with Satan.

The shooting script for *The Black Cat,* dated February 27, 1934, was complete with a warning foreword from Carl Laemmle, Jr., that the script was "the property of Universal Pictures Corporation," and that anybody who lost a script owed the studio $25.00. And Shirley Kasseler Alexander — who was to become Shirley Ulmer a year later — was delighted to be assigned to *The Black Cat* as an assistant to the script girl.

On Wednesday morning, February 28, 1934, the morning broke over the mountain at Universal City — and *The Black Cat* began shooting.

On Saturday, March 17, 1934, shooting "wrapped."

On Sunday, March 25, 1934, shooting began again.

In those 19 days, Universal City created the decade's sickest (and, in many ways, most fascinating) horror film — and provided the backdrop for the first glorious teaming and sadly emotional relationship of Karloff and Bela Lugosi.

*   ACT I   *

.on't play down the sensational angles — capitalize on them! Flash the town with sensational ballyhoo! Send your message searing through the city, cry to the skies that you have the biggest triple-barreled, non-stop, emotion-wrangler that ever stalked across a screen!
— from Universal's pressbook for *The Black Cat*

Compartment F, Car 96, the Orient express. Pruned from the script was the wedding of Peter and Joan Alison in a Vienna cathedral; instead, *The Black Cat* opens, with a flourish from Liszt's "Hungarian Rhapsody," in a dark, gloomy train depot, where food is being loaded onto the train. A patrolman holds the passport of Joan Alison close to the camera. He lowers the passport, and there, snug in the compartment sit our newlywed heroes — David Manners and Jacqueline Wells.

David Manners had made a splendid Hollywood bow as the doomed Raleigh in 1930's *Journey's End,* directed by James Whale (who "discovered" the stage actor at a Hollywood party); the climax gave him a great death scene in the skeletal arms of Colin Clive ("To me, his face was a tragic mask," remembers Manners). Too quickly, Manners became Hollywood's storybook horror hero of *Dracula* and *The Mummy*, and self-effacing counterpart to such high-powered, high-heeled cinema deities as Ruth Chatterton, Barbara Stanwyck, Kay Francis, Constance Bennett and Katharine Hepburn. In 1934, the privacy-craving actor was only two years away from retiring from the screen forever—"Wherever I went, I seemed to be on show. I didn't feel free." A cynic might argue that Manners' effete, Beau Brummell type (he once beseeched Eva Le Gallienne to help him get effemininety out of his acting) was obsolete by 1936. Still, never did Manners play with more dash, humor and style than he did as writer Peter Alison in *The Black Cat*. "I had a good director in that one," Manners told me. "Edgar was most helpful and friendly."

As for Jacqueline Wells ... Peter Ruric describes Joan Alison in his script as "hyper-virginal," and indeed, there's a deadly coy look in Miss Wells' eyes and grin (directed by Ulmer?) that well-suits the beleagured bride who proves a nemesis for both Poelzig and Werdegast. Miss Wells had an odd career in Hollywood. She had begun her career at age nine in 1923's *Maytime*, acted on the California stage, studied dance with Theodore Kosloff (who would stage the "Spirit of Poe" ballet for *The Raven*), and signed with Paramount, where she played in such 1933 releases as *Alice in Wonderland* and W.C. Fields' *Tillie and Gus*. In 1939, she married money in the person of Walter Brooks, whose mother was multimillionairess Louise Cromwell, who had later married Gen. Douglas MacArthur—and was then married to Lionel Atwill. The marriage didn't last, and she would sign with Warner Bros. under the name of Julie Bishop, winning her special footnote in Hollywood history: by reportedly signing a $25,000 policy with Lloyd's of London, insuring her against gaining four inches or more around her waist and or hips during the seven-year pact.

The romantic leads clinch for John Mescall's camera (which seems smitten with Miss Wells); under jazzy thirties music they laugh how their wedding luncheon was made of papier-mâché (Manners gives it the French pronunciation), and they decide to dine romantically in the compartment. "Elegant!" flirts Joan.*

The script also featured an overt sign of Joan's "hyper-virginal" fears when, looking up at Peter with "shy, frightened" eyes, she begs him, "Please—don't lock the door." The fear is only suggested by glances in the release print. "Ulmer was a great one for using glances," says Shirley Ulmer, "thus defying censorship!"

There originally followed a comic episode (doomed to the cutting room floor) with the Maître D'Hôtel, played by plump Herman Bing, whom Ulmer knew was a part of F. W. Murnau's entourage. Bing (who had played the German who claimed Erik the Ape was speaking Italian in Universal's Murders in the Rue Morgue), woos the newlyweds with promises of such epicurean delights as Chateaubriand, crêpes Suzette, and a 1911 Tokay wine. "I congratulate you, sir, on ordering a dinner that you will never forget!" announces Bing's Maître D'—then, according to the script, "belches slightly—a frail feather of a belch." This entire character was cut from the release print; Bing, whose dialectic comedy soon faded from movie fashion, committed suicide in 1948.

The train stops at Budapest. There is an interruption. Space has been sold to a gentleman in the newlyweds' private compartment.

"Do please forgive this intrusion," intones Dr. Vitus Werdegast.

"Oh, he looked beautiful in that!" Lillian Lugosi once signed about her husband in *The Black Cat.* Indeed, Bela is tall, distinguished, dynamic; oddly, his dramatic entrance is partially blocked by the porter — as opposed to the various baroque entrances enjoyed by Karloff in the movie. As if to punctuate this first bit of sexual repression, Werdegast bumps into the phonograph, and the needle scratches across the jazz record that's been serenading the newlyweds. Then a bag soon falls from the rack above, seemingly destined for Joan's brunette head before the gentlemen intercept it.

"Sorry I frightened you, darling," says Manners.

"It is, after all, better to be frightened, than to be crushed!" smiles Lugosi in Hungarian charm.

There are polite, charming introductions; but with Werdegast's "intrusion," Ulmer has set the film on its wild and sexually aberrant course. And, as Lugosi, after ominously announcing his intent to visit "an old friend," asks if he may open the shutter to look out in the night, his own reflection — diabolical in the dark, and shrouded with smoke from the train — glares back at him, accompanied by Liszt's brooding *Tasso* theme, which becomes Werdegast's leitmotif. . . .

The train races through the stormy night, itself diabolical with its blazing furnace and billowing smoke. And, as the strains of Tchaikovsky's *Romeo and Juliet* serve as the Alisons' theme (nicknamed "Cat Love" by the mischievous Roemheld), Manners' Peter Alison awakens to find Lugosi's Werdegast stroking the hair of his sleeping wife. Bela movingly builds a passionate monologue:

> I beg your indulgence, my friend. Eighteen years ago I left a girl — so like your lovely wife — to go to war. For Kaiser and country, you know. She was my wife. Have you ever heard of — Kurgaal? It is a prison below Omsk on Lake Bakail. Many men have gone there. Few have returned. I have returned. After fifteen years — I have *returned!*

Was Lugosi thinking of his own war wounds? Or how he finally escaped World War I (according to one source) by persuading the Army that he was insane? Whatever his "method," the delivery has wonderful intensity, his face seemingly ready to convulse with emotion as the scene fades out. Ulmer, however, found Bela's overplaying to be a problem.

"You had to cut away from Lugosi continuously," Ulmer told Bogdanovich, "to cut him down."

It is 2:00 a.m. The train arrives at a hellishly stormy Vizhegrad. The scene was shot at night on the Universal lot, with rain machines and requiring 75 "Midnite Meals" catered for the company. There, Werdegast and the Alisons board a bus, accompanied by Vitus's servant, Thamal — a giant mute, reminiscent of Ulmer's old friend, the Golem. Harry Cording well suits the role. In portentous thunder and lightning, the bus rolls off into the Carpathian Mountains, over a road built by the Austrian army, as the splendidly moustachioed driver narrates:

> All of this country was one of the greatest battlefields of the war. Tens of thousands of men died here. The ravine down there was piled twelve deep with dead and wounded men. The little river below was swollen — red — a raging torrent of blood. That high hill, yonder, where engineer Poelzig now lives, was the site of Fort Marmaros. He built his home on its very foundations. Marmaros! The greatest graveyard in the world!

As the driver hugely enjoys his grim tale, Ulmer focuses on the passengers' reactions: the Alisons, laughing at the driver's dramatics; Thamal, enigmatic, expressionless; and Werdegast, blinking back emotion. However, the bus rolls out of control.* In a $250 John P. Fulton miniature special effect (filmed during the retake period), the bus crashes through a fence. The effect is bizarre — a prop tree falls over like a shot ballerina — but it's strangely in touch with the surreal film itself. Joan screams, the passengers topple . . . after a dissolve, we learn that the driver is dead. Thamal carries the unconscious Joan, and Werdegast and Peter join them as they look up the mountain in the storm

There, atop a Carpathian crag, introduced with a blast of Liszt's *The Rakoczy March,* looming over a graveyard and with storm clouds racing in the sky, is Fort Marmaros — the lair of Hjalmar Poelzig.

"It was very, very much out of my Bauhaus period," said Ulmer of Fort Marmaros, a scenic masterwork — a modernistic glass and marble mausoleum, sleekly sinister, and totally unique from the gothic creations usually a part of Universal's horror shows. For all the Bauhaus influence, the opening shot of the Marmaros exterior (a $175 process created by the team of Lawson and Cosgrove, also shot during the retake period) perhaps owes its major inspiration to Hollywood: the Ennis-Brown House, 2607 Glendower Avenue in the Hollywood Hills, designed by Frank Lloyd Wright, completed in 1925, and popularly known today by horror buffs as "The Black Cat House." A Los Angeles landmark, it also was *The House on Haunted Hill* (1958), played a part in such movies as *The Day of the Locust* and *Terminal Man,* and offers house tours. Ulmer, of course, designed the great hall, with its sinuous staircase and avant-garde arches — created for $3700, plus $1000 worth of objet d'art props.

---

*It was here that the Black Cat was to appear for the first time, over the injured Joan; "The cat slowly stretches its lean throat," noted Ruric's script, "sniffs delicately — its thin wisp of tongue darts out and it very delicately licks at the dark trickle of blood from a wound on Joan's white shoulder." Werdegast was to grab the cat by the throat and fling the cat "savagely against a rock." After the group departed for Marmaros, the camera was to reveal that the black cat, apparently deathless, was no longer there.

The stranded trio enter Fort Marmaros, accompanied by Chopin's *Second Piano Prelude,* admitted by Egon Brecher's Majordomo—stooped, gnarled, and wearing a $100 made-to-order hairpiece especially designed for the film. Lugosi briskly demands a place to dress the lady's injury, as the Majordomo announces, via intercom, a visitor. . . .

The shooting script noted the ominously sensual effect as we see the Poelzig bedroom:

> CAMERA slowly approaches grey mass which takes gradual form in the dim light as a very large low square bed. Smoke colored gauze descends in smooth vertical sheets to almost entirely enclose it. . . .
> As the CAMERA approaches the bed the upper part of a man's body rises slowly, as if pulled by wires, to a sitting position. In rising, one arm sweeps backward and covers with a gauze thin sheet the nude body of a woman. We are not shown her nudity but know it from the curve of her body under the thin sheet. . . .

Werdegast treats the still unconscious Joan; Manners winces as the psychiatrist injects a narcotic. The door opens. . .

There stands Karloff's Poelzig—a modern Lucifer, festooned in satanic hairdo and black robe, and introduced with a flurry of *Sonata in B Minor* by Liszt—"The Devil Sonata." "The earthly incarnation of Satan," is how the shooting script hailed Poelzig; those magnificent eyes ravage the sleeping Joan, as Ulmer treats Karloff's Devil to a reverential entrance, Mescall's camera virtually genuflecting before him. High Priest Poelzig will be Karloff's most slyly perverse performance; indeed, the actor prowls through *The Black Cat* like a great, satanic wolf, yet with a feline touch. . . .

On the set, "Dear Boris" was a devil, too—but in a different way. As Ulmer remembered:

> . . .Karloff was a very charming man . . . . Very charming. And he never took himself seriously. My biggest job was to keep him in the part, because he laughed at himself. . . . One of the nicest scenes I had with him, he lies in bed next to the daughter of Lugosi, and the young couple rings down at the door, and he gets up and you see him the first time in costume, in that modernistic set . . . he got into bed, we got ready to shoot, and he got up, he turned to the camera, after he put his shoes on, and said "Boo!" Every time I had him come in by the door, he would open the door and say, "Here comes the heavy. . . ." He was a very, very lovely man . . . a very fine actor. Five star. As you know, he lisped—but the way he used that lisp—he knew exactly how to overcome the handicap.

In Poelzig's study, the Satanist sits behind his desk, framed by white flowers; Werdegast stands before him. "You sold Marmaros to the Russians," sneers Lugosi. "Scuttled away in the night and left us to die. Is it to be wondered that you should choose this place to build your house? The masterpiece of construction—built upon the ruins of the masterpiece of destruction—the masterpiece of murder. The murderer of 10,000 men returns to the place of his crime!" (The script had put it into the vernacular, "scene of his crime"; it was an expression with which the Hungarian Lugosi was perhaps not familiar.)

Lugosi's face and tone become haunted as he remembers, "Those who died were fortunate. I was taken prisoner—to Kurgaal. Kurgaal, where the soul is killed—slowly. Fifteen years I've rotted in the darkness—waited. Not to kill you—to kill your soul—slowly." And then, demanding: "Where is my wife, Karen? And my daughter?"

Werdegast then accuses Poelzig of stealing his wife after betraying Marmaros—and tells how he traced them to America, Spain, South America—and finally, back to Marmaros.

"Vitus," says Karloff, dramatically rising, "you are mad!"

The leer on Karloff's face becomes a sick smile; Manners has entered the study. "I'm sorry if I'm intruding," says the hero.

"Not at all. Do come in," smiles Karloff, punching the comedy of the line. "We were just going to have something to drink!"

The three men pour on the charm; the Majordomo gets Alison a whiskey, and Karloff turns on his modern radio, offering a bit of Schubert's *Unfinished Symphony.*

"Engineer Poelzig is one of Austria's greatest architects," smirks Lugosi.

"And Dr. Werdegast," smiles Karloff, in a line that taxes his lisp to the limit, "is one of Hungary's greatest psychiatrists."

Manners melodramatically whispers he's an author of "mysteries!"—and Bela proposes a toast. "To you, my friend. To your charming wife, and to Love!"

A Black Cat runs across the room.

For all the ballyhoo of Universal's Black Cat Contest, the records reveal a dispatch to the studio ranch, engaging "1 Special Black Cat" for two weeks' work and a Depression salary of $200. Fifty dollars was allotted for "Additional Cats," perhaps those prize winners selected on that gala day on the back lot. Certainly, it was good money in 1934 for an animal. "In those days," says Shirley Ulmer, "I was making $50 a week and considered *very* highly paid!"

Impressively, at the sight of the cat, all of Werdegast's continental charm escapes; the anguished soul drops his glass, grabs a knife and hurls it fatally at the cat. Almost swooning, his face in his hands, Lugosi's Werdegast tries to recover, as Karloff's Poelzig slinks around him—clearly enjoying this abnormal fit. (Strangely enough, Bela himself had a fear of black cats—as his fifth wife, Hope, revealed in a 1957 interview, a year after his death: "He was afraid of cats. He hated them. Now I have a black cat sitting in front of his painting. If he knew that he'd die all over again.")

Meanwhile, in *The Black Cat,* the title feline isn't the only one slinking. So is Joan, who enters the room, in her nightgown, in a sexy trance. What Ulmer had wanted here—only implied in the film—was clearly noted in the script:

> As she stands above the cat her eyes close and a faint tremor disturbs her body. . . . A strange and at first indefinable change has come over her face; by means of makeup and lighting, her chaste beauty has taken on a sensual, faintly animalistic contour. . . . There is something distinctly feline in her expression, in the way she moves. . . .

"You are frightened, Doctor?" she asks Werdegast, almost mockingly, with a hint of the "faintly malicious smile" called for in the script. Then she oomphs to Karloff. "You are our host," she flirts. "At your service, Madame," says Karloff suggestively, clearly enjoying the metamorphosis that has overwhelmed Joan's soul. Karloff takes her hand, kisses it, and purrs:

> You must be indulgent of Dr. Werdegast's weakness. He is the unfortunate victim of one of the commoner phobias, but in an extreme form. He has an intense and all-consuming horror—of cats!

Karloff's delivery of this line is a masterpiece of villainy; as he lisps of Lugosi's little secret, his eyes roll and his mouth curls in a way that makes the line sacrilegious, erotic and sinister all at once.

The possessed Joan glides to Peter—and gives Manners the most passionate kiss he ever received in the movies. It is a superbly sensual touch; the camera watches it, almost voyeuristically, from beneath the robed sleeve of Poelzig, who has grasped a statue of a nude woman atop his desk. As Joan kisses Peter, Poelzig's arm passionately grips the statue, Mescall's camera focusing back and forth from the lovers' kiss to the clutching arm. Manners scoops his suddenly sensual bride in his arms. "Good night, gentlemen!" he says. (Once again, the shooting script provided a bizarre bonus to this wicked scene: the Black Cat, again, has resurrected, and as Joan lies in bed, ". . . CAMERA draws back to take in the black cat which has jumped onto the bed and is rubbing itself luxuriously against Joan's body.")

With Joan back to sleep, the three men meet in the hallway. Manners mentions the "curious change" in Joan, and Lugosi superficially blames the narcotic. However, he does partially explain the erotic proceedings with, "Sometimes these cases take strange forms. The victim becomes, in a sense, mediumistic—a vehicle for all the intangible forces in operation around her."

"Sounds like a lot of supernatural baloney to me," says ingenuous Peter.

"Supernatural—perhaps," replies Lugosi, masterfully. "Baloney—perhaps not. There are many things—under the sun."

The question of the cat arises—"Joan seemed so curiously affected when you killed it," says Peter. "That was — coincidence, I think," says Werdegast. "However, certain ancient books say that the black cat is the living embodiment of evil. At death that evil enters into the nearest living thing. It is . . ."

"The black cat does not die," interjects Poelzig. "Those same books, if I am not mistaken, teach that the black cat is deathless — deathless as evil. . . ." The High Priest shows the men to their bedrooms.

"Good night, Vitus," purrs Poelzig. "Sleep well . . ."

The 1934 digital clock reads 4:37 a.m. The scene dissolves into the dynamite-fraught cellars of Fort Marmaros. The music is a strange, classical 5/4 "three-legged waltz," which Roemheld entitled *Morgue*. And the insinuation is one of the most ghoulishly baroque of all Universal's horror shows. . . .

To the romantic strains of *Morgue,* Karloff's Lucifer, lovingly stroking a black cat, haunts the Marmaros cellars, his own kinky kingdom of hell, slyly eyeballing the embalmed female sacrifices preserved in vertical crystal caskets. And it is here, we soon discover, where Poelzig keeps his special trophy. Looking like a morbid Frederick's of Hollywood mannequin, hanging from a blonde, wildly-teased wig in her exotic, see-through coffin, is the corpse of Karen — Werdegast's wife.

"The sex scene of sex scenes!" laughs Shirley Ulmer of this fantastic perversity, shot during the retake period. Six anonymous actresses, whose dreams probably embraced snapping their garters for Busby Berkeley, found themselves as Poelzig's erotic corpses in this necrophiliac fantasy, earning $12.50 each; Lucille Lund, cast as Karen the daughter, here posed as Karen the mother. The brazenly macabre episode delicately suggested more than it stated. These ladies had been Poelzig's brides of Satan, raped at his Black Mass altar, murdered, and, by some wicked embalmment magic, preserved forever for his lustful review; Karen, apparently slaughtered by her husband, has joined them. The script itself seemed frightened of this idea as it noted ". . . Poelzig's embalming room, where he immortalizes the bodies of his women after having immortalized their souls in other, perhaps gentler, ways. . . ."

"I love that scene," says Shirley Ulmer. "Naughty, but nice!" Surely, if Karloff nursed any bitterness about his own previous three (or four) wives, he might have exorcised it in this sensually nightmarish vignette. . . .

Into these cellars, past the old gun turrets, Poelzig guides the vengeance-craving Werdegast. And there, framed against a looming glass gun chart, Werdegast sees Karen, posed in her casket. Karloff illuminates the coffin; with a strange, graceful, almost balletic gesture, he touches the glass coffin and looks up at the body.

"You see, Vitus. I have cared for her tenderly, and well. You will find her almost as beautiful as when you last saw her. She died two years after the war."

"How?"

"With pneumonia." (A blink betrays Poelzig's lie.) "She was never very strong you know."

Bela never looked so handsome in the movies as he does in this close-up, mournfully lovesick at the sight of his Karen.

"And the child? Our daughter?"

"Dead."

"And why is she . . . ," asks Bela, heartbreakingly, ". . . why is she — like this?"

"Is she not beautiful?" hisses Boris. "I wanted to have her beauty, always. I loved her too, Vitus."

"Lies! All lies, Hjalmar! You killed her! You killed her, as I am about to kill you!"

The Black Cat runs into the scene. With a scream, Werdegast falls back with his pistol, crashing into the glass charts of Fort Marmaros.

Beethoven's *Seventh Symphony* begins, like some hallowed hymn of the damned; Mescall's enchanted, voyeuristic camera begins a tour of the cellars, up the twisting staircase as Karloff's disembodied voice beautifully speaks the movie's most memorably sinister soliloquy:

> Come, Vitus. Are we men or are we children? Of what use are all these melodramatic gestures? You say your soul was killed, and that you have been dead all these years. And what of me? Did we not both die here in Marmaros, fifteen years ago? Are we any the less victims of the war than those whose bodies were torn asunder? Are we not both — the living dead? And now you come to me — playing at being an avenging angel — childishly thirsting for my blood. We understand each other too well. We know too much of life. We shall play a little game, Vitus. A game of death, if you like. . . .

Back upstairs, Werdegast retires to his room, and Poelzig enters his boudoir. The blonde sylph in his bed awakens, and we hear Brahms' *Sapphic Ode* — Karen's theme.

"What is it, Hjalmar?"

"It's nothing. Only an accident on the road below."

Karloff slides into the bed. His face nears hers, and his hands glides sensuously over her face. Her eyes close . . .

"I want you to stay in this room all day tomorrow, Karen. You are the very core and meaning of my life. No one shall take you from me. Not even Vitus. Not even your *father*."

But Poelzig's thoughts stray from Karen. They embrace Joan. And the High Priest of Satan opens his missal, *Rites of Lucifer,* and reads:

> In the night, in the dark of the moon,
> the High Priest assembles his
> disciples for the sacrifice.
> The chosen maiden is garbed in white . . .

*   INTERMISSION   *

"We don't stay young and lovely forever!" David Manners warned me in 1976, when he granted my wife and me one of his very rare interviews. The actor, who had retired from Hollywood in 1936 and from public life after a 1949 tour in *Lady Windermere's Fan,* was living in a lovely house high in Pacific Palisades, overlooking Will Rogers State Park, where he wrote on metaphysics; he greeted us on a beautiful summer day in his garden, and it was a relief to find the mysterious septuagenarian trim, turtlenecked, and still classically handsome. My immediate emotion was joy at shaking the hand of this man who was a legend in horror cinema—a legend he was quick to dismiss.

"I *hated* doing those things," Manners winced. "I never dreamed they would become classics!"

He was gracious, and laughed easily. And, when I mentioned *The Black Cat,* he gave one of his louder laughs.

> Lugosi and Karloff—those two in the same picture!
> They weren't very much alike—Karloff, delightful; Lugosi, a mystery and distant. How did they get along? They got along very well, as far as Karloff was concerned. With Lugosi, though, I think there was some jealousy. Lugosi was a big star—in his own mind!

During the eventful 19 days of the shooting of *The Black Cat,* Karloff and Bela Lugosi were the talk of Universal City. The stars hosted the famous "Black Cat Contest," delighting the cat-cradling contestants. PR boys flocked to the set, begging for candids, posing Karloff on a ladder looking down at Lugosi—who defied superstition by sitting under it. Every day there was the 4:00 p.m. tea break, Universal's special concession to star Karloff, and Boris enjoyed a cigarette and his tea while Bela peacefully puffed his omnipresent cigar.

Nevertheless, gossip soon spread under the mountains of Universal, around Hollywood, and through posterity for over half-a-century: the "Twin Titans of Terror" were not hitting it off. Rumors of hot "hostility" circulated.

And—as David Manners crystallized it—there truly was trouble.

Eight years after Bela Lugosi's death, a serene Boris Karloff, in a *Films in Review* story by Robert C. Roman, delicately discussed the problem:

> Poor old Bela. It was a strange thing. He was really a shy, sensitive, talented man who had a fine career on the classical stage in Europe. But he made a fatal mistake. He never took the trouble to learn our language. Consequently, he was very suspicious on the set, suspicious of tricks, fearful of what he regarded as scene-stealing. Later, when he realized I didn't go in for such nonsense, we became friends. . . .

Karloff looks down upon Lugosi, on the set of *The Black Cat*.

According to Lillian Lugosi Donlevy, who drove Bela to Universal and back home every day (he never learned to drive), Lugosi never considered Karloff his "friend." When I asked this low-key (but candid) lady if her husband was ever friendly with Boris, her response was immediate and dramatic: *"No!"* She elaborated, giving insight into how her late husband had regarded "Dear Boris":

> Bela didn't like Karloff; he thought he was "a cold fish." And Karloff was *ugly!* He *lisped!* Really, in life, without any makeup or anything, he really was a *very* unattractive man.... Bowed legs.... Oh! *everything* against him!

Boris would diplomatically blame Bela's English problems for the conflicts—"He had real problems with his speech, and difficulty interpreting lines. I remember he once asked a director what a line of dialogue meant. He spent a great deal of his time with the Hungarian colony in Los Angeles, and this isolated him."

However, it appears certain that a problem, at least equal with the language, was ego.

Shirley Ulmer, the assistant script clerk on *The Black Cat,* was on the set every day. As such, she enjoyed a ringside seat at the sideshow of the Boris and Bela offscreen relationship:

> Karloff was the "intellect with the lisp"—he was a very well-educated, intelligent guy, with a great sense of humor. The Karloff I first knew at Universal was very posh, dressed immaculately, a bit mysterious, very drawn into himself—*unless* he met somebody he considered his equal; then you got to know him. I guess I would never have gotten to know him, except for how he opened up to Edgar. Karloff was a hell of a good actor. Of course, he had that damned lisp! We had a terrible time, because he couldn't say "black cat"—he'd say, "black cath!" But he understood the undercurrents that Ulmer was trying to bring out, with the Black Mass, and so forth.
> And Bela didn't.
> There *was* a certain rivalry, because Boris was the "intellect" and Bela was the "performer." To me, Lugosi seemed like a very lower-middle class guy, whom people didn't take seriously; I think he was a very insecure man. On *The Black Cat,* Karloff really became the director's "pet," and Lugosi did resent that. You see, when Edgar would start talking in a Kafka-like manner, about music, about psychiatry (Edgar was a Jungian)—things that Lugosi didn't understand—he and Karloff could talk with each other. Karloff and Edgar would go off, and Edgar would spend evenings with him, and they would have big dissertations. Bela just didn't belong.... So, since he couldn't get involved in those conversations on the set, Bela would tell stories—how he had been a hangman back in Hungary! They were *weird* stories, and I can only wonder how they affected Karloff, who was the perfect gentleman....
> You could never call Edgar a "snob"; but in this instance, without meaning to, he might have insulted poor Bela a little bit. Bela couldn't join in the fun Edgar was having with Boris, I guess it made him mad—and, thinking about it now, I don't blame him!"

On *The Black Cat,* Bela Lugosi, a sensitive man, resented Karloff, the "cold fish," who had top billing, a superior salary, and that p.m. tea break— which Bela detested. (All his life he bitterly ridiculed Boris's tea ritual when reminiscing with admirers.) He mistrusted the Krafft-Ebing conversations Boris enjoyed with Ulmer. He worried that Karloff would steal their scenes. And, no matter how charming Boris was to him on the set, Bela always had the memory of the summer of 1931, the *Frankenstein* test debacle, and how, as Lillian Lugosi put it, "Bela created his own monster...."

Shirley Ulmer vividly harbors a revealing off-the-set memory of Bela Lugosi:

> I'll never forget my visit to Bela Lugosi's home, right as we began work on *The Black Cat!* He lived in the Hills somewhere. Edgar, who took me there, had not properly prepared me—and it really was like the worst horror film you ever could imagine! He had this huge painting of himself, in bold, full regalia. His dogs were there. His poor little wife had to serve us, and every time she came in, he insulted her, and screamed at her—I'll never forget it ... and I was so scared of him I was really shaking in my pants, too! I wonder if he got a kick out of scaring me....

Bela Lugosi, by nature, was a dominating man—but, on *The Black Cat,* he was finding himself dominated. The difference in the stars of the film was more than that of simply an Englishman and an Hungarian (with all those stereotypes suggest). Boris Karloff was so intoxicated with becoming a star after so many real-life melodramas that he simply loved his work—even affectionately regarding a man who clearly had no affection for him. But Bela Lugosi took stardom as his due—indulging a large ego, and naturally resenting the monstrous cold fish who was such a threat to that ego.

"Karloff was definitely the shrewder of the two," wrote John Brosnan in *The Horror People,* "but probably his main advantage was that he never took himself very seriously, while poor Lugosi never got the joke. And a rather cruel one it was." Boris, through it all, always regarded Bela as "a kind and lovable man," but, after *The Black Cat,* he would always refer to his costar the same way; he always called him, "Poor Bela."

*   ACT II   *

> It will be a good idea at least for the first few showings of *The Black Cat* to plant a few women in the audience with instructions to scream at certain high spots of the picture. Screams put the audience into the right mood for enjoyment of the picture and also serve to start word-of-mouth advertising which spreads like wildfire...
> —advice to the exhibitors from *The Black Cat* pressbook

The shooting script of *The Black Cat,* Universal's production estimate for "Additional Scenes for the Black Cat," and the final release print all relate that the second half of this film, for all its wild aberrations, was a milder shocker than Edgar Ulmer plotted — or filmed.

Morning has dawned. In a comic scene, also destined for the cutting room, David Manners has breakfast at Marmaros. Realizing the servants can't understand what he's saying, the frustrated bridegroom, his voice "dripping with acid and honey," insults the house, Poelzig, the Hungarian language, Hungary, the food, and the servants — who, fooled by Peter's expression, beam like fools at the insults. A still from the scene survived; the scene itself did not.

Meanwhile, Joan Alison has awakened after her wedding night, virginity intact, and back to her normal self — sans feline slinks and stares. Werdegast comes to examine the dressing and learns that Joan remembers nothing after the bus accident. Another Liszt flourish — and Karloff enters, to inquire as to the health of his "charming guest." In a wonderfully sinister touch, Karloff turns on profile to leer at his potential sacrifice — "Poelzig might well be contemplating a very delectable piece of French pastry," noted the script — his look so lascivious that Miss Wells needlessly adjusts her negligee.

However, Karloff is not the only one leering in the original footage. So was Lugosi — for, originally, Werdegast had ascended from the Poelzig cellar partially unhinged, and lustful. In the original, he too leers at Joan, as does Karloff, with an expression "which leaves even less to the imagination. . . ."

Then came the famous chess game. In the release print, as Karloff's Poelzig suggestively plays with a chess queen, leering all the while, Lugosi's Werdegast challenges him to a game — to decide the fate of Joan. In the release print of the film, Werdegast intones, "I intend to let her go."

It was a line, and a reshot scene, not originally filmed. Indeed, the original chess game had Poelzig and Werdegast challenging each other for Joan — for Werdegast, unhinged by their trip to the cellar with Poelzig and the sight of his mummified wife, wants Joan for himself.

Manners and Miss Wells, meanwhile, have a brief love scene — without the opening detailed in the script. Peter was to come to the bedroom as Joan was showering. He was to press against the bathroom door, and Ruric added the dialogue, with parenthetical directions:

JOAN: (very much the blushing bride) Darling! . . . I'm not dressed!
PETER: (very much the unblushing bridegroom) Joan!

None of this survived, but there is a scene, with the "Cat Love" music, in which the newlyweds embrace, and plan to leave Fort Marmaros. . . .

And there follows the comic relief, in comic opera style, with a toy-like Sergeant ("Henry Armetta if possible," noted the script, and it was) and sleek Lieutenant (Albert Conti, who, in Fox's 1930 *Such Men Are Dangerous,* had been billed above Lugosi), sporting capes and accents and debating (for Peter

Alison) the glories of honeymooning in Goomboos or Pisthyan. Adding to the
effectiveness of the relief was Roemheld's music, a spoofed confectionary rendition of *The Rakoczy March* which the composer entitled *Hungarian Burlesque.*

The chess game goes on. Peter wants to leave—but the car, mysteriously, is out of commission. And the phone is dead. "You hear that, Vitus?"
leers Karloff, his face a Renaissance devil mask. "The phone is dead. Even
the *phone* is dead!"

Poelzig wins the chess game. The Alisons try to leave—and Thamal,
blocking the door, knocks out Peter with a blow to the neck; the groom
is tossed into the cellars below, while Thamal carries the fainted bride
upstairs to the bedroom. Close-ups of Lugosi, later made in the retake
session, transformed his reaction from one of "morbid interest" to one of
sympathy.

The night is approaching. Karloff, his eyes almost in an unholy trance,
plays a Bach Toccata and Fugue at his organ. Lugosi, grabbing the key to
the room, races upstairs to the ingenue. In one of Bela's best scenes in the picture, he warns the terrified girl, while trying to comfort her. "Definitely
underplayed, if you please, M. Lugosi," noted the script, betraying Ulmer's
fear of Bela's overacting. With "a vague, partly cruel, partly tender, partly
impersonal expression," Werdegast warns:

> Poelzig is a mad beast. . . . Did you ever hear of Satanism, the worship of
> the devil, of Evil? Herr Poelzig is the great modern priest of that ancient cult,
> and tonight, in the dark of the moon, the Rites of Lucifer are celebrated . . . if
> I am not mistaken, he intends you to play a part in that ritual—a very important
> part. . . . Dear child . . . be brave . . . it is your only chance. . . !

Once again, the three-and-half days of retakes altered this speech. The
"Dear child. . ." section was added—replacing a scene in which Wedergast's
shadow looms over Joan on the floor as he almost surrenders to his lust—but
controls himself as he hears Karloff's organ-playing cease.

There follows the brief but perversely evocative Karen vignette. Lucille
Lund, as mentioned earlier, was to appear as a Siamese cat, permutated by
her moral decay as Poelzig's wife; however, as Ulmer related, "Censorship in
the thirties was even worse than now, and people couldn't take things like the
character of Karen resembling the physical characteristics of a cat." Nevertheless, as originally filmed, Karen—a fetishistic Grand-Guignol pinup in her
long blonde hair and flowing black negligee—meets Joan:

> KAREN: You are new here, aren't you?
> JOAN: What do you mean?
> KAREN: I have not been out of this house since I was brought here nine
>   years ago. In that time, many women—young, beautiful like you,
>   have come.

JOAN: Who are you?
KAREN: I am Karen — Madame Poelzig.
JOAN: Karen?
KAREN: You know my name? My father died in prison during the war. Herr Poelzig married my mother — she died when I was very young.
JOAN: And he married you? You are his wife?

There is the sound of the three-tone bell downstairs, where the devil-worshippers are arriving.

JOAN: What is that?
KAREN: (hysterically) Another bride for the devil! Another offering to the gods of my master. (dominating — on a crest of hysteria) Prepare!

This chilling hysteria, too, was doomed to the cutting room floor. Instead, Ulmer cut Karen's diabolic ravings, keeping her cool and calm, and adding for Joan, "Karen, listen to me. Your father is *not* dead. I know . . . he's here in this very house. He's come for you. Karen, do you understand me? Your father has come for you!" (Actually, this dialogue was sickly chilling — in a private way. According to Paul Mandell's "Edgar Ulmer and *The Black Cat*" in the October 1984 issue of *American Cinematographer,* Ulmer had taunted his sister Elly with the rumor that she was illegitimate, and that her real father had come to the house to take her away.)

At any rate, Karen is doomed; Poelzig, hearing this exchange, enters carrying his black cat, orders Karen out of the room. We hear her scream piteously, "Don't Hjalmar. *Please!*", followed by a heartrending scream . . .

It is time for the Black Mass. The devil worshippers, meanwhile, had been arriving downstairs, with Werdegast playing host. The script had wanted to make more of the Satanists than was possible in the release print. One select passage:

> A Man and woman of extremely strange appearance and expression enter, followed at a little distance by a youth. The man is about fifty, fat in the soft pasty way of self-indulgence — his face a puffy mask of greed and lust. The woman is as emaciated as the man is fat — her eyes, burnt, black holes in her dead white face. The youth is a loose-lipped, pimply, bespectacled mistake with the vacant smile of a congenital imbecile. . . .

The script wanted the satanic cult to resemble Aubrey Beardsley woodcuts, "as odd and freakish as possible — all to have the suggestion of some kind of abnormality about them. Members, for the most part, of the decadent aristocracy of the countryside."

While the "Satanists" who answered Universal's $20.00 per-day casting call were not quite so exotic as Ulmer had hoped, there were some unusual faces in the crowd: bald, moustached Russian Michael Mark, father of Little Maria in *Frankenstein* and hanger-on in a number of Universal horror shows;

The Black Mass begins. Lugosi, Karloff, and the coven of cultists in *The Black Cat*. (Barely glimpsed, far left: John Carradine?)

Paul Panzer, villain of silents; Lois January, a stock contractee at Universal; King Baggot, who had starred in the title roles of Universal's 1913 *Dr. Jekyll and Mr. Hyde;* and a tall, cadaverous 28-year-old actor named John Peter Richmond — who, in 1935, would begin attracting notice under the name of John Carradine.

The dark of the moon. From above, Karloff's Poelzig, in his $50

Ulmer-designed high priest robe, descends the great staircase. The actor stares, his eyes gaping, unholy; the pentagram jewelry around his neck reflects in the light, and his step, again, is wolfish. There is a magnificently wild, bestial look in Karloff, one that portends that the dapper guests are fated to become shrieking, orgiastic disciples as the rites proceed to their climax — where the high priest will rape the maiden, and kill her.

Inside the chapel, there is a blasphemously cockeyed cross; the worshippers don robes as an organ eerily plays the "Adagio in A Minor" from Bach's *Toccata, Adagio and Fugue in F.* Karloff's Lucifer mounts the altar, his arms waving in ritualistic gestures, and hauntingly chants the prayers of the Black Mass:

> Cum grano salis, Fortis cadre, cedre non potest. . . .
> Lupis pilum mutat non mentem.
> Magna est veritas, et pro evolebit.
> Acta exteriora indicant interiora, secreta.
> Ac quem memento rebus
> In adriis servare mentem.
> Amissum quod nescitor non amitor.
> Brutem fulmen.
> Cum grano salis. Fortis cadre, cedre non potest.
> Fructus non foliis arborem estima.
> Insanus omnis furere credit ceteres.
> Quem poenitet
> Piccasso paene est innocens.

Actually, the translation is hardly sinister — as Karloff was really praying,

> With a grain of salt. The brave may
> fall, but cannot yield.
> The wolf changes its skin, but not its mind.
> Great is truth, and it shall prevail.
> That which I admit I do not know I cannot lose.
> The loss that is lost is not lost at all.
> Bright lightning. . . .
> Judge a tree by fruit not leaves.
> Every madman thinks everyone is crazy.
> He who repents is almost innocent. . .

Meanwhile, Joan, in her white sacrificial maiden gown, is battling the diabolists who have come to deliver her to the Black Mass; they prevail, and the swooning virgin is lashed to the crooked cross. The satanic Poelzig turns to her, his eyes wild, and reaches for her. . . .

A female Satanist screams, overcome by what is about to happen, and faints. Naturally, Ulmer wanted her to have an orgasm ("She goes into hysterical paroxysms, screaming loudly . . . her hands upraised, her whole

Satanic high priest and sacrificial virgin; Karloff with Jacqueline Wells (later known as "Julie Bishop").

body trembling violently...."). Nevertheless, the faint suffices to distract Poelzig from his ritual rape and murder—and Werdegast moves to save her.

Save her? Not in the original script! Lugosi's Vitus was to abscond with the swooning girl—and try to rape her!

It is Joan's knowledge that Karen, whom Vitus believes to be dead, is alive that saves her in the script. In the film, to the music of Brahms' *Rhapsody in B Minor,* Werdegast, Joan and Thamal run through the cellars. In the escape, the Majordomo fatally shoots Thamal, and Thamal fatally beats the Majordomo; as each is dying, Joan, hoping to delay Werdegast so as to find Peter, informs Werdegast that Karen, his dauger, is Poelzig's wife—and alive. Getting directions from the dying Majordomo, Bela runs to find Karen, pulls back a sheet, and finds his daughter—apparently killed hideously by her husband/stepfather. (Once again, the original idea was even more horrific; Ulmer wanted Werdegast to discover his dead daughter hanging from a hook.) In one of his greatest moments in the film, Lugosi trembles—and lets out a howl of horror.

Poelzig, ripping off his ceremonial robes, stripped down to basic black, now races in—and wildly grabs Joan. In a crowd-pleasing battle, Werdegast attacks Poelzig, and Boris and Bela fight it out, Lugosi wincing, Karloff evoking a repertoire of bestial expressions as the dying Thamal helps Werdegast drag his "old friend" to a rack. That mission accomplished, Thamal collapses and dies. (Ulmer originally wanted him to speak a dying word or two—hence surprising the audience with the news that he wasn't really dumb.)

The infamous skinning alive scene of *The Black Cat* merits a special place in the cinema of sadism; it served, ironically, not only as a sick climax to a satanic picture, but a bizarre climax to the Karloff and Lugosi relationship as well. It's one of the greatest, most haunting vignettes of all horror movies: Karloff, stripped to the waist, hanging on the "embalming rack"; Lugosi, wildly, vengefully mad, ranting to his nemesis as the "Sempre Forte ed Agitato" of Liszt's *Devil Sonata* exhorts the madness:

> Do you know what I'm going to do to you now? No? Did you ever see an animal *skinned*, Hjalmar? Ha, ha! *that's* what I am going to do to you now. Tear the skin from your body—slowly—bit by bit!

It was Bela's big scene of the movie, and he couldn't wait. Ulmer called, "Action." Bela, so enjoying the dramatics and so thrilled at skinning his top-billed, tea-break nemesis, ripped into "Did you ever see an animal *skinned*, Hjalmar?"—and garbled his English.

"Cut," called Ulmer.

"Dear Boris," hanging half-naked on the rack, smiled politely as his emotional costar prepared for a new take. Once again, Ulmer called, "Action!" and the star ranted, "Did you ever see an animal *skinned*, Hjalmar?"

Bela garbled his English again.

As Boris kept hanging on the rack, Bela kept battling his emotions and the English language. Finally, Bela controlled his abandon sufficiently for Ulmer to get a "take"; however, even in the release print, Bela gives "slowly" a whole new pronunciation. Many years later, actor/mimic/game-show-host Richard Dawson recalled meeting Karloff, and discussing his (Dawson's) Karloff/Lugosi impersonations. Boris recalled Bela's troubles with English in that famous scene—and suggested Dawson watch the skinning alive episode in *The Black Cat* to perfect his Lugosi imitation!

The skinning alive is done in Kafka shadows, with Jacqueline Wells screaming (only after getting a good eyeful in Pandora fascination), the Liszt

A candid from *The Black Cat:* Karloff hangs on his "embalming rack" (as Lugosi prepares to skin him alive).

Sonata booming, a close-up of Boris's hand writhing in the manacle, and Bela ranting, "How does it feel to hang on your own embalming rack, Hjalmar!" To cap the sadism, Karloff lets out a lupine yelp — bizarre, but totally in keeping with his wolfish portrayal. Sadistic as the skinning alive may be, it is a gloriously gothic demise for Karloff's Poelzig — surely the most exotic villain of the Golden Age of Horror.

It's now that Manners reappears on the scene, free of the cellars and brandishing a revolver. Bela, transformed in the retakes from mad rapist to tragic hero, aids the heroine. Misinterpreting Werdegast's actions as he tries to help Joan free the key from Thamal's rigor-mortised hand, the "hero"

"It has been a good game!" says Lugosi, climactically pulling the "red switch," in *The Black Cat*.

warns Lugosi, and then shoots him — in the back. "You poor fool," says Lugosi, with great sadness. "I only tried to help you. Now go. Please — *go!*"*

*Ulmer's original ending, according to the shooting script: "An effect as if Werdegast was splitting the scalp slowly, pulling the sheath of skin over Poelzig's head and shoulders... Werdegast finishes, straightens and surveys his work with eminent satisfaction; his insane eyes turn to Joan. He starts toward her... Peter raises the Luger and fires... Werdegast staggers, falls. Joan is still trying to pry the key out of Thamal's hand in background. Poelzig, sans skin, is struggling on the rack. By a superhuman effort he frees himself and falls to the floor... Werdegast raises himself on one elbow and stares at Poelzig. He laughs hysterically, insanely... Poelzig raises his hideous body — his eyes focused dully, expressionlessly, on Joan. He laboriously, painfully crawls toward her. As he comes closer, Joan, with redoubled strength, gets the key, rises and runs to the door... Poelzig with the last vestige of his strength, turns and starts crawling toward Werdegast..."

The honeymooners flee. Werdegast props himself against the wall. "It's the red switch, isn't it Hjalmar? The red switch ignites the dynamite. Five minutes—Marmaros, you, and I, and your rotten cult—will be no more!" The dynamite begins to sputter. "It has been a good game," says Bela's Werdegast—a cynical, dramatic curtain line to a wonderfully melancholy and intense performance.

Manners and Wells, her sacrificial gown torn, running in her high heels, showing a 1934 flurry of thighs and the tops of her stockings, escape. To rhapsodic chords of Tchaikovsky's *Romeo and Juliet*, Fort Marmaros explodes, apocalyptically, amidst wild flashes of dynamite...

Down on the road, in the night, the young man in his torn suit and the lady with her exposed thighs easily attract headlights. The script originally offered a tag in which a bus—piloted by no less than Edgar Ulmer, in white beard and goggles—stops.

"Will you take us to Vizhegrad?" asks Peter.

"I'm not going to Vizhegrad," replied the disguised Ulmer. "I'm going to a sanitarium to rest up after making *The Black Cat* in fourteen days! However, it will be a long walk. For you, I shall make an exception."

While this never made the film either, a comic ending did. Back on the Orient Express, a refreshed Peter and a bundled Joan settle down as Peter picks up his paper. There's a review of Peter's latest book, *Triple Murder*. It claims Peter Alison has fulfilled his promise, but overstepped credibility bounds:

"These things could never by the furthest stretch of the imagination actually happen. We could wish that Mr. Alison would confine himself to the possible, instead of letting his melodramatic imagination run away with him!"

The *Romeo and Juliet* theme swells. THE END.

A good cast is worth repeating...

*   *   *

...put your faith and your hope and your bets on the big three in *The Black Cat*—Karloff, Lugosi and Poe! You can be sure that by not pussy-footing about them—you will fill to complete satisfaction, your house, your box office, and the public's appetite for excitement. *The Black Cat* is coming—sock it!
                         —from Universal's pressbook for *The Black Cat*

The Black Cat had completed shooting Saturday, St. Patrick's Day, 1934—one day over schedule. And from Universal's front office, and Bela Lugosi, and especially "Uncle Carl" Laemmle, there was a great gnashing of teeth.

Bela was unhappy. After all, he had been promised a "benign" role, and the film had him try to rape the heroine. Ulmer's horror show, with two madmen at each other's throats, rampant sexual perversity, and flourishes of

Satanism, seemed doomed by the censors. And one can only imagine the face of Uncle Carl as he watched the original climax, with Karloff, a skinned and bloody pulp, wriggling on his belly toward the hysterical Lugosi. To placate Bela, save Laemmle Senior from a stroke, and fashion a marketable film, emergency action had to be taken.

On Sunday, March 25, 1934, *The Black Cat* began three-and-a-half days of additional scenes; "It drove Edgar crazy," says Shirley Ulmer, who recalls Uncle Carl's apoplexy at the original film. A Production Estimate dated the next day called for 9000 feet of film and a $6500 budget to make the sick movie marketable. Shot in that time:

•A new scene, following the trip to the cellars, where Werdegast stops Thamal from going to knife Poelzig. Bela's new dialogue plugged many holes in the altered plot: "Not yet, Thamal. Put that away. We will bide our time. Other lives are involved — and this place is so undermined with dynamite that the slightest mistake by one of us could cause the destruction of us all. Until I tell you different — you are his servant, not mine."

•Process shots of the bus accident, and the introductory shot of Fort Marmaros.

•New shots of the chess game, with Werdegast avowing himself on the side of the angels — "I intend to let her go!" — and his ensuing close-ups of remorse when Thamal knocks out Peter.

•The new, milder scene between Karen and Joan.

•The new tag for Werdegast's boudoir scene with Joan, and the shots of his climactic self-sacrifice in the finals.

•Of course, for all the antisepticizing, the irrepressible Ulmer also added at this time one of *The Black Cat's* most horrifying episodes: Karloff's stalk through the cellars, staring at his embalmed raped-and-murdered sacrifices in their glass coffins as he cradles his black cat. The director gambled that the Universal front office wasn't intellectual enough to recognize the full perversity of the scene. He was right.

Comedy scenes of the Maître d'Hôtel on the train, and Peter's badinage with the servants, were cut, along with many Lugosi leers, and the retakes and new scenes saved the film — and, naturally, fattened the wallets of the players. Aside from dividing $75 among the six beauties in the glass coffins, the new scenes for *The Black Cat* paid Egon Brecher $83.35 (for one day), Harry Cording $83.35 (for two-and-a-half days), Lucille Lund $87.50 (for three-and-a-half days), Jacqueline Wells $125 (for two-and-a-half days), and David Manners $417.30 (for two days). Karloff went along collecting his weekly Universal pay, and Lugosi picked up $583.35 for his three-and-a-half days — thereby properly becoming the second-best paid actor of *The Black Cat,* and earning slightly more than half of Karloff's fee. Ulmer simply picked up another weekly Universal check of $150, making his total remuneration for *The Black Cat* $1050.

It was now that Heinz Roemheld and Edgar Ulmer worked closely, Herr

Roemheld playing the piano with his classical music ideas as Ulmer watched the rough cut on a movieola. While production reports called for an orchestra of 28 players (as well as a 1–6 hour session for an organist), the April 13, 1934, *Hollywood Reporter* claimed that Roemheld conducted a 50-player orchestra in scoring *The Black Cat*. Once again, Uncle Carl was apoplectic, hating the idea of the classical music; he wanted to rescore the entire picture. This time, however, Junior Laemmle stood behind Ulmer—and they won.

All in all, *The Black Cat* had taken an official 19 days to shoot; the final cost sheet, dated 7/14/34, computed the final expense at $95,745.31—actually $1879.69 below the revamped budget allowing for the extra scenes. (Curiously, a revised cost sheet, dated 2/16/35, tallied the final budget at $92,323.76; the $3400 difference came under "General Overhead.")

Now, Universal City had to sell *The Black Cat* to the public.

Of course, the exhibitor's handbook accented the first teaming of Karloff and Bela Lugosi in one of Poe's "most outstanding masterpieces." Also among the dozens of PR promotional gimmicks:

•"Giant Cat Ballyhoo." This called for two "ballyhoo men" to dress up in a giant black cat suit, emblazoned with:

Frankenstein   Dracula
KARLOFF   LUGOSI
in
"BLACK CAT"

•"In walking through the streets," the pressbook suggested, "have these men cavort, leap and carry on in such a way as to attract extra attention. You can be certain of stopping crowds with this stunt."

•Black Cat costumes (made of black sateen, and complete with tails) for the ushers, doorman, or barker—only $3.75 each.

•"Life-size fur cats with realistic black hair," for prizes. "Just the thing for a kiddies matinee, and adults would appreciate a gift like this too." Only $19.75 a dozen.

•"Can You Find *The Black Cat*" puzzle, Black Cat lucky charms, atmospheric slides, poster cut-outs. . . .

The pressbook even noted a still of Karloff and Lugosi playing chess, and exhorted exhibitors, "Use it for chess tie-ups—a pastime more popular now than ever . . . !"

Thursday, May 3, 1934. *The Black Cat* filled the screen at the 3000–seat Hollywood Pantages Theatre, where Boris, Bela, and Jacqueline Wells all appeared opening night. If anyone at Universal expected the conventionally-minded critics of the day to appreciate this shocker, they were in for a proverbial rude awakening. The *Los Angeles Examiner* said

> If you have ever wondered what would happen should Frankenstein meet Dracula on a dark night, the Pantages Hollywood Theatre now offers an

opportunity to find out. . . . Throughout most of the movie both try to outstare each other, with Karloff having a bit of an edge. Lugosi never concedes victory — for he can stare, too. . . .

The Black Cat opened at New York's Roxy Theatre Friday, May 18, 1934, complete with a "Gala New Stage Show" featuring the Park Central Revue, with Teddy Bergman, Wesley Eddy & His "Gang," and the Foster dancing girls. The premiere was chillingly-timed; two days before, Norman Mudd, a disciple of Aleister Crowley, had grimly fulfilled a prophecy of "the Beast" by drowning himself in the English Channel. There were a number of hit movies in New York City that spring: Columbia's Gable and Colbert in *It Happened One Night,* MGM's *Tarzan and His Mate* and *Manhattan Melodrama,* Paramount's version of Lugosi's Broadway play *Murder at the Vanities,* and 20th Century's *House of Rothschild,* with Karloff. *The Black Cat* was a box office hit, despite the *New York Times,* lambasting the movie as "A clammy and excessively ghoulish tale of hijinks in a Hungarian horror salon. . . ." Meanwhile, *Variety,* the show business bible, pontificated:

> Because of the presence in one film of Boris Karloff, that jovial madman, and Bela Lugosi, that suave fiend, this picture probably has box office attraction. But otherwise and on the counts of story, novelty, thrills and distinction, it is subnormal . . . skinning alive is not new. It was done in a Gouverneur Morris story, *The Man Behind the Door,* filmed during the war. A truly horrible and nauseating bit of extreme sadism, its inclusion in a motion picture is dubious showmanship. That devil-worshipping cult is also close to the border. . . . Karloff and Lugosi are sufficiently sinister and convincingly demented. Jacqueline Wells spends most of her footage in swoons.

For all the outraged reviews, a magic accompanied Universal's release of *The Black Cat.* The awesome, ominous billing, "KARLOFF and Bela LUGOSI," looming on the posters and marquees, lured a public that lined up to see the screen's master bogeymen in action. *The Black Cat* proved to be Universal's hit of the season, with a profit of $140,000.

The Black Cat had survived to become Universal's darkest horror tale.

And it had presented the public the first glorious teaming of Karloff and Lugosi.

*   *   *

> . . . *The Black Cat* is a fascinating dark landmark in the cinema of the fantastic. . . . Never were the rituals of witchcraft more completely presented. . . . Never has Karloff had a more suavely evil role, sensuous and demonic. . . . Rarely was Lugosi to enjoy as sympathetic a part, although by the finish he too is completely mad and caught up in the grotesque spirit of the plot. . . .
> — from *Cinema of the Fantastic,* by Chris Steinbrunner and Burt Goldblatt

At five o'clock in the morning of October 7, 1849, Edgar Allan Poe, wracked by alcohol and drugs, roused himself in Washington College

Hospital in Baltimore, cried out "God help my poor soul!" and died. Many believe he would have reacted the same way had he somehow lived to see *The Black Cat*.

True, Poe's tale of revenge is suggested only by the black cat pet of Poelzig. Nevertheless, Poe probably would have found much to admire in this moody, sinister movie; indeed few films have ever evoked the twisted, nightmarish Evil that haunted Poe's stories as did *The Black Cat*. The motifs of revenge, souls that have been "killed," and the demonic flamboyance would have fascinated Edgar Allan — as would have the marriage of Poelzig and stepdaughter Karen. Poe, after all, had married his beloved Virginia (who was truly the "core and meaning" of his life, and whose death destroyed him) when she was only 13 years old; and, as Philip Van Doren Stern noted in his introduction to *The Portable Poe*, Poe's personality indicated "he was sexually abnormal, but there is no way of proving it."

Frankenstein is the most beloved and classic of horror films, *The Mummy* the most poetic and romantic, *Bride of Frankenstein* the most theatrical and misanthropic; *The Black Cat* is the most sinister and perverse. Its shadows and fetishist fascination with necrophilia and sadism and Satanism can instill fear in audiences who know nothing of the Krafft-Ebing catalogue it presents. An actress acquaintance recently told me how, as a child, she sat with her older brother, watching *The Black Cat* on television late one night; she begged him to turn it off, but he refused, and she kept watching, fascinated. By the time the film reached its skinning alive sequence, she was almost hysterical, and he was delighted.

Yet, in perspective, all the morbid quirks of *The Black Cat* serve as the ideal backdrop for the first teaming of Karloff and Lugosi, a wonderful showcase for the macabre chemistry which would make the unions of these two men vital movie history. Although, as Carlos Clarens noted in his tome, *An Illustrated History of the Horror Film,* "Lugosi was dominated by Karloff's lisping, wolfish performance...," *The Black Cat* would be their most glorious teaming. Karloff's Lascivious Lucifer versus Lugosi's Avenging Angel makes *The Black Cat* transcend the horror movie genre, and become a grand, lunatic fairy tale, sparked by a wickedly imaginative director, a bewitched camera and a properly epic romantic score.

Edgar Ulmer would never work with Karloff and Lugosi again; indeed, his days at Universal were numbered. One can only imagine the cataclysmic consequences when Shirley left Uncle Carl's favorite nephew to marry the man who had directed *The Black Cat*. Ulmer's legendary career went on to such Yiddish films as 1938's *The Singing Blacksmith,* and his famous work at Producers Releasing Corporation during World War II, creating such striking movies as *Bluebeard* (starring John Carradine) and *Detour.* "We worked day and night," remembers Shirley Ulmer, who assisted Edgar on all his films at PRC (and later), and is the mother of their daughter Arianne. "You didn't get to eat or sleep — you just had to be crazy!" The fifties found him crafting such films as *The Man from Planet X* (1951) and *Daughter of Dr. Jekyll* (1957). When François Truffaut visited the United States in the sixties, he praised the "classicism" of Ulmer's work. Indeed, Ulmer became a cult figure. To the end of his life he was a passionately creative man, as Shirley movingly remembers:

> My poor, dear Edgar — he had three strokes. He was so terribly ill, I almost prayed that God would take him. But, as ill as he was, he still had the brain. At the very end, all he could move was the forefinger of his right hand; but I would bring him an ink pad, and put the pen in his hand, and he would write his thoughts. I still have them...

Edgar George Ulmer died at the Motion Picture Country House on September 30, 1972. He was 72 years old.

Poe's tale *The Black Cat* was bastardized worse than ever in Universal's 1941 *The Black Cat,* which wasted such players as Basil Rathbone, Gladys Cooper, Anne Gwynne, Claire Dodd, Alan Ladd (in a small pre-*This Gun for Hire* role) — and Bela Lugosi, who played a caretaker named Eduardo, referred to as "the keeper of the cats." Rumor claims that Broderick Crawford and Hugh "Woo-Woo" Herbert ad-libbed their way through most of it. In 1962, American-International sandwiched *The Black Cat* as the middle piece of its *Tales of Terror,* in a spoofy treatment in which drunken Peter Lorre, à la the Poe tale, walls up wine expert Vincent Price and buxom spouse Joyce Jameson in his cellar.

There was little chance for the stars of 1934's *The Black Cat* to celebrate socially as their movie became Universal's moneymaker of the season. Bela Lugosi left the lot with little more than contempt for his costar, a contempt nurtured by intimidation, resentment, and second billing. And Boris Karloff bid "Poor Bela" a temporary goodbye, feeling more sympathy than animosity toward a proud, emotional star whom Karloff would remember as "a charming man — but in some ways a fool to himself."

4
The Meager Gift of Gab, 1934

"Incidentally," said Lugosi, "I was originally signed as the monster in *Frankenstein*, but I convinced the studio that the part did not have meat enough."

It was this role that made Karloff his principal rival for the throne of King of Horror.

Lugosi, however, considers Karloff primarily a make-up artist, and a man inwardly too gentle and kind to be suited for grisly portrayals.

— from "Big Bad Bela," *Picture Play,* July, 1934.

In the sensational wake of *The Black Cat,* Universal promised that Karloff and Lugosi would soon haunt theatres in such spine-tingling properties as *The Suicide Club, The Return of Frankenstein* and *Dracula's Daughter.*

Instead, 1934 audiences seeking Boris and Bela together had to settle for Universal's *Gift of Gab.*

This dated, forsaken, and very rarely-seen curiosity was basically a love tale of a radio announcer and braggart Gabney (Edmund Lowe) and his long-suffering girlfriend Barbara (Gloria Stuart). However, to pad the 71-minute "show," Universal added "30 stars and Five Hit Tunes," all under the director-ship of none other than Karl "Papa" Freund (1890–1969).

Gift of Gab began shooting July 2, 1934, at Universal, on an 18-day schedule and a $230,000 budget. Over 25 percent of the budget went to Radio Guest Stars, who included, in order of their salaries: Phil Baker ($10,000), Ruth Etting ($7000), Ethel Waters ($2500), Gene Austin ($2250), Gus Arnheim ($1200), the Beal Street Boys ($1000), the Downey Sisters ($375), Winnie Shaw ($250), Leighton Noble ($250), and Graham McNamee ($225). The footage of Miss Waters reportedly was shot in New York, as was the cameo of Alexander Woollcott.

Inevitably, Universal decided to toss its own array of stars into the hodgepodge: Paul Lukas, Douglass Montgomery, Chester Morris, Binnie Barnes, KARLOFF, and Bela Lugosi. The vehicle for them was a radio mystery play, conceived by hotshot Lowe, with the Universal attractions burlesquing Radio and themselves.

For the record, Boris camped it up as "The Phantom," sporting a black cape, top hat and fright wig. Bela chose a costume reminiscent of his sexy

Portion of the lobby card for *Gift of Gab* (1934). Kneeling, Karloff, Roger Pryor and Paul Lukas. Standing, Lugosi, Chester Morris, Douglass Montgomery, June Knight and Binnie Barnes.

Fernando the Apache of Broadway's 1922 *The Red Poppy,* but now looked more like a Transylvanian procurer in the black velvet smoking jacket and rakish cap, merely glimpsed standing in a closet as he asks, "What time is it?"

Freund completed *Gift of Gab* July 24, 1934, three days over schedule and at a cost of $251,433.79 — over $21,000 over budget. Cut from the film was a gag opening of Billy Barty, as a baby Edmund Lowe, talking to his parents; added was footage from Universal's 1933 *Saturday's Millions,* of Johnny Mack Brown in football action. Dave O'Brien and Dennis O'Keefe were extras in a dance sequence, and, with virtually everybody else getting into the picture, columnists Sidney Skolsky and Radie Harris appeared as themselves.

Gift of Gab opened at New York's Rialto Theatre on September 25, 1934.

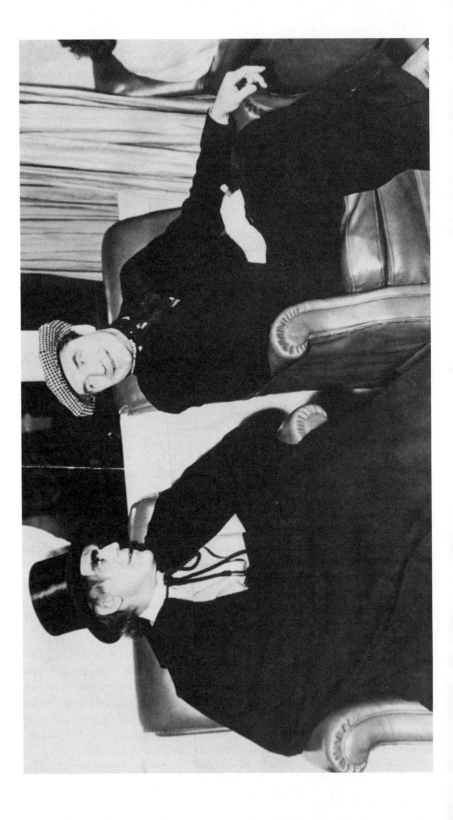

The *New York Times* said, "It constitutes a minor miracle that the sum of so much talent should be such meager entertainment."

The cameos of Karloff and Lugosi did little for their screen popularity—nor did it add significantly to their bankrolls. Karloff received a flat fee of $500; Lugosi, a very flat $250.

*   *   *

Also in 1934, movie audiences saw Karloff and Lugosi—sharply dressed, and in straight makeup—glaring at each other, a skull observing the square-off from atop a fireplace ledge:

KARLOFF: Ready for the test, Dracula?
LUGOSI: I'm ready, Frankenstein!
KARLOFF: Then—let us begin!

The camera retreats, the stars break up—and there they are, playing chess.

"You understand, Bela, don't you," smiles Karloff, "that the one who wins this little game of chess is to lead the parade at the Film Stars' Frolic."

"Okay, Boris," says Bela. "Your move."

"Right!" says Karloff, and spoofy music ends the clip. For years, historians have had fun misidentifying this gag—one claiming it a teaser for *The Black Cat,* another calling it their work from *Gift of Gab.* Actually, it's from Columbia's 1934 short subject, *Screen Snapshots #11,* a coverage of Hollywood charity work which also featured Genevieve Tobin, Pat O'Brien, James Cagney, Maureen O'Sullivan and Eddie Cantor.

Boris Karloff spent the rest of 1934 collecting his Universal salary and awaiting the special deluxe vehicles his home studio was preparing for him. Bela Lugosi, while awaiting Universal's callback, visited some of RKO's old *King Kong* sets for Principal Pictures' *The Return of Chandu,* in which he glowered the starring part, and signed to play a bearded and bespectacled heavy (to Edmund Lowe's hero) in Columbia's *The Best Man Wins.*

Come the Christmas holidays of 1934, the Los Angeles *Examiner* prepared its gala Christmas Benefit, staged at the Shrine Auditorium on the night of December 14. "SCINTILLATING STARS, Beauties in Benefit," proclaimed an *Examiner* headline, promising Clark Gable, Jeanette MacDonald, Bing Crosby, Dick Powell, Al Jolson, Burns and Allen, Wini Shaw, Jimmie Durante and many others. "In battalion strength," reported the *Examiner,* "the numerous great stars of Universal Studios will make an impressive appearance...." Karloff, "the man who made the world shudder," would be there, as would Gloria Stuart, Henry Hull, Chester Morris, Heather Angel, Roger Pryor, John Mack Brown, June Clayworth, and Phyllis Brooks. And,

Opposite: **Boris (left) and Bela trade pleasantries on the set of Universal's *Gift of Gab,* in which they guest-starred in the summer of 1934.**

while the *Examiner* promised that "Universal Notables Join 100%" in the show, there was no mention (at this point, at least) of Bela Lugosi, despite his picture deal with the studio.

Universal, apparently, hadn't thought to ask him.

5
The Bride of 1935

I protest against the labelling of my melodramas as "horror pictures." They are bogey stories, that's all. Just bogey stories with the same appeal as thrilling ghost stories or fantastic fairy tales that entertain and enthrall in spite of being so much hokum. And contrary to the general belief, children love the menace man as much as the grown-ups. The greater part of my mail, with the exception of the requests for photographs or autographs, comes from youngsters—little girls as well as boys. I stir their imaginations in the same manner of Gulliver . . . or the Giant of the Jack and the Beanstalk fable, or the Big Bad Wolf.
— Boris Karloff

. . . This typing is overdone. I can play varied roles, but whenever some nasty man is wanted to romp through a picture with a wicked expression and numerous lethal devices, Lugosi is suggested. Why, they even wanted to cast me as the Big Bad Wolf in *The Three Little Pigs!*
— Bela Lugosi

On January 2, 1935, Universal began shooting the masterpiece of Hollywood's "Golden Age" of Horror — *Bride of Frankenstein*. Crucified high on a pole, waved about a forest by sadistic villagers, Karloff's monster became the screen's most bizarre Christ symbol; his Pilate, of course, was Jimmy Whale, elegantly posing with cigar in the soundstage shadows, scourging the hapless monster with bitter bravado.

It was a magnificent, blasphemous, wickedly funny, movingly tragic fairy tale, with a splendidly eccentric cast: the decaying Colin Clive, his Christ-like face becoming chillingly satanic, again a tormented Frankenstein; Ernest Thesiger, of the Olympian nostrils, mincing and smirking as the serpentine Dr. Pretorius; Dwight Frye, prissy and muggy as Karl, a grave-robbing heart-procuring ghoul; and, of course, Elsa Lanchester, classic in her performance(s) as precious Mary Shelley and the nightmarish monster's mate (sporting the classic makeup, designed by Whale and Thesiger, and fastidiously applied, of course, by Jack P. Pierce). Miss Lanchester, who based her female monster on a hissing swan who terrorized the lake at London's Regents Park (and who once coached me in performing that hiss), died the day after Christmas, 1986. To the end, she fondly remembered *Bride's* director, and her "mate."

89

"I thought Karloff's monster was a marvelous creation," she told me. "That gentleness!"

The new Elizabeth, pious, screaming bride of Clive's Frankenstein, was Valerie Hobson, dressed up by Whale in a $125 wig and a magnificent, satin bridal gown with fur train—beneath which, by director's dictate, she could wear no underwear. At home in the countryside of England, Valerie Hobson told me in 1989:

> ...I remember that, the very first time I saw Boris Karloff, he was in full gear as the monster! I had been warned what he was going to look like, and I thought he was absolutely extraordinary; I hadn't realized his boots were so built up, and he'd be so *huge*. And then to hear this very gentle, English voice coming out of this awful makeup—and with a pronounced lisp!
>
> ...Boris's kind eyes—he had the kindest eyes! Most monsters have frightening eyes, but Boris, even in makeup, had very loving, sad eyes. The thing I remember best about him was his great gentleness . . . he was awfully quiet, softly-spoken, always interested in one's problems, but still had his reserve. He was a dear man.
>
> ...Karloff was so moving—like some of the great clowns who make you cry, he made you cry. The makeup was wonderful, but it was almost clownlike in its extremeness. You really felt that here was one whose heart was absolutely bleeding to get out of his monstrous self and find someone to love and who would love him. Very moving. . . .

As the monster talked, smoked a cigar, drank wine, hiccuped, wept beneath a crucifix and overturned a bishop's statue, Whale ran amok as well—merrily running the long-promised sequel over its $293,750 budget and 36-day shooting schedule. Junior Laemmle pampered his prize director and star (both now earning $2500 weekly); after all, the monster show was a bonanza of Universal publicity.

Interestingly, ever since Universal had announced the sequel as *The Return of Frankenstein* in 1933, it was rumored that Bela Lugosi would join Karloff in the melodrama. There have been reports that Junior Laemmle considered Lugosi (as well as Universal's Claude Rains, who instead won the showy role of evil, opium-addicted choirmaster John Jasper in *Mystery of Edwin Drood*) for the Pretorius part. In truth, Whale had tailor-designed Pretorius for his friend Thesiger (who, although by no means a "name" in Hollywood, demanded and received the same salary that Lugosi received—$1000 weekly). Whale was no more interested in working with Bela than he had been in the summer of 1931. Certainly the director would never have found in Bela the same kinky nuance that he so admired in Thesiger (whose scene with Clive's Frankenstein, where he seduces him into creating

Opposite: **Poster art for *Bride of Frankenstein*, 1935.**

a mate for the monster, has been called an allegory of a homosexual blackmailing scene).

While Universal showcased Boris in *Bride,* the studio showed no signs in affording Bela his own vehicle (*Dracula's Daughter* was still on the nebulous horizon). However, Metro-Goldwyn-Mayer did sign Bela for *Vampires of Prague*—Tod Browning's revamping of his 1927 Lon Chaney vehicle *London After Midnight,* and fated to be released as *Mark of the Vampire.* The thriller was set to begin shooting January 14, 1935, and Bela's "Minimum Contract for Artists" in Metro's archives records the terms: MGM would pay "Bela Lugosa" (sic) $1000 per week for no less that three weeks. Also, with Universal emblazoning KARLOFF on Boris's vehicles, it's interesting to note how Metro handled the issue of Bela's billing:

> ...the artist's name will be accorded not less than second male billing and that the name of no other member of the cast will appear in type larger than that used to display the artist's name except the star or costars provided, however, that should the producer elect to feature the name of Lionel Barrymore his name may appear in type larger than that used to display the artist's name...

Premiering on Broadway in May, 1935 (just days before *Bride of Frankenstein*), *Mark of the Vampire* is one of the most schizophrenic of horror movies: there are James Wong Howe's wonderfully blood-curdling atmospheric shots, with peasants singing below a church steeple, a baby playing with a sprig of wolfsbane, a horrid graveyard, a wonderfully decaying castle, Bela's mute but magnificent Count Mora (with bullet hole in head) and his daughter, "Luna" (Carroll Borland), in her shroud by Adrian, looking anemic and ethereal. On the other hand, there is the dominant talky footage, with Lionel Barrymore desperately trying to wheeze life into the proceedings as a professor of demonology, a dapper but wasted Lionel Atwill as an inspector, and a juvenile lead (Henry Wadsworth) so feeble that Browning has him play almost constantly upstaged by leading lady Elizabeth Allan. Omitted were the sinister flashbacks of Mora and Luna becoming vampires via incest (they committed suicide—hence Bela's bullet hole); retained was the infamous cop-out ending, in which the vampires are only actors, playing to trap Jean Hersholt, and giving Bela his only lines in the film:

"This vampire business—it has given me a great idea for a new act. Luna, in the new act, I will be the vampire. Did you watch me? I gave all of me! I was greater than any real vampire!" To which Miss Borland replies, "Sure, sure, but take off your makeup!"

Carroll Borland recalls that Bela tried to discourage her from auditioning for Luna; "If you do," he told her, "you'll be stuck in that as I have been." However, when she was determined, Bela helped her get the part. MGM was concerned she was too small to play opposite Bela, so he tested with her in

Mark of the Vampire, 1935: Carroll Borland as Luna, Lugosi as Count Mora (complete with bullet wound on the side of his head), and the MGM peasants.

his cape, scrunching down while she wore her high heels. On the set, Miss Borland found the relationship had changed:

> By the time we did *Mark of the Vampire,* he was married, and very cozily involved in being a family person. Everybody on the set was calling him "Mr. Lugosi," so I did. We had ceased to have this sort of incredible playmate relationship. But he was kind and friendly and helpful and indulgent. . . .
> We would be tired at the end of the day; I had my hair glued to the side of my face with spirit gum, and Lugosi had this bullet wound stuck on him, and we would just pile into the car and Lillian would drive us home. And it was so funny! This truck pulled up, with a crate of chickens. I was sitting on the right

hand side, in the back seat, and Lugosi never drove, so he was on the right hand side in the front seat. The truck driver looked at us—and did the most beautiful double take I've ever seen! He looked first at Lugosi with this bullet wound, then me in the back seat, and then his foot must have slipped—and he *shot* right up on the sidewalk, on someone's yard! The chickens were screaming their heads off! And Lugosi said, "Why did he do that?" I was laughing so hard, I couldn't stand it; if it had been staged, you would have said, "That's just slapstick comedy!"

Meanwhile, back at Universal, the studio indulged one of its more aberrant decisions. With Boris busy on *Bride* and Bela occupied at Metro with *Mark of the Vampire,* Universal decided to launch a "second Karloff"—despite the fact that it already had a contractual commitment with the "first" Bela Lugosi.

The actor was Henry Hull; the film was *Werewolf of London.* Junior had blueprinted it as a Karloff vehicle, and the author was John Colton (who had dramatized that immortal hooker, Miss Sadie Thompson, in his Broadway play *Rain*). *Werewolf of London* began shooting January 28 (26 days after *Bride* began), wrapped February 23 (12 days before *Bride* ended), and cost $195,393.01 (about one-half of *Bride's* final cost). Hull was a fiery, Kentucky-born character player who had created the role of Jeeter Lester in the original Broadway cast of *Tobacco Road* in 1933; he had played Magwitch in Universal's 1934 *Great Expectations* and acted in such Universal films as *Midnight* and 1935's *Transient Lady.*

The "second Karloff" hardly came cheaply. For *Werewolf of London,* Hull received $2750 per week—$250 more than even Karloff was receiving. In addition, a "special arrangement" paid Hull's agent $82.50 per week, and there was even a mysterious additional allowance of $1375 included for Hull's "trick shots."

One can only marvel at why Laemmle paid such money to Hull; if he had waited a week, Bela Lugosi would have been free of *Mark of the Vampire,* and would have been ready, willing, able, and much cheaper than Hull. And, for all this expense, Hull's performance was unsympathetic. His famous refusal to allow Jack P. Pierce carte blanche with his face resulted in a light, bat-like makeup which retrospectively suffers in comparison to Lon Chaney, Jr.'s *The Wolf Man* of 1941. As things evolved, *Werewolf of London* proved to be Henry Hull's swan song at Universal; so much for the "second Karloff." (Ironically, a few years before Hull died on his Connecticut farm in 1977, *Famous Monsters of Filmland* offered to forward fan mail to the old, retired actor, who, according to the magazine, was desperate for attention.)

For a spell, Universal had eyed *Werewolf of London* as a possible Karloff/Lugosi vehicle. Even after Hull was cast, the studio did consider Lugosi (significantly) for the second banana role of Dr. Yogami—a part ultimately played by Warner Oland. Bela would have given a more zesty portrayal than did Oland (then "Charlie Chan," of course, at Fox); he also undoubtedly would have worked for far less than the guaranteed $12,000 that Oland received.

Meanwhile, *Bride of Frankenstein* finally "wrapped" March 7, 1935, after 46 days of shooting and at a final cost of $397,023.79 — Universal's most expensive horror film of the era. During its shooting, movie fans saw Bela Lugosi in two new releases: Columbia's *The Best Man Wins,* with Bela as a bespectacled heavy menacing Edmund Lowe, and Monogram's *The Mysterious Mr. Wong,* with Bela's tall, Hungarian-accented Wong madly seeking "the twelve coins of Confucius."

On May 10, 1935, *Bride of Frankenstein* premiered at New York's Roxy Theatre, complete with its awesome Franz Waxman score. It proved to be the outrageous climax of Universal Horror; "Mr. Karloff is so splendid in the role," reported the *New York Times,* "that all one can say is 'he is the monster.'" Karloff was at the apex of stardom. Yet, for all of Boris's dominance, and Universal's executive myopia, it was a good life for Bela Lugosi.

"Bela was getting sacks of wild — and I mean wild — fan mail," remembered Lillian, "and none of Bela's pictures ever lost a dime."

*   *   *

No, we really didn't socialize. You see, our lives, our tastes, were quite different. Ours was simply a professional relationship. But I have warm recollections of him as a fine actor and a great technician....
— Karloff on Lugosi, 1967

During these palmy days of Hollywood glory, did Karloff and Lugosi ever really socialize?

"Hell, no!" said Lillian Lugosi Donlevy. "No way!"

For Karloff, home was an old, Mexican farmhouse — a bizarre aerie, high amidst the oak trees and honeysuckle of Coldwater Canyon. 2320 Bowmont Drive, with its pool and rambling gardens, had been the address of Katharine Hepburn, who believed the house haunted by a "ghost" who moved the furniture, jiggled the latch on Miss Hepburn's bedroom door, and loomed over the guest bed — reportedly scaring Miss Hepburn's brother Richard so badly that he couldn't sleep "one single night" during his visit. After Miss Hepburn's friend, Laura Harding, tried to have her dogs ferret out the ghost — to no avail — Boris and Dorothy moved into the haunted hacienda.

Perhaps Boris scared away the ghost; perhaps they were kindred spirits. At any rate, the star loved his "little farm." There, "Dear Boris," a pastoral bogeyman in top hat and swim trunks, cigarette in mouth, pitchfork in hand, paraded about the farm, reading English poetry, splashing in his pool, feeding his turkeys, pruning 20 varieties of roses, tending to his plum trees (900 pounds of plums in 1935!) and romping with his beloved zoo of Bedlington terriers, a giant turtle, and his prize, 400-pound pig, Violet. Marian Marsh,

Bela Lugosi and canine companions.

Boris Karloff and friend on the Coldwater Canyon farm.

Trilby to John Barrymore's *Svengali* (1931) and Karloff's leading lady in
Columbia's 1935 *The Black Room,* remembers Violet—and Violet's loving
master—vividly.

> Boris had a pet pig, whose name was Violet. She was the cleanest, pinkest
> pig I've ever seen, and always wore a violet bow. And the pig had a playpen,
> with little rails, and a spread over the floor, inside the house...
> Well, many a time we would be invited to Boris's house for dinner, and
> sometimes, Boris would be late from the studio ... when the pig heard his car,
> it would start bouncing, forward and back, forward and back.... It was
> amazing—just like a dog who knew the master's car! The pig would make little
> squealy sounds, and everyone would turn and say, "Well, what's the matter with
> Violet? Is Boris coming home?" The more the pig heard the name "Boris" and
> the longer it waited, the more excited it would get, and its little eyes would be
> just huge!
> So, in would come Boris. "How's my little Violet today?" he'd ask, and with
> his long legs, he would climb into the playpen with the pig, and they would romp
> together. It was really a sight to be seen. But the funny thing was, my name at
> birth had been Violet—and I never did tell Boris, because I was afraid it might
> upset him!

Away from the farm, Boris, of course, played cricket, and fought
courageously as an officer of the Screen Actors Guild. All in all, Boris's intelligence, humor, and concern for his fellow actors—as well as the uncanny
grace with which he played his macabre movie roles—won Karloff the affection of the movie colony.

Bela Lugosi, meanwhile, was "lord and master" (Lillian's description) of
a stately mansion high in the hills above Beachwood Drive, under the
HOLLYWOODLAND sign. Lights burned every night in every window as
Bela puffed his Havana cigars, studied astrology, philosophy and sociology,
enjoyed a giant stamp collection, and lavishly savored his fame—treating
Hungarian friends to gala parties with Gypsy music and rich Bavarian beer.
Lillian remembered those exciting days:

> Of course, we went to the Hungarian restaurants in Los Angeles. Bela
> loved the Gypsy musicians—and boy, did they love him! Many of them had fol-
> lowed him from New York to Hollywood, because Bela was such a great "tipper"
> that they couldn't make it without him! In the restaurant, he'd point right at them
> when he wanted them to play, and signal exactly when he wanted them to stop.
> Then, after closing time, we'd bring the Gypsy musicians home with us, closing
> the draperies at dawn, as the music went on and on...
> Bela loved "nature hikes," too. We used to hike up to the HOLLYWOOD-
> LAND sign, and to Mulholland Dam. Bela would hike up first, and I had to re-
> main at the car with the great Danes. Then, when he was ready, Bela would
> signal to me, and I was to let out the dogs, so they could run up to him. I'd
> follow!

Bela also followed soccer, and generously sponsored a number of
Hungarian teams. And he, too, was active in the Screen Actors Guild, serving

on the Advisory Board. In truth, he was a warm, generous, stimulating friend to his European confreres who shared his old country nostalgia. However, his ego, temperament, and preference for Hungarian company and custom did, as Karloff put it, "isolate" him in the eyes of Hollywood.

In 1935, the very convivial Peter Lorre, now in Hollywood for MGM's *Mad Love,* hosted a stag party, and invited Karloff and Lugosi. When Bela found out Boris would be there, he almost declined. Only Lorre's Hungarian blood, and the fact that countrymen would be there, convinced him to attend — politely.

6
The Raven of 1935

"Prophet!" said I, "thing of evil! — prophet still, if bird or devil!
By that Heaven that bends above us — by that God we both adore —
Tell this soul with sorrow laden if, within the distant Aidenn,
It shall clasp a sainted maiden whom the angels name Lenore —
Clasp a rare and radiant maiden whom the angels name Lenore."
Quoth the Raven "Nevermore."
— from Edgar Allan Poe's 1845 poem, *The Raven*

In a Haunted House of Horror, a Half-Corpse Stalked, His Face a Crazy-
Quilt of Death, Transfixed in Mocking Grimace of Terror!
His Ugliness Bred In Him Monstrous Hate of Humanity and Made of Him
the Perfect Slave of Dr. Vollin — The Man Who Destroyed All Who Crossed
Him!
— Universal Display Lines for *The Raven*, 1935

Poe, you are avenged!
— Bela Lugosi, in *The Raven*

Since the summer of 1934, Universal had been battling *The Raven*, trying
to adapt Poe's lyrical poem of the lost Lenore into a Karloff and Lugosi
screenplay.

Guy Endore, author of *Werewolf of Paris* and one of the scriptwriters for
MGM's *Mark of the Vampire*, earned $700 for the first draft, submitted August
31, 1934. Clarence Marks earned $887.50 and Michael Simmons $2133.35 for
their stabs at it later that year; Jim Tully earned a hefty $5083.35 for bastard-
izing the poem further; John Lynch dallied with it and took home $1750 for
his trouble. With all this time and expense thrown into the adaptation,
Universal was hell-bent on producing *The Raven*, and at length, David Boehm
wrote three full screenplay versions — receiving $5375 and the only screenplay
credit on the film. Even Dore Schary, who, over 15 years later, would usurp
Louis B. Mayer as potentate of MGM, earned $233.36 for some last-minute
flourishes on *The Raven's* script.

The final result: Lugosi won the dominating role of Dr. Richard Vollin,
a gloriously mad surgeon with a Poe obsession, a torture chamber in his
cellar, and a lunatic glint in his eye; "a God," as he describes himself in the
melodrama, "with the taint of human emotions!" Karloff landed a virtual supporting part (with the consoling bonus of two special makeups) as Edmond

Bateman, a pathetic, on-the-lam murderer who ponders, "Maybe if a man looks ugly, he does ugly things..."

Once again, Universal placed most of its faith in the "KARLOFF and Bela LUGOSI" box office power. *The Raven* received a 15-day shooting shedule and a grand total budget of $109,750 — almost $19,000 more than *The Black Cat* (the various fees paid to the writers making up a large share of the difference). This time, Junior Laemmle didn't produce personally, and the honor fell to David Diamond, who would supervise the production for $150 per week.

Universal played it safe this time in selecting a director. They wanted no kinky Ulmer flourishes, and assigned Louis Friedlander (1901-1962, later known as Lew Landers), who had directed such Universal serials as *Tailspin Tommy*, to make his feature bow as director. Friedlander received the same pay as Ulmer — $900 for the picture.

The studio quickly picked its cast of supporting players:

• For dancer Jean Thatcher, Lugosi's "Lenore" of *The Raven*, Irene Ware (who had acted with Bela in Fox's 1932 *Chandu the Magician*) signed for $250 per week and two and a half weeks' work — total, $625.

• For her beau, Dr. Jerry Halden, Lester Matthews, who had just completed *Werewolf of London*, signed at $461.50 per week for two and a half weeks — total, $1,153.76. Both Miss Ware and Mr. Matthews had been set for *The Raven* for some weeks, and the various delays forced Universal to split a $2830 bonus for "idle time" between the romantic leads. (A trade notice had originally slated Chester Morris for this role.)

• For Judge Thatcher, Jean's father, Universal picked Samuel S. Hinds, a former lawyer who sparked many Universal films over the years (*Destry Rides Again, Man Made Monster, The Spoilers,* et al.). Hinds' fee: $500 per week for two weeks and four days — total, $1333.35.

• For the various eccentric sophisticates who join Jean and Jerry and the Judge for that horrific night at Vollin's, the studio's Inez Courtney, a cute character comedy actress as Mary; Ian Wolfe, then just beginning his awesomely prolific career as her husband Geoffrey (aka "Pinky"); and Spencer Charters and Maidel Turner as Bert and Harriet, who sleep through the mayhem.

Charles Stumar, who had been Karl Freund's cinematographer on *The Mummy* (and would tragically die shortly after *The Raven* in a plane crash while securing aerial photography) was the cameraman.

John P. Fulton's Special Effects were easy this time: the budget sheet called only for one miniature — of the Elevator Room, with a preparation/construction/photographing allowance of $825.

Once again, however, the real significance in the Production Reports concerns the salaries of the two stars.

Karloff's weekly Universal paycheck had jumped to $2500; set for four weeks' work as Bateman in *The Raven,* his fee totaled $10,000.

The uncanny master of make-up in a new amazing thriller!

CARL LAEMMLE presents

KARLOFF

and

Bela (DRACULA) LUGOSI

IN AN ADAPTATION OF EDGAR ALLAN POE'S

"The Raven"

with IRENE WARE · LESTER MATTHEWS
INEZ COURTNEY

Directed by
LOUIS FRIEDLANDER

Associate Producer
DAVID DIAMOND

A UNIVERSAL PICTURE

Lugosi settled for the same weekly fee as Vollin that he had received for *The Black Cat*—$1000 per week—but now for a five-week period. So, although Bela enjoyed almost double the screen time Boris did, he got exactly half the salary—and, once again, was forced to take second billing.

On Wednesday, March 20, 1935, two days after David Boehm turned in his final script, *The Raven* began shooting.

* * *

> Dr. Vollin, Suave, Fascinating,—Demon of Medicine! A Law Unto Himself! Great Lover and Rabid Hater! Madman Who Exerts A Strange Spell—and Lasting Fascination!
>
> His Name Was Bateman—This Beast-Like Man That Roamed the Eerie Corridors of Dr. Vollin's Crazy Mansion, Forced to Deeds of Torture, But Struggling, Insanely to Save From Disaster—Himself, and the Other Victims In That Dark and Dungeon Like House!
>
> —display lines for *The Raven*

The shooting script of *The Raven* began with Jean Thatcher leaving her theatre after a triumphant dance performance; two autograph seekers were to beseech her for her signature. Instead, the release print of *The Raven* opens with W. Franke Harling's *Destination Unknown* music, a shot of a car racing over treacherously slippery roads, and a close-up of our heroine, Irene Ware.

Miss Ware was an attractive actress, with bedroom eyes, who had just played in the Universal films *Night Life of the Gods* and *Rendezvous at Midnight;* she would vanish entirely after the decade. Unfortunately, she had very fine hair, and for *The Raven,* the studio furtively budgeted Miss Ware a $125 wig.

The car crashes. With serial-like speed, Friedlander rushes us into the emergency room, where Jean lies on an operating table. Close-ups of her desperate fiancé, Jerry Halden, and her heartsick father, Judge Thatcher, set up the situation. Oddly, the pencil-thin moustached Mr. Matthews, other half of the romantic interest, also sports a hairpiece (which he occasionally discarded later in his career as he gave up horror heroes for a prolific character player career); Mr. Hinds as Judge Thatcher instantly suggests the authority he gave all his screen roles.

Drs. Hemingway and Cook can offer no hope. Meanwhile, up on Hillview Heights, a stuffed raven sits on a desk, and a Hungarian accented voice declaims:

Suddenly, there came a tapping,
as of someone gently rapping,
rapping at my chamber door.

Opposite: **One-sheet poster for *The Raven*, 1935.**

Open then I flung the shutter,
when with many a flirt and flutter,
in there stepped a stately raven. . . .

Dr. Richard Vollin—brilliant surgeon, worshipper of Edgar Allan Poe—
recites the immortal lines; we first see him on profile, as the script called for
a "Close Shot . . . Emphasizing a certain sinister bird-like quality." Lugosi's
maniacal surgeon might well be a passionate descendant of Count Dracula; the
role, in many ways, will be the apotheosis of his screen persona.

Adding to the menace of Bela's introduction in *The Raven* is "Raven
Theme," a sinister motif by Clifford Vaughan, who had orchestrated Franz
Waxman's magnificent score for *Bride of Frankenstein*. Vaughan, who composed
and orchestrated about 15 minutes of original music for *The Raven,* adds a delightful touch here: a xylophone, suggesting the sound of a pecking raven.

The real treat, however, is Bela Lugosi. Shortly after completing *The
Raven,* Bela told a *New York Times* reporter:

> You can't make people believe in you if you're playing a horror part with
> your tongue in your cheek. The screen magnifies everything, even the way you
> are thinking. If you are not serious, people will sense it. No matter how hokum
> or highly melodramatic the horror part may be, you must believe in it while you
> are playing it.

Seated next to Vollin's desk is little Mr. Chapman, who has come to ac-
quire Vollin's Poe collection for his museum. He notes on the desk the large,
stuffed raven—which Vollin claims is his "talisman."

"Curious talisman," says Chapman, "the bird of ill omen, a symbol of
death."

"Death *is* my talisman, Mr. Chapman," replies Vollin. "The one indestructible force, the one certain thing in an uncertain universe. Death!"

The telephone rings. It is Judge Thatcher, who begs Vollin to operate
on his dying daughter. But Vollin has retired from actual practice, and has
devoted himself to research; he declines and hangs up. As Chapman leaves,
Vollin tells him of the various torture devices of Poe's works which Vollin has
built in his own cellar.

"Imagine building those things!" marvels Chapman. "A very curious
hobby."

"It's *more* than a hobby," says Vollin, in an intense close-up.

Chapman leaves, Judge Thatcher arrives. He begs Vollin's aid in saving
his daughter's life.

> "I'll pay you any amount of money, Dr. Vollin."
> "Money means nothing to me."
> "But someone is dying! Your obligation as a member of the medical
> profession—"

Bela Lugosi as Dr. Richard Vollin in *The Raven*.

"I respect no obligation. I am a law unto myself!"
"But have you no human feeling? My daughter is dying."
"Death hasn't the same significance for me as it has for you."

Thatcher keeps pleading. All the doctors at the hospital say that Vollin is the only man with the brilliance to save Jean.

"So they do say I am the only one!" beams Vollin. He departs for the hospital. And, as he stares behind his surgeon's mask at the lovely patient on the table, beneath his knife, passion enters Vollin's eyes and we see him, as the script desired, "his stature tremendous, his face like a god or demon..."

Vollin saves Jean's life. Fascinated by the genius, she visits his house; Miss Ware lounges on the couch in an attractively eccentric dress and hat one might expect a modern dancer to wear, while Bela serenades her with the Bach Toccata on the organ. (Once again, exactly as in *The Black Cat,* the budget allotted $30 for an organist, to put in a one to three hour session.)

"You're not only a great surgeon, but a great musician too," says Jean. "Extraordinary man! You're almost *not* a man. Almost—"

"A god?" suggests Vollin; "...a god—with the taint of human emotions."

Vollin stares at the surgical miracle he performed on Jean's neck. The scar is almost gone. "When I touch it," asks Lugosi with wonderfully sinister fascination, "does it still hurt?"

Jean gratefully expresses her debt to Vollin for his saving her life. She wishes there was something she could do to show her gratitude.

"There is," says Lugosi, and we suddenly get insight into how he must have played Romeo on the stage in Hungary. "The restraint that we impose upon ourselves can drive us mad!"

Jean, clearly attracted to her savior, nevertheless cowers from Vollin's passionate advance. She reminds Vollin of her fiancé, Dr. Jerry Halden, whom Vollin has made his assistant since Jean's operation. Now she and Jerry can be married sooner than they thought.

"I did it," says Vollin, reaching for Jean, "to give him something to take the place of what he's losing!"

Jean withdraws. But she has invited him to her new dance performance, where she has a surprise for him...

From a balcony on the old Universal "Phantom Stage," Lugosi's Vollin watches raptly as Jean performs an original ballet, "The Spirit of Poe," accompanied by a narrator reciting *The Raven.* Forty "dress people" earned $15 each for sitting in the theatre, pretending to be the audience, while 12 men (at $12.50 each) apparently really played in the orchestra pit. It's not much of a ballet, staged by Theodore Kosloff; the fact that Jean, in a mask and costume, merely bounds around the stage in strange leaps makes one presume that the bewigged Miss Ware did her own dancing. At any rate, Vollin is ecstatic. Backstage, he enters Joan's dressing room, and takes her hands.

"Whom the angels call Lenore!" he says with rapture.

Judge Thatcher notes the attraction between Jean and Vollin, and calls on the surgeon at his home. When Thatcher reveals the nature of his visit—to ask the doctor not to see Jean again—Vollin crushes a test tube in his own hand.

"Not see her again!" says Vollin. "Listen, Thatcher. I'm a man who

Irene Ware and Lugosi in a tense moment from *The Raven*.

renders humanity a great service. For that my brain must be clear, my nerves steady, and my hand sure. Jean torments me. She has come into my life, into my brain."

And so Thatcher's pleas fall on deaf ears. Vollin demands that the Judge send his daughter to him.

"You're mad!" cries Thatcher.

"I *am* mad!" cries Vollin.

The Judge leaves. And Vollin's thoughts turn to revenge...

In a grimy saloon, a bearded figure in a porkpie hat sits at a table, looking like a melancholy hedgehog. We hear Clifford Vaughan's "Bateman Theme," and meet fugitive bank robber–murderer Edmond Bateman — KARLOFF.

"Why it was nothing but a bloody stuffed bird on Bela Lugosi's desk!" lamented Boris of *The Raven*. The star was put off by Universal's script — "Here was an attempt to pile on the thrills without much logic" — and hardly could have been delighted by the role, which, for all the makeup bonanza, was a stooge.

What Karloff did with his part, therefore, was novel.

Noted film historian William K. Everson once analyzed Karloff's acting in a 1964 issue of the late and long lamented *Screen Facts* magazine:

> He also developed two very distinct approaches to acting. Roles that he ob-
> viously respected — through the years these ranged from *The Mummy* to *The Body
> Snatcher* — he played seriously and creatively. Other roles — and *The Mask of Fu
> Manchu* and *The Raven* are key examples — that he saw as basically idiotic but
> grand fun, he played in marvelous bravura style, revelling in every absurd
> line. . . .

Indeed, Boris makes Bateman an outrageous character, almost out of Disney; he suggests some awful, overgrown, eye-rolling problem kid, who any minute might petulantly suck his thumb. There's a bit of the monster there, too; if Lugosi's Vollin shows lineage from Count Dracula, Karloff's Bateman might be a descendant of some of Dr. Frankenstein's original source material. Karloff's approach works wonders in *The Raven;* rather than patronize the penny dreadful, Karloff hits the movie's tone at its most outrageously silly level, helping to stylize it while providing a sly, comic relief from the Lugosi bombast.

Bateman has been told Vollin can perform plastic surgery; after we see him lurking sheepishly on some back lot streets,* he invades the Vollin mansion — for one of the best Karloff and Lugosi scenes of all their movies.

The mad doctor recognizes Bateman, who quickly grabs his beard, like a trick-or-treater, disappointed that a neighbor had recognized him so easily. Vollin agrees to the operation — if Bateman will return the favor.

"Like what?" asks Bateman.

"It's in your line."

"*Like what?*"

"Torture. And murder!"

---

*In the original script, Bateman was to spy on Vollin, getting into his chauffeur-driven car in front of the hospital; "That's him . . . getting into the car," the drug clerk was to say. Karloff was to start across the street toward Lugosi, and "a car has to swerve suddenly to miss him." Bateman was to stand bewildered in the middle of the street, and a policeman was to call out to him from his passing car, "Where do you want the flowers sent?"

Bateman protests, but Vollin, who has followed Bateman's criminal career, reminds him of his deeds.

LUGOSI: You shot your way out of San Quentin. Two guards are dead. In a bank in Arizona a man's face was mutilated — burned — cashier of the bank. . . .
KARLOFF: Well, he tried to get me into trouble! I told him to keep his mouth shut. He gets the gag out of his mouth and starts yellin' for the police. I had the acetylene torch in my hand. . . .
LUGOSI (appreciatively): So you put the burning torch into his face! Into his *eyes!*
KARLOFF (petulantly): Well, sometimes you can't help things like that. . .

Pouting, Bateman blames his nefarious deeds on his ugly face. "I'll tell you somethin', Doc," growls Karloff, his eyes shining in a great close-up. "Ever since I was born, everybody looks at me and says, 'You're ugly.' Makes me feel mean. . . Maybe because I look ugly, maybe if a man looks ugly, he does ugly things. . . ."

"You are saying something profound," grins Vollin. "A man with a face so hideously ugly. . . !"

Bateman pleads for a handsome face — "Fix me so I look good, will ya'?" — and Vollin leads him through a secret passageway to surgery. The great surgeon puts on his smock, and informs the fugitive that he can change his face in a ten-minute operation by adjusting the roots of the seventh cranial nerve.

". . . I, who know what to do with these nerve ends" says Lugosi, employing his famous use of pauses to the maximum, "can make you look any — way — I — choose. . . !"

The stars themselves appear to be enjoying themselves hugely in this episode, which adds all the more to *The Raven*'s fun. Candid set shots show the bearded Karloff, with cigarette, and the surgeon-smocked Lugosi, with cigar, cuddling on a couch, slyly perusing the script as if reading each other a bedtime story. Of course, Bela had to tolerate the tea breaks again, but his meaty role of Vollin seemed to boost his security, and he even told reporters how he and Karloff had "laughed" about the *Frankenstein* saga of 1931.

"We became very good friends," said the high-spirited Bela, telling the PR boys what he thought they wanted to hear while tolerating yet another tea break.

Vollin completes the operation. As Clifford Vaughan's "Bateman Theme" reaches a chilling crescendo, Lugosi removes the bandages from Karloff's new face. . .

Universal proudly publicized that Jack P. Pierce's inspiration for the new Karloff makeup was *The Man Who Laughs,* and the twisted smile of Gwynplaine. Boehm's shooting script, however, had described it quite originally, and accurately:

His face is a horror. Certain muscles have been paralyzed through cutting of the nerve ends. Certain others have been permitted to remain — giving life to

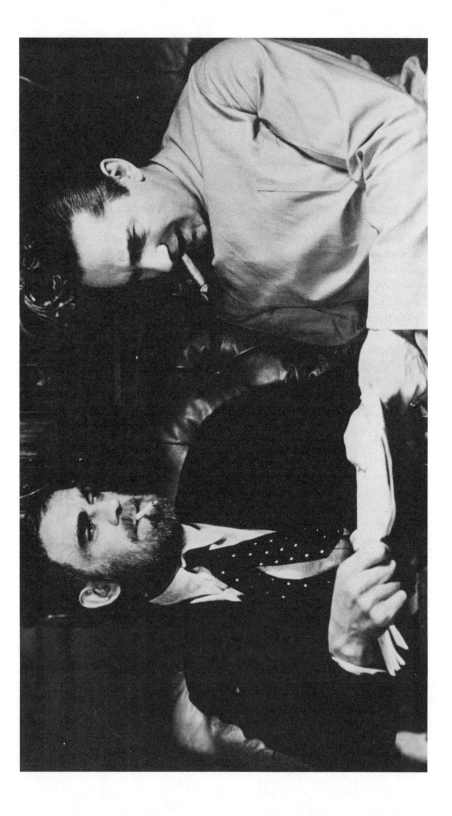

the part of the face they control, so that here is a face — a crazy quilt of death and life. One part of his face remains fixed in a horrible dead grimace, while the other remains alive — side by side with the corpse. One eye remains open, unblinking — staring straight ahead.

Actually, the final effect in the movie makes Karloff look like a five-day old jack o'lantern — outrageous, but in tune with the melodrama itself.

"Do I look — different?" smiles the Halloween pumpkin.

"Yes," smiles Vollin.

The doctor leaves the room. Suddenly, under the surgeon's control, curtains fly back to reveal a series of full-length mirrors. To his savage horror, a new swelling of the "Bateman Theme," and shades of the monster's mime by the pool in *Bride of Frankenstein,* Bateman sees his new and hideous face. Karloff roars. He madly shoots each mirror, and along with the crashing glass, we hear the mad laughter of Lugosi, enjoying it all from a dungeon window above.

Karloff growls, à la the monster. He hurls his empty pistol at the mocking face of Lugosi.

"Fix my mouth!" demands Karloff's Bateman. Not surprisingly, with the actor's famous lisp now aggravated by that slack mouth, the line comes out, "Fix my mouse!" The fact that the budget sheets note $200 for "Karloff Dental Work for Makeup" probably didn't help either.

"You're monstrously ugly!" exults Lugosi. "Your monstrous ugliness breeds monstrous hate! Good. I can use your hate..."

Invitations go out to a weekend at the Vollin mansion. The guests include tubby Sir Bertram (Spencer Charters) and tubbier Harriet Grant (Maidel Turner), Mary Burns ("a Gracie Allenish or Una Merkelish sort," noted the script, and Inez Courtney is delightful), and her English husband Geoffrey (whom Mary calls "Pinky" — played by Ian Wolfe). Jerry Halden is there too — and Jean and Judge Thatcher.

Ian Wolfe, who became one of Hollywood's most recognizable, busy and best character players, won the part of "Pinky" — one of his first Hollywood roles. He remembers Karloff on *The Raven* as "a pussy-cat — kindly and charming," and Lugosi as "a real European gentleman." He also remembers Karloff's irreverence toward his home studio. Making his Universal debut in *The Raven,* Wolfe arrived at Universal extra-early his first day; in fact, so early was Wolfe that, upon his arrival at the studio, the only person he could find was Karloff, who had also arrived early so to have his face prepared for the makeup. The makeup assistant hadn't shown up. As Karloff waited, Wolfe approached him.

"Mr. Karloff," asked Wolfe, "could you please direct me to a toilet?"

"This *whole* place," said Karloff, waving at the studio-at-large, "is a toilet!"

Opposite: **Tobacco break on the set of** *The Raven.*

The guests are cheering at a spinning horse game. Screams interrupt the gaiety. As Miss Ware primps at the mirror in her guest boudoir (careful not to disturb her wig), she sees the horrific reflection of Bateman. Vollin assures the guests that his "servant" (who has dressed for the part, in tuxedo and bow tie) was mutilated by Arab bandits while serving in Vollin's regiment. The guests return to Vollin's study, where they ask Vollin why he is so fascinated by Poe. In a very dramatic soliloquy, Lugosi, again on profile, Stumar's camera clearly trying again for that "sinister bird-like quality," wonderfully builds:

> I will tell you. Poe was a great genius. Like all great geniuses, there was in him the insistent will to do something big, great, constructive in the world. He had the brain to do it. But—he fell in love. Her name was Lenore...
> "Longing for the lost Lenore," sighs Jean.
> "Longing for the lost Lenore," sighs Vollin in return.
> Something happened. Someone took her away from him. When a man of genius is denied his great love, he goes mad. His brain, instead of being clear to do his work, is tortured—so *he* begins to think of torture. Torture for those who have tortured him...!

Realizing he has perhaps overplayed his hand (if not the scene), Lugosi adds, lightheartedly, "My interest in Poe, the way I speak about torture and death, you people being laymen perhaps do not understand. As a doctor, a surgeon, I look upon these things differently." And then the villainous tone returns: "A doctor is fascinated by death—and pain. And how much pain a man can endure..."

The guests retire for the night. On the way to her bedroom, Jean apologizes to Bateman for screaming—and he's touched by her kindness; somehow, behind that pumpkin face, Karloff manages to look lovesick. And, as the guests close their doors, Vollin, debonair in smoking jacket and cravat, takes Bateman on a tour of his cellar torture chambers.

It's a reversal of the cellar visit in *The Black Cat;* Bela is now escorting Boris through his cellar, and the music is Chopin's *Second Piano Prelude*—the music which introduced the Marmaros interior in the 1934 film. (Tracks of music from *The Black Cat* become increasingly a part of *The Raven* as the film goes on toward its climax, which was a surprise to the film's composer/arranger, Clifford Vaughan.) Proud of his sinister handiwork, Vollin can't resist showing Bateman his Pit and Pendulum device. The doctor lies on the slab, sets the great pendulum knife in motion, and shows Bateman a switch that operates manacles, which imprison the wrists and ankles.

"In fifteen minutes," boasts Vollin, "the knife reaches the heart."

Suddenly the manacles close—on Vollin.

"Gotcha!" rasps Bateman's goblin face.

However, Vollin reminds him that, if anything should happen to him, Bateman remains "the hideous monster that you are." Bateman releases Vollin—and soon, the madman's scheme of vengeance begins.

Bateman wrestles Judge Thatcher from his room. The Judge, in his pajamas, finds himself manacled to the slab and looking up at the giant, swinging knife.

"What's that thing?" gasps Thatcher.

"A knife," replies Vollin.

"What's it doing?"

"Descending."

"What are you trying to do to me?"

"Torture you!"

"Oh, try to be sane, Vollin!"

"I am the sanest man who ever lived! But I will not be tortured! I tear torture out of myself by torturing *you!*"

Vollin explodes into maniacal laughter. "Torture, waiting, *waiting!* Death will be sweet, Judge Thatcher!"

The Judge stares at the knife, waiting to be disemboweled. "Do you mind if I smoke?" asks Vollin.

Vollin has other plans too. At a great control panel, he pulls a switch— and Jean's room, really an elevator, descends to the cellar. Other switches cause iron shutters to cover the windows, and phone lines to be cut off. Jerry, Geoffrey, and Mary all run to aid Jean and the Judge, but Vollin traps them all at gunpoint, as Karloff contents himself, rolling his one mobile eye as he watches the swinging pendulum.

Vollin offers the engaged couple a wedding gift.

"My gift to you two," sneers the madman. "The place in which you will live. A humble place, but your love will make it beautiful... It will be the perfect marriage, the perfect love. You will never be separated! Never... Forever and ever!" It is the room Poe concocted in *The Pit and the Pendulum*— the room where the walls come together.

At gunpoint, the lovers have entered the room. Vollin orders Bateman to pull the switch that sets the walls in motion.

"What torture!" exults Lugosi. "What a delicious torture, Bateman! Greater than Poe! Poe only conceived it! I have done it, Bateman! POE," climaxes Bela, his voice so choked with emotion that he sounds just like Ygor in *Son of Frankenstein,* "YOU ARE AVENGED!"

Vollin waves his arms insanely and laughs. Fortunately, the lines he is to say in sing-song, according to the script—"The Raven... Symbol of Death... Nevermore... Nevermore... The lost Lenore!" are cut.

"You've done nobly, Bateman," says Vollin. "Now, I'll do nobly by you. Ha, ha ha!"

But Bateman isn't comforted by the promise of a new face—not if the girl who was kind to him, and has offered to help him, is about to be killed. Impulsively, Bateman pulls the switch to stop the walls. The outraged Vollin shoots him in the back. But the fatally wounded Bateman is still strong enough to attack Vollin...

The pendulum swings: Karloff, Lugosi and Samuel S. Hinds in *The Raven*.

While the budget had allotted $17.50 each for two doubles to fight for Boris and Bela, the stars themselves appear to be performing the very limited brawl. Bateman knocks Vollin out. And, after releasing the lovers from the room, Bateman drags Vollin's unconscious body into the chamber. With final energy, the dying Bateman, our pitiful tragic hero, falls back upon the switch — and sets the chamber walls back into motion...

Jean, Jerry, Mary and Geoffrey save Judge Thatcher, seconds before the great blade can reach his heart. Vollin awakens in the torture chamber he created, becomes hysterical as the walls close against him, covers his face, screams, and falls...

The shooting script was to end with the Colonel and Harriet awakening. "Hasn't it been a marvelous night!" says Harriet. "I don't know when I've had such a good sleep..."

"Nor I, my pet," says the Colonel.

Instead, we only see them snoring away. And the released version offered a new tag. Matthews and Miss Ware, each keeping their wigs under their hats, are driving in a car. "Poor Bateman...," says Jean. "Yes, darling, he saved us from being crushed...," says Jerry. And then, putting his arm around Jean, "I think I better finish the job—don't you? Only a little more gently."

"So *you're* the big bad Raven, hmm?" says the heroine flirtingly. "Hmmm!" responds the hero. The Tchaikovsky *Romeo and Juliet* theme from *The Black Cat* swells. THE END.

And once again, a good cast is worth repeating...

* * *

TO SHOCKER FANS

For Those who enjoyed *Dracula, Invisible Man, Bride of Frankenstein* and other screen shockers, we announce a new sensational goose-pimple thriller entertainment—Karloff in Edgar Allan Poe's *The Raven* with Bela (Dracula) Lugosi.

WARNING!

In keeping with this theatre's policy of frankness, WE WARN YOU that this is a picture of the wild shocker type. Highly nervous, timid people should stay away. Those, however, who enjoy excitement and having their hair stand on end, will love this horrific sensation! THE MANAGEMENT
—suggested lobby easel from Universal's pressbook for *The Raven*

The Raven came in right on the 15-day schedule—wrapping Friday, April 5, 1935. The final cost was $115,209.01, putting it $5450 over budget—running most significantly over in editing, synchronization, and retained time.

Due to Karloff's contract, and growing popularity (Universal was previewing *Bride of Frankenstein* as it prepared *The Raven* for release), his studio awarded him the dominant space in promotion: "The Uncanny Master of Makeup in a New Amazing Thriller," said the one-sheet posters (see page 102 above). "Karloff Crowns His Terrific Screen Achievements With A New Role," crowed *The Raven* publicity, "More Remarkable Even Than His Former Triumphs!"

Clearly somebody at Universal recognized the inequity of the Karloff promotion. Therefore, the opening screen credits list the stars as KARLOFF and LUGOSI. However, on the opening/closing cast list, Karloff remains Karloff, but Lugosi became Bela Lugosi. So much for the intricacies of Hollywood billing!

Naturally, Universal had a whole new sideshow of promotions as *The Raven* came a-tapping to theatres in the summer of 1935:

> •A "Chamber of Chills" in the Movie Lobby. "Partition off a space in your lobby, or any nearby empty store and set it aside as a 'chamber of horrors.' The chamber should be concealed by a heavy velvet curtain and admission offered free. Inside, exhibit blow-ups of the stills set into frames using, of course, the most thrilling shots!!! Focus on each one of these stills a green light for mystery effect... You can easily fix up a pendulum by hooking up a broomstick to a curved chopping knife..."
> •"Winged Ballyhoo." A theatre employee would wear a raven head, and a wing-like cape. When he opens the cape, one side read, "Edgar Allan Poe's *The Raven*" and the name of the theatre, while the other side read, "With Karloff, Bela Lugosi..."
> •A "Curtain Teaser Stunt." "Suspend a small curtain over the cut-out face of Karloff which you will get from the poster and paint on the curtain this message: 'This Curtain conceals a Face that Is a Crazy-Quilt of Horror! Look at it Before You Dare See *The Raven*.' Have a small pull cord arranged so that courageous people can try the experiment."

With a respectful nod to Poe, the pressbook even offered a form letter for high schools and colleges.

> Dear Sir (or Madam): We feel that your students will be interested in seeing on the screen a remarkable entertainment, inspired by Edgar Allan Poe's literary classic, *The Raven.* Karloff and "Dracula" Lugosi are the featured players ... the pit yawns, the pendulum swings... The great writer's lines are frequently quoted throughout the picture, and you and your students will feel a new interest, and appreciate more keenly the dramatic power of this famous verse....

The pressbook called for art contests in drawing the face of Poe, reciting *The Raven* on local radio, and even Raven hat feathers: "Local novelty dealers should be able to supply small black feathers to distribute to people with tags attached advising them to wear the feathers in their hats and join the new *Raven* faddists..."

Universal opened *The Raven* literally with a bang—on the Fourth of July, 1935, at New York's Roxy Theatre, with a "Big Revue on Stage" boasting Herman Timberg, Tip, Tap & Toe, The Digitanos, The Gae Foster Girls, and Freddie Mack's Orchestra. Also playing in New York that holiday: Columbia's Grace Moore musical *Love Me Forever;* Warner's *In Caliente,* featuring Dolores del Rio and Busby Berkeley dances; and Hollywood's first full Technicolor feature, RKO's *Becky Sharp,* starring Miriam Hopkins. In Manhattan too, at this time, was Bela Lugosi himself—en route to England with Lillian to star in *The Mystery of Marie Celeste.* "Mr. Lugosi will appear in person tonight on the stage of the Roxy," reported the July 4 *New York Times.* Bela arrived, as he put it, to "take some bows," and the audience warmly greeted the star. However, Bela wasn't ready — nor was Universal — for the critical roasting of *The Raven.* The *Times* said

> ... the Roxy's current tenant should have no difficulty in gaining the distinction of being the season's worst horror film. Not even the presence of the screen's Number One and Two Bogeymen, Mr. Karloff and Bela (Dracula) Lugosi, can make the picture anything but a fatal mistake from beginning to end.... Of course, it must be said that Lugosi and Karloff try hard, even though, both being cultured men, they must have suffered at the indignity being visited upon the helpless Edgar Allan....

"Stars Karloff, features Bela Lugosi" reported *Variety,* which naturally rated the film's box office power over everything else: "With both Karloff and Lugosi in the cast, it should scare them into the b.o.'s in spades..."

However, Universal executives couldn't help being nervous as critics attacked the sadism, torture and ugliness of *The Raven.* *Time* magazine booed the film as "stuffed with horrors to the point of absurdity." When *The Raven* opened at the Pantages Theatre July 10, 1935, the female critic of the *Los Angeles Herald-Examiner* dutifully reviewed the new vehicle of the "No. 1 and 2 horror men of the movies," panned *The Raven* as "their most dreadful effort to date," and distastefully noted that a little boy in back of her kept sliding out of his seat in fear. She even bypassed using a short of Karloff or Lugosi in her review, preferring a portrait of Irene Ware (whom she panned for her screaming — "It was too delicate").

Censorship problems came in from all over the country. New York and Ohio demanded cuts of the scenes of Samuel S. Hinds beneath the swinging pendulum, and Lugosi's line, "Torture waiting, waiting. It will be sweet, Judge Thatcher." Virginia demanded the cutting of Karloff's line, "I had the acetylene torch in my hand," and Lugosi's rejoiner, "So you put the burning torch into his face — into his eyes!" "The Old Dominion also insisted on cuts in shots of Hinds under the pendulum. Pennsylvania ordered the acetylene torch dialogue cut, insisted that the close-up of Karloff after the operation (and "of his hand reaching to his face and feeling it") go out of the picture, eliminated a close-up of Karloff watching the pendulum swinging rhythmically, axed Lugosi's climactic laughing fit, cut his line "Yes, I like to torture!" — and, of course, condemned those infamous shots of Hinds under the knife.

Meanwhile, outside the U.S., Quebec insisted on the exact same changes as Pennsylvania, as well as cutting the pendulum swinging over Hinds' face out of the trailer. British Columbia rejected *The Raven* outright until it was reconstructed by Film Exchange. Alberta shortened the shots of Karloff's disfigured face after the operation, and insisted that all advertising note: "The Alberta Censor Board advise nervous and excitable people to avoid this picture as it is a HORROR PICTURE." Ontario rejected it totally, and their reason almost surpassed the work of Universal's PR department: "Featuring horror and shuddering melodrama. Full of fiendish and diabolical doings." And overseas, Holland rejected it outright, coming right to the point: "Because of degrading effect on the public."

Bela's glowing sadist and Boris's fidgety hobgoblin were the overnight bad boys of the international cinema, and naturally, all these attacks made *The Raven* all the more appealing to many thrill seekers. However, Universal couldn't laugh off the ominous hissing that came from England. The British Board of Censors cut five minutes — and vowed to ban future films of similarly sadistic content. With the British market such a boon to Hollywood, Universal City, Hollywood's prime horror exponent, felt a truly cold shiver of its own.

The Raven fulfilled *Variety's* prediction of a powerful box office. However, it rapidly won the dubious distinction as Universal's least distinguished horror film, offending the sensitivities of so many critics that critical evaluation of the genre was never quite the same again.

Hollywood's big parade of horror movies was hardly over that summer of 1935. In August, MGM released the exotic *Mad Love* — the last film directed by Karl Freund, who then returned to cinematography. One can only wonder how Louis B. Mayer winced at this shocker, with bald-pated Peter Lorre's mad Dr. Gogol transplanting the hands of a guillotined knife murderer onto the train-wrecked limbs of pianist Colin Clive — making a neurotic's feast day of his role. *Mad Love* also offered a lovingly sadistic perusal of the Grand Guignol Theatre of Paris, where Frances Drake is branded nightly on a rack, to the thrills of the wide-eyed audience.

August of 1935 also saw the release of Columbia's *The Black Room,* featuring Karloff's fascinating *coup de théâtre* as the de Berghman twins — noble Count Anton, and depraved Count Gregor. It is a lovely gothic melodrama, directed by Roy William Neill with striking religious flourishes; indeed, with its cathedral, choir, and crucifixes, *The Black Room* must be the most Catholic horror movie ever made! It was a brilliant showcase for Karloff, while one of Neill's touches — a wicked black bird, cawing on a graveyard fence — returned when he directed Universal's *Frankenstein Meets the Wolf Man* (1943). Some historians have noted a resemblance between *The Black Room* and James Whale's horror fairy tales. Part of the reason: according to Marian Marsh, the film's storybook blonde leading lady, Columbia visited Universal to shoot the scenes in the Tyrolean village.

The *New York Times* predicted correctly: *The Raven* had won the "distinction" of being the season's most dreadful horror movie. In time, this distinction would bring on the wrath of censors and the British film industry, snowballing until it buried alive the horror genre — and the career of Bela Lugosi.

"We all thought," Ian Wolfe told me, speaking of *The Raven*, "that with the two 'scare-mongers' as stars, and author Poe, it would be a lalapalooza; but it was something of the latter syllable, with one 'o' out — *loser!*"

* * *

The Raven . . . was at heart an old-fashioned serial, memorable mainly for Lugosi's unwitting self-burlesque. When the script has him exulting in such lines as "Poe, you are avenged!" without a shadow of tongue in cheek, the movie becomes its own deadly parody.
— Carlos Clarens, *An Illustrated History of the Horror Movie*

The Raven survives not only as a Poe homage, but a Karloff and Lugosi homage. Of the three Universal films they appeared in together, this one survives almost entirely on their presence; there is no clever direction as in *The Black Cat*, no distinguished cast and special effects as in *The Invisible Ray*. Friedlander (who, for Columbia, later directed Karloff in 1942's *The Boogie Man Will Get You* and Lugosi in 1943's *Return of the Vampire*) keeps a very low directorial profile, supplying only a breakneck pace to the plot; the supporting players and camerawork dress the film well without really adding to it; the musical score, initially impressive with Clifford Vaughan's "Raven Theme" and "Bateman Theme," but later dominated by scavenged cues from *The Black Cat*, keeps reminding the viewer of the earlier film.

Nevertheless, *The Raven* is a movie one regards with much affection, if little admiration. It is almost a celebration of Bela and Boris — Lugosi's sleek, sexy, sadistic Vollin with Dracula nuances, believing in his mad role with touching, almost childlike relish, wringing the juice out of a fiery role tailor-made to his gifts, makes one wish he could have seen Bela in one of his great classical roles on the stage in Europe. And Karloff's weird, pumpkinhead Bateman, playing an oddball, almost absurd performance, nearly burlesquing the role with touches of his "dear old monster," yet achieving a real pathos, makes one marvel that this is the same actor who satanically chanted the Latin in *The Black Cat*.

However, *The Raven*, seen today, has an extra dimension to it. Horror fans have long known the outcome of the Karloff vs. Lugosi rivalry, still alive (or at least Bela believed so) in 1935. With the final score so disastrous for the loser, *The Raven* takes on a special charm; for 61 memorable minutes, Bela was able to dominate Boris. The dominance proved merely academic, as *The Raven* in its original release did nothing to fill in the gap in their studio clout and box office power; yet it seems only right in the legendary mythos of Karloff and Lugosi that Bela deserves his own special showcase — and one that Karloff, with his own quirky presence, makes all the more rich and enjoyable.

It's ironic that Bela's Dr. Richard Vollin, so loved today because of the actor's unbridled dramatics, probably did the star more harm than good in the days of *The Raven's* original release. Karloff's versatility, his makeups, his touches of theatrics and humor made his horror rogue's gallery the stuff of great make-believe for 1935 audiences; he was a welcome guest in their nightmares. But Lugosi's real-life intensity, accent and bombast seemed all too real, all too much of the man himself; and this, in strange irony, made him all the more difficult to take seriously.

Boris Karloff, in the 12 years he outlived Bela Lugosi, frequently praised him (curiously) the same way; he called him "a wonderful technician." It was the theatre term for a player who carefully "used" his voice and gestures and mannerisms, and Lugosi's great presence in this area was not lost on Karloff. However, Karloff also saw the great pitfall in Lugosi's acting, one which would disastrously limit his Hollywood career while strangely endearing him to his many, many fans today. Late in life, Karloff said of his costar, who in 1935 was "the No. 2 Man in horror films":

> Poor Bela... I think he remained slightly old-fashioned in his acting. He didn't really grow with the times — and I think one must...

7
The Invisible Ray, 1936

Every scientific fact accepted today once burned as a fantastic fire in the mind of someone called mad. Who are we on this youngest and smallest of planets to say that the *Invisible Ray* is impossible to science? That which you are now to see is a theory whispered in the cloisters of science. Tomorrow these theories may startle the universe as a fact.

> — foreword to *The Invisible Ray*

The people were so nice on that picture, all of them...

> — Frances Drake

My son, you have broken the first law of science!

> — Violet Kemble Cooper to Karloff, in *The Invisible Ray*

A picture with greater magic than *The Invisible Man,* with a central character more demonic and dramatic than Dr. Jekyll and Mr. Hyde, with Karloff given a chance to look handsome and yet more terrifying than ever, sounds like the definition of a picture impossible to produce. And it was the definition until Universal made the impossible come true the other day with *The Invisible Ray...*

> — from Universal's pressbook for *The Invisible Ray*

The last of the "KARLOFF and Bela LUGOSI" Universal horror tales, *The Invisible Ray* is, in many ways, the most unusual, prophetic melodrama of Horror's Golden Age. Romancing gothic horror with the maiden realm of science fiction, it is a movie crafted in the glorious tradition—yet years ahead of its time.

Karloff's poisoned, lunatic scientist, Dr. Janos Rukh, in dark cloak and broad-brimmed hat, a Machiavellian villain, tormented by a woman and on a vengeful killing spree in Paris, is a gothic, romantic Jekyll/Hyde creation foreshadowing later science fiction; he raves, "I could destroy a nation! *All* nations...!" Bela Lugosi's Dr. Felix Benet, symbol of housebroken science, almost a Van Helsing hero, makes the film (especially in its star casting!) an epic battle of Science Amok vs. Science for the Betterment of Human Life. The leading lady is Frances Drake, horror's most lovely heroine, a Raphaelite beauty inspiring her mad husband's baroque vengeance. And the John P. Fulton special effects, mixed with Universal's traditional back lot sights such as the European village and the Notre Dame Cathedral, make it a grand finale to Universal's "Golden Age" while stretching toward a genre not destined to flourish until the postwar years.

Unusual is its content and style, and unusual was its production, at a time when horror was at its cinema peak, yet on the precipice of a downfall. Its shooting history would contain much that would affect the output of Hollywood—and the lives of the artists of *The Invisible Ray*.

*   *   *

WOMEN—COULD YOU LOVE A "LUMINOUS MAN?"

A genius whose face and hands
shone in the dark? Whose body
exuded the mysterious
rays drawn from planets
and stars of millions of
years ago?
—PR for *The Invisible Ray*

In August, 1935, Karloff and Lugosi were each at a climax of stardom.

High in Coldwater Canyon, Karloff, in his top hat and "wickies," harvested his vegetables and fruit, spoiled Violet the pig and reviewed new contract overtures from Gaumont-British and Warner Bros. In England, where he had completed *The Mystery of Marie Celeste*, Bela Lugosi was so assured of his stardom that he rejected $25,000 worth of British film offers because he didn't want his beloved dogs quarantined for the time he would be needed in London.

The year 1935 was the zenith for horror in Hollywood, and classic horror memories freshly swirled in moviegoers' nightmares: Elsa Lanchester's horrific Bride and Karloff's heartbroken monster, Lugosi's Count Mora and his Carroll Borland's "Luna," Henry Hull's snarling lycanthrope of London, Bela's mad Vollin and Boris's eye-rolling Bateman, Lorre's leering Gogol and Clive's agonized Orlac, Karloff's baroque de Berghmans...

In the spring of 1935, Universal had paid $1250 for a story titled *The Death Ray*, by Howard Higgin and Douglas Hodges. It joined the slate of Karloff vehicles, and told the story of a Belgian scientist named Koh, whose discovery of a radioactive meteor in Africa transforms him into a poisoned madman whose very touch is death. When *Bluebeard*, Karloff's next announced project, ran into trouble with the Bayard Veiller script, Universal rushed *The Invisible Ray* (as the production was dubbed) into the works, blueprinting an August shooting date.

Once again, Junior Laemmle would *not* produce. Indeed, rumors ran rampant through Hollywood about the physical and emotional state of little Junior—and his inability to lead Universal into profits. "As an executive," wrote Hollywood historian Charles Higham of Junior, "he had about as much skill as the average janitor." Despite Junior's success with *All Quiet on the Western Front,* and the horror films, many were professing a similar opinion as Universal failed to make profits — despite hits like *Bride of Frankenstein.* Meanwhile, as rumor insisted that Warner Bros. would buy Universal City (cheerfully denied by Uncle Carl), there were stories that Junior, having suffered so long under his father's tyrannical wrath, having lost Alice Day and Constance Cummings (both of whom had married) due to Uncle Carl's command, regretted his years of obedience — and that his "spirit was broken."

Universal City, in its imperiled financial state, was in the manicured hands of a little lovesick hypochondriac.

Desperate for moneymakers, Universal rushed *The Invisible Ray* into production, via Edmund Grainger's production unit. The studio entrusted the screenplay to John Colton, Broadway adapter of Somerset Maugham's *Rain* and author of *Werewolf of London.* The man who had so winningly dramatized Maugham's Miss Sadie Thompson constructed an exciting continuity, and accented the role of the woman — whose unfaithfulness to her husband largely inspires his maniacal killing spree.

There was also in Colton's work a "legitimacy" that Universal desperately wanted. The summer of 1935, for all the profits of the horror films, had brought vociferous attacks from critics. *The Raven,* in particular, had been roasted by the reviewers — and the British censors' growing sensitivity worried the Laemmles. Colton earned $7791.60 for his screenplay for *The Invisible Ray.*

Fashioned for Karloff, of course, was the flamboyant part of Dr. Janos Rukh, a misanthropic scientist who lives in a Carpathian castle, is poisoned by his literally earth-shattering discovery of Radium X, becomes a Jekyll/Hyde scientific monster, and goes on a berserk killing spree in Paris. It was a showy role — with a neurotic twist; Colton managed to have Rukh's emotions taunted not only by his wife Diane, but by his mother, Madame Rukh, whose blinding in a scientific accident by Janos has left him a guilt-ridden mother's boy.

Meanwhile, Universal once again, in an afterthought, decided to boost the stock of *The Invisible Ray* by making it a vehicle for Karloff and Lugosi; it would toss Bela the role of Dr. Felix Benet (called "Dr. Felix" right up to the shooting), the socially-adjusted humanitarian scientist who served as a dramatic foil to Rukh's paranoia and madness.

Universal tracked down Lugosi in London, where he and Lillian were planning their festive trip to Hungary. An abrasive telegram curtly ordered Bela to return to Hollywood immediately — "they really made a stink about it," recalled Lillian of Universal. The dream vacation was ruined; angry, Bela and Lillian sailed for home. They would never have that vacation.

Arriving in Hollywood, Bela got madder. Universal, in its panic to get *The Invisible Ray* into the works, had misjudged its own resources — and

Poster for *The Invisible Ray*, 1936. Note the billing.

informed the incensed Bela that production would be delayed for about three weeks!

As Bela consoled himself, seeking backing to finance his own production company, Grainger began recruiting a respectable cast. What Universal envisioned that summer—and what it got—were considerably different.

The studio originally set Gloria Stuart for the pivotal role of Diane. However, the lovely Miss Stuart, having spent over four years as Universal's most versatile and talented female contractee, was fed up. "I finally got tired of making those lousy movies," she candidly told me, "and I told my agent, 'Get me out of my contract.'" She managed to escape *The Invisible Ray* and Universal, and signed with new 20th Century-Fox—beginning her stay as the long-suffering wife of Dr. Mudd (Warner Baxter) in John Ford's superb *The Prisoner of Shark Island* (1936).

Universal needed ideally a fine actress and a great beauty for the part of Diane. Fortunately it got both—Frances Drake, who had driven Peter Lorre to rhapsodic madness in Metro's wild and woolly *Mad Love*. A Paramount star, Miss Drake had visited Universal for James Whale's *Remember Last Night?*, which starred a significant actress at Universal—Constance Cummings; the studio shifted Frances instead to *The Invisible Ray*.

A calamity followed.

Universal had assigned Stuart Walker, stocky, middle-aged, bespectacled, to direct *The Invisible Ray*. Walker had been doing competent work for the Laemmles: he had brought in *Mystery of Edwin Drood* in 30 days at a cost of $253,631.37 (three days over schedule and $38,256.37 over budget); he had delivered *Werewolf of London* in 24 days and a cost of $195,393.01 (four days and $36,393.01 over budget). Walker himself was earning over $2000 weekly at Universal, as he took on *The Invisible Ray*.

Then, as the production date neared, Walker asked the front office for a three-day delay: he felt the script needed repairs. The front office refused absolutely. Walker walked off the picture. A later conference failed to appease either faction, and Walker not only walked off *The Invisible Ray*, he walked out of Universal City. Walker never directed another movie; he died March 13, 1941.

Desperately, Universal searched for a new director—and settled on Lambert Hillyer (1895–?), who had been directing movies since 1917 and whose chief claim to fame was helming at least 25 William S. Hart westerns. There was, however, one notable horror credit in his past: Lon Chaney's *The Shock* (Universal, 1923). Why so odd a choice? There were two primary reasons: Hillyer would shoot fast, and he signed to direct the movie at a price tag of only $3750.

Actually, Hillyer (not to mention Edgar Ulmer and Louis Friedlander) perhaps thought Stuart Walker something of a prima donna, considering what Universal had lavished on *The Invisible Ray* as compared to the previous Karloff and Lugosi fright fests. The Universal production estimate for *The*

Invisible Ray budgeted the movie at $166,875 — almost double the cost of *The Black Cat* and *The Raven;* the shooting schedule was 24 days — nine days more than afforded the previous Karloff and Lugosi vehicles. About 25 percent of the budget went toward a high-priced cast — engaged by Universal to add "legitimacy" to its beleaguered genre:

•Frances Drake, as Diane, was set for four and a half weeks at $500 per week, for a total of $2250; she also picked up three weeks' extra due to the film's various delays.

•Frank Lawton, who had starred in Whale's 1934 *One More River* for Universal and had played the grown David in *David Copperfield* for MGM, was signed to play Drake, for four weeks at $1250 per week.

•Walter Kingsford, the noted legitimate stage actor, signed for two weeks at $850 per week to play Sir Francis Stevens, head of the African expedition.

•Beulah Bondi, the great character actress who would win a 1936 Best Supporting Actress Academy nomination for Metro's *The Gorgeous Hussy,* played Lady Arabella Stevens — signing for two weeks at $1000 weekly.

•Violet Kemble Cooper, who had played Basil Rathbone's unspeakable sister in *David Copperfield,* played Madame Rukh, Janos's mother, and was engaged for two and a half weeks at $1150 per week.

The cast budget was $40,500, with an additional $6200 allowed for extras. Sets and scenery were afforded $15,750, over double the allowance for *The Black Cat* and *The Raven.* And if Hillyer's $3750 was peanuts compared to the salaries of Stuart Walker or James Whale, it was still about four times what Ulmer and Friedlander had reaped for their Karloff and Lugosi work. Furthermore, John Fulton, Universal's special effects wizard, was entrusted all of $4500 to create the early science fiction effects of *The Invisible Ray.*

Once again, however, the most intriguing aspects of the budget sheets were the terms of the two stars. Karloff had surpassed another salary option at Universal, and now was earning $3125 weekly. *The Invisible Ray* originally set him for five weeks' work — at a total of $15,625. Lugosi signed to play Dr. Benet at a flat fee — three weeks' work for $4000. Frank Lawton was earning more!

Meanwhile, as *The Invisible Ray* began shooting, the production gained a major bonus. Franz Waxman, who had so magnificently scored *Bride of Frankenstein,* was assigned to *The Invisible Ray,* and created a moving, highly dramatic romantic score.

On September 17, 1935, Universal began shooting *The Invisible Ray.*

*   *   *

I'll tell you a real "horror story" about my days in Hollywood...

Opposite: **Boris, right, sans makeup and costume, seems mercifully unaware of a telling glance from Bela, on the set of *The Invisible Ray*.**

I was doing *The Trumpet Blows* (1934) with George Raft at Paramount. There was a man on the set named Steve Clemente, partly black and partly Mexican or Indian, and he was a knife thrower. He had once had this act, I suppose, in a circus — a very interesting man. So he told me all about his act, and said to me, "I could bring my knives tomorrow, if you'll stand for me." I thought he was joking, so I said, "Of course I will."

My dear, he brought the knives! So during the lunch hour, outside, he said, "I'm all ready — you stand there," and he was going to outline my head, if you don't mind, with the knives! I thought, "I'll trust this man, I'm sure he's all right," and I felt I should do it because I said I would. So he said, "Let's do the profile first," and I said, "That's a good idea," and as I was standing there, he did the profile. Then he said, "Now we'll do your front face" . . . so he threw a knife, about six inches from the face. Well, just then the director, Stephen Roberts, appeared, and he said, "You stop that at once! I don't care what you do when the picture's finished, but not during the picture!"

Well, it turned out that this knife thrower had killed his wife in his act — and that's when he had to stop. Of course, he didn't mean to — but he didn't tell me that before!

—Frances Drake

For all of Hollywood's decay, there are areas of the movie colony still regally beautiful. One such vista is Summit Drive in Beverly Hills. The grandly prestigious address runs up into the mountains, past the old movie star mansions of Ronald Colman, Constance Bennett, William Wyler, Charles Chaplin. Ascend a bit higher and you pass the legendary Pickfair.

The road curls higher up the mountain; Summit Drive ends, and now Summitridge Drive snakes high up into the hills, where coyote, deer and raccoons run wild and happy. On a peak, there is a lovely mansion, above a canyon which falls dizzyingly and magnificently down to a breathtaking view of Los Angeles. There lives the son of the Countess of Suffolk; she is very well-remembered by movie fans all over the world as Frances Drake.

In the Golden Age of the thirties, Frances Drake was one of Hollywood's great exotics; with those incredible, hazel moon eyes, and that Victorian beauty, she looked like a sexy archangel. She was her best in parts such as the vamp of the Gable/Crawford/Montgomery *Forsaking All Others,* seducing Montgomery to leave Crawford waiting at the altar ("I *adored* playing bitches!" she says); *Les Miserables,* as a strikingly tragic, self-sacrificing Eponine; and, of course, Metro's 1935 *Mad Love,* as Yvonne Orlac, the Grand Guignol star, screaming nightly on the rack as she's "branded" and driving bald Peter Lorre to bravura insanity. Her last film was MGM's *The Affairs of Martha,* in 1942; very wealthy, she has lived in her Beverly Hills aerie for decades, very happily and socially, with a magnificent cat named Roman.

Still strikingly lovely, Miss Drake candidly recalls her Hollywood career. She remembers (charmingly) how she outfoxed Fredric March's plan to seduce her on the set of *Les Miserables.* She'll talk of *Mad Love;* how Peter Lorre insisted on meeting her before his head was shaved so she knew he really had hair, and how he'd destroy one of her big scenes ("He didn't want

Frances Drake, leading lady in *The Invisible Ray.*

you to be *too* good!") by suddenly ad-libbing, "Don't you know me? I'm your little Peter!" Or, she'll puncture the myth that Karl Freund was a great director, remembering that the director of *Mad Love* wanted to be cinematographer simultaneously, leaving the actors on their own while he harassed Gregg Toland. "And Gregg Toland was a marvelous cameraman! Such a dear little man, and he looked rather hunted when this wretched big fat man would say, 'Now, now, we'll do it *this* way!'"

On *The Invisible Ray,* however, Frances Drake has happy memories of the entire company—especially Karloff and Lugosi.

> Both Karloff and Lugosi were delightful!
> Boris was a darling man . . . Beautiful eyes! The most gorgeous brown eyes you've ever seen in your life. You could drown in them! Boris was a very charming man, and a quite brilliant man. He was very busy with the Screen Actors Guild, of which he was a founder, on that set . . . .
> He was so good-natured, too. Remember when he's in Africa in the film, up on that sort of "lift," the platform which lowers him into the radium pit? They played a trick on him, while we were shooting out on the back lot. I was not in on it, because I don't really like those sorts of jokes; but after they raised him

up, very high on the platform, they went off, during the lunch hour — and left Boris up there! And he was such a good sport about it! Absolutely charming! He never punched anyone, he never roared at anyone, he was so darling about it. I thought, "I wouldn't have been quite so pleasant!"

As for Bela Lugosi, Miss Drake recalls him with both warmth, and a flushed embarrassment:

> Bela Lugosi and I shared an adjoining bungalow at Universal, and one day, this pretty young girl came and said, "Would you please tell Mr. Lugosi on the set that I'm here to drive him home?" So . . . I told Bela Lugosi that his daughter had come to call for him, and he said, "She is my wife." I wanted to sink through the floor for being so tactless! It might have hurt him, and I wouldn't have done that for the world, because he was such a charming man, very soft and very congenial. . . .

As Miss Drake recalls, *The Invisible Ray* was a very happy set. After all, Boris and Bela were in their prime; for all the intrigues at Universal, life was very promising.

Any signs of rivalry between Karloff and Lugosi? "No, not at all," says Frances Drake. "They worked well together. I thought they were probably friends. I liked them both very much!"

*   *   *

> A storm over the mountains, lightning, thunder, screaming wind. . .
> A mountain top retreat, not unlike the castles of the old German feudal barons which mark the shores of the Rhine. . . The place is silhouetted against a lightning shot sky. . . This is, of course, miniature.
> — from the shooting script of *The Invisible Ray*

The Invisible Ray opens with a wonderfully gothic flourish, Hillyer capturing the scene described above, the storm crashing about the great Carpathian castle (a painting, to which the budget had afforded $275). Franz Waxman's music, which he called "Castle in Hungary," erupts along with the storm; actually, it's a revamping of Harling's *Destination Unknown* composition (also used in the opening scene of *The Raven*).

Inside the great hall, with its roaring fireplace, a Tyrolean servant lights a candle, and Diane Rukh keeps a vigil. "Yes, I did have quite a nice part in that, didn't I?" says Frances Drake. The actress enjoyed the most lavish and expensive wardrobe of any Karloff and Lugosi heroine; in her introduction, she is strikingly garbed in flowing white Grecian robe, designed by Brymer. She is, as ever, the pictorially perfect horror heroine. A Great Dane looms beside her ("Wasn't he wonderful!" exclaims Miss Drake, a great animal lover). And, in a large chair sits an old blind woman.

"It was on such a night," says Mother Rukh, "that Janos first caught his ray from Andromeda. Your father worked the guides, I held the detecting lens, and — never saw again... My son will not learn until too late, I fear, that the universe is very large — and there are some secrets we are not meant to probe!"

Violet Kemble Cooper, gaunt, florid, is a very effective Greek chorus in this tragedy, her dramatics in tune with those of her screen son. In truth, Miss Cooper was terrified of the camera. "She was so nervous," Frances Drake remembers, "that the moment the camera started, she started shaking — very, very nervous."

Car lights appear. "Pygmies — that scoff at a giant!" is how Mother Rukh describes the pilgrims Rukh has invited to witness his great discovery. Originally, the budget had afforded $100 for a process car, showing Dr. Felix Benet, Ronald Drake, and Sir Francis and Lady Arabella Stevens en route, rising above a snowstorm as they near Rukh's laboratory.*

Diane goes to inform her husband, venturing out into the storm; in a terrific scene, with wild, foreboding music by Waxman, Miss Drake crosses the old castle battlements, ascending to the laboratory. Our leading man is curled beneath his giant telescope. "Janos," calls Diane gently. "Janos..."

Karloff's Rukh looks up — wild-eyed, feverish, romantically demonic. It's a marvelous "entrance" for Karloff. The Jack Pierce makeup is striking — dark, curly hair, a moustache, and the costume of a futuristic, scientific cape; and, according to Universal's *The Invisible Ray* pressbook, "the erstwhile monster is revealed as a handsome gentleman who might well have posed for a portrait of Edgar Allan Poe." In fact, Universal played up Karloff's Poe-esque appearance here, and reported:

> Those who have seen the film screened for its entire length in rough continuity, predict that the former master movie monster is going to find many perfumed notes in his fan mail from feminine admirers after *The Invisible Ray* is released...

Bela Lugosi must have gagged if he read this one.

Karloff gives Rukh a strange, tragic loneliness. After a gentle moment with Diane, Karloff quickly lashes into a bitter soliloquy, under Waxman's stormy music: "Sir Francis Stevens. And the great Dr. Benet from the University of Paris. What do they know? What will they *ever* know? ... They'll *never* laugh at me again!"

Actually, somebody did laugh at that moment — Frances Drake. As she remembers,

---

Inside, Dr. Benet confirms Lady Arabella's inquiry as to Madame Rukh's having been "one of Madame Curie's assistants at the time radium was discovered," and Sir Francis gives exposition on Rukh as "a crazy, unbridled genius that tried to twist science into bases for improbable conjectures." Twenty years before, Stevens and company had (supposedly) disproved Rukh's theory that a great meteor, containing an element more powerful than radium, had crashed into Africa. "Rukh flew into a rage and disappeared," says Sir Francis. "No one has really seen him from that day to this...." Production stills show the group departing the car, but whether this interior exposition was shot is a mystery.

It was the first day, and Karloff was in his laboratory, and I had to go in and call his name. Well, I hadn't realized that he had a slight speech impediment — a lisp. And when he launched into his speech, and I heard the lisp — I had to laugh! Well, it was the first day, so fortunately we just put it down to "first day nerves!"

Down in the hall, Rukh greets his skeptics. Walter Kingsford ("Sweet" recalls Miss Drake) plays Sir Francis with just the right undercurrent of the British fuddy-duddy; Beulah Bondi ("A darling!" recalls the leading lady) as Lady Arabella, is the garrulous dynamo of the couple. Frank Lawton ("Very charming!") plays Ronald Drake (Lady Arabella's nephew, and a famed explorer, described by Miss Bondi as "one of the few men who have ever crossed the Mountains of the Moon"). Lawton, an excellent actor who later became a top British character player (he died in 1969), plays with intelligence and style — and a fine chemistry with Miss Drake.

"Would anyone ever expect to find something like this on top of the Carpathian Mountains?" asks the ebullient Miss Bondi.

"No," says Lawton, delicately eyeing Miss Drake.

Most impressive of all, however, is Dr. Felix Benet — played by Bela with a striking goatee (the budget sheets allotted $25 for "Hair Goods for Lugosi"), a stiff, stoical charm, and a palpable temperament clash with Karloff's Rukh. "It is instantly apparent that there is deep enmity between these two men," noted the script. "They face each other with the smouldering appraisal of pack leaders."

"We have never seen eye to eye," says Lugosi to Karloff, ominously.

"That is because I've always looked 200 years ahead of your theories!" volleys Rukh.

The Invisible Ray pressbook contrasted the two stars' offscreen lives:

> More than an acre of Karloff's Hollywood estate is a solid profusion of flowers, and here, as well as in the adjoining orchards, the screen's most menacing villain spends practically all his spare time....

As for Bela, the pressbook headlined him as "Strangest Man in Hollywood," reported about his "secluded house nigh in the Hollywood Hills and "six unfriendly canines," and quoted the star:

> It is true that I am not as other men. To me, life is very stern and very real, and I believe that by intense application a man can be complete master of his own destiny. I am a stern taskmaster over myself, disciplining my mind no less than my body. Often I take long hikes through the hills before dawn... My only meal of the day that is worthy of the name is evening dinner, at which I eat one pound of meat, either boiled or broiled, green vegetables and fruit... I shut myself up in my room and give myself over entirely to thinking, analyzing the day's problems and working out their solutions. I take no part in the so-called

Opposite: **"They'll never laugh at me again!" Karloff, with giant telescope, and Frances Drake's best side in *The Invisible Ray*.**

nightlife of Hollywood. Life is too grim and cruel to permit such frittering away of time that might better be spent in meeting its rebuffs...

Bela's Dr. Felix Benet suggests just such a man. Also, at this time, Bela was hoping to finance his own film productions, so to showcase his talents, and — presumably — avoid the kind of treatment he had suffered at Universal with *The Invisible Ray.* On the day that *The Invisible Ray* began shooting, September 17, 1935, the Los Angeles *Illustrated Daily News,* covering the star's bold and doomed plan, quoted Bela as saying, "I'll finance my own company and star in pictures that I want to play in." Bela's dream project: *Cagliostro.*

The guests all visit the great laboratory. It is a magnificent set by Albert S. D'Agostino, who had designed *Werewolf of London* and would festoon *Dracula's Daughter.* Universal's Set Estimate sheet estimates the tab for Rukh's laboratory at $4000, with $550 for the observatory.

"This is the nebula of Andromeda," announces Rukh at his telescope. "A ray from this nebula will be caught here, and electrically transferred to the projector in my laboratory. There I will recreate what is recorded on that beam of light."

"From Andromeda?" says Dr. Benet, skeptically.

"From Andromeda," vows Rukh; "three-quarters of a million light years distant."

As Rukh prepares, he puts on a bizarre protective lead helmet with a glass vision piece; "the entire effect is like looking upon a visitor from another planet," noted the script. The visitors all sit behind a wall of protective glass, to safeguard them from renegade rays such as those which destroyed Mother Rukh's vision. They watch spellbound as Rukh performs a scientific miracle...

Universal had advanced John Fulton $350 for "Miscellaneous Preparation." The trick work for "The Battle of the Elements"* was budgeted at $1000. *The Universal Weekly,* sent to exhibitors to tub-thump new releases, reported that Fulton was working so secretly that the set was closed, the cast under strict silence — and the daily production reports to the front office had stopped. Uncle Carl advised, "Watch for the technical effects, especially in a certain scene which will be discussed all over the world," and the pressbook reported:

In truth, what the script originally wanted was impossible to achieve with Universal's budget. "Billions of years ago," Rukh told his guests in the original script, "the sun roamed through space. There were no planets. Then another sun emerged out of the vastness and began to approach...." The script detailed: "As the other sun draws near, the surface of the sun becomes greatly agitated. Great fiery tides are raised — indeed the sun seems to pulsate with fear and fury like a live thing. It shoots forth great fingers of fiery atmosphere as though to tear the enemy apart and the intruder replies in kind... There is a terrific tussle but the second star outdoes the sun in gravitational pull, with the result that a whole stream of matter shoots out from the sun... These drops, however, do not fall back into the sun because the pull of the other star now receding in the distance has set them in motion and already they have begun to describe orbits around the parent body they have been torn from...."

For 19 days recently one of the sound stages at Universal studios stood in lonely isolation . . . Watchmen were placed at every door, to bar entrance even to studio attachés who under ordinary circumstances enjoyed the freedom of the entire plant. Only those actually working on the picture were permitted to enter the stage . . .

Fulton created Rukh's "Tour of the Universe" — wonderfully impressive. As George Robinson's camera seemingly floats past the swirling miniatures, and Waxman reprises his "heaven music" from Germany's 1933 *Liliom,* cinema fantasy itself takes a time trip, gliding out of Rukh's Carpathian castle observatory and into a futuristic filmic realm of science fiction — actually over a decade away from blossoming in the cinema. It wa a vision Fulton wanted desperately to produce to its fullest impact; indeed, his $4500 budget on *The Invisible Ray* ultimately would run triple his allotment, and his painstaking perfectionism would soon push the film over schedule.

"Years ago," says Rukh, "Sir Francis, I voiced the belief that a great meteor bearing an element even more powerful than radium had struck an uncharted spot somewhere on the continent of Africa. If you will bear with me for a moment, I will show you how I *know* this to be a fact!"

Rukh's (and Fulton's) vision climaxes — a colossal meteor tumbles through space, and crashes into Africa "with a detonation," quoth the script, "that seems to shatter the laboratory."

"That is all," proudly announces Rukh.

"A trick?" asks Sir Francis.

"No," replies Lugosi's shaken Benet. "A reality!"

The guests sip brandy and marvel at what they have witnessed. They invite the triumphant Rukh to join them in an expedition to Africa, where they might perhaps pinpoint the locale of the meteor's crash. Rukh agrees.

"No, Janos!" speaks a voice from the shadows. It is Mother Rukh. Karloff approaches and bends down to her. "I'm listening, Mother," he says with a strange tenderness.

"Even though you may make a great discovery, you'll not be happy. You're not used to people, Janos. You never will be. Your experiments are your friends. Leave people alone!"

In this little speech, so dramatically underscoring Rukh's misanthropy and eccentricity, *The Invisible Ray* hits a profound moment. Tragically, Janos Rukh doesn't listen. A science magazine announces that he has joined with his colleagues in a trip to Africa. And accompanying him is the woman who, pivotally, along with Radium X, will prove the great tragedy in his screen life.

*   *   *

A bit of African jungle was set down on the famous "back ranch" at Universal studios in California for the scenes in *The Invisible Ray* . . . giant ferns and other tropical vegetation formed the setting for the main camp of a scientific

Karloff as Dr. Janos Rukh in *The Invisible Ray*.

expedition, housed in bamboo huts and large tents.... Chattering monkeys
swung through the trees, and strange birds fluttered and called in the jungle...
It was difficult to realize that Hollywood was only a mile away.
— from Universal's pressbook for *The Invisible Ray*

The Invisible Ray moves to Africa's Mountains of the Moon, in deepest
Universal City. Rukh has set out on his own with native guides to seek the
meteor, with the blacks who played Rukh's "Safari boys" at the fee of $7.50
a day. Back at camp, Sir Francis bathes his swollen ankles, Lady Arabella
hunts wild game, and Dr. Benet, humanitarian that he is, turns his
astrochemistry to cures for the local natives.

Indeed, Lugosi's major humanitarian scene today appears almost comic—due to the actor's curious interpretation. We find him in a tent, treating (in the words of the script) "a wizened, deformed Negro baby." "See, Stevens," intones Bela—"the little creature is going to live!" He was then to carry the baby to its mother, who was to breast feed it as Benet watches with, as the script directed, "clinical satisfaction."

Bela's attitude differs sharply. After curing "the little creature," he lifts the baby like Dracula handling a case of garlic; face intensely distasteful, he hands the baby to its mother, glaring all the while. When the baby's swaddling clothes get caught, he frees himself—and then, for a parting shot, gives the mother and child a final farewell glare!

Also, in Rukh's departure, the melodrama thickens—Diane and Drake are falling in love. In the original script, in an African twilight, Drake saved Diane from a charging rhino. An adjustment was made, as Frances Drake recalls:

> There's a scene they cut out where a lion chases me. It was great fun! The lion was a darling—I think her name was Margie, and she was from MGM, where the children used to ride on her back. I didn't mind being chased by her at all—in fact, I hoped she would catch up with me, so I could pet her!

Only a dissolve shot of the finale of this scene remained in the release version.

There is a dinner scene, where the assemblage dines on antelope stew. "What new secrets did you draw from the sun today, Dr. Benet?" asks lovesick Drake, definitely on edge.

"Proof—that the sun is the mother of us all," responds Lugosi, deadpanning perhaps the most painful line of the movie.

Meanwhile, in the forlorn Mountains of the Moon, Karloff discovers the site of the meteor crash—and Radium X. A geyser explodes from the cave, and the grand effect is that he's discovered the pits of hell, wonderfully empowered by Waxman's swelling of an ominous organ theme to a grand climax of the Rukh leitmotif. Universal enjoyed describing the site in the pressbook:

> ...The "set" covers almost three acres, with lofty cliffs of solid rock surrounding a gaping hole 200 feet in diameter. Jets of steam issue from the seething substance below, and tropical vegetation has begun to encroach again on this great wound literally seared out of the heart of the jungle...

Karloff races to the site—then turns, a wild, lunatic light in his eye...

Rukh's letter arrives—word that he has made a great discovery. Diane prepares to go to him.

"He's a great man, Ronald," she tells her admirer. "I'm his wife—he needs me—I can't let him down."

John P. Fulton's radium pit, in *The Invisible Ray*.

"You wouldn't," says Drake, "You're not the sort to let any man down — ever."

High in the Mountains of the Moon, Karloff's Rukh prepares to descend into the radium pit. "It is a grim spot, horrifying, infernal," noted the script. The vignette is infernal, indeed, as Karloff seems to be descending into the flames of hell itself. Fulton's magic matched shots of Karloff, sporting what looks like a 1950s space suit and helmet, on the platform on the back lot (where the crew played that trick Miss Drake described, high on a crane) with his special effects of the wicked fiery pit. It's a great sequence — and later was employed in Universal's 1939 serial *The Phantom Creeps,* in which Karloff "stood in" for Lugosi in a similar episode!

"Power!" marvels Karloff's Rukh. "More power than man has ever known!"

The safari boys are frightened. They want to leave this unholy place. Incensed, Rukh decides to terrify them into staying.

"You see that rock?" . . . I want you to keep your eyes on that rock . . ."

Rukh aims his Radium X gun at the boulder — and it spouts into a pool of jelly, as the natives scream and wail in terror.

"You can all go if you want to — but you won't go far!" raves Karloff. "All that will be left of you will be like that!"

That night, however, Rukh enters his tent. In the dark, his flesh glows with radiation. After a native enters, takes one look, and lets out a rolled-eyed screech that delighted the not-so-racially-conscious audiences of the thirties, Rukh looks in the mirror at his glowing reflection.

"It's poisoned me!" he laments, as harp, cymbals, and finally a full orchestra accent the tragedy.

The budget of *The Invisible Ray* had allowed $250 for Fulton and Jack Pierce to create a luminous makeup for Karloff. This, apparently, was the cause of much experimentation and delays on the set; in the end, Fulton added a pulsating glow to the negative — just as he would do in Universal's 1941 *Man-Made Monster* for Lon Chaney, Jr.

Meanwhile, that handsome Great Dane senses Rukh's misery and moves to him. Rukh pets the dog. It falls over — dead.

Minutes later, Diane arrives in the camp. Rukh, terrified that she will see him in so ghastly a state, refuses to see her, or allow her to enter his tent. "This is no place for you! You must leave here at once!" As Diane weeps in another tent, Rukh stifles his urge to embrace her and races instead through the jungles, and back to the camp — and Benet.

Sweaty, wild-eyed, Karloff reaches Lugosi. "I've discovered an element a thousand times more powerful than radium" gasps Rukh, "but it's done something to me — something horrible!" Out in the dark, Benet sees the terrible glow of Rukh's body. Hiding him in a supply tent, the astrochemist works to discover a counteractive to treat Rukh's poisoned system. At midnight, Benet injects Rukh with the counteractive.

A few hours later, Rukh awakens. The glow is gone.

"I can touch people now?" exults Rukh, clearly thinking of Diane.

"Yes," answers Benet, "but remember what I told you. Nothing can ever cure you. . . . And now that the counteractive has gone into your bloodstream, you can only live if you use a small amount of it at regular intervals each day — all the days of your life . . ."

"And if I exceed the time?" asks Rukh.

"Your body again becomes the deadly machine it was. Your touch will kill ... if you do not use the counteractive in time," says Lugosi with marvelous foreboding, "you will literally crumble to an ash!"

There is another risk as well. "I don't know," says Benet, "enough yet to say what effect the violent surcharge of poison and antidote will have upon the brain." Swearing Benet to secrecy, and taking the antidote, Rukh returns to his camp to complete his experiments as quickly as possible.

Some time later, Benet arrives in Rukh's camp—having followed the sound of drums, which told of a white man who made magic in the mountains. Inside a tent, Karloff strangely strokes his Radium X gun ray—and has a mad look in his eye...

"I've harnessed it at last, Benet!" says Karloff, gleefully and effectively overacting. "I could crumple up a city a thousand miles away. I could destroy a nation—*all* nations!"

"You have harnessed its power to destroy," responds Lugosi. "Have you harnessed it to heal?"

It's a memorable scene—Karloff, curly-haired and wild-eyed, going "over the top"; Lugosi, brooding and censorial, in cool dramatic control.

"That'll come later, when I devise a filter to curb its power. But in the meantime, it's mine to experiment with—*mine!*"

Benet had feared this—which is why Sir Francis is en route to an International Scientific Congress to reveal the discovery of Radium X to the world.

"Thieves!" shrieks Karloff. "THIEVES!"

There is more. Benet delivers Rukh a letter—from Diane. "She doesn't believe I love her... She loves someone else... Drake?"

"Yes," answers Benet softly.

"You come like thieves in the night!" rants Rukh. "You steal everything from me! Get out of here, Benet! Get out before I..." Benet leaves—leaving Rukh with his hands madly clasping his ray gun.

The discovery of Radium X stuns the world. While Benet and Stevens reap honors, Rukh cannot be found. He is cloistered in his Carpathian castle, where he has harnessed Radium X—and aims his ray gun at Mother Rukh, to cure her blindness. "It renders the body of Mme. Rukh translucent. WE SEE THROUGH HER," noted the script. As Ms. Cooper counts her fingers, and makes the "strange little sounds of delight" called for in the script, the acting is heavy-handed, but effective, and Karloff emotionally places his head in her lap. The scene almost reminds one of Cagney's Cody "Top of the world, Ma" Jarrett of *White Heat* (1949).

"You have work to do that will take you all of your life," says Madame Rukh. But Janos wants to go to Paris. Mother Rukh prophesizes tragedy, yet Janos is determined to go. He leaves his secret with her—"More power than man has ever possessed—power to heal—power to destroy..."

Rukh arrives in Paris—at Benet's house, just in time to see a family thanking Benet for using Radium X to cure their blind daughter. This time, Bela is a bit warmer about it all—but his expression is austere when he turns and sees Karloff—staring, in the script's words, "like a Viking of Vengeance."

"All Paris is waiting to pile honors on you," salutes Benet. "You know, of course, the Nobel Prize was awarded you?"

"Yes ... I know. Everybody considers you and Sir Francis Stevens *very* generous men."

Rukh learns from Benet that Diane has become Lady Arabella's secretary—and that Diane and Drake plan to marry, although she will do nothing until she hears from Rukh. Rukh claims he'll not stand in the way of her happiness—and promises she will soon hear of him.

"You see, I was right, Rukh," says Benet as his guest leaves. "Your discovery's too great for one man to control."

"Someday you will realize," says Rukh bitterly, "that you haven't even scratched the possibilities of Radium X—and I'm still the only man to control it fully!"

Soon, we see Karloff's Rukh, in cloak and broad-brimmed hat, loping at night through the village streets—where the monster had chased the villagers in *Bride of Frankenstein*. He selects a derelict who slightly resembles him. "I want to do you a benefit," says Karloff with a bravura bitterness; "...the greatest benefit one man can do another..."

Shortly afterwards, the incinerated remains of a man believed to be Janos Rukh are discovered. Diane and Drake are free to wed, and they do so at the Notre Dame Cathedral—which, of course, still loomed on the Universal back lot from Lon Chaney's 1923 *The Hunchback of Notre Dame,* and received an $850 facelift for *The Invisible Ray.* As they leave the church, Franz Waxman makes the traditional Mendelssohn *Wedding March* music something sinister as Karloff spies at them—then looks at the figures of six holy statues on the cathedral wall. "Six of us," he remembers—and the six religious figures transform in his eyes to those of his expedition companions.

A series of shocking murders soon appalls Paris. First, Sir Francis Stevens, then Lady Arabella—both offscreen, in shades of *Dracula*. At the time of each death, a statue of the cathedral wall had horribly melted into ashes, the populace hysterically falling to its knees to pray at the blasphemous sight. The strange, religious touch (also referred to but never seen) is worthy of James Whale.

Benet, who never believed the cremated corpse found in Rukh's clothing was really the scientist, had employed an ultraviolet camera to photograph the pupils of the dead Stevens' eyes—and found on them an image of Rukh. Though he unfortunately dropped the glass negative and broke it, he convinces the police that Rukh is alive and hell-bent on killing all those who were part of the African expedition. To lure Rukh, Drake and Benet plan to hold

The Notre Dame set returns to service for the wedding in *The Invisible Ray*. From left: Walter Kingsford, Frank Lawton, player, Frances Drake, Bela Lugosi.

a scientific congress at Benet's home, where both of them — and Diane — will be the bait.

"...At midnight," says Benet, "bolt all doors and darken the entire house. His face and hands will appear like phosphorous, regardless of any disguise."

"And — if he touches anyone?" asks the Chief of the Surete.

Lugosi shrugs, and replies — with superb timing — "They die."

The night arrives—with a terrible storm. Looming in the village streets, in dark cloak and slouch hat, is the mad Karloff. Also in the storm, is Dr. Meiklejohn (Frank Reicher, the skipper of *King Kong*). Rukh, posing as "Jones, of the University of Wales," offers the old man to step into an alley for a Napoleon brandy—and kills him. With Meiklejohn's pass, Rukh gains entrance to the grounds.

The time arrives to bolt the doors. As Benet approaches the door of his laboratory, the outside door opens with a burst of Waxman's music—and there stands Rukh.

> "We expected you," says Benet.
> "I knew that. Five thieves—two are gone, three are left."
> "Do you intend to kill us all?"
> "Yes!"
> "I felt it was better to have left things alone when you were first poisoned. I warned you about your brain!"
> "It began to affect my brain almost immediately. I could feel it coming—*crawling* for cells!"
> "Aren't there ever moments when you think as you used to think? When you are human?"
> "Not often now. Not often."
> "And because of that—we must die!"　·
> "*No!* Because you are thieves—*all* thieves—*five* thieves! It will be *easiest* just to shake hands. It will all be over in a second."

Lugosi impulsively reaches for his pistol; Karloff touches him. It is one of their finest, best-played scenes.

A few minutes later, Diane, upstairs in a boudoir, is pacing; Miss Drake, strikingly lovely in a $125 Brymer black negligee, holds a candle, when...

"Diane..."

She turns—and drops her candle at the sight of her "dead" husband. The light extinguished, Karloff, looking his most Poe-esque in his cloak and dark hat, glows luminously and horribly, as Miss Drake's magnificent eyes stare in horror...

John Colton had composed a morbid, final soliloquy for Karloff as he prepared to kill his wife:

> I want to get my eyes full of your loveliness first, full of your loveliness. Cool hands—put them close to my forehead—but don't touch me, don't touch me. All the fires that burn inside my head are going, going. There's only a little time left for me, only a little time. Don't move Diane—don't move... I want to hold you in my arms, just once. I want to destroy you, but I can't, I can't... You are too beautiful to kill—but he—he must die—

Only the tag of this speech survives in the picture. Yet so eloquent are Karloff's pantomime and expressions, even behind the Fulton glow, that he conveys all the mad emotions as he fails to slay his wife.

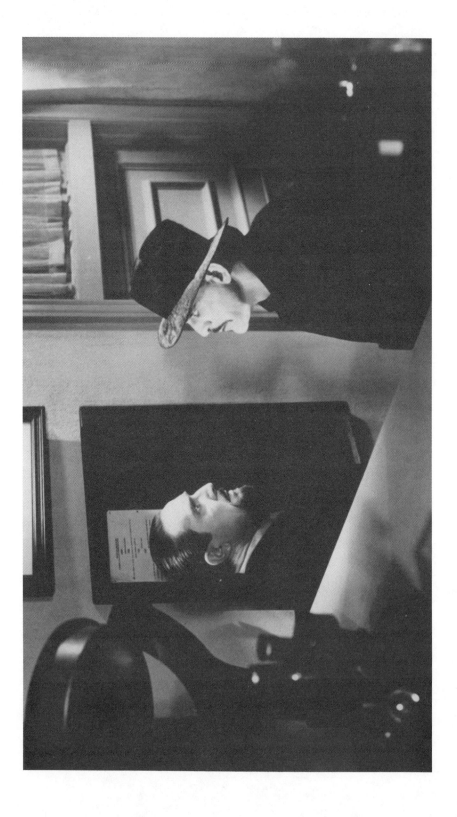

Meanwhile, at the door below, there is a visitor — Madame Rukh, who has come to Paris at Benet's request. As Karloff seeks Lawton, Miss Cooper intercepts him; shamed that his Diane, and now his beloved mother, have seen the freakish monster of science he has become, Karloff rolls his calf eyes and wrings his hands in shame.

It is near midnight — the radiation poisoning needs the daily antidote. "I must go on to reach one more," rasps Karloff. "DRAKE!"

Rukh opens his packet to get the injection. Mother Rukh lifts her cane — and smashes the lifesaving drug to the floor.

"My son," she says, in a pitying voice, "you have broken the first law of science!"

"Yes, you're right," says Karloff, smoke ominously rising from his poisoned body, "it's better this way." His body is cremating itself. "Goodbye, Mother," cries Karloff, racing across the room (while strains from Waxman's *Bride of Frankenstein* score play), hurling his flaming body through a window and falling, a fireball, into the streets below.

Janos Rukh's ashes lie in the wet street.

Drake and Diane embrace.

And, as Franz Waxman's music offers its final, swelling theme, Madame Rukh offers her tragic son a brief, telling eulogy, one to be paraphrased in many a science fiction film of the future:

"Janos Rukh is dead. But part of him will go on eternally — working for humanity."

Frances Drake has her own final lines on the melodramatics of *The Invisible Ray:*

> Oh yes, I love that sort of thing! If you're just the sweet young girl in the movies, it's so blah! Nothing to get your teeth into. Of course, Karloff was awfully easy to work with, you know. A real professional. So was Lugosi... They were both totally darling!

* * *

100 YEARS AHEAD OF ITS TIME!
Here's an awe-inspiring drama
that leaps a century ahead of
its time ... to show the world
the scientific wonders that will
mold or terrorize human life
and love!
— poster copy for *The Invisible Ray*

During its final stages of shooting, *The Invisible Ray* already was terrifying Universal's front office. The melodrama finally "wrapped" Friday, October 25, 1935, after 36 days of shooting — 12 days over schedule!

Opposite: **The stars' third death scene together — the climax of *The Invisible Ray*.**

This was almost unheard of for a film of this calibre; the previous Karloff and Lugosi movies had come in almost right on schedule and budget. Universal was appalled. The cast fees ran $14,044.75 over budget; General Set Expense, $4895.90 over estimate; Director Hillyer collected $1266.65 extra fee for his extra days. The only one not to enjoy the extra pay was Bela Lugosi — who, after all, had signed on for a flat fee.

None of the delays had bothered the cast in the least. Boris had his tea breaks, and Frances Drake remembers the on-the-set atmosphere as totally genial. "Lugosi, Frankie Lawton and I all had birthdays at the same time," says Miss Drake. "We're all the same sign. So we all had a birthday party on the set!"

The actors and director went home. Boris Karloff reported to Warner Bros., commencing the first of five melodramas at that studio with *The Walking Dead,* one of his most haunting performances. However, *The Invisible Ray* stayed in production — as John P. Fulton mastered the special effects. Adding the pulsating Radium X glow to Karloff on the negative was a painstaking and agonizingly slow process. On Wednesday, November 20, 1935, almost four weeks after the cast had dispersed, studio manager M.F. Murphy dispatched this emergency memo to Fulton:

> There is no need to go into any long story about the urgency of finishing up *Invisible Ray.* We have done everything in our power to help you push this work. It is now absolutely essential that I advise both Mr. Laemmle and Mr. Meyer something definite on when we expect to finish this job so that we can advise New York of a shipping date and they in turn set the release. We must have this information by Thursday morning. I am personally in one very embarrassing spot on this picture and must admit that I am depending on you to perform miracles, if necessary, to get this picture finished up...

At length, Fulton finished his work. Allotted $4500 to work his magic, the special effects wizard ran about $6000 over budget. *The Invisible Ray,* set for a 24-day shoot on a $166,875 budget, ran 36 days and tallied a grand cost of $234,875.74 — $68,000.74 over budget, and more expensive than the final budgets of *The Black Cat* and *The Raven* combined!

However, the need to sell *The Invisible Ray* to the public would be even more desperate than it originally appeared.

The year 1935 had been glorious in Hollywood. All studio front offices hungrily eyed the fiscal profits. MGM made a profit of $7.5 million; Darryl Zanuck's new 20th Century–Fox, $3.1 million; Columbia, $1.8 million; Warner Bros., $700,000.

Universal, in the 53-week period ending November 2, 1935, had lost $474,053.

Then came ominous news: Universal had arranged a loan from Standard Capital of $750,000. J. Cheever Cowdin and Charles R. Rogers engineered the deal, with a lethal option: they could buy Universal City from

Uncle Carl if they could raise the money by February 1, 1936. Always the gambler, Uncle Carl now staked his empire.

Meanwhile, Junior, whose emotional state hardly could have been helped by the presence of Constance Cummings on the lot playing in Whale's *Remember Last Night?*, was stranger than ever — producing the lavish musical *Show Boat*, to be directed by Whale, while rumor insisted he would play prodigal son and run away to MGM after the extravaganza was completed.

As such, *The Invisible Ray* became a release of special significance — Universal needed moneymakers to battle the advances of Standard Capital. But how to promote it? The studio didn't want to wave a red flag at the sensitive antihorror factions, or the apoplectic British censors; at the same time, they wanted to draw the melodrama fans.

"NOT A HORROR PICTURE! BUT A REVELATION IN THRILLS AND TERRIFIC SUSPENSE !" headlined PR about *The Invisible Ray*. Yet the poster copy heralded melodrama:

DESTRUCTION
To All He Touched Or Looked Upon!
Monster of Science! Drawing his world shattering rays
from distant heavenly bodies! . . . Fearing no man nor thing
but his own unearthly powers! . . . Paying for his unholy
secrets with the woman he loved!

And:

A HUMAN EARTHQUAKE. . . !
His Scientific Discoveries Were Turned to Diabolical
Ends To Avenge His Stolen Love. . . !

The copy blazed on and on. . . "100 Years Ahead of Its Time!" . . . "A Blazing Monster Walking the Earth" . . . "Most Unusual Love Story Ever Filmed!" . . . "The Strangest, Most Sensational Picture Ever Filmed!" . . .

The trailer, too, promised thrills, but lacked one of the picture's most memorable special effects: John P. Fulton's luminous glow on Karloff. Universal clearly rushed the trailer out while Fulton still meticulously added this effect to the negative.

Naturally, the pressbook had its own bizarre variety of publicity stunts. One was "Mechanical Man Bally," which advised exhibitors to dress up some poor soul in a black shirt (bearing the words "KARLOFF as the Luminous Man in THE INVISIBLE RAY"), put a large corrugated cardboard box over his shoulders (featuring hype like "Delving Into New Strange Depths of MYSTERY!" and "The Most AMAZING Sight You Ever Saw!"), and place a large aluminum pot on his head (with mesh cloth around the rim, to cover the man's face while still allowing him to see). This "Mechanical Man" was to carry a flashlight in each hand (covered with extra-light cotton gloves), and turn the lights on and off ("thus making his hands seem to glow") as he marched around the streets nearby the theatre. "This street bally can be easily made," promised the pressbook, "and should prove a good attention attracter."

Finally, Universal added a climactic element of hype. To add legitimacy, suspense, and box office allure, Universal billed its star on posters of *The Invisible Ray* as

The Great
KARLOFF

Tellingly, the words "and BELA LUGOSI" were dwarfed beneath this monolithic billing, and in size about one-half that of Boris's name. Other Universal posters proclaimed, "KARLOFF As The Luminous Man in *THE INVISIBLE RAY*"—tucking Bela Lugosi's name beneath the title.

The Invisible Ray premiered at New York's Roxy Theatre on January 10, 1936, with a "Big Stage Revue" featuring "Music Goes Round and Around." It competed for Broadway audiences with such movies as MGM's *Riffraff*, starring Jean Harlow, RKO's *Sylvia Scarlett*, starring Katharine Hepburn, and Warner's *Captain Blood*, with Errol Flynn and Olivia de Havilland versus villains Basil Rathbone and Lionel Atwill. "Boo right back at you, Mr. Laemmle!" snapped the *New York Times* of *The Invisible Ray*. The *New York Tribune*, too, was intimidated by the film's foreword,

> ...which is perhaps not to be denied, but what follows is so palpably nonsensical that one suspects that the grave foreword and the impressive opening, with its gleaming astronomical instruments, were such a subterfuge for taxing the property departments of the film studios, and whisking Messrs. Karloff and Lugosi into the heat of melodrama involving a new way for Karloff to annihilate...

Oddly, it was *The Cinema*, a British revue, which gave *The Invisible Ray* the most fair endorsement:

> ...It is this combination of laboratory possibility with film studio extravagance that makes the picture—finely staged and powerfully portrayed as it is—of considerable appeal to the masses, many of whom may even enthuse over its melodramatic abnormalities. Boris Karloff makes a curiously sympathetic figure of the stricken Rukh, and gives us no small insight into the tortured brain responsible for his later atrocities.

The Invisible Ray proved a box office winner; indeed, the week of January 22, 1936, proved to be the most successful week in Universal's history, thanks to national business from *Magnificent Obsession* (starring Irene Dunne and Robert Taylor, and which world-premiered at NYC's Radio City Music Hall December 30, 1935), *Next Time We Love* (with Margaret Sullavan and James Stewart, which followed *Magnificent Obsession* at Radio City) and *The Invisible Ray*.

Uncle Carl was optimistic. He had no idea that, within weeks, he would be toppled from his kingdom of Universal City.

And the stars of *The Invisible Ray* had no idea that they had completed the last of the Karloff and Lugosi vehicles.

*   *   *

> While on a scientific expedition to Africa, Boris Karloff discovers a meteorite containing an element a thousand times more powerful than radium. The scientist is poisoned by the element and inherits the uncanny ability to deliver death with the mere touch of his hand. Despite his friend Bela Lugosi's efforts to develop an antidote, the screen's master of mayhem is again on the loose, unable to control the urge to kill at will. No one is safe from the effects of *The Invisible Ray* in this classic thriller.
>
> — from the video cassette package of *The Invisible Ray*

The Invisible Ray is a striking curiosity. As the final Karloff and Lugosi vehicle, and one of the very last Universal horrors of the Laemmle regime (only *Dracula's Daughter* would follow), it has a great aura of nostalgia; in its stylized forecast of science fiction, it is prophetic and fascinating; in its production — the beauty of Frances Drake, the John P. Fulton effects, the music of Franz Waxman, the grand tour of the Universal lot — it is a slick, stylish, exciting melodrama, offering a full reel more thrills and escapism than the previous Boris and Bela outings.

As ever, though, the real "astrochemistry" of *The Invisible Ray* is in the performances of the stars.

Karloff (never again would he be billed only by surname) clearly relished the showcase role of Dr. Janos Rukh. It's a wild, feverishly played, bravura portrayal; those eyes Frances Drake so admired are mad and apocalyptic when he strokes his gleaming, ominous (and yes, phallic) Radium X gun and raves, "I could destroy a nation! All nations!"; he is truly Poe-esque, dashing in his cloak and slouch hat, vengefully haunting the rainy village streets, mysterious and menacing; and, of course, he's nightmarish as the Luminous Man. However, there is a unique, moving tragedy about Karloff's Rukh, which gives *The Invisible Ray* its real power.

"Your experiments are your friends," says Mother Rukh. "Leave people alone..."

The vision of the glowing Karloff, hovering over the orb-eyed Miss Drake, movingly miming his inability to kill her, is haunting; but he tops it with his quirky shame when Mother Rukh confronts him. Before the audience, Karloff wrings his hands and rolls his eyes and — in a superbly eccentric touch — transforms his glowing, Radium X Luminous Man into a pathetic, horrific mama's boy.

In a rather audacious performance, Karloff at times goes "over the top"; frankly, the actor hadn't sliced the ham so thickly since John Ford had set him loose on the Yuma sand dunes as the religious lunatic of *The Lost Patrol.* Yet his broad strokes leave some unforgettable images, and Dr. Janos Rukh of *The Invisible Ray* is one of Karloff's greatest characterizations.

Of course, Karloff's Radium X madman totally overshadowed Lugosi's Dr. Felix Benet — yet the good doctor also survives as one of Bela's finest portrayals. Wise, cool, stable, Bela never once overacts in *The Invisible Ray;* none of the ham that creeps into Karloff's performance ever invades Lugosi's. Lugosi splendidly suggests the great man, and, despite his death in the film, his appearance reassures the audience in a way reminiscent of Peter Cushing's Van Helsing in the Hammer *Dracula* films.

Of course, Bela's portrayal, too, has its oddities: his almost comic distaste of "the little creature" he cures in the jungle; his heavily foreboding line, "I hope they will be happy," after the wedding of Drake and Diane; his censorial glances at Karloff's Rukh, subtle in the beginning, memorably bitter in the finale. Yet it's a change of pace for Bela Lugosi, and he, too, clearly enjoyed the dramatic challenge of playing an unconventional force for good.

In all, the offbeat stylized confrontation of Karloff's dark, eccentric Rukh versus Lugosi's white, stoically moral Benet makes this not only a harbinger of science fiction cinema, it makes *The Invisible Ray* an offbeat acting climax to the most palmy Hollywood days of Boris Karloff and Bela Lugosi.

A whole new act was about to begin in the lives of Karloff and Lugosi, and in Hollywood history. The late thirties would bring many surprises in the lives and careers of both men, and add a whole new dimension to their odd relationship.

In her book *Dear Boris,* Cynthia Lindsay, Karloff's longtime friend, offered this story:

> I personally remember Boris's attitude toward Lugosi. In the late 1930s, the Karloffs, Jimmy and Lucille Gleason, Russell (Gleason, her husband) and I were riding in the Santa Claus sleigh down Hollywood Boulevard, which becomes "Santa Claus Lane" during the holiday season. Every night the sleigh carries so-called celebrities who wave to the populace as Santa "Ho-ho-ho's" through a scratchy microphone. The night we rode, Santa was very, very drunk and commenting loudly on people in the profession, neglecting at times to switch off the microphone. Suddenly a voice from the crowd cried, "Boris! Boris! Down here!" It was Bela Lugosi, loudly applauding his "compatriot." Boris waved back and shouted, "Bela! How are you, old boy?"
>
> "Boo!" hiccuped Santa.
>
> As we passed, Boris said quietly, "Poor Bela." He always called him "Poor Bela."

8
In Limbo, 1936 and 1937

> Horror is knowing that you won't find anybody to give you a hand when you are down. A down-and-out actor is already a ghost haunting the corridors where he once walked a star.
>
> —Bela Lugosi

January 24, 1936

Bela Lugosi, acting in Republic's *House of a Thousand Candles,* grows so ill with a bad cold that he must leave the picture. Irving Pichel replaces him in this Arthur Lubin–directed movie.

February 4, 1936

Universal begins shooting *Dracula's Daughter,* destined to be the final curtain on Hollywood's most prodigal era of horror. The film has a 29-day schedule and a $230,425 budget. Long planned for Lugosi, once envisioned for Karloff, Lugosi and Colin Clive, drafted by John Balderston, the moody film starred Gloria Holden (who played the Countess for $300 per week), Otto Kruger (the hero Jeffrey, at $2500 a week) and Edward Van Sloan (reprising his famous Van Helsing of *Dracula* for $600 a week). It also had production problems which mirrored the disorganization and waste of the doomed Laemmle regime:

•R.C. Sherriff, author of *Journey's End* and screenplay adapter of *The Invisible Man,* was set to pen *Dracula's Daughter*'s screenplay. The prestigious writer earned $10,932.62 in "London payments," $4756 in studio payroll, and even $961.95 in transportation fees—all for a screenplay which was never used. A writer named Peter Dunne followed, earning $2350 for his time, before Garrett Fort (who had worked on *Dracula* and *Frankenstein*) took over, receiving sole screen credit and $6375. This set the cost of the script alone at $25,675; $5000 had already been paid for the story.

•Eddie Sutherland had been set to direct *Dracula's Daughter.* The various delays while the studio got the production ready caused him to bail out. The studio had to pay him $17,500 for his retained time—then hired old reliable Lambert Hillyer, fresh from *The Invisible Ray,* to take over, at a salary of $5400.

•Right up to the production date, Universal had envisioned *Dracula's Daughter* to star Bela Lugosi. And, because of the time the star forfeited, Universal—rightly—had to pay Bela $4000.

At length, *Dracula's Daughter* wrapped March 10, 1936, seven days over schedule and at a cost of $278,380.96. By the time this low-key film, well-remembered for the implied lesbianism of its title character, and beautifully scored by Heinz Roemheld, premiered, life had changed drastically at Universal.

February 20, 1936

Boris Karloff and wife Dorothy set sail for England, where the star had contracted for *The Man Who Lived Again.* Boris soon signed for another British film, *Juggernaut,* and in all would stay in his beloved home for nearly six months. It was a lovely time for Karloff: acting in his movies, walking through the London fog at night, hiking through the snow in the countryside, attending the London premiere of Universal's *Magnificent Obsession.* The couple leased "Malt House" in the village of Hurley, and had a lovely time sailing on the river, playing darts in the neighboring inn called "The Old Bell." Still, Boris was homesick for Coldwater Canyon. In his diary, he referred to a telephone call back home as "the biggest thrill of our trip," and jubilantly recorded, "The dogs are all well and Violet, my pig, is 'expecting'!"

February 29, 1936

Warner Bros. releases *The Walking Dead,* first of Karloff's five star vehicles for the studio. Karloff gave one of his most moving performances as John Elman, framed for murder, resurrected by Edmund Gwenn, sadly haunting his gangster enemies with a plaintive, "Why did you have me killed?" The baroque vignette at the piano, as Karloff plays Rubinstein's *Kammenoi Ostrow,* staring into the souls of his hoodlum foes, is one of the classic scenes of his career; and his death scene, in a rainy graveyard, advising Gwenn, "Leave the dead to their maker. The Lord our God is a jealous God," is one of his most powerful.

March 14, 1936

An era ends in the history of Hollywood: Carl Laemmle loses Universal City to usurpers. Ever the gambler, "Uncle Carl" had wagered his kingdom,

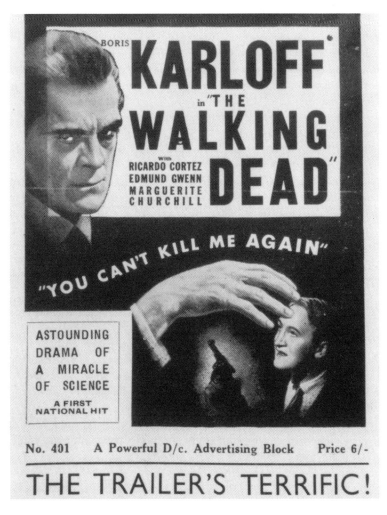

British Trade advertisement (including two lines at bottom meant for the theatre, not the public) for Karloff's *The Walking Dead,* 1936, the first of his star vehicles for Warner Bros./First National.

giving the J. Cheever Cowdin forces an extension when they failed to raise the $5,000,000 early in 1936. Uncle Carl and Junior went into what would be a permanent exile, but with a grand finale: James Whale's *Show Boat,* one of the greatest hits of Universal's history, would be their swan song.

The new power figure at Universal City was Charles R. Rogers, formerly of Paramount, a shrewd, money-minded, bespectacled man whose new reign at Universal was one of purging the Laemmle hangers-on (some of whom reportedly lived in sets on the back lot) from the studio. Hollywood legend insists that Rogers cut over 70 Laemmle family members, friends and moochers from the payroll—which had been providing weekly checks to at least two parties who were dead. It was Rogers who tried to claim credit for *Show Boat,* publicized as a product of the "New Universal"; he did the same with *My Man Godfrey,* the classic Carole Lombard/William Powell screwball comedy which actually had been blueprinted by Junior Laemmle and which, like *Show Boat,* reaped a $1,000,000 gross. In truth, Rogers had no eye for talent—and his major "discovery" at Universal, and one which would help save the studio, was a total fluke.

One of Uncle Carl's protégés was producer Joseph Pasternak, who in 1936 had been producing films in Budapest. Uncle Carl offered him a new two-year contract in Hollywood, with a one-year pact for Pasternak's favorite director, Henry Koster. As James Bawden reported in his piece on Pasternak in *Films in Review* (February 1985):

> The day Pasternak arrived back in Hollywood, Laemmle was ousted in a power play and the new regime at Universal tried to break the contract or buy Pasternak out. He refused and together with Koster camped out on the front lawns. The studio heads ordered the water sprinklers turned on. Pasternak and Koster retreated to vacant offices behind the horse stables where they concocted a fable about a teenage girl trying to bring her parents back together....

The film turned out to be *Three Smart Girls,* and the star would be Deanna Durbin. "She came to my office in a white cotton dress and white socks and held her mother's hand," recalled Pasternak. "I knew she'd be perfect." Deanna Durbin, plump little songbird, would prove the studio's salvation, and over the next 12 years, one of Universal's greatest legends. And Rogers, having lucked into the wake of *Show Boat* and *My Man Godfrey,* and *Three Smart Girls,* decided he had developed a "style" for family entertainment—and one in which there was no room for horror movies.

June 1, 1936

Universal begins shooting *Postal Inspector,* a $175,174.43 "B" in which Bela Lugosi took third billing (under Ricardo Cortez and Patricia Ellis) as a heavy named Benez. Bela was set for three weeks' work at a flat fee of $5000.

September 7, 1936

Boris Karloff arrives back in Hollywood after the wettest summer in England in twenty years. "It rained constantly," said Boris. "I'm not expressing a mere pleasantry when I say that I am glad to be back in the sunshine." Boris was set to start immediately on 20th Century–Fox's *Charlie Chan at the*

Opera, and to follow at Universal with *The Man in the Cab,* a new horror film, which (as scripted) was to team Karloff and Lugosi. Boris was to be an Electric Man, wearing a costume of glass, rubber, steel, metal, aluminum and insulation, and electrical equipment, "so I can shoot sparks in every direction, like the rays of the sun"; Bela was to play the mad doctor who caused the aberration.

The film, perceived by Rogers as a hangover from the crazy Laemmle era, is shelved. It would lie in the script morgue until 1940, when a new management at Universal revived it for *Man-Made Monster,* with Lon Chaney, Jr., and Lionel Atwill inheriting the Karloff and Lugosi–designed roles.

October 26, 1936

Lillian Lugosi goes before a notary public and signs a "Quitclaim Deed," promising to "remise, release and forever quitclaim to Bela Lugosi, as his sole and separate property," their new mansion at 2227 Outpost Drive in the Hollywood Hills. The colonial house, which still stands today, was Bela's pride and joy, a showplace he reportedly had made both bombproof and earthquake proof. What could have been behind this odd domestic situation?

January 1, 1937

Great Britain, appalled by such horrors as *Bride of Frankenstein* and *The Raven,* slapped the genre with the infamous "H" certificate — hence greatly limiting their audience. With the British market so valuable to Hollywood profits, it seemed an official death decree for horror movies.

February 1, 1937

James Whale begins shooting *The Road Back,* the long-awaited sequel to *All Quiet on the Western Front.* Whale had signed a new Universal pact; Rogers figured he needed him. However, in the kingdom of Deanna Durbin, a homosexual director with a flair for misanthropic horror films and a reputation for carte blanche with the Laemmles, could only be doomed to disaster.

Whale began shooting all-night battle scenes, garbed in the military waistcoat of a German captain, high boots, and a beret. Rogers invited the press corps to watch the shooting, many of whom found Whale's aloof nature and military costume subjects for raucous catcalls and printed jibes. Whale banned them from the lot. Rogers allowed them to return.

Above: Boris Karloff as Santa, while the dog does a comic "take." *Opposite:* Bela Lugosi as Claus too.

Karloff and Lugosi

However, the real horror of *The Road Back* was Rogers' cowardice in the ugly face of the Nazis. Whale had made a picture passionately anti–German; the denouement originally showed a repulsive dwarf, sadistically drilling Teutonic youths in skills needed to regain the glory of the Motherland. The German Nazi Party responded so strongly that Rogers, fearing the loss of a major European market, ordered 21 separate cuts, absurd comedy footage, and a new ending. Whale was outraged (Ted Sloman directed the new footage), accused Rogers of sucking up to Hitler — and hence sealed his fate with the New Universal.

It was an appalling situation. Only years before, Uncle Carl Laemmle was destroying Junior's spirit by tyrannically ordering him not to wed a gentile girl. Now this studio, founded by Jews, was virtually falling into goose step with Nazi mandates.

It was also in February, 1937, incidentally, that Karloff began his new Universal picture, *Night Key* — a "B" melodrama with Boris as a kindly old inventor.

March 22, 1937

Bela Lugosi, his Hollywood offers shriveling in the wake of Universal's sale and Britain's horror ban, opens as Commissar Gorotchenko in the play *Tovarich* at the Curran Theatre in San Francisco. Osgood Perkins and Eugenie Leontovich had the star roles, played in the 1937 Warner film by Charles Boyer and Claudette Colbert; Bela had the major supporting role, played in the film by Basil Rathbone.

Aside from a week's work in Republic's serial, *S.O.S. Coastguard,* in which Bela had the curious character name of Boroff, it would be the only work Bela would get for over a year.

*   *   *

For years, Karloff fans have based major parts of their arguments about Boris versus Bela on this sad era: Karloff, after all, was still busy, with his Warner Bros. films, while Lugosi faced a well-publicized and humiliating round of unemployment. Why?

The popular reason is that Karloff, having created a versatile parade of horror characters, was now permitted to be a versatile character star. Universal, in an October, 1936, publicity release, hailed him still as "the outstanding character actor of the screen." Lugosi, after all, was always Count Dracula to many audiences who couldn't accept him (or at least casting directors thought) doing anything that wasn't macabre.

Still, the situation demands more analysis. First of all, Karloff had commitments with Universal and Warner Bros., which were not about to lose their investments. Lugosi had no studio alliance; his original three-picture commitment with Universal was long over, and he was independent — perhaps good for an actor's soul, but a dangerous thing in the Hollywood of the 1930s.

Also, one must not overlook the power of the great Hollywood agencies, which proverbially made and broke stars in this era. Karloff was a member of the very aggressive Leland Hayward/Myron Selznick Agency, which, in 1936, represented such major stars as Gary Cooper, Carole Lombard, Fredric March, Myrna Loy, Fred Astaire, Ginger Rogers, Charles Laughton, Merle Oberon, Henry Fonda, Kay Francis, Katharine Hepburn, William Powell, Margaret Sullavan, Miriam Hopkins, Pat O'Brien, Fay Wray; such busy character players as Dudley Digges, Edmund Gwenn, Eugene Pallette, Binnie Barnes, Billie Burke, Stanley Ridges, ZaSu Pitts; and such prestigious directors as William Dieterle, Fritz Lang, Rowland V. Lee, Leo McCarey, William Wellman, William Wyler—and James Whale.

The 1936 *Film Daily Yearbook* lists Bela Lugosi's agent as Al Kingston— who, that year, was representing talent like Ward Bond, Arthur Aylesworth, Granville Bates, Noah Beery, Jr., Spencer Charters, Berton Churchill, June Collyer, Frankie Darro, Russell Gleason, Porter Hall, Nedda Harrigan, Louis Jean Heydt, Ivan Lebedeff, George Meeker, Moroni Olsen, Addison Richards, Charles Starrett, George E. Stone, Henry *(Mark of the Vampire)* Wadsworth, Irene *(The Raven)* Ware and John Wray.

Bela blamed his agent for his career slump, and the 1937 *Film Daily Yearbook* listed him as a client of William Merklejohn, Inc. Bela's fellow clients included Eddie "Rochester" Anderson, Mischa Auer, Monte Blue, Herman Brix (aka Bruce Bennett), Harry Carey, Hattie McDaniel, Jack Mulhall, Tom Tyler and Toby Wing.

Things grew worse. The 1938 *Film Daily Yearbook* listed Bela's new agent as William Stephens, Inc., representing such popular character players as Jean Hersholt, J. Carrol Naish, Margaret Dumont (the Marx Bros.' ever-flustered friend), Gloria *(Dracula's Daughter)* Holden, and John Miljan.

Three different agents apparently couldn't help the cause of Bela Lugosi. And now, the bitterness of Lugosi toward Karloff increased. After all, Bela was a widely admired European Shakespearean actor when Karloff was just being booted out of England—and now Karloff was finding steady stardom in Hollywood while Bela sat in his library at 2227 Outpost Drive, worrying about the payments on his mansion—and worrying how he would support the baby that Lillian would have in early 1938.

Curiously, while Karloff kept busy, while Lugosi sought solvency, two of the major figures in Hollywood's horror history did nothing. "Uncle Carl" Laemmle played cards, looked after his charities, and finally died September 24, 1939, at his Benedict Canyon showplace (demolished in the mid-fifties).

Junior Laemmle vegetated. After a brief visit to MGM in the summer of 1937, he retired completely, never producing another picture. The broken little producer of *Dracula* and *Frankenstein* lived on his savings and inheritance, served in the U.S. Army Signal Corps (as a private) and lived in Hollywood, where he bet on the horses and fanatically avoided anything related to his old career. He never married, but reportedly entertained a bevy of prostitutes who regularly visited him — which must have shocked the shade of Uncle Carl. In the early sixties, Junior contracted multiple sclerosis, living a severely reduced life but hosting traditional New Year's Eve parties.

"I saw him in the mid-seventies," says Shirley Ulmer. "We did a lot of reminiscing. He had his wits, but he didn't want to talk about the past too much. He was a poor soul, really. After he left Universal, he was just going to enjoy life. But he got sicker and sicker — it was very sad. He was a very sad boy...."

On the 40th anniversary of Laemmle, Sr.'s death — September 24, 1979 — Junior Laemmle died, at his house, 1641 Tower Grove Drive, high in the mountains above Beverly Hills, near the old mansions of John Gilbert and John Barrymore. He was 71. Two days later, there were services at the Home of Peace Memorial Park, in Whittier, California, just as there had been for Uncle Carl 40 years before, and Carl Laemmle, Jr., was buried in the Laemmle family mausoleum — with Carl Laemmle, Sr.

9
Son of Frankenstein, 1939

My Son—
   . . . if you, like me, burn with the irresistible desire to penetrate the unknown, carry on. Though the path be cruel and torturous, carry on. Like every seeker after truth, you will be hated, blasphemed and condemned; but maybe, where I have failed, you will succeed.
      —letter to Wolf von Frankenstein from his father, Baron Henry (deceased), in *Son of Frankenstein*

Two p.m., June 29, 1937. It looked like a gala Hollywood premiere. Three hundred people had gathered under the summer sun, outside the Edwards Brothers Colonial Mansion, 1000 Venice Boulevard, a Southern Gothic domicile à la Tara of *Gone with the Wind.* There were starlets, striking in their dark dresses and sunglasses and bonnets; actors, slicked and dapper; directors, producers, agents, all eyeing each other, anticipating the show inside.

But the Colonial Mansion was not a theatre—it was a mortuary. And this was not a premiere, but a funeral—the wake of Colin Clive, the cinema's most famous Dr. Frankenstein, who had died alone at the Cedars of Lebanon Hospital on the morning of June 25.

The corpse of Clive, his "face of Christ" lacquered to masquerade the ravages of alcohol and disease, had lain in a baroque funeral bed at the Colonial Mansion, where the curious public had paraded reverently past. The English actor's final days had been truly horrific. As Jean Arthur's demonically jealous spouse in United Artists' *History Is Made at Night,* Clive had broken into hysterical sobbing during a dramatic scene; as a Lafayette Escadrille captain in RKO's *The Woman I Love,* he was so intoxicated by noon that two men had to hold him up for close-ups. Mae Clarke recalled a new nightmare that plagued her *Frankenstein*—and one chillingly reminiscent of his role in *Mad Love:*

> James Whale told me that Colin had suffered a leg injury in the army. After many years of agony as he "trod the boards" of England and New York, and his Hollywood films, the old leg wound worsened, and he was hospitalized in Los Angeles. There was the chance they would amputate—and it broke his spirit.

The *Los Angeles Examiner* noted a floral wreath from Clive's estranged wife, Jeanne de Casalis, who didn't bother to make the trip from London; years later, she would write a memoir without once mentioning her tragic husband. Nor did James Whale attend. In fact, he had refused to be a pallbearer; the man who directed *Frankenstein* was in life frightened by funerals and cemeteries.

Only hospital staff were at the forsaken Clive's bedside when death mercifully took the actor who would personify Mary Shelley's Modern Prometheus for generations. Yet now, 300 Hollywoodites filled the Edwards Brothers' chapel, playing the bereaved mourners as Peter Lorre, Alan Mowbray and the other pallbearers marched with the coffin. The Rev. Philip Easley prayed for a man whom actress Rose Hobart (Clive's costar in Broadway's 1933 *Eight Bells*) told me was "a most sensitive actor, but a very private person who would not let you in his private world."

After the funeral, the hearse drove Clive's body down the boulevard to Rosedale Cemetery, where, that day, it was cremated. Newspapers theorized that the ashes would be sent to his native England. Whether they ever were is a mystery. The Rosedale Crematory informed me that an Edwards Brothers undertaker picked up the ashes almost two weeks after the cremation. No record was made of how they were to be disposed.

The Abbott and Hast Mortuary, now housed in the Colonial Mansion, wrote me that the California State Board of Funeral Directors took away the Edwards Bros. license in 1969. At that time, in the mortuary cellar, the Board had found the cremains of approximately 300 people, never claimed by loved ones. Mr. Hast informed me it was "remotely possible" that Clive's ashes were among those forgotten tins. And although a list of names was filed at the time, with the State Board, nobody can (or will) validate if the actor's ashes were among them or not.

If they were, Colin Clive's ashes rest in an anonymous community grave in the Los Angeles County Crematorium Grounds. It would be a fate pathetically but poetically in the spirit of the "hated," "blasphemed" and "condemned" Henry Frankenstein.

*   *   *

> If there's a power of good, it follows that there must be a power of evil. And I've seen evil. Years ago, Hollywood used to be one of the most evil places on earth. No, I'm not joking.
>
> — Vincent Price

As 1938 began, the political caldron brewed by Charles R. Rogers at Universal bubbled and spat. February presented a new Deanna Durbin hit: *Mad About Music,* a slick Pasternak production, with Universal's gussied little songbird trilling "Ave Maria"—backed up by the Vienna Boys Choir, no less. The family entertainment fare also offered the Bob Baker westerns, Oswald

Rabbit cartoons, and the 65-minute musical *Reckless Living*, in which Nan Grey (victim of *Dracula's Daughter's* lesbian tendencies) now raised her voice in song.

If Universal was the picnic ground of La Durbin (who received a special 1938 Oscar), it was a purgatory for others—such as James Whale. In early 1938, the Laemmle's "Ace" returned to the New Universal, bloody but unbowed after his misadventures at Warner Bros. (1937's *The Great Garrick*) and MGM (1938's *Port of Seven Seas*). Rogers, disliking Whale and still vindictive over the scandal of *The Road Back,* slapped him with two "B" projects: *Sinners in Paradise* and *Wives Under Suspicion* (a remake of Whale's 1933 *The Kiss Before the Mirror*). The goal was to make Whale's ego rebel, so he'd refuse the assignments, so Universal could fire him. Instead, Whale shot them rapidly and coolly, took his salary, and left the studio where he had directed some of Universal's historic successes.

The Laemmles had always protected Whale, hailing him as a genius; the New Universal allowed an ugly problem to overtake Whale: his homosexuality. It became a convenient nail to drive into his career coffin; as Vito Russo wrote in his book, *The Celluloid Closet:*

> ...a man who, like Whale, openly admitted his love relationship with another man ... did not stand a chance.... Whale's Frankenstein Monster was the creation that would eventually destroy its creator, just as Whale's own "aberration" would eventually destroy his career....

Whale had invested his money wisely. "The James Whale Company" dealt in real estate and investments, and he could afford an elegant exile in Pacific Palisades. Junior Laemmle, taking refuge in his Sunset Towers apartment, also could afford to relax, play the horses, and avoid entirely the pressures of the industry.

What of the horror stars?

Boris Karloff, once the pride of Universal, didn't play in a single Universal release of 1938. However, he was busy: starring in several *Lights Out!* radio shows from Chicago, touring vaudeville performing Poe's *The Tell-Tale Heart,* commencing the *Mr. Wong* series at Monogram, continuing his Warner contract, starring in the summer of 1938 in *Devil's Island* as the dapper, sympathetic hero, saved from the guillotine in the climax. The *Los Angeles Examiner* reported that two female visitors to the set fainted while watching Boris perform an on-screen operation. Also, early in 1938, the Karloffs learned wonderful news: they were about to become first-time parents.

However, for Bela Lugosi, the horror blackout continued agonizingly. On January 5, 1938, Bela George Lugosi, Jr., was born at Cedars of Lebanon Hospital. The Motion Picture Relief Fund paid the hospital bill, and Louella Parsons (whose husband was a doctor on the relief board) proclaimed the Fund's magnanimity in her popular column, with the headline, "Bela Lugosi Jobless."

For a man of Bela's pride, it was a terrible humiliation. Even after the news of the baby's birth, no producer offered a part, and Bela sat reading in his library, wondering how he could support Lillian and Bela Jr., and save 2227 Outpost Drive from the finance company.

Then came a series of surprise events. At the close of 1937, ancient Robert Cochrane resigned as Universal's president, and Nate J. Blumberg, formerly of RKO, took over. *Film Daily* reported Blumberg's "frequent trips to the studios and burning the midnight oil in New York"; he also reviewed Universal's books—and the staggering figures spoke for themselves. In Charles R. Rogers' two-year reign, Universal had lost over $3,000,000. On May 19, 1938, Rogers "resigned" as vice president in charge of production, managing to depart with a $297,000 "contract" and the face-saving allowance of continuing on the company's directorate. Knowing no shame, Rogers would take a full-page advertisement, with portrait, in the 1939 *Film Daily Yearbook*.

In marched a new New Universal. Replacing Rogers was Cliff Work, a beefy, no-nonsense industry veteran, whose previous post was RKO's divisional chief in San Francisco, where he managed the Golden Gate Theatre. Work, who would supervise Universal throughout the colorful World War II years, conferred with Blumberg and the producers as they sought a path to lead the studio into the novelty of profits.

Then came a miracle. On August 5, 1938, the Regina Theatre, facing bankruptcy, cast its luck with a triple feature: *Dracula, Frankenstein,* and *Son of Kong.* The attraction became the overnight talk of Los Angeles; manager Emil Ullman kept the theatre open 21 hours a day, and police had to control the crowds—the last departing at 3:00 a.m. All of Hollywood read of the sensation, and joining the mob was none other than the fly-eater Renfield of *Dracula,* and hunchbacked Fritz of *Frankenstein*—Dwight Frye. He attended with seven-year-old Dwight, Jr., who, over forty years later, told *Midnight Marquee:*

> My father took me alone, just the two of us ... my mother later told me that she thought he had devilment in his mind. He was hoping I'd come home terrified out of my skull and apparently I came home and started criticizing the films for not having been terrified at all! From what I am told he was very disappointed that the films hadn't scared the pants off me....

Universal deliriously struck 500 new prints of *Dracula* and *Frankenstein,* complete with new, lurid trailers, and released the double bill nationally. "Breaking box office records from New York to San Francisco," reported *Look* magazine, which gave the double feature a giant spread, "they may outgross, as a double dose of horror, the figures they rolled up separately in 1931."

It was all Universal needed. A new horror show was in order—and one of the studio's first moves was to negotiate with Boris Karloff and Bela Lugosi. Sadly, in one way, it already was too late. While crowds were waiting in

Poster for *Son of Frankenstein, 1939.*

monstrous lines to see the *Dracula* and *Frankenstein* double feature, the mortgage company was foreclosing on Bela's earthquake-proof Outpost Drive
mansion. The star moved with Lillian, baby Bela and the dogs to a rented
house in the Cahuenga Pass of the San Fernando Valley — almost on the property of Universal Studios.

                              *   *   *

INT. TOMB — NIGHT — WIDE ANGLE

   ...It is impossible to see the bearer of the lantern; the light is always held
so that it casts nothing but a shadow behind it. The light comes closer and closer,
and its approach is accompanied by heavy, dragging footsteps, footsteps that we
identify with the monster... In the unsteady light from the lantern the incised
lettering is disclosed:

                            Hier ruht in Gott
                   HENRY, BARON FRANKENSTEIN
                               1874–1919
                                R.I.P.

   ...In the center of the tomb stands the coffin of Baron Frankenstein on a
sort of dais, the dim light from the high barred window falling across it... The
sound of the coffin lid being wrenched off is heard... The figure fumbles with
the interior of the coffin for a moment, then turns. In the light from the lantern
we can dimly make out a small metal box in its hands ... it contains papers...
There is the sudden sound of a rat scurrying across the floor, and the figure turns
its head sharply into a CLOSEUP that fills the screen sharply lighted by the
lantern on top of the coffin. It is the monster, leering ferociously at us....
                   — from the original shooting script of *Son of Frankenstein*

On October 17, 1938, Universal rushed film #931, *Son of Frankenstein,* into
preproduction. All originally set was the title and a release date — January,
1939 — the earliest the studio could hope for to "cash in" on the re-release success of *Dracula* and *Frankenstein.*

   The new Frankenstein saga was to proceed without the quirky, brilliant,
intensely personal guidance of James Whale. Universal made no overture to
him, and he probably would have rejected the project if they had. As far as
Whale was concerned, *Bride of Frankenstein* had climaxed the monster's
tragedy.

   Instead, Universal entrusted *Son of Frankenstein* to Rowland Vance Lee,
who had just joined the studio as a producer/director. The Ohio-born,
47-year-old Lee had been a Broadway actor, a silent film player, a wounded
World War I soldier; he began his directorial career with Trangle-Ince's 1920
His Own Law (both director Irvin Willat and assistant Roy Marshall became
ill, so Lee, an actor in the film, took over). He was a contract director for
William Fox Studios during the silent period, later joining Paramount on the

eve of sound. Lee hit his peak with Fox's 1933 *Zoo in Budapest,* starring Loretta Young and Gene Raymond, a pastoral love tale featuring a wild climax of escaping zoo animals. Reliance's 1934 *The Count of Monte Cristo,* 20th Century's 1935 *Cardinal Richelieu* and RKO's 1935 *The Three Musketeers* all revealed Lee's graceful sweep as a director of costume epics.

Rowland V. Lee had profound ideas on the movies:

> Every time a director looks through his camera lens, he is looking directly into the eyes of millions upon millions of people all over the world. . . . The vast audience is countless times greater than all the persons who saw and heard Moses, Buddha, Jesus, Mohammed and all other prophets combined. What a privilege! What an obligation!

A charming, easy man, Lee owned "Farmlake," a 214-acre ranch in the San Fernando Valley with a two-mile lake and tree-lined ponds, which he rented for location shooting. Hans J. Salter, Universal's famed musical director (who began his legendary horror output orchestrating *Son of Frankenstein*) warmly recalled Lee for *Cinefantastique:* "Very charming fellow. A typical Yankee. He embodied the best things in America. He had a wonderful sense of humor, and a wonderful outlook on life which was very heartening."

Lee's first production for Universal had been 1938's *Service De Luxe,* starring Constance Bennett and (in his film debut), 27-year-old Vincent Price. Production had gone smoothly. However, as Universal would learn, Lee was a gutsy man with an almost heroic defiance of front office politics. It was news Universal would be quick to learn as *Son of Frankenstein* neared a shooting date.

The October 13, 1938, *Variety* had reported that *Son of Frankenstein* would star Peter Lorre (to be borrowed from 20th Century–Fox), Boris Karloff and Bela Lugosi. Meanwhile, engaged to write the screenplay was Willis Cooper, who had been cranking out scripts for Lorre's *Mr. Moto* series at Fox, and who had created the popular radio show, *Lights Out!* Cooper familiarized himself with *Frankenstein* and *Bride of Frankenstein,* rushing to meet Universal's time demand.

What Cooper completed on October 20, 1938 — Bela Lugosi's 56th birthday — bore only slight resemblance to what would appear on the screen.

In the original, Wolf von Frankenstein, his wife Elsa, and their child Erwin all return to the ancestral castle on a stormy night. Henry Frankenstein's will had dictated:

> If, after twenty-five years have passed since my death, there has been no sign or indication that the monster still lives, then it is my wish that my son and his wife, if he be married, return unto their inheritance.

That night, as Wolf reads his father's diary aloud to the terrified Elsa, recapping plot from *Frankenstein* and *Bride of Frankenstein,* lightning strikes the old laboratory ruins — resurrecting the monster, who escapes his tomb, kills a mounted gendarme, and wipes out a peasant family. Then, eavesdropping on Wolf, learning that Frankenstein's records were buried with him, the monster raids his creator's tomb — stealing from the coffin the infamous *Records of Life and Death.*

The plot takes the expected path: the talking monster demands that Wolf create a friend for him — or he will kill Elsa and Erwin. Karloff, who had been unhappy with the monster's speech in *Bride of Frankenstein,* must have winced at this original dialogue:

> Listen — me — you — got — woman. You — got — baby. You — do — what — I — say — I — not — kill — them... Make — friend... Ah! Then — we — rule — whole — world. Like — your — father — say... Ha! Friend!

A cigar-smoking inspector named Neumuller, whose father had been killed by the monster, suspects monster-making is in the blood. He realizes the creature committed the murders on the night Wolf and family arrived, and hounds Wolf unmercifully. Curiously, the role of Ygor appears nowhere in this script — which means Cooper must have envisioned Bela in the Inspector Neumuller role!

Meanwhile ... the "giant" befriends Erwin, kills Fritz the servant, trades Erwin Fritz's watch for his storybook — a nice touch which survived in the film. The climax saw an army, with machine guns and grenades, answering Neumuller's cry for help; the monster kills a young soldier, and wants Wolf to use the body to create his "friend." But the brain is useless, so the monster kidnaps Erwin — and decides to perform the brain surgery himself. Wolf gets the scalpel, and wildly stabs the monster; the monster gets Wolf by the neck — but he cannot bring himself to kill him. "A look of sadness comes into its eyes," noted the script of the monster, "and it mutters — 'Friend.'" The army attacks, blasting the monster, who backs away and topples into a deep, dark pit. "Far below is heard the splash of water, and a groan of agony from the monster...." Neumuller drops a grenade into the pit. "In a moment, there is an echoing explosion. Music picks it up, and we FADE OUT. THE END."

The script featured some clever touches, such as the monster studiously reading Erwin's *Cock Robin* book, and recognizing the word "dead"; there was also a black comedy scene of the monster enjoying Fritz's lunch after killing him, and throwing away the salad in disgust. (A still of Karloff's monster, lunching over the "body" of Edgar Norton, exists, although no such episode is in the movie.) There also were echoes from the earlier films, as Wolf found the skeletons of Pretorius, his homunculi and the female monster in the ruins of the laboratory. And Cooper even offered some historical tidbits on the Frankensteins: how the first Baron Frankenstein built the ancestral castle in 1194; how Wolf was the 27th Baron Frankenstein; how some of the Frankensteins were womanizers.

"Hugo and the first Wolf each had two wives," Wolf tells Elsa, "and Lothar had five — Hedwig, Theresa, Elise, Hertha, and Beatrix. He died in 1401."

"I should think he would," replied Elsa.

Universal's front office was waiting to pounce on the finished script. The studio had publicly allotted *Son of Frankenstein* a budget of only $250,000 — $40,000 less than the final cost of *Frankenstein,* and $150,000 less than the full tab of *Bride of Frankenstein.* As was the custom the studio wanted to get the script, draw up a schedule to shoot the scenes of the top-paid stars first (to get them off payroll) and take advantage of the sets, supporting cast and crew as economically as possible.

Rowland V. Lee knew it. He had his own vision of *Son of Frankenstein* — an epic celebration of the monster's legend. Aware that the front office would never sanction this expensive conception, Lee slyly plotted to achieve it. . . .

First, Lee vetoed Peter Lorre for the title spot. For Wolf von Frankenstein, Lee pictured Basil Rathbone — then Hollywood's top free-lance actor, at a price tag of $5000 weekly. A former Broadway Romeo, Rathbone was the screen's most colorful villain, a dashing classical player who seemed to leap out of the pages of great literature as he lashed Freddie Bartholomew in *David Copperfield* and won Oscar nominations for Tybalt in MGM's *Romeo and Juliet* and Louis XI in Paramount's *If I Were King.* Of course, Rathbone was at his most beautifully wicked when he crossed swords with Errol Flynn as pirate Levasseur in *Captain Blood* and as wonderfully evil Sir Guy of Gisbourne in *The Adventures of Robin Hood.*

There was an irony in this sensitive, dog-loving, athletic actor excelling as Hollywood's top-paid villain. After taking rod to master Bartholomew in *David Copperfield,* Rathbone had hugged the child actor, and kissed him; and, in his screen duels, the very skilled swordsman could have run through Errol Flynn at any time. Basil Rathbone was top Hollywood society, residing regally at 5254 Los Feliz Boulevard in the Hollywood Hills, working almost nonstop in the studios to fund the elegant soirées of his wife, Ouida. Lee had directed the popular actor in UA's *Love from a Stranger* (1937), filmed in England; he loved working with Basil, and would star him in two Universal follow-ups of 1939, *The Sun Never Sets* and *Tower of London.* Rathbone savored the chance to be heroic in *Son.* After all, he had just lost two leading roles he had deeply wanted: Dr. Steele in Bette Davis's *Dark Victory,* and Rhett Butler in *Gone with the Wind.*

Karloff, his own weekly salary now $3750, signed on for the monster. No longer just "KARLOFF," he now agreed to second billing under Basil Rathbone. Boris, however, scored his own victory. He had voiced his objection to the monster's dialogue in *Bride of Frankenstein* ("Stupid!"), and Lee, respecting his opinion, restored the monster to his eloquent pantomime.

Lugosi as Ygor, Karloff as the monster and Basil Rathbone as Wolf von Franken-stein, that is, the *Son of Frankenstein*.

Lee boosted *Son's* box office power. He signed Lionel Atwill for the role of Inspector Krogh; hence, the star of *Doctor X* and *Mystery of the Wax Museum* made his first of five appearances in a Frankenstein melodrama. For Elsa von Frankenstein, Lee engaged red-haired Josephine Hutchinson, who had won a certain following as a Warner Bros. star of the mid-thirties, and was now on a picture deal at Universal. Four year-old Donnie Dunagan won the pivotal role of Peter—agreed by all to be a far more winning name for the moppet than Erwin.

Meanwhile, there was a serious problem: there was no part for Bela Lugosi! Hence, Lee and Cooper created the role of Ygor, and began planning to incorporate the part into the script. Universal responded in character. Aware of Bela's financial woes, the studio offered a merciless dictate to the humbled actor: his salary, $1000 per week, would be cut to $500—and Lee was to shoot all of Bela's scenes in one week. The Lugosis appealed to Lee, and for the rest of her life, Lillian relished his response:

> "Those God-damned sons of bitches! I'll show them. I'm going to keep Bela on this picture from the first day of shooting right up to the last!"

As the stars signed their contracts, Lee pulled a new stunt: he toyed with shooting *Son of Frankenstein* in Technicolor. Tests began, to see how the monster's gray-green complexion would photograph. George Turner, editor of *American Cinematographer* magazine, recalls reading in a journal that the studio had abandoned the Technicolor idea after evaluating the tests.

With the Technicolor tests, the conception of the Ygor role, and various changes, Lee threw the front office totally off balance. With the stars on contract, collecting salary, Universal did exactly what Lee hoped would happen: it rushed *Son of Frankenstein* into production with no further dictates. And now, on the eve of shooting, Lee guaranteed his autonomy with a very audacious move.

He threw away the script.

*   *   *

> Due to the necessity of meeting release date and in order to get value of cast already on salary, this picture started in production Wednesday, November 9. Operating under conditions like we are, without script, is extremely difficult for all departments concerned in physical production, and, more improtant, most expensive.... However, on the basis of Rowland Lee's performance during the shooting of *Service De Luxe,* we figure it might be possible to finish the picture December 10. This would make a 27-day shooting period, and according to some rough figuring, we believe the cost will be somewhere in the neighborhood of $300,000...
>
> —report from Universal Studios Production Manager
> Martin F. Murphy, November 12, 1938

BASIL RATHBONE
BORIS KARLOFF
BELA LUGOSI

The star names loom, mighty and monolithic, as Frank Skinner's magnificently epic score heralds the credits for *Son of Frankenstein.* The movie

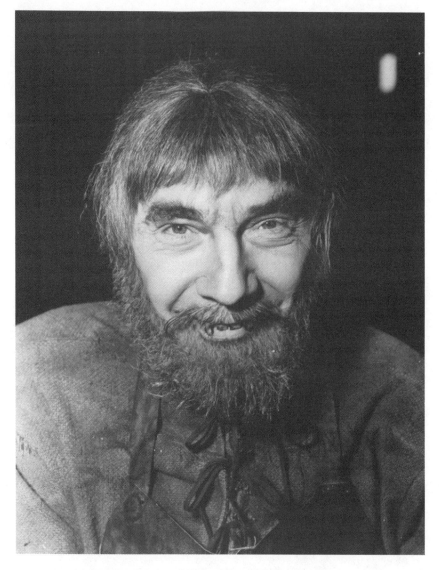

Bela Lugosi as Ygor, in *Son of Frankenstein*.

opens on the old, ancestral Castle Frankenstein — giant, Gothic, a fairy tale fortress set on a mountain crag. "Eingang Verboten," warns a sign at the gate as peasants, crossing themselves, pull their cart past the unholy site.

Up in the tower, at the gate, leering down at the peasants, is Old Ygor.

"God, he was cute!" rejoiced Bela of this wonderful part. Scraggly in his four-hour Jack P. Pierce makeup of beard, snaggle teeth and that petrified broken neck, Bela is almost unrecognizable; certainly, proud Count Dracula would never have stooped to biting the broken neck of this horrible old blacksmith/shepherd/body snatcher. "He loved it!" recalled Lillian of Bela's feelings for Ygor. "He loved any challenging part."

"Ain't you afraid?" asks one peasant boy of another. "Of old Ygor? No!" responds his friend, about to hurl a rock at the tower window — until he sees Bela's Ygor glaring at him — and runs in terror. It was the kind of little episode Lee created to keep Bela on the picture — and which helps give *Son of Frankenstein* its magic...

That stormy night, a train roars through the countryside. Inside, snug in a compartment with his family, is the new Baron Frankenstein. Basil Rathbone is Wolf von Frankenstein: Sir Guy of Gisbourne, as modern hero. Forty-six years old, the elegant Rathbone was at his movie peak, and one movie away from becoming Sherlock Holmes. Outside the European scenery is smoky, bleak, haunting; it's as if the monster's legend has warped nature itself.

"What strange-looking country!" marvels Elsa von Frankenstein. Josephine Hutchinson, sleek, sophisticated, is elegant in her Vera West dress and a smashing fur hat. There is something almost too brittle, too *très chic* about Miss Hutchinson's Elsa; one imagines her keeping her fur hat on while lounging in her bubble bath. In 1978, Miss Hutchinson, still slender, red-haired, ethereal, sat in her New York penthouse, charmingly recalling her days as the pride of Eva Le Gallienne's Civic Repertory Company, and her Warner stardom in movies like 1935's *Oil for the Lamps of China*. *Son of Frankenstein*, however, seemed to perplex her:

> I had beautiful clothes in it — that was fun, as was working with Basil and Pinky, both pros and charming men... Of course, doing a Frankenstein film is kind of phony — you don't have to delve too deeply...!

Actually, this slightly cavalier attitude made her a perfect Baroness Frankenstein, who regards the in-law's blasphemy with fear, a mild distaste, and — climactically — hysterical, screaming horror.

Finally, there is little Peter (Erwin of the script) — four-year-old Donnie Dunagan. Poor little Donnie (who later played in Lee's *Tower of London*); with his moppet curls and that "Well, Hell-ooo!" cry, he has become the child actor-you-love-to-hate with many horror fans. Actually, he fits the tale well, looking like he could have been twin brother to Shirley Temple (then the top box office draw in the United States).

"Out there, in the darkness, a new life lies before us!" exults Wolf. The heir is finally able to depart his career as a college teacher; he and Elsa joke about the castle they have inherited, and Elsa wonders if there might be "a haunted room."

"Oh yes, there's sure to be a haunted room!" volleys Wolf. The castle itself

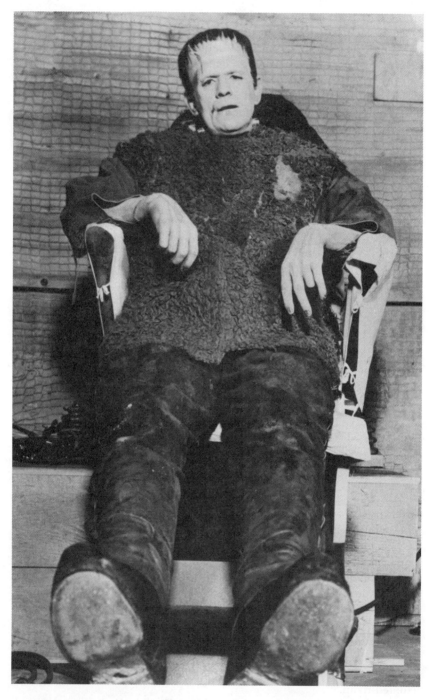

Boris Karloff as the monster relaxes on the set of *Son of Frankenstein*.

is supposed to be haunted—by the blasphemous ghost of Wolf's father and the Frankenstein monster. Rathbone begins a soliloquy on his father's tragedy, giving off sparks of Frankenstein passion and Rathbone ham:

> It wasn't my father's fault that the being he created became a senseless, murderous monster—he was right! You understand that, don't you, dear? He was right! ... How my father was made to suffer... His name has become synonymous with horror and monsters. Why, nine out of ten people call that misshappen creature of my father's experiments...

"Frankenstein!" announces the conductor.

In this scene, Universal made peace for all time with the cinema misdemeanor of referring to the (nameless) monster by the name "Frankenstein." It also established a poetic fact: the village—Goldstadt in the 1931 film—has now taken on the name of the man who made it famous. It was a scene whipped up shortly before shooting—as Lee blithely proceeded to make up the movie (with Willis Cooper, who received sole screenplay credit) from day to day.

The storm is magnificent, as it was the night the monster came alive; the Frankenstein heir and his family depart the train. The villagers, broodingly menacing under umbrellas, stare at the family. "We-come to meet you. Not to greet you," rhymes the Burgomeister—staunchly British Lawrence Grant, an early pillar of the Motion Picture Academy. He presents Wolf with two boxes: a large one with papers relevant to the estate, the small one holding the key that will open it.

Wolf, with the theatrics of a Frankenstein, launches into a speech to the townspeople: "...it was my father's misfortune to be the unwilling, unknowing cause of tragedy... I'm so sorry I don't remember him, because I've been told he was a good man..."

The crowd moans and begins filing away in the rain.

"...And I know how greatly your tragedy must have weighed upon his mind... My wife and I, and our son—we want so much to be your friends...!

The crowd is gone. Only a gendarme stands in the street.

A car bears Wolf, Elsa and Peter up the mountain to Castle Frankenstein; the headlights spy Ygor in the shadows. Inside, we behold Universal Art Director Jack Otterson's magnificent "Psychological Sets": the climax of German expressionism in Universal's horror shows. We meet Amelia (Emma Dunn, best remembered as *Dr. Kildare's* mom at Metro), and Benson, the butler (Edgar Norton, who had made a career of playing Poole, Dr. Jekyll's butler, on the stage, and in the Fredric March 1932 *Dr. Jekyll and Mr. Hyde*). Elsa goes upstairs to prepare Peter for bed, where she remarks on the oddly-built beds. A Tyrolean maid offers this couplet:

> If the house is filled with dread,
> place the beds at head to head.

In Otterson's Gothic library, a beautiful, full-length portrait looms above the fireplace. It is Henry Frankenstein — an emotional sight for Wolf, and for fans of Colin Clive (more than one of whom have wondered what Universal ever did with this painting).*

"Here he planned a miracle," says Rathbone, "and saw it come to pass — a miracle that the good people of Frankenstein called a monster."

"They call it a lot worse than that, Sir!" chimes in Norton.

Beneath the portrait, Wolf finds, with the estate papers, all of his father's records, charts and secret formulas. He reads aloud, with the backup symphony of thunder, lightning, and Frank Skinner's music, his father's last letter...

> ...Even though the path is cruel and torturous, carry on... You have inherited the fortune of the Frankensteins. I trust you will not inherit their fate.

A bearded, broken-necked, soaking-wet figure, with a radiantly evil grin, peeps in the library window. Wolf, sensing it, turns, but the ghoul has gone. He lifts his brandy to the portrait.

"To you, sir!" toasts Wolf von Frankenstein.

*   *   *

> This picture will complete their 10th shooting day tonight. Progress has been unusually slow, chiefly due to the nature of the scenes calling for many special effects. While we are still operating without completed script, receiving only a few pages spasmodically just before we start a sequence, we hope it will still be possible to finish up by December 15th and that our cost will be somewhere in the neighborhood of $300,000....
> — production report from M.F. Murphy, November 19, 1938

A cavernous booming echoes throughout Castle Frankenstein. Benson admits a stiff, cloaked visitor, who looks and moves like the puppet of a general. The visitor enters the library.

"Inspector Krogh," salutes the visitor, clicking his heels, cocking his right arm into a military salute by hitting it with his left one. "Of District Police."

Lionel Atwill — Hollywood's kinky, Krafft-Ebing villain of the 1930s. Who can forget Atwill's abashed vanity after Fay Wray cracks his wax face in *Mystery of the Wax Museum*, revealing his Westmore, blistered-persimmon

---

*Perhaps no star of the horror genre enjoys the intensity of admiration from such sensitive fans as does Colin Clive. Over the years, this author has received (most gratefully) everything from art work to a prayer book from people who have read of my own admiration for Clive, and responded most generously to it.

Opposite: **Portrait of actor Colin Clive (who died in 1937) as Henry Frankenstein haunts Lionel Atwill (left) and Basil Rathbone,** *Son of Frankenstein.*

makeup? Or that evil little smile on his face in *Murders in the Zoo*, just before he tosses his spouse, slinky Kathleen Burke ("The Panther Woman" of *Island of Lost Souls*), into a pool of alligators? Or his primping in *The Song of Songs*, smoking, humming, perfuming himself, leering at a portrait of a naked Dietrich before he enters her bedroom to make love to his weeping bride? "Pinky" Atwill loved such roles:

> Do you realize that the two characters of drama that have survived and made the most money for producers and actors have been Richard the Third and Hamlet? Richard the Third, that deformed man, with his horrible attitude toward women, his lust for killing and then more killing—and Hamlet, with his pitiful diseased mind, his ability to conjure up nightmare pictures of his mother and uncle... There is something about horror that is horribly compelling...

As Inspector Krogh, perhaps his most famous role, Atwill is in his glory. He and Rathbone were old stage friends, had already played together in 1935's *Captain Blood,* and were lofty celebrities of Hollywood society. They serve each other their lines with glee, just as they volleyed tennis balls at Atwill's popular Sunday buffets in Pacific Palisades.

"I've come here, Herr Baron," says Atwill's Krogh, "to assure you of protection ... from a virulent and fatal poison."

"Oh... Am I to be poisoned, then?"

"You're poisoned already—by your name."

Rathbone begins a spirited defense of his father; after all, did Krogh really know of one crime this "poor creature" ever committed? Did he ever even see him? Atwill's response—delivered as he wedges his monocle into his gloved right "hand" and polishes the eyepiece—is one of the classic soliloquies of the horror genre:

> The most vivid recollection of my life. I was but a child at the time—about the age of your own son, Herr Baron. The monster had escaped and was ravaging the countryside—killing, maiming, terrorizing. One night he burst into our house. My father took a gun and fired at him, but the savage brute sent him crashing to a corner. Then he grabbed me by the arm...

Krough impulsively smacks his wooden prosthesis into the wall.

> One doesn't easily forget, Herr Baron, an arm torn out by the roots!

If not for his wooden arm, Krogh might have been a general—instead of commander of seven gendarmes in a little mountain village. He certainly acts like a general—strutting and posing with military flourish. One would almost suspect he's lampooning General Douglas MacArthur—at that time,

Opposite: Universal studios art director Jack Otterson's sketch for the main hall of Castle Frankenstein, showing its huge scale. *Son of Frankenstein,* 1939.

Atwill was married to multimillionairess Louise Cromwell — MacArthur's first wife! At any rate, Atwill's black comedy bits throughout *Son of Frankenstein* are one of the joys of the Universal series, as is his pained demeanor toward it — like a vain playboy aware his toupee is crooked while he visits the chorus girls' dressing room.

Wolf apologetically offers Krogh a brandy, Krogh apologizes for arousing Wolf's sympathy, and tells Wolf of six men of the village, all of some prominence and all of whom are recently dead. Cause of death: a concussion at the base of the brain, and a ruptured heart. "In fact," says Atwill of those ruptured hearts, "they had burst!" — at which point he toasts Wolf and downs his brandy. Neither Scotland Yard nor the French police have been able to solve the crime — hence the superstition of the murdering ghost. "Need I add," purrs Krogh, "that it is always alluded to as — Frankenstein?"

Wolf assures Krogh he is not about to make a monster, and he will not need Krogh's help.

"*When* you need help," replies Krogh, "you have but to ring the alarm bell in the tower, and I shall hear it; wherever I may be, and hasten to your assistance."

As Krogh leaves, he meets Elsa, in a perfectly splendid negligee; she offers her right hand, he takes it with his left one. She invites Krogh to dinner one evening, and then joins her husband at the library window to watch the storm. "Nothing in nature is terrifying when one understands it," says Wolf, proudly. "My father drew that very lightning from heaven and forced it to his own will to bring life to a being he created with his own hands. Why should *we* fear anything?"

It's a splendid curtain line for this vignette. However, neither Wolf nor Elsa are aware that, upstairs, that bearded, broken-necked peasant glimpsed in the car lights is peering through a door, grinning villainously at the sleeping Peter...

> Progress during the past week on this production has only been fair, the company averaging a little better than two pages each day. We are still operating under the most difficult conditions to make pictures, that is, without script which prevents us from laying out schedule or figuring a budget.... From what has been accomplished to date we do not believe it will be possible to finish shooting much before Christmas Eve.... This would make a total shooting period of 39 days and in all probability the cost would exceed our hoped for $300,000 mark...
> — production report from M.F. Murphy, November 26, 1938

The next morning is beautiful; more like the sunny day when the monster met Little Maria by the mountain lake. Wolf and Elsa dine in the great hall, each beneath a ferocious mounted boar's head. "Well, Hell-ooo!"

Opposite: **Jack Otterson's sketch for the library, with huge slanting beams and massive furnishings, *Son of Frankenstein*.**

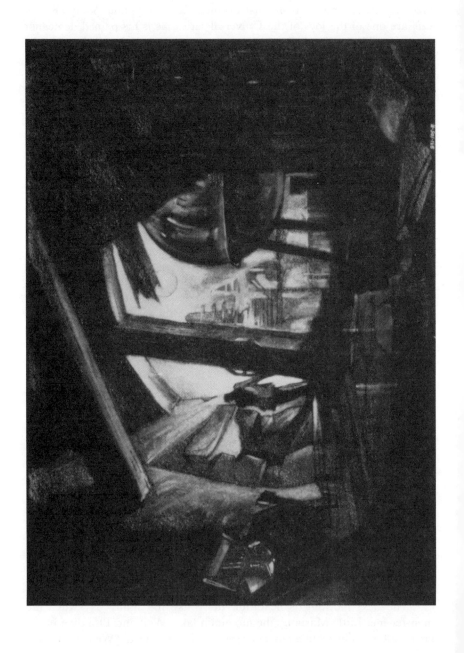

announces Peter, who asks what those creatures are, leering aside the balcony.

"That? That's a boar," responds Wolf.

"Like Aunt Fanny?" asks Peter.

Elsa is intrigued by that "weird-looking structure across the ravine"; it is the old laboratory, and Wolf, rifle in tow, heads off to explore it. The laboratory is Jack Otterson's masterpiece: a cavernous, smoky hell, seemingly designed by Satan himself in tribute to Frankenstein's blasphemy. Indeed, the ruins follow a *Paradise Lost* motif; in Milton's masterwork, we first meet Satan on a horrific, boiling lake — and the set piece of the Frankenstein laboratory, with its wreckage of electrical equipment, is the magnificent, 800-degree sulphur pit. The *Philadelphia Inquirer* (February 5, 1939) would regale readers with data on the perilous pit:

> Technicians worked for two weeks creating the lava pit . . . smearing on the plaster that later was covered with strained mud to simulate the boiling mass. Pipes, attached to garden hose, were run under the mud in the pit. Air and steam were pumped through, making huge bubbles and heavy vapors arise from the "lava." Pulleys and ropes were attached to all the workmen while preparing the unique set, so they could be fished out promptly if they skidded into the mud . . .

Suddenly, a boulder falls from the roof, missing Wolf narrowly. Wolf aims his rifle at his erstwhile assassin, who slides down a chain to his captor.

"My name — is Ygor," announces Bela Lugosi. The Jack P. Pierce makeup, detailed by Al Taylor and Sue Roy in their book *Making a Monster,* is remarkable:

> Because of Karloff's popularity as a result of his heavy character makeup as Frankenstein's monster, Bela Lugosi was willing to don the makeup of Ygor. . . . Pierce employed a rubber neck form to simulate the broken neck Ygor received from being hanged. . . . Pierce fit the rubber neck brace snugly to Lugosi's neck and head, securing it with an elastic strap which ran under Lugosi's right arm. The application of neck appliance and hair took Pierce well over four hours. Once the neck appliance was secured, Pierce began laying layers of yak hair upon Lugosi's face and on the rubber appliance. Once the necessary layers were completed, a wig was added. . . . Pierce then, carefully and diligently, clipped, combed and curled the hair until he had completed a most realistic beard. . . . A moustache was added, and appropriate teeth. . . .

More remarkable, than the makeup, however, is Lugosi's brilliant performance, delivered in that unforgettable raspy, gruff voice: "They hanged me once, Frankenstein. They broke my neck. They said I was dead. Then they cut me down . . ."

"Why did they hang you?" demands Wolf.

Opposite: **Jack Otterson's sketch for the laboratory of Castle Frankenstein.**

"Because I stole bodies . . . er . . . they said. . . . They threw me in here, long ago. They wouldn't bury me in holy place, like churchyard. . . . So, Ygor is dead!"

Cackling, wicked, yet possessing an almost childlike, mischievous glee, Bela's Ygor is superb; Count Dracula might celebrate Lugosi the Personality, but Ygor celebrates Lugosi the Actor.

"Nobody can mend Ygor's neck," boasts Bela. "It's all right" — and he mirthfully raps on the bulging skin and bone.

Tickled that Wolf is a doctor, Ygor pulls away a slab in the wall and leads the leading man into the catacombs of the laboratory. There, Wolf finds the coffins of his grandfather, and his father; like Ygor, they have been deemed unfit to be buried in a holy place, and their remains rest in this forsaken tomb. Henry Frankenstein's coffin bears vindictive villager graffiti *Maker of Monsters.*

However, deeper in the catacombs, is the real sight to see. As Skinner's music ominously swells, George Robinson's camera draws back — and there, atop a large bier, is Frankenstein's monster — Karloff.

The effect is grand, the camera surveying the monster reverentially, as if here were some revered, legendary wonder of the macabre world — which, indeed, he is. The monster also has "a new look": a curly, sheepskin jersey — perhaps a gift from Ygor the shepherd, perhaps a concession from the costume department when the picture was proposed for Technicolor. By now, Karloff was almost obsessed with devotion and respect for his "dear old monster," and the actor resented much in *Son of Frankenstein:*

> In the third one I didn't like it because they changed his clothes completely . . . wrapped him up in furs and muck, and he just became nothing. I mean the makeup, like the clothes, had become part of him. If you accepted the convention that he lived or came to live, as it were, at the end of the film . . . after practically being destroyed . . . you could accept that he wore the same clothes to meet the script . . .

"He's alive!" shouts Wolf, as the monster's hand moves.

"He's my friend," says Bela's Ygor. "He . . . he does things for me."

Boris, for all his concerns about the monster, was in jolly good humor on the set, and he and Basil Rathbone gave each other the giggles. The monster remembered this particular episode:

> In the scene where Bela slowly tells Basil, "He — does things for me," and there I am, all stretched out on this dais — well, we all just doubled up, including everyone else on the set, the entire cast, crew, and even Rowland, who said he didn't mind the extra takes for the chuckles it gave everyone.

Bela laughed too — but he failed to see much of the humor. Not only was he working for $500 per week, not only was he forced each day to behold

Karloff in the very guise of the Frankenstein monster, but he developed a sharp dislike for Basil Rathbone. Lillian Lugosi was outspoken on it:

> Basil Rathbone was verrrry Brrrritish. He was a cold fish, and Karloff was a cold fish. Bela, who actually was very warm, couldn't tolerate either of them!

Actually, Rathbone, a very gregarious man, had a way of dominating his sets, regaling the cast and crew with stories. Once again, Bela probably bristled at the domination; he puffed his cigar stoically on the set, while Basil and Boris played the Rover Boys, hooting at practical jokes and blowing up surgeon's gloves like balloons.

Bela comforted himself by throwing himself passionately into the role of Ygor, and his dialogue to Rathbone is chilling: how the monster was struck by lightning (Bela cleverly imitates the lightning with a bizarre hand move) one night while out "hunting" (Bela reads the word with wonderfully sinister intonation); how the monster *cannot* be destroyed; how Wolf von Frankenstein has the duty to make the monster well.

"Your father made him," says Bela, "and Heinrich Frankenstein was your father too!"

"You mean to imply then," says Rathbone distastefully, "*that* is my — brother?"

Ygor slyly nods. "But *his* mother was — the LIGHT-E-NING!"

Naturally, Wolf cannot resist. The scientific wonder is too potent. And, as the music swells, Rathbone takes a torch, stands above his father's coffin, and changes MAKER OF MONSTERS to read — MAKER OF MEN.

*   *   *

> Progress on this picture during the past week has been only fair. Although Mr. Lee is firm in his belief of being able to complete the production by Christmas Eve, we cannot help feeling a little dubious on the possibility of accomplishing this, considering we have only two weeks left from today. Of course, we still have no script upon which to base this contention, and unquestionably Lee should be in a better position than we are to know just how much he has left to do because the story appears to be altogether in his mind. We have compiled a definite estimate amounting to $347,100, based upon finishing December 24 (which we are now putting through regular channels)...
> — production report from M.F. Murphy, December 10, 1938

In a series of wonderfully impressive shots, beautifully dramatized by the Skinner score, Wolf raises the monster up from the catacombs, to a giant platform above the lake of sulphur. The shot of the monster, rising on his table, chains hoisting him up through a catacomb hole and onto the platform is magnificent; here the monster looms at his most legendary, and although Karloff says nothing, there is a striking melancholy about him; we can almost sense his nightmares.

The new electrical equipment of Kenneth Strickfaden, who supplied the laboratory equipment from *Frankenstein* and *Bride of Frankenstein,** once again buzzes and crackles as Wolf makes his discoveries: the abnormal pituitary, accounting for his great size; bullets, pocking his still-beating heart; superhuman blood cells, battling each other, as if they were conscious and bitter enemies...

Ygor has been assisting, and now the Gentlemen of the Council call him into their gingerbread courtroom. It's an interesting assemblage: besides Burgomeister Lawrence Grant, and Atwill's Krogh, who suavely smokes throughout this scene, adjusting his prosthesis, we meet Emil Lang, played by plump, white-haired Lionel Belmore — the Burgomeister from *Frankenstein.* Then there's Ewald Neumuller — played by bald, moustached Michael Mark, who was Ludwig, Little Maria's grieving father in *Frankenstein.*** Also sitting on the council is Gustav von Seyffertitz — Barrymore's Moriarty from 1922's *Sherlock Holmes,* and the evil one who tried to consign Mary Pickford to quicksand in 1926's *Sparrows.*

Bela, in one of his best scenes, is all innocence as the council debates if he can be hanged again. "He was pronounced dead by Dr. Berger," rules the Burgomeister, "and all the others Berger has pronounced dead for the last 30 years have been dead! ... If Ygor came to life again, it's the devil's work — not the courts!" But we also learn that, of the eight men who ruled that Ygor would be hanged, only two are alive. The other six are all dead — victims of the "ghost."

"They die — dead!" cackles Ygor. "I die — live!"

The council has had enough. They dismiss Ygor, who leaves coughing. Suddenly, he spits on Neumuller. "I'm sorry. I cough. You see," says Bela, pointing to his broken neck, "bone get stuck in my throat!"

In the laboratory, the experiments continue. Wolf has decided to revive the monster, to make him well. "That would vindicate my father," he proclaims, "and his name would be enshrined among the immortals!" Benson turns on the generator, and as the Skinner score again soars, the Strickfaden machinery zaps and jolts the monster. In a nice touch, concerned Ygor grabs the monster — and gets an electrical shock. Karloff's monster awakens, snarls at Benson — then lapses back into his coma.

---

* *Strickfaden, who had supplied the electrical effects for such films as* The Mask of Fu Manchu, *created the supernatural charge that stung Margaret Hamilton when she tried to remove Judy Garland's ruby slippers in* The Wizard of Oz, *and contributed his wizardry to about 60 other movies (as well as CBS's* The Munsters*), later revived his Frankenstein apparatus for Mel Brooks' 1973* Young Frankenstein. *Late in life he was still touring Southern California during summers with his "electrical sideshow." Once asked what his wife's opinion was of his profession, he replied: "She is no fan. I remind her that she is living in a house built and paid for by Frankenstein!" He died in 1984.*

** *By Universal magic, Mark and Belmore returned to the council (once again headed by Lawrence Grant) for 1942's* The Ghost of Frankenstein — *even though both were fated as monster victims in* Son.

Back in the castle, Wolf finds Krogh, sipping tea with Elsa. The inspector and Wolf spar, as Krogh learns Wolf has been experimenting in "the monster's home."

"Haven't seen him stalking about by any chance, have you?" asks Krogh.

"No, I fear he'll never stalk again," replies Wolf.

Peter enters. Krogh offers his hand. "You're not supposed to shake hands with your left hand," corrects Peter. "You're not supposed to wear gloves in the house, either."

"You see," says the abashed inspector, "I only have one real arm. This one isn't mine."

"Well, whose is it?" asks Peter.

Wolf makes peace, telling Peter that Krogh lost his right arm in the war. "He's something more than a general—he's an inspector," says Wolf, and Krogh clicks his heels in thanks. But Peter disturbs both men when he announces that a giant—a nice giant—came into his room and woke him up. Peter gave him his storybook. "Are there lots of giants around here?" asks Peter.

"Only one that I ever heard of," responds the suspicious Krogh.

Wolf, racing to the laboratory, calls for Ygor. In the smoky ruins, a giant figure approaches Wolf from behind—and places his giant arm on his shoulder. Wolf turns to look into the face of Frankenstein's monster.

There is a lovely pantomime, musically scored, of course, as the melancholy monster studies Wolf; seeing the fear in Rathbone's face, Karloff takes his hand and twists his costar's face into a smile. Clearly ill and dazed, the monster strides away, and sees his own reflection in a mirror—the same face that had grimaced at him from the little pool where he had hoped to befriend the shepherdess in *Bride of Frankenstein*. Humiliated by his horrific appearance, the monster drags Wolf over, and compares their reflections— groaning dismally at the reflected awful truth. It's a clever scene, played by Karloff with all his magic.

Ygor appears. "He just do what I tell him—always!" boasts Ygor. Before Wolf, Ygor orders the monster, who pathetically follows his directions to come and go. Wolf hopes to experiment more—but Ygor will have none of it.

"He's well enough for me," snarls Ygor, "AND YOU NO TOUCH HIM AGAIN!"

As Wolf watches in horror, Ygor laughs wickedly, patting the monster's huge chest. The musical score soars into a theme of evil enchantment. And Karloff's monster looks at his broken-necked friend, his sad face reflecting— love.

*   *   *

The *Son of Frankenstein* stage was the talk of Universal City, the circus sideshow of the lot. The shooting of this movie was also the closest that Boris Karloff and Bela Lugosi would ever become.

Everybody at Universal wanted to visit the soundstage of *Son of Franken-stein*. Even the "Queen," Deanna Durbin, paid a call, and Edgar Bergen and Charlie McCarthy, then sparring with W.C. Fields on *You Can't Cheat an Honest Man*, took time to parry playful insults at Karloff and Lugosi. Universal's PR office fielded a deluge of requests for passes to the set—mainly from females, yearning for a look at the monster and Ygor. One lady who visited, Elizabeth Copeland, reported in her column, *Reel News from Hollywood:*

> It would be a sight for all of you to have gone to the studio at 4 P.M. every day during the shooting of the picture to see Karloff, Bela Lugosi and Basil Rathbone drinking tea. . . .
> Karloff in his fantastic makeup balanced a cup and saucer on his knee, look-ing like a demon from the pit and conversed smilingly with the cast in a voice that sounds like it is emerging from a correct English drawing room. . . . Lugosi wasn't a bit less hideous. He has the role in the picture of a broken necked shepherd. Except for his piercing eyes, his features are mostly concealed by a matted beard and unkempt hair. Lugosi's continental bearing, his Chester-fieldian manners and his meticulous grammar, were somewhat out of keeping with his appearance. . . .
> Little 4-year old Donnie Dunagan . . . wasn't afraid of any of them, although he didn't like the whiskers on Lugosi's face. He shied away from them the first two days on the set, but he soon became accustomed to them and before the picture was half over, he was sitting on their laps and regarding them as his pals. . . .

As Lee mischievously and defiantly fought the front office, Boris and Bela became relaxed with each other. "On the set," reported Copeland, "each displays a surprising sense of humor. Karloff's is of the dry, English variety. Lugosi's is more along American lines." The stars laughed to the press about their fan mail. Bela quoted a letter that went, "Recently I saw a revival of *Dracula* and it was like seeing an old friend again. If one can call *Dracula* a friend." Boris quoted one of his recent missives: "Dear Mr. Karloff. I am 12 ½ years old. You don't scare me!"

For once, the actors were playing misfit friends, not arch foes. On the *Son of Frankenstein*, a friendship appeared to be growing, solidly and surely. And then a very happy event occurred that seemed to cinch it.

On November 23, 1938, Boris Karloff turned 51, and the *Son of Franken-stein* gang had a surprise for him. Lee set up the famous pantomime scene, with Karloff stalking up behind Rathbone, and placing his arm on Basil's shoulder. Rathbone moved—and there, on a laboratory table, was a giant birthday cake! Boris beamed. Rathbone and Bela surrounded him, all three smiling and laughing as the photographers had a proverbial field day.

However, November 23, 1938, was another special day for Boris Karloff: that morning, wife Dorothy gave birth to their daughter, Sara Jane, at Hollywood Hospital. The monster heard the news—and broke into tears. The *Los Angeles Examiner* reported:

Rathbone (left) and Lugosi flank Karloff at his surprise birthday party, November 23, 1938, on the set of *Son of Frankenstein.*

> Elated at the news that he was a father, Boris Karloff rushed off the set of his new picture yesterday and appeared in Hollywood Hospital still wearing his makeup. After reassuring nurses and attendants that he was not a man from Mars, Karloff saw his baby daughter for the first time. . . .

Naturally, Universal took note of Boris's absence, and responded in kind in M.F. Murphy's production report of November 26, 1938:

> This unit was forced to change plans last Wednesday, due to the absence of Boris Karloff because of the birth of his first born. Fortunately, the company was able to carry on without Karloff and Dan Kelley has made arrangements to obtain the gratis services of Karloff on the last day of his engagement in lieu of the one day he was absent. . .

Bela Lugosi was delighted for Boris. The next week, Bela, Lillian, and 10-month old Bela, Jr., visited the *Son of Frankenstein* set with a present for baby Sara Jane. Years ago, Lillian Lugosi showed me her wonderful scrapbook, with pages of photographs from *Son of Frankenstein*. There was "Ygor,"

looking proud as could be of his wife and baby son; there was "the monster," sans sheepskin jersey, relaxing in his visible body padding and suspenders, smiling widely as he accepted the gift. There was something wonderfully warm about Karloff and the Lugosis on those snapshots; and there, on a full page, was the famous still (it had appeared in the January 9, 1939, *Life* magazine) of little Bela, Jr., standing under the feet of Karloff, just about to burst into tears. It was autographed:

"To Bela Jr. — from his friend, the Monster — Boris Karloff."

As shooting ran into the Christmas season, Lee assured the front office that all would be completed by Christmas Eve. Then he promised that December 28 would be the completion date, but that he would finish up with Rathbone ("and some other principals") by Christmas Eve night. Meanwhile, both first-time fathers, each looking forward greatly to baby's first Christmas, worked closely: meeting early every morning in Jack Pierce's makeup studio, acting on the set, the camaraderie transferring to their scenes.

They had never been so close. A few months later, Bela, in New York before sailing to Europe for *Dark Eyes of London,* gave Hy Gardner an interview.

"I became a daddy 14 months ago," boasted Bela, "and I've never been happier."

Gardner remarked that Boris Karloff had become a father of a baby girl.

"Yes, he did," said Bela. "We often get together and talk about when our children grow up and how nice it would be if they fell in love with each other."

*   *   *

Although this unit worked on Christmas Eve until 6:15 P.M. (a somewhat unusual procedure for this day of the year when all studio work as a rule stops at noon), all our plans and calculations of last week were entirely shattered by Lee not living up to promises made of finishing this production Wednesday, December 28. Rathbone and other high-salaried players, whom we had expected to close on the payroll Christmas Eve, had their engagements extended over the Holiday until December 28th and 29th. In addition to this, unexpected demands were made upon us for sets and various other requirements which we had no way of contemplating in advance due to lack of script. And so our approved budget of $347,000 on this production proves up as nothing more than a guess figure and a rather poor one at that. . . .

With the exception of Karloff, Lugosi, and Donnie Dunagan (nominal salaried child actor), the entire cast was closed out as of December 29th. It is now expected shooting will continue until Wednesday, January 4. . . .

— production report from M.F. Murphy, December 31, 1938

Opposite: **Boris Karloff and Bela Lugosi, Jr., on the set of *Son of Frankenstein.***

There was very little peace-on-earth or goodwill toward Rowland V. Lee in Universal's front office come Christmas, 1938. The stars went home with the Yuletide bonus of extended engagements, while the studio despaired how to meet the soaring cost and the shipping date for release. Still, there was no doubt about how impressively Lee's work was shaping up in the "dailies" in the screening room.

Ewald Neumuller drives his cart past Castle Frankenstein. High in the tower, Ygor and the monster peer down at him—and as Neumuller rides under a tree on a mountain road, the monster, with a gracefully acrobatic move, swings from the branch of a tree with one hand—strangling Neumuller with the other. Then he places the body on the road, and leads the horses and cart over it. . . .

Benson is missing in Castle Frankenstein. "He went up to the nursery for the baby's supper tray," says Fritz, a servant spying for Krogh, "and we haven't seen him since!" Wolf suspects Ygor, and goes to the laboratory, where the rogue is patting the monster, plagued by a nightmare. Ygor plays innocence regarding Benson.

"I *scare* him to death," laughs Ygor. "I don't have to *kill* him to death!"

Night. Ygor sits in the castle tower, playing his shepherd's horn. The monster pays a call in the village. He slyly pulls down the blind in the tobacco shop of Emil Lang. We see the shadow of Lang, sitting under his cloak; he senses something behind him, rises, turns, and. . .

The villagers are in an uproar. They storm the castle gates, as Krogh meets Wolf on the steps of the castle. As Krogh lights a cigarette—wedging the matchbox on his gloved wooden "finger" as he strikes a match—a cat-and-mouse game begins, Atwill making Wolf listen to the bloodthirsty crowd at the gate,* and hounding Rathbone (who now surrenders to some ripe overacting).

Nevertheless, Wolf visits the laboratory. He sees the sleeping monster. Fearing the worst, giving up his dream of vindicating his father, the son of Frankenstein picks up a rock—and is about to crush the monster's skull.

"No touch him, Frankenstein!" shouts Ygor. "No touch him, or something happens to you—*worse* than dying!" Bela is marvelous as Ygor exults his guilt: "Eight men say—Ygor hang. Now—eight men deaaad! All dead!" Wolf orders him off the estate, but Ygor refuses, Bela ranting like some awful child with a temper tantrum.

"He's *mine*. He no belong to you. *You* go away—not *me!*" The monster snarls and rises, and grabs Wolf by the throat, in support of his friend. Ygor intervenes—with a sinister smile.

Curiously, a guard at the gate is Ward Bond, who had a great year in 1939, playing major roles in John Ford's Young Mr. Lincoln and Drums Along the Mohawk, as well as character parts in such films as Gone with the Wind. Here, he's glimpsed only for a bit, and has one line, to Lugosi: "Ygor! Shut up! You've been playing that thing all night!" Could more footage have been filmed of Bond, and left on the cutting room floor?

Back in the castle, Krogh keeps his hat on — he has officially placed Wolf under arrest. Krogh dismisses Ygor as the murderer — after all, wasn't he up in the castle tower, playing his horn, at the time of the murders? Still, with Krogh's permission, Wolf visits the laboratory, with his pistol. Ygor, suspecting the worst, attacks fitfully, and throws his hammer at the hero. Wolf shoots him dead.

Wolf boasts to Krogh that he "got rid" of Ygor.

"How did you get rid of him?"

"I killed him! . . . What are you going to do about it?"

"Compliment you. For it was undoubtedly he who killed Benson!"

Wolf is at a loss for words, but Krogh is not. He has found Benson's body in a secret passageway, off the nursery. Little Peter had told him the monster came through the wall. Benson's watch had been found in the possession of Peter — a gift to him from "the giant." Boiling, Atwill's Krogh rips into one of the dramatic joys of the movie:

> But Ygor didn't do it. Nor did you! Nor was it done by any ghost! There's a monster afoot, and you know it! He's in your control! By heaven, I think you're a worse fiend than your father. Where is this monster? Where is he? I'll stay by your side until you confess. And if you don't I'll feed you to the villagers — like the Romans fed Christians to the lions!

And out in the laboratory, the monster sees Ygor on the floor. He kneels tenderly over him; fearful, like a small, frightened child, he moans, and rocks back and forth on his knees. Then he sees blood.

In one of the classic vignettes of all horror movies, Karloff's heartbroken monster looks up — and screams.

The most classic scene of Karloff's monster is in the 1931 film, when Karloff looks toward the heavens, and reaches so pitifully for the ray of sun from the skylight. "It was as though man," Karloff had said so beautifully of his monster, "had been deserted by his God."

And now, in Karloff's farewell monster performance, the star hits this profound chord again, kneeling over the dead Ygor, looking to the sky and unleashing that heartrending scream. The God who did not make him does not reply — and Karloff's abandoned monster plays a wild, final *Son of Frankenstein* act that is unforgettable. . .

Karloff's monster roars through the smoky old laboratory, madly destroying the works of his creator and the son of his creator, hurling the giant operating table into the sulphur pit which encouragingly flames and explodes, howling and storming and giving Frankenstein's monster his last great showcase in the movies. It is a super, awesomely bitter climax to Karloff's monster portrayals, as if he's hysterically defying God himself to acknowledge him; and Karloff, who realized by now he would never play his "dear old monster" again, gave the episode everything he had.

Then he sees Peter's fairy tale book. The monster grins an evil smile, crumples the book in his hands—and conceives his plan for revenge.

Wolf and Krogh are playing darts; Atwill carries them by sticking them into his wooden arm. Amelia screams. The monster kidnaps Peter and takes him through the passageway—to the laboratory. Elsa, losing her cool totally, screams magnificently (only Evelyn Ankers of the Frankenstein heroines emitted a better yell) and runs to the laboratory, as do Wolf and Krogh. The action is almost choreographic, the music thrilling, and what a climax!

The monster and Peter climb to the sulphur pit. The monster raises Peter to throw him into the sulphur pit, but he cannot do it. "Here we are," says trusting Peter, who offers to help his "giant" friend and erstwhile murderer up to the platform.

Krogh reaches the laboratory, through the passageway; Wolf, the screaming Elsa and Amelia are trapped outside, the door blocked by wreckage from the monster's wrath. As Krogh goes for his gun, the monster roars, reaches—and, in sinister irony, rips off the inspector's wooden arm! Pinning Peter under his boot, the enraged monster waves Krogh's destroyed wooden arm like a club, as the inspector fires bullet after bullet into him. Wolf, meanwhile, has climbed up the walls of the laboratory, and in through the wrecked roof.

"Daddy! Daddy!" cries Peter.

And Basil Rathbone, who always wanted to be a movie hero, performs his greatest heroic stunt: he swings down on a chain, à la Tarzan, and to a climax in the music, he kicks the creature, knocking the screaming monster into the 800-degree sulphur pit, for his third and most magnificent demise.

Wolf and Krogh look down into the blazing pit, and see the monster sinking.* Elsa and Wolf embrace their son.

The epilogue shows the Frankenstein family at the village train station. Wolf's climactic heroics apparently absolved him of any guilt in the deaths of Neumuller and Lang; and, for penance, he has deeded the castle and estates of Frankenstein to the village.

"And may happiness, and peace of mind, be restored to you all," says Wolf. "Goodbye!"

The villagers cheer. The family boards the train. And, as the Burgomeister and surviving Gentlemen of the Council call their goodbyes, Inspector Krogh—with his new prosthesis—snaps his farewell salute.

*   *   *

As Rowland V. Lee completed his last few days of shooting with Boris, Bela, and Donnie Dunagan, work was already progressing literally round the

---

* *The fall into the pit was performed by stuntman Bud Wolfe, who also played the robot in Lugosi's 1939 Universal serial,* The Phantom Creeps. *The cry, however, is a re-recording of the scream Boris unleashed beside the dead Ygor.*

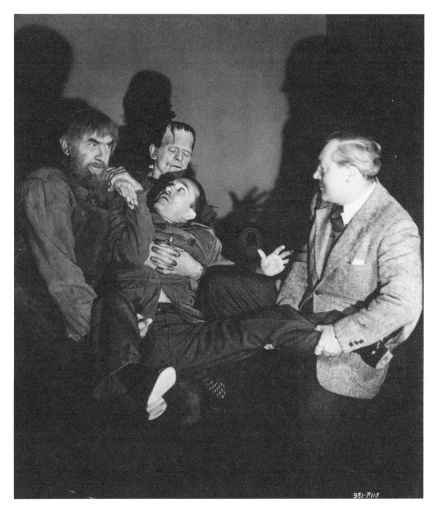

Hijinks on the set of *Son of Frankenstein:* **Bela and Boris take their revenge on makeup wizard Jack P. Pierce, while director Rowland V. Lee referees.**

clock in the editing and scoring departments on the completed scenes of *Son of Frankenstein.* Lee had promised to complete the production Wednesday, January 4, 1939 — three days before Universal planned to preview the picture.

At 1:15 a.m., Thursday, January 5, 1939, Rowland V. Lee completed *Son of Frankenstein.*

> Produced on a vast scale, *Son of Frankenstein* presents the most fearsome cast in the History of the Screen!
> — from the trailer for *Son of Frankenstein*

The final days of *Son of Frankenstein* had been total mayhem. Frank Skinner, composer of the score, and Hans J. Salter, who orchestrated it, found themselves virtually prisoners of the studio as they raced frantically to compose and score the film. "I remember," Salter told *Cinefantastique,* "there was one stretch, pretty close to the recording date, where we didn't leave the studio for 48 or 50 hours." Skinner would compose a sequence, while Salter napped on a couch; then Salter would orchestrate it while Skinner napped. Overtime rolled in all departments, and the musical score itself ran $5000 over budget.

However, on Saturday, January 7, 1939, M.F. Murphy triumphantly reported:

> What appeared to be an impossibility has been accomplished and all credit should be given Maurice Pivar and his Editorial Department, Charles Previn and his Music Department, and Bernard Brown and his Sound Department for making it possible to preview this picture tonight and ship the first group of prints on the scheduled dates next week. This is an unbelievable accomplishment . . .

In rushing the picture for preview and release, some cuts were made, and additional recutting took place on the first prints. Legend notes that Dwight Frye was consigned to the cutting room floor in footage as an angry villager; other odd, assorted scenes have shown up in a renegade print of *Son of Frankenstein,* shown at the Vagabond Theatre in Los Angeles in 1976.*

The original *Frankenstein* had been shot in 35 days, at a cost of $291,129.13; *Bride of Frankenstein* had been shot in 46 days, at a cost of $397,023.79. *Son of Frankenstein* tied *Bride's* shooting schedule — 46 days — but surpassed *Bride's* cost with a final tab of $420,000, establishing itself as Universal's most expensive horror show of that era. Lee had defied Universal by going over budget by 19 days and $120,000.

No figures are available on the respective salaries of Karloff and Lugosi. However, if Karloff received his usual weekly fee of $3750, his *Son of Frankenstein* salary was about $30,000. If Bela got his Lillian-reported, cut-rate fee of $500 per week, he earned about $4000.

Now Universal was hell-bent on recouping its investment. The surviving trailer for *Son of Frankenstein* reveals the rush of preparing the film for release; it features Waxman's score from *Bride of Frankenstein* (and even a mob shot from Whale's film!), and discarded footage from *Son* — a long shot of laboratory sequence given close shots in the release print. Still, the trailer proclaimed the movie's powerhouse cast:

---

*In the print: a scene of Josephine Hutchinson, sensing something is wrong in Peter's bedroom, rushing in and nearly catching Ygor spying; a scene of Ygor and the monster, roaming through a castle passageway as Wolf tells Benson that the monster is alive; some scenes of the Burgomeister leading the mob; and a shot of Rathbone brooding in his library before Atwill interrogates him.

BASIL RATHBONE — In his heart, warm human emotions.
In his mind — the Monster Mania!
KARLOFF — Rising from the past to spread new terror!
LUGOSI — Sinister — Mysterious — Evil!
LIONEL ATWILL — Grim hatred in his blood!

It was an effective trailer; when the Byrd Theatre of Richmond, Virginia, ran the coming attraction, a gentleman complained that his sons couldn't sleep afterwards.

The *Son of Frankenstein* posters baited crowds with lurid lines:

ALL NEW! . . . FIVE TIMES AS THRILLING AS FRANKENSTEIN — A shadowy hand reached out of the past . . . But its touch was REAL! . . . Transformed Terror . . . Dormant for 20 years . . . Unleashed by this Half-Man Half-Demon . . . Plagued by the mania of his Father . . . The Monster Maker!

On Friday, January 13, 1939 — less than nine days after Lee completed the film — Universal premiered *Son of Frankenstein* at the Hollywood Pantages Theatre. Fortunately, for everybody, the 99-minute result surpassed all of Universal's expectations; *Son of Frankenstein* was a glorious smash hit, and the *Los Angeles Examiner* reported:

Did you ever see a nightmare walking? That's Frankenstein's little monster, Boris Karloff, back again to scare the mischief out of kids and grownups in *Son of Frankenstein*. . . . He has a "buddy," Ygor . . . played to the hilt by Bela Lugosi. . . . Sets, photography and acting are all calculated to carry out the creepy effects. Makeup of Karloff is still superb. His appearance, and that of the broken-necked Ygor, will stick in your memory. Lionel Atwill is outstanding. . . .

On January 28, 1939, *Son of Frankenstein* opened at New York's Rivoli Theatre, Broadway at 49th Street. There were some big shows in town, including 20th Century–Fox's Technicolor blockbuster *Jesse James* at the Roxy, and RKO's *Gunga Din* at Radio City Music Hall. "Filmdom's Fearful Four!" proclaimed publicity as *Son of Frankenstein* packed the Rivoli, playing special "Midnite Shows." Universal soon took a trade advertisement, heralding how *Son of Frankenstein* broke all studio records in Los Angeles, Boston, and Richmond. *Look* magazine ran a pictorial spread of the movie, and the *New York Times* published a long interview with Jack P. Pierce.

Michelangelo had his "David," Auguste Rodin had his "Thinker," and Jack Pierce has profited by their example. He has his "Frankenstein Monster." If this be sculpture, Pierce is making the most of it. Using the unfortunate Boris Karloff again for a lay figure, he reconstructed the good gray monster for a third time in Universal's *Son of Frankenstein*. . . . And thereby hangs a tale, which is about the only thing Bela Lugosi does not wear in the picture. . . .

As *Son of Frankenstein* broke box office records, the antihorror vigilantes stormed in protest. The California Congress of Parents and Teachers, for one, ranted:

> Not recommended for any audience is this horror picture which returns to the screen the monster of two previous pictures. Although well produced and well acted, the subject matter is gruesome, unnatural and revolting. There are several violent deaths, objectionable mob scenes, and the whole has an atmosphere of ominous foreboding that is nerve wracking.

Son of Frankenstein, however, was too powerful a hit — so powerful, in fact, that the movie stormed England, where it defied the "H" certificate. "Grand Guignol melodrama," reported Britain's *The Cinema,* "all colorfully emphasized by Karloff's characterization of hideous monster who yet inspires pang of pity, and Bela Lugosi's portrait of misshapen and crazy fiend. Whenever the pair are together the incident is interesting indeed."

All in all, *Son of Frankenstein* raised from the dead the horror genre. The movie's box office performance, along with such hits as the W.C. Fields/Edgar Bergen and Charlie McCarthy *You Can't Cheat an Honest Man,* Deanna Durbin's *Three Smart Girls Grow Up* and Bing Crosby's *East Side of Heaven,* aided Universal in reaping a $1,000,000 profit for 1939 — the first year of profit in front office memory. By front office decree, Deanna Durbin would have to coexist with horror movies.

Boris Karloff had more offers than he could handle. Continuing his *Mr. Wong* series for Monogram, Boris won the role of Mord, the bald-pated, club-footed Executioner in Universal's *Tower of London,* toplined by Basil Rathbone's Richard III and produced/directed by Rowland V. Lee; he also began his "Mad Doctor" series at Columbia with *The Man They Could Not Hang.* Bela Lugosi signed a multipicture contract with Universal, commencing with the starring spot in the studio's 1939 serial, *The Phantom Creeps.* He also joined Lionel Atwill as a red herring in 20th Century-Fox's *The Gorilla,* with the Ritz Brothers; visited England to star in *Dark Eyes of London* (aka *The Human Monster*); and played the supporting part of the Commissar in MGM's *Ninotchka,* enjoying what was virtually every Hollywood actor's dream — a scene with Garbo.

And what of Rowland V. Lee? Universal's recalcitrant producer/director began shooting *The Sun Never Sets* on March 13, 1939 — with only 30 pages of revised final script. Studio reports note that Lee had "definitely promised" to complete this silly melodrama (which pitted brothers Basil Rathbone and Douglas Fairbanks, Jr., against warmonger Lionel Atwill) "within a figure of $525,000." Lee finished the film May 3, began shooting additional scenes May 18, and finished *The Sun Never Sets* at a cost of $586,000. Lee began *Tower of London,* starring Rathbone and Karloff, August 11, 1939, on a 36-day schedule and a $490,000 budget; he finished the film October 4 (10 days over schedule), only to insist again on additional scenes, completing the picture at a cost of $577,000.

Departing Universal, Lee made only a few more films: United Artists' *The Son of Monte Cristo* (1940), starring Louis Hayward, Joan Bennett and George Sanders; RKO's *Powder Town* (1942), starring Victor McLaglen; UA's *The Bridge of San Luis Rey* (1944), based on Thornton Wilder's best-seller; and UA's 1945 *Captain Kidd*, starring Charles Laughton. He retired ("All the fun had gone out of making pictures"), but came back to produce 1959's *The Big Fisherman*, based on the Lloyd C. Douglas religious novel. Frank Borzage directed, but the film (which Lee coscripted with Howard Estabrook) was a failure. Lee retired to Palm Desert, with his wife of over 40 years, Eleanor. "I greet each day and thank God for my wonderful experiences in the movie industry," wrote Lee late in life.

Rowland V. Lee died in Palm Desert December 21, 1975, at the age of 84.*

* * *

This starkly stylish film, which features Karloff's third and last appearance as the monster, sparked off the new spate of horror movies that ran through the early forties. . . . Lugosi gives one of his very best performances. . . . Slow the film may be, but it has a kind of architectural solidity that matches the dreamlike labyrinthine massiveness of the sets (designed as a sort of realistic equivalent to UFA expressionism), and builds to a stunning climax as the monster, at bay on the brink of the sulphur pit into which he will be toppled by Rathbone, still with his foot clamped firmly on the hostage body of the latter's son, once more rips Atwill's (false) arm out by the roots.
— from *The Encyclopedia of Horror Movies,* edited by Phil Hardy

The 1931 *Frankenstein* is about souls, blasphemy, the dynamics of an alcoholic young actor named Colin Clive, and the beauty of a 43-year-old British black sheep born William Henry Pratt. 1935's *Bride of Frankenstein* is about theatricality, misanthropy, the cinema's most infamous female monster, and the wonder that a beloved actor could create as Mary Shelley's hapless monster. Both films, too, were about James Whale — the feminine beauty of his visual sense; his wonderful theatricality mixed with pioneering, filmic style; his sly, wicked humor; and finally, his own sense of isolation, alienation, bitterness.

The audacious Whale had taken the monster about as far as he truly could go; indeed, in *Bride of Frankenstein,* the drinking, smoking, hiccuping

In February, 1939, Warner Bros. announced in the Hollywood Reporter *that Karloff would star in* The Return of Dr. X; *in March, the studio publicized plans to negotiate with Universal to costar Bela Lugosi with Karloff. But nothing came of the deal, and in May, the* Hollywood Reporter *noted that Humphrey Bogart was replacing James Stephenson as the lead of* The Return of Dr. X.

monster had tiptoed on the brink of burlesque. "There was not much left in the monster to be developed," Karloff had sadly stated; "we had reached his limits."

As such, Rowland V. Lee's *Son of Frankenstein* was a blessing. Via the new director's sense of epic, this movie respectfully treats the monster as a great legend, the classic ogre of a classic fairy tale. Rather than taxing the character with new dimensions that might have made the monster ludicrous or laughable, it surrounds him with reverent backdrops — the ancestral castle, the wonderfully smoky laboratory, the bleak, misty countryside. Here, the monster is like a hallowed relic in a macabre cathedral, showcased with reverence; yet he enjoys enough meaty scenes — the pantomime, the murders, and classic climax — to make the role worthy and rich. True, there isn't the Whale miracle of the evolving monster, the cinema's most horrific baby; certainly *Son* has none of the eccentric, quirky genius of the first two misadventures. However, never has the monster loomed so legendary as he does in *Son of Frankenstein;* and nor would he ever again — at Universal, or anywhere else. (Oddly, Mel Brooks' 1973 *Young Frankenstein,* described by the director as a "homage to James Whale," ended up resembling *Son of Frankenstein* more than the others.)

However, the true charm of *Son of Frankenstein,* the most classic element, is that the monster (long separated from the hermit of *Bride of Frankenstein*) has, at last, found a friend. And in Bela Lugosi's Ygor, Karloff's monster has found an almost perfect friend. True, Ygor cruelly uses the monster for vengeance; yet, they exist in the same fantastic, fairy tale realm: both horrific to the eye, both despised, both bitter, and — most of all — both children. With his merry eyes, scruffiness, sly humor, and that Hungarian baby talk ("I scare him to death! I don't have to kill him to death!"), Ygor is an ideal companion for the lonely, unhappy, ever-forlorn monster, who loves him. And this makes the most powerful scene of *Son of Frankenstein,* the monster howling over Ygor's dead body, all the more emotional — and magnificent.

Of course, the fact that Karloff and Lugosi are playing these roles makes it all the more legendary, all the more powerful. In past films, the stars climactically turned on each other; but in *Son of Frankenstein,* they are unholy allies. And as Ygor cackles and pats the monster's chest, as the two gargoyles peek down from the castle tower at a prospective victim, as the monster cries over Ygor's corpse, the two stars are at their very finest, transcending the realm of horror to create two of the most splendid misfits of Hollywood history.

Basil Rathbone, as the highly-strung, heroic Wolf, made himself a major star of the horror genre for all time (much to his later shock) via *Son of Frankenstein.* Lionel Atwill, as his most floridly bizarre, created his most famous role as the one-armed Krogh (so memorably lampooned by Kenneth Mars in *Young Frankenstein,* as Inspector Kemp, with wooden arm and monocle over his eyepatch). Rathbone and Atwill provide classic characters in *Son of Frankenstein,* generating their own sympathy; the villagers, too, are less barbaric than in Whale's films.

Yet, in the end, the overwhelming sympathy still goes to the monster and Ygor, to Karloff and Lugosi, whose genius made these villains of *Son of Frankenstein* two of the best-loved visitors to our movie-inspired nightmares.

*   *   *

In November, 1987, Universal/MCA had just discovered an "uncut" lavender printing negative of *Son of Frankenstein,* long forgotten in the Library of Congress. In the summer of 1988, MCA Home Video was debating whether or not to release the familiar version of this beloved horror movie, or to release the "uncut" version, which runs only slightly longer.

Of greater fascination, however, were the rumors about Universal's discovery of the long-lost, legendary Technicolor makeup tests for *Son of Frankenstein.* Originally, MCA claimed the test no longer existed. Then came a well-circulated account that Universal *had* found the Technicolor tests — only to drop them in an unmarked film can and accidentally sent them back East, where the tests were reportedly lost in a New Jersey warehouse the size of a football stadium.

However, in August of 1988, Mike Fitzgerald of MCA Video confirmed to me that the *Son of Frankenstein* Technicolor tests *had* been found — by Mike Frend of the American Film Institute. Karloff and Lugosi fans greeted the news like the discovery of King Tut's tomb, and Fitzgerald promised that the Technicolor tests will be packaged eventually — perhaps with the future Home Video release of *Son of Frankenstein.*

Then came word that the Technicolor test footage had disappeared — again! And, on April 13, 1989, MCA Home Video released the traditional 99-minute *Son of Frankenstein.*

10
Black Friday, 1940

Isn't it amazing? *The Wolf Man,* for example — a 1941 film! I wish I had 1 percent of its profits. I made about $2800 for writing it, and the studio must have made millions upon millions of dollars on the damn thing.

But, I don't mind. Writers care about their stories, not money. Besides, when *The Wolf Man* and all those other horror movies I wrote come on television and I look at the credits, most of those guys are dead, and I am alive. So!
— Curt Siodmak, author of *Black Friday, The Wolf Man, Donovan's Brain,* etc.

"IT'S TIME for HIT TIME!" trumpeted Universal's spread in the 1939 *Film Daily Yearbook.* In the wake of box office hits like *Son of Frankenstein,* the studio was operating at full blast in the midsummer of 1939, defying an historic heat wave.

In was on August 11, 1939, that Rowland V. Lee began filming *Tower of London.* For this medieval melodrama, a new landmark arose on Universal's back lot: the Tower set, still standing today. Inside the castle courtyard was Karloff, as Mord, bloodthirsty executioner, in bald pate and club foot, wielding a giant axe and yearning to kill "in hot blood"! Basil Rathbone, as crookbacked Richard III, and a crowd of sweltering costumed extras, all watched in the gallery as Karloff leered. Vincent Price enjoyed his first movie melodrama role here as the doomed Clarence — drowned in a vat of wine by the star villains.

"Jimmy" Whale was back on the Universal lot (albeit temporarily), directing a ridiculous Inca temple headhunter saga titled *Green Hell,* which began shooting August 21. It was a big, $700,000 production, with a magnificent jungle set which took over one of Universal's largest stages. However, despite a cast featuring Douglas Fairbanks, Jr., Joan Bennett, George Sanders and Vincent Price, *Green Hell* would prove a disaster. Audiences would laugh so raucously that Whale fled the preview in Oakland, and Harvard would vote *Green Hell* Worst Film of 1940.

"Most of us," Mr. Fairbanks once told me, "agreed!"

On September 7, 1939, Universal began shooting *Destry Rides Again,* a $750,000 Joseph Pasternak production, and one of the great wild west melodramas of all time. Marlene Dietrich's Frenchy — primping before her mirror in bonnet and corset, cat-fighting with Una Merkel, belting out "See

What the Boys in the Back Room Will Have" in cowgirl costume — is unforgettable; James Stewart, as the pacifist gunfighter Destry, found one of his most winning characterizations, and Brian Donlevy, slick, evil, hat cocked back over his toupee, was (as ever) the perfect saloon villain. *Destry Rides Again* was filming during the peak of the heat spell, and Miss Dietrich would relax between takes, rolling down her stockings and bathing her feet in a tub of cold water. . . .

It was the best of times at Universal. And, to keep the ball rolling, along with serials like Lugosi's *The Phantom Creeps* and a fresh batch of Walter Lantz Andy Panda cartoons, the studio wanted a new program of horror movies.

*   *   *

Today, Curt Siodmak is a feisty, candid survivor of Hollywood and German cinema. The legendary octogenerian author/director of fantasy–horror–science fiction lives on the Old South Fork Ranch, in the mountains of Three Rivers, California. "Every night I say "Heil Hitler!" says the salty Siodmak, "because without that son-of-a-bitch, I'd still be in Berlin!" After exploits in Germany (where he wrote 1933's science fiction classic *FP1 Antwortet Nicht* for UFA, based on his novel), France (1935's *La Crise Est Finie*), and England (1935's *Transatlantic Tunnel*), Siodmak came to the United States, where he won his greatest fame as author of *The Wolf Man* screenplay and the classic 1943 novel *Donovan's Brain*. Brother of the late-lamented director Robert Siodmak (1900–1973), Curt Siodmak is proud of the popularity of his vintage horror films:

> Yah, they hold up. They were classic tales; the violence was implied, the menace was implied. It wasn't like today, where you cut people open and see the blood flying all over the floor. We only had the menace — which was much more tempting and frightening.

Siodmak first visited Universal for *The Invisible Man Returns,* which starred Vincent Price as the Invisible One and a host of special effects Siodmak had cunningly defied John P. Fulton to create. The movie started shooting October 9, 1939, with a budget of $253,750. The trick shots caused problems; perfectionist Fulton's final effects cleared the laboratory on the night of December 22, and *The Invisible Man Returns* ran about $16,000 over budget. (Still, Martin Murphy was quick to point out to the front office that Whale's 1933 *The Invisible Man,* "made six years ago, when the cost of operations was much more economical than at present," had cost approximately $312,000.)

Still, in the tradition of Universal, the top names of horror were Karloff and Lugosi. In the wake of *Son of Frankenstein,* Universal desired a new vehicle for the stars — and called on Siodmak to create a script.

The result (coscripted with Eric Taylor) was *Friday the Thirteenth,* later
retitled *Black Friday*—an intriguing precursor to Siodmak's masterwork,
Donovan's Brain. Siodmak had (and has) very definite opinions on the men for
whom he was fashioning the screenplay:

On Karloff: "He was very, very nice—very soft-spoken, and he loved to
read children's stories to little boys and girls. . ."

On Lugosi: "He could never act his way out of a paper bag!"

As Siodmak recalls, Lugosi was "a pest," who implored him repeatedly
to use his influence at Universal to get him meaty parts. In the tradition of
Universal, Siodmak had little respect for Lugosi, artistically or personally.

"How can a Hungarian be a nice guy?" laughs Siodmak.

Brain-swapping was not an entirely new idea. Universal, it will be
remembered, had toyed with it in an early draft of *The Black Cat,* and
Gaumont-British had pioneered the concept cinematically in Karloff's 1936
The Man Who Lived Again. Curt Siodmak, however, would parlay brain
transplants into a melodramatic fine art and a virtual career trademark—
while, in *Black Friday,* simultaneously fashioning two marvelous roles for
Karloff and Lugosi.* For Boris, the writer created the part of Dr. George
Kingsley—a gentle, aesthetic professor of English literature, transformed by
a brain transplant into a Jekyll/Hyde monster who permutates back and forth
from Kingsley to a bloodthirsty gangster named Red Cannon. For Bela, the
screenplay offered the part of Dr. Ernest Sovac—a European refugee, whose
scientific mania causes the operation and perpetuates the tragedy as he hopes
to get Cannon's hidden $500,000 so to create his own research center.

Burt Kelly, who had been producing Jackie Cooper vehicles for Universal, was associate producer. Arthur Lubin, who had joined Universal in 1937
and would win glory as director of such all-time Universal hits as Abbott and
Costello's *Buck Privates,* the 1943 *Phantom of the Opera,* and the *Francis the Talking
Mule* series, was set to direct. The front office smoothly cast the supporting
parts from the studio contract roster: Anne Nagel, a fine brunette actress—

---

*The first draft of the script differed in several aspects. The story opened at the State Hospital for the
Criminal Insane, where Dr. Ernest Sovac is an inmate. One Dr. Small reads Sovac's notorious medical
diary to three other doctors, and the story (as in the released film) plunges into flashback. The top gangster
here is named Red Banning (not Red Cannon); after Kingsley is run down by the gangsters, Sovac argues
at the hospital with a Dr. Warner about brain transplantation. "I was chief surgeon at the Franz Joseph
Hospital in Vienna," says Sovac—exposition missing in the final film; Warner arrogantly reminds him
that he is only an intern in America, not a surgeon, and has no right to operate. Afer the first murder,
Sovac goes to a newspaper morgue and learns about the $500,000.*

*In the original script, the primary gangster is Miller (not Marnay). Also, after Miller's death in
the broom closet, Sovac had meaty dialogue, telling daughter Jean that the human brain requires 300 years
of life to achieve full development. If one transplanted the brain of an old scientist into the head of a child,
again and again, that brain could solve the riddle of the cosmos and bring happiness to all mankind.*

*At the film's close, Dr. Small completes reading the diary, and it's clear that Sovac has won no allies.
Sovac is outside, waiting with Jean, and "his whole bearing radiates the egotistic superiority of the insane."
As he goes in to hear the verdict, Jean, "bleak and hopeless," instinctively knowing the outcome, leaves
quietly.*

Ad for *Black Friday,* **Universal, 1940.**

perhaps best remembered as the nightgowned heroine leered at by Lionel Atwill and carried off by Lon Chaney, Jr., in 1941's *Man-Made Monster* — received the role of Sunny, Red Cannon's chanteuse moll; Anne Gwynne, Universal's Texas-born ingenue who became one of the lot's most attractive fixtures of the war years, played Sovac's daughter, Jean.

As Christmas approached, Universal looked forward to what promised to be a very effective Karloff and Lugosi chiller. And then something very strange happened. There was a change in roles.

For reasons never clarified by the studio, Karloff vacated the Jekyll/Hyde Kingsley role. Suddenly, he took Lugosi's Sovac part, a role reminiscent of the "Mad Doctor" series he had just begun at Columbia with 1939's *The Man They Could Not Hang.* Curt Siodmak states most definitely why this happened:

> Karloff didn't want to play the dual role in *Black Friday.* He was afraid of it . . . It was too intricate . . . Karloff was smart enough to know that he might not come off too well in the role . . .

Siodmak's statement is controversial among Karloff fans. True, Karloff was one of the screen's most versatile character stars, toplining nine releases in 1940; he ultimately played many kinds of challenging roles right up to the end of his life. However, in truth, Karloff was always a hoot in his early '30s gangster roles (catch him in Columbia's 1932 *Behind the Mask,* in derby and dark suit, smiling a cocky grin, smoking a cigar, and snapping at a nurse, "That's all right, baby. The doc expects me!"). His English accent and lisp made him quite the exotic gangster. Now, after years of the horror films, perhaps Karloff felt he no longer had the luxury of escaping type so dramatically; certainly, he must have had a hard time imagining himself flirting and smooching with Anne Nagle.

One must remember, too, that Karloff was a very humble actor; a man who, one year later, would walk through New York City all night, trying to concoct a graceful way of dropping out of his Broadway debut in *Arsenic and Old Lace,* which terrified him. Certainly no other explanation has been offered for the switch — which, of course, created a domino effect.

If Karloff took Sovac, could Lugosi play Kingsley?

Not according to Universal! Instead, the *Black Friday* company recruited Stanley Ridges (1892-1951), a British stage and screen actor of low profile. Ridges had recently played in Paramount's *If I Were King* (1938) and de Mille's *Union Pacific* (1939); he would be best remembered as the villainous Gestapo agent in 1942's *To Be or Not to Be.*

So — what for Lugosi? Since *Black Friday* was conceived as a Karloff and Lugosi picture, Universal tossed Bela the only male part of any size — Eric Marnay, Cannon's rival gangster. It was an embarrassingly secondary part — one which Lugosi would have bitterly scorned in palmier days; still, the humbled actor accepted. The fact that Karloff's humility had cost Lugosi a dynamic role hardly could have bettered his attitude toward his dominating costar.

Once again, Bela's pride was hurt, and whatever bond he had formed with Boris on *Son of Frankenstein* sadly crashed on the casting problems of *Black Friday.*

Black Friday was set to begin shooting three days after Christmas, 1939. So eager was Universal to keep the cost and shooting schedule as cheap and modest as possible that the major flaw of the recast *Black Friday* apparently didn't bother the producer, director, or the front office.

Karloff and Lugosi didn't share a single scene together.

*   *   *

Universal archives reveal a merciless front office attitude toward *Black Friday.* Once again, the studio, having paired Karloff and Lugosi, was traditionally determined to add as little else as possible in time, money, and studio resources. M.F. Murphy's report of December 30, 1939 stated:

> This picture started on Thursday, December 28, with an 18-day shooting schedule and an approved budget running $130,750. This schedule is particularly

tight, considering the number of stage moves necessary to take advantage of standing sets—there can be no elaboration or changes in our plans to meet schedule demands. The budget, being based upon this schedule, is comparatively just as conservative and will have to be watched most carefully in order not to run over....

At a time when the average cost of an "A" feature at the studio ran $500,000 to $750,000, *Black Friday's* budget was almost as absurdly small and its schedule as stringently tight as that of *The Black Cat* and *The Raven.*

Black Friday opens impressively. As the main titles appear, accompanied by Hans J. Salter's melodramatic music, a calendar madly sheds its pages— and ends on Friday the 13th. The film opens at the state prison: "SOVAC TO DIE IN CHAIR TODAY," shouts a newspaper headline, and we have a grim montage tour of the electrical paraphernalia all shiny and primed for the execution. Inside the prison, an ancient priest intones the Lord's Prayer; reminiscent of Warners' *The Walking Dead,* we see Karloff—now in a sleek gray wig, and dapper mustache—calmly walking the last mile. Inside the press room, Karloff's Dr. Ernest Sovac approaches one reporter (James Craig, who thereafter became an MGM star.

"I'd like you to have my notes and records," says Sovac. "Of all the newspapers, yours was the only one which was fair to me."

"Thanks, Doctor," says Craig, in his one line of the entire movie.

As Karloff's Sovac enters the death chamber, the notes reveal his tragedy in flashback. "I go to my death as a scientist," reads the records, "leaving behind this record with the hope that it will benefit mankind...."

It is Friday, June 13, at the University of Newcastle, a small, rural college. Dr. George Kingsley is lecturing to his English class. Stanley Ridges is dreamy, distracted, sporting pince-nez; instantly he suggests the clichéd image (although charmingly and winningly) of the absentminded professor. He recites a little 1547 poem about Friday the 13th, and claims it established its author as a poet of the first rank—"In fact, I should say he possibly was the *rankest* poet...!" He sadly announces to his class that he might not be back next term—he is to appear before a Board of Regents of a very large university in the East. "I sincerely hope the board does not like me," he tells his students.

As he leaves, Professor Kingsley is intercepted by his friend, Dr. Ernest Sovac's daughter, Jean. This was the first horror film for Anne Gwynne, who had signed with Universal in 1939 after what was publicized as "the shortest interview on record" (47 seconds). A charming and versatile actress, Miss Gwynne had legs almost as lovely as Betty Grable's (though we scarcely get a peek at them in *Black Friday*), and a scream almost as lush as Evelyn Ankers' (who became her good friend and dressing-roommate at Universal); she would appear with everybody from Abbott and Costello to Lon Chaney to Deanna Durbin, and play in 40 Universal pictures between 1939 and

1944—when she suddenly and mysteriously walked off the lot after completing her role in *House of Frankenstein*.

Ridges and Gwynne share a bit of dialogue giving evidence of the original characterizations envisioned by Siodmak. "Most of all, I'm going to miss your father," says the professor. "A brilliant man, Jean. It distresses me to think that such a great brain surgeon should be so utterly wasted in Newcastle."

"Newcastle is a very welcome port in a very bad storm," replies Jean. For, as scripted, the Sovacs were supposed to be European (and presumably Jewish) refugees—a point almost lost due to Karloff's British accent and Miss Gwynne's Texas beauty.

Karloff appears, very dapper in a homburg and sharp suit, the first of a fashion parade of costumes that he sports in *Black Friday*. He picks up Jean and Kingsley in his open car; Mrs. Kingsley is in the back seat. There's a cute "bit" in which absentminded Kingsley keeps forgetting to close the car door, and they stop so he can pick up his hat. However, as he crosses the street, there is the sound of gunfire—and two cars blast into town. In a thrilling sequence, one of the cars goes out of control, and smashes poor Kingsley into a wall.

"Mr. Red Cannon now belongs to the history of crime—past tense," announces Eric Marnay in the getaway car. Bela Lugosi looks puffy and uncomfortable in his first appearance in *Black Friday;* it looks as if the other well-cast gangsters in the film have their old uncle out for a Sunday drive. He assures the hoodlums that he knows where Cannon hid his money—then doesn't appear again for 25 minutes.

Kingsley is dying; Red Cannon has head wounds and a broken spine but is fully conscious as he reveals his neurotic fear of sirens: "Turn that thing off! I can't stand it! It's driving me crazy!" It appears Sovac will lose his friend. But, back in the hospital, Sovac gets an inspiration...

"The only possible way to save George Kingsley's life is by a brain transplantation!" reveals Sovac's diary. Sovac secretly performs the illegal operation, the music from *Son of Frankenstein* underscoring the surgery. Kingsley survives; Cannon, of course, is dead. And, relaxing after the operation, Sovac picks up a newspaper, and reads of Cannon's hidden fortune of $500,000.

"$500,000! With that money I could build my own laboratory and continue with my experiments!" notes Sovac's records. And, in a later entry: "Kingsley's convalescing and seems to show some of Red Cannon's traits. Does the Cannon brain in Kingsley's head retain the knowledge of the hidden money?"

Karloff's Sovac swings into action. He suggests that Kingsley accompany him on a trip to New York—and takes him to stay at the Midtown Hotel, where Cannon had hidden from the police. Once again, we see Boris in sartorial splendor, garbed in a dark suit, bow tie, sharp blazer handkerchief and black derby. In the Manhattan environment, Kingsley asks for Cannon's old rooms—505 and 506. He remembers the special knock of the comic bellboy. And, in an effective touch, he dreamily recites lines from Tennyson's "The Brook":

> I chatter, chatter, as I flow,
> to join the brimming river.
> For men may come, and men may go,
> but I go on forever.

And, in a crucial test, Sovac takes Kingsley to a nightclub where the chanteuse is Sunny Rogers, Cannon's old girlfriend.

Anne Nagel was a very attractive, sad-eyed actress with an aura of melancholy. It was probably genuine. She was the widow of actor Ross Alexander, a stage actor who had arrived in Hollywood in the mid-30s as a Warner Bros. star and played in such films as 1935's *A Midsummer Night's Dream* and *Captain Blood.* As Alexander succumbed to the lure of easy ladies, his bride of four months, actress Aleta Alexander, took a rifle into the yard of their home at 7357 Woodrow Wilson Drive on the night of December 6, 1935, and killed herself. Alexander, stricken with guilt, began drinking heavily, but his marriage to Anne Nagel on September 16, 1936, caused his friends to wish him a new and happy life as the newlyweds settled on a ranch at 17221 Ventura Boulevard.

However, on the anniversary of Aleta's death, Alexander's black butler had to fight his guilt-stricken master to get gun cartridges away from him. On the night of January 2, 1937, Alexander took the same rifle that Aleta had used on herself, climbed into the hayloft of his ranch and, as his friend Henry Fonda wrote in his autobiography, "Ross put it into his mouth and blew his head off." Newspapers reported how Miss Nagel became "hysterical" and "prostrate" when the butler brought her the news.

Hollywood threw work Miss Nagel's way, and now she was on contract to Universal. She was one of the studio's busiest actresses in such fare as 1939's *Legion of Lost Flyers,* with Richard Arlen, 1940's Mae West/W.C. Fields *My Little Chickadee,* 1941's *Never Give a Sucker an Even Break* (as "Madame Gorgeous"), again with Fields, and 1942's *The Mad Doctor of Market Street,* with Lionel Atwill. She also graced such Universal serials as 1940's *The Green Hornet,* 1941's *The Green Hornet Strikes Again,* and 1942's *Don Winslow of the Navy.* Her second marriage to an Air Force officer ended in divorce in 1951; she died July 6, 1966, at age 49 after an operation, survived by a brother.

As for Ross Alexander, his tragedy had a definite impact on Miss Nagel, Hollywood and world history. After his death, Warners signed a new young sportscaster/actor because his voice sounded like Ross Alexander's. The new contractee: Ronald Reagan.

At the nightclub, Kingsley watches strangely as Sunny Rogers soulfully sings. "Could she be one of my former students?" he wonders. However, the sight of one of Cannon's rival gangsters — Kane — plunges Kingsley into a terrible headache which forces him to leave the club with Sovac. "My sleep only seems to tire me," the frightened professor tells Sovac the next morning, "and I'm haunted by the most horrible dreams." Sovac, however, persuades his friend to stay—and then, in a very effective scene, hypnotically attempts to bring the personality of Cannon out into the open:

> Red! Red Cannon! You were the leader of a gang! They tried to kill you. You came back to get revenge! Red—do you remember the name, "Marnay?" Marnay! He's the one who took your place. Marnay! Miller! Kane! Devore! Why did they try to kill you Red? To get your money? They didn't find it, did they? It's safe, just where you hid it! Where is it Red? Marnay! Miller! Kane! Devore!

As Salter's music swells, and ghostly images of Lugosi and the gangsters swirl around Ridges' bowed head, the actor raises his face to the camera—and there is a subtle, very effective transformation into Red Cannon. The Jack Pierce makeup is expertly slick, and as Karloff villainously grins in triumph, Ridges begins an equally slick portrayal of Cannon. Sovac explains what has happened; Cannon/Kingsley studies his new features in the mirror.

"I never saw plastic surgery like that before," marvels the gangster. He realizes the anonymity of his new body, and laughs at the identity of his donor body. "Well, how are ya, Prof?" he asks his reflection.

"What a disguise! What a break for—Red Cannon," rejoices the gangster. In no time, he escapes the Midtown Hotel. And that night Cannon brutally murders gang member Louis Devore (played by an unbilled Raymond Bailey, who later became "Mr. Drysdale," the banker of television's long-running *The Beverly Hillbillies*).

The next morning, Cannon/Kingsley awakens in his hotel bed—as Kingsley. Sovac informs him of the morning newspaper's top story. "Here's a curious thing, George. It seems that Louis Devore, one of the Red Cannon gang, was found early this morning in a deserted building, dying from the effects of a brutal beating. His back had been broken."

"Good heavens, Ernest," says Kingsley. "Why on earth bother me with that gruesome stuff?"

*   *   *

> Our mention last week of this 18-day shooting schedule being particularly tight has proven a reality for this unit. Although we have worked the last two nights and intend putting in a rather long session tonight, if not stopped by threatening rain, this company is running a full ½ day behind schedule. It will be necessary to keep extreme, heavy pressure on this outfit from now on in order to finish upon schedule, January 18th, and for a cost somewhat close to the approved budget of $130,750....
> —production report from M.F. Murphy on *Black Friday*, January 6, 1940

The closest Boris and Bela came to working together on *Black Friday* was on the nightclub set. There, the two stars posed for the publicity boys with leggy chorines who capered briefly in the sequence.

Meanwhile, the pressure that Universal poured on the *Black Friday* company was outrageous. Lubin often kept his company on call well into the night after supper, madly racing from one standing set to another to indulge the studio's mania for a low budget production. The pressure took its toll on everybody—and then came a rebellion. Karloff, after all one of the 13 founders of the Screen Actors Guild, announced he would refuse to work over eight hours on any day. The front office was incensed, but Boris kept his word—as well as stopping every day at 4:00 p.m. for tea. It was a brave strike against the studio's tyrannical demands, and one sourly noted in the studio reports. By Saturday, January 13, 1940, Murphy filed this report:

> With weather conditions very much against us during the past two weeks—Karloff refusing to work over eight hours in any one day—and the constant changing of pace in progress shown by Lubin, this picture has been somewhat of a problem child. They will finish up tonight running about a ½-day behind schedule. We believe if weather holds out Monday our revised schedule will be possible to fulfill by next Thursday night, the end of their 18-day schedule....

Fortunately, *Black Friday* had a very resilient director.

On Valentine's Day, 1988, 87-year-old Arthur Lubin sat in his lovely house, up in the Hollywood Hills near Mulholland Drive, watching the Olympics. The congenial survivor directed some of the greatest money-makers in Universal's history: 1941's *Buck Privates,* with Abbott and Costello (as well as their four follow-up hits); the 1943 Technicolor *Phantom of the Opera;* and (also in Technicolor) 1944's *Ali Baba and the Forty Thieves,* with Maria Montez; and 1949's *Francis the Talking Mule,* and the sequels. When one ventures that he must have made millions for Universal City, Lubin laughs.

> Well, I think I did—but they don't like to say it! The only time I hear from Universal is when they have to pay me the small percentage I had on several of the pictures I brought to them, like *Francis.*

By his own count, Lubin has directed 62 feature films and over 500 television shows—including 143 episodes of the famous *Mr. Ed* teleseries. Over the years, he directed some of Universal's most "difficult" attractions—Abbott and Costello and Maria Montez, alone, are legendary for their temperament and antics. Yet Lubin was famous for keeping his cool:

> Did I enjoy working with Bud and Lou, or Maria Montez? Well, I enjoy working—period. With actors, you can't yell at them: you have to treat them like human beings. Most of the young directors get so excited! They start yelling and screaming, and they lose the confidence of the actors.

For all the pressure of *Black Friday,* Lubin found it easy to keep his famous "cool," because of the two stars:

As far as Bela is concerned, I first met him when I got out of college, in 1922. I went to New York to get a job, and became assistant stage manager of a stage play called *The Red Poppy*. Bela at that time was a very famous star in Budapest. But when they signed him for the play, they forgot to ask him if he spoke English! So my job, as assistant stage manager, was to coach him as frequently as possible in his English; in three weeks, he spoke English, with, of course, a Hungarian accent. So we became very close friends during those years at Universal.

Karloff only lived about a mile away from where I live now, above Hollywood. He was a real gentleman. He was a scholar — he was high class! Both Bela and Boris were gentlemen. They were both fine men . . . and I don't remember anything unpleasant ever happening with either one of the two boys. They were just wonderful, wonderful guys to work with.

Lubin mercifully remembers the rigors of *Black Friday* only in general terms, and he doesn't resent them: "It was wonderful training for me to be able to do pictures of that budget, because when I got to the big feature pictures, I was very sure of myself."

It's been an incredibly prolific career — "I hope it's not over with," chuckles Lubin. As we spoke, he was looking forward to doing a two-hour television revival of *Mr. Ed,* which, with Arthur Lubin at the helm, most assuredly will come in on time and budget.

* * *

Black Friday gets grimmer. A siren changes Kingsley into Cannon. Lugosi's Marnay, suspecting Sunny knows who the vengeful killer is, visits the nightclub with his gang. Kane offers Sunny a fancy watch if she agrees to meet him in her apartment and put together what they know. But in his car, Kane finds a visitor — who breaks his back . . .

With Kane's watch, Cannon/Kingsley shows up at Sunny's apartment, reveals knowledge only Cannon could have known, and, in his new body, moves to make love to Sunny . . .

Cannon climbs into Marnay's apartment. Marnay isn't there, but two policemen are, and Cannon kills them — and then is wounded in an exciting rooftop chase . . .

Marnay, meanwhile, is visiting Sunny. She says she had a visitor last night who insisted he was Red Cannon. "What did he drive up in," asks Lugosi, "a hearse?"

And to make matters totally haywire, Margaret Kingsley and Jean Sovac arrive in New York. Sovac smoothly convinces them not to interfere, but as he ushers them out, Cannon appears — and the women glimpse him. "Who were those women?" demands Cannon as Sovac notes his wound. "My daughter and your wife!" responds Karloff.

Opposite: **Bela and Boris appear delighted to honor a PR request for a chummy pose with the chorines of *Black Friday*. The stars did not share a single scene in this picture.**

As Sovac slips and gives away the fact that he knows about the hidden fortune, the gangster threatens the doctor. Karloff, however, masterfully regains dominance: "How would you like to be George Kingsley for good? ... You're walking around in Kingsley's body all right—but part of your brain is his and you can't control it! ... I CAN MAKE YOU FORGET YOU EVER WERE RED CANNON! ... From now on, you'll do EXACTLY as I say..."

Jean Sovac confronts her father, and he confesses to the brain transplant. Karloff is terrific as he barnstorms his gleeful pride: "I've proved what I always knew to be true. Transplanted human brain cells will live and function! What a triumph! *Think* of it!" That night, Sovac—and Cannon—will get the money...

In a bar at the nightclub (the bartender is Jack Mulhall, onetime leading man of the silents who was reduced to playing bits), Sunny agrees to meet Cannon after the show—they will flee with the money to South America ("for a starter"). But Sunny has turned traitor, tipping off Marnay and Miller, who follow Cannon to the reservoir where he has hidden the money. There's a fight, Cannon tosses Marnay into the reservoir, but as Cannon and Miller grapple, Marnay grabs the money—and makes his way back to Sunny's...

Perhaps by this juncture, Universal had realized just how sorry a part they had tossed Bela. At any rate, despite the tight shooting schedule, Universal approved a wild publicity brainstorm (hatched by PR agent Evan Hoskins) that Bela Lugosi be truly hypnotized for his death scene—being locked in Sunny's closet by the vengeful Cannon. As the trailer for *Black Friday* would proclaim, "Reporters saw Dr. Manley Hall hypnotize actor Lugosi to give reality to a scene in *Black Friday*. Horror-struck, they witnessed the hypnotized actor's mortal agony as Lugosi actually experienced the terror of suffocating to death in a closet!"

On the big evening, a select 25 reporters ("who could be depended upon to regard the affair in its proper light," theorized the *New York Times*) arrived on Soundstage 14 at Universal City. Arthur Lubin was master-of-ceremonies, introducing Bela, as well as costars Karloff, Ridges, Nagel and Gwynne. The hypnotist was Bela's close friend Dr. Manley P. Hall, fated to perform Bela's fifth and final marriage in 1955. Dr. George Esker and his nurse, Peggy Bell, checked Bela's pulse—72—and Hall went to work. Douglas W. Churchill documented the adventure for the *New York Times:*

> Lugosi, looking like a benign Irish cop, was placed in a chair before Hall while the spell was woven. Hypnotized, Lugosi made his way to a two-sided set which was the closet in which the actor was locked and in which he was to suffocate.

Opposite: **Manley P. Hall (who officiated at Lugosi's last marriage) puts Bela into an hypnotic trance (or does he?) for his death scene in *Black Friday*. Stanley Ridges, Anne Nagel, Anne Gwynne and Karloff look on.**

Hall went over the script with the hypnotized man, the cameras turned, Hall whispered, "Now you're suffocating," and Lugosi began to nose the cracks in the door, demanding, "Let me out!" As hysteria began to overcome him he shouted, "Let me out. I'll tell you where the money is. It's in the oven." His voice became shrill and he screamed his lines. With his shoulder against the door, the set began to give, and he slumped to the floor. A doctor who was in attendance stepped in, took his pulse, which had increased from normal to 160, which, the physician said, would be actual in a suffocating person. They carried Lugosi to a chair, where Hall awakened him. Examination showed that the player's pulse was again normal. Arthur Lubin, the director, said that the scene was 100 percent better than it had been in the afternoon without hypnosis....

According to Churchill's account, the "one flaw" was that cameraman Elwood Bredell ran out of film before the show was half over—which is perhaps why only a couple of shots of the disheveled Bela appear, almost lost in shadow, merely as a backdrop for the grim action of Ridges preparing to break the screaming Miss Nagel's back. Churchill apparently thought the whole show a humbug, opining that hypnosis would probably now be used to make writers finish scripts, critics give good notices, and stars behave; still, he included this notice:

> To reassure doubters, Boris Karloff, costar of the epic, stated he was positive Lugosi was hypnotized because he had never seen his fellow actor keep his back to the camera for so long.

Was the hypnosis stunt real? Not according to Lillian Lugosi. She recalled that Bela had threatened to fire his agent if any actual hypnosis took place; in fact, when Hall visited Lugosi's home before the stunt to rehearse, Bela insisted that Lillian be the guinea pig! As Lillian remembered, Bela would have nothing to do with hypnosis—fearing Hall might take advantage of the actor's trance to discourage his drinking.

Back to the movie: Cannon, with the money, has an adventure with a comic taxi driver. He goes to the airport, but when he arrives, he's transformed back to Kingsley. He returns to the Midtown Hotel—and gives the taxi driver a $1000 bill. Back at the hotel, Karloff, sporting a magnificent polka-dot dressing gown, hypnotically suggests that Cannon become dormant—and gets the money...

After some confusion, in which Kingsley is interrogated after the taxi driver tries to pass his $1000 bill ("The guy I was talking about was a GANGSTER...!" barks the cab driver), the professor is free to return to the University of Newcastle. He resumes his teaching. Sovac plans to create "a great laboratory and give the world the benefit of my scientific knowledge." We see Kingsley back in his lecture room with his students; there is something haunting about his face, almost eerie; and as he apologizes for cutting class short to bid goodbye to Sovac, a sound comes from outside...

It is a police siren.

In agony, Kingsley collapses at his desk. His students gather around him, and he sees the spectres of the gangsters. He rises—and has become Cannon. The students scream, and he takes off for the Sovac home. He demands his money from Jean; Miss Gwynne (in a close-up she recalls Karloff requesting for her), looks terrified, and the gangster attacks her. Sovac, hearing her incredibly sustained scream, runs in and shoots him.

"Ernest—why?" asks the dying Ridges, having passed a sharp dissolve from Cannon to Kingsley. "Why did you do it? Why, Ernest?"

"I think you know the answer now, George," reads Sovac's journal.

The music swells. In the prison, the electrical switches are pulled. "I pronounce this man—dead," says a disembodied voice as the reporters remove their hats.

"I am leaving all my notes in the hope that, in better hands than mine, some good may come of them," reads Sovac's journal.

The End. A Universal Picture.

M.F. Murphy was able to report:

> After considerable struggle and working the last four nights of production, this company finished up Thursday, January 18, right on our 18-day schedule. We encountered a great variety of difficulties during the shooting period—weather conditions requiring changes of plans—Karloff on some occasions refusing to work over eight hours in one day—and the spasmodic change of pace in progress on the part of the director. During the 18-day shooting period they were compelled to work nine evenings after dinner until 10:00 P.M. and later, and on one Saturday night until 3:15 A.M. Sunday morning.
>
> We figure, if retakes or added scenes are not found necessary, the probable final cost should come out to approximately $129,000 on the 25 percent basis, this being $2000 under approved budget.

To Universal's delight, when all figures were tallied, *Black Friday* actually came in about $7000 under budget. In that sense, already, the studio's fifth Karloff and Lugosi chiller was a success.

*   *   *

> BORIS KARLOFF... BELA LUGOSI... At their fiendish best in *BLACK FRIDAY*... The sinister hand of science bares a new and dangerous experiment. Into the body of a gentle scholar is grafted the brain of a criminal—and a new and deadly monster is born to ravage an unsuspecting world!
> —from the *Black Friday* trailer

"A man-made monster is on the loose!" screamed the promotional teasers for *Black Friday.* The trailer luridly played up Lugosi's hypnotic trance, which incidentally, also found its way into a *Universal Newsreel. Black Friday* opened Thursday, March 21, 1940, at New York's Rialto Theatre, just in time for Easter. Universal's new Deanna Durbin show, *It's a Date,* opened at the Rivoli the next day, while other holiday attractions in New York included Warner's super western *Virginia City,* 20th Century–Fox's Shirley Temple in *The Blue Bird,* and Disney's *Pinocchio.* Bosley Crowther, of the *New York Times,* apparently liked *Black Friday* in spite of himself:

> As a treat for the kiddies, the Easter Bunny left Boris Karloff and Bela Lugosi on the stoop at the Rialto Theatre yesterday in a fluffy and pink beribboned basket labeled *Black Friday.* Lugosi's terrifying talents are wasted in the role of a mere gangster, an unsupernatural thug, but Karloff is in exquisite artistic form as a surgeon who "transplants" the brain of a killer into the timid cranium of an aging professor of English Literature and then morbidly watches the fun in "English A" . . . Stanley Ridges plays the scholarly Schizophrenic.

Curiously, just a short time later, April 12, 1940, the *New York Times'* esteemed editorial page took time to examine the popularity of the horror melodrama. Besides *Black Friday,* Paramount's Technicolor *Dr. Cyclops* had opened at the Paramount Theatre, the play *Ladies in Retirement* was drawing full houses at Henry Miller's Theatre, and United Artists' *Rebecca* — fated to win an Academy Award for best picture of 1940 — was at Radio City Music Hall. "Broadway is all a-tingle with chills down the spine," noted the editor, and suggests escapism wasn't the only reason for such popularity:

> [It] might have something to do with Aristotle. He had something to say about tragedy on the stage being a catharsis, a release for the emotions. . . . [I]t is just conceivable that a good murder story or play does offer one way of escape from Hitler and Stalin in Finland and the Japanese. It shows us horror and madness and violence in operation, but there is always the saving knowledge that it isn't real. . . .

Ironically, just as the *New York Times* was making an official peace with the horror genre (a peace its film critics would be soon to break), *Black Friday* would be the final Universal collaboration of Karloff and Lugosi. The film, after all, was a misfire; Stanley Ridges ("in a performance you will long remember" promised the trailer) generally received the best notices. Expecting a Karloff and Lugosi frightfest, the film's presold audience found Boris and Bela not sharing a single scene together, and the picture's most ghoulish moments enacted by an actor many had never heard of. *Black Friday* was only just profitable and by no means a sensation. For a time, Universal hyped its new Karloff and Lugosi project, *The Monster of Zambor,* but it was never made.

Arthur Lubin would go on to become one of Universal's most prolific and happy directors, his masterwork in the horror genre being the Technicolor 1943 *Phantom of the Opera.*

And, as for Curt Siodmak — the famed fantasist penned a fascinating Universal output: *The Invisible Woman* (starring John Barrymore) and the powerhouse hit *The Wolf Man,* both in 1941; *Invisible Agent,* starring Jon Hall and Ilona Massey, in 1942; the Chaney, Jr./Lugosi *Frankenstein Meets the Wolf*

Man, and Chaney's *Son of Dracula* (scripted with Eric Taylor—Curt's brother Robert Siodmak directed), both in 1943; the Karloff/Susanna Foster *The Climax* (scripted with Lynn Starling), and the story for the "monster rally" *House of Frankenstein*, both in 1944. Siodmak also scripted such nonhorror Universal titles as the 1945 Susanna Foster vehicle *Frisco Sal*, as well as visiting Monogram for Karloff's *The Ape* (1940) and RKO for Val Lewton's *I Walked with a Zombie* (sharing credit with Ardel Wray, 1943). It was also in 1943 that Siodmak's classic novel *Donovan's Brain* was published.

Later, Siodmak scripted Warner's *The Beast with Five Fingers* (1946), as well as such films as RKO's *Berlin Express* (1948) and *Tarzan's Magic Fountain* (1949); still later, he became a director, contributing to the scripts of his films *Bride of the Gorilla* (Realart, 1951), *The Magnetic Monster* (United Artists, 1953), *Curucu, Beast of the Amazon* (Universal, 1956), *Love Slaves of the Amazon* (Universal, 1957), *The Devil's Messenger* (actually a frame he shot in Sweden with Chaney, Jr., for an unsold series titled *13 Demon Street*), and *Ski Fever* (Allied Artists, 1969). He also penned more novels.

However, the prolific Siodmak has come back time and again to the brain-swapping idea he originally used in *Black Friday*. It was the core of *Donovan's Brain* (made into a movie at least three times); he also employed it in his story of Universal's 1944 *House of Frankenstein* (Edward T. Lowe wrote the screenplay) as Karloff vengefully plotted to pop one enemy's brain into the skull of Frankenstein's monster and another's into the cranium of the Wolf Man. Various forms of brain perturbation figured in Siodmak's screen stories for *Creature with the Atom Brain* and *Earth vs. the Flying Saucers;* he revived it yet again for the 1958 television pilot, *Tales of Frankenstein*, on which he was associate producer, writer and director. In this unsold pilot, Frankenstein (Anton Diffring) transplants the brain of a dead man (Richard Bull) into the head of the monster (Don Megowan, of *The Creature from the Black Lagoon* fame), only to have the abashed monster see himself in a mirror and rampage after his loving wife (Helen Westcott). One bit of climactic dialogue bears repeating.

"The life you had was brief, but it was decent and good," the wife tells her monster spouse. "Don't destroy everything now because of a hideous face and grotesque body—that aren't yours!"

*   *   *

Because of the artistic misfire exploded by the recasting of roles, *Black Friday* perhaps was doomed to receive the most absurd critical evaluations of all the Karloff and Lugosi films.

Some writers have employed that puerile cliché that Stanley Ridges "stole the picture" from Karloff and Lugosi—not knowing or recognizing that Ridges was actually playing the starring part in the picture.

Others have praised Lugosi's offbeat casting as a gangster, opining that it gave new insight into his talents—totally missing the grim discomfort the actor shows in his very supporting role and modified zoot suit.

In summary, *Black Friday* is a sharp, brisk, exciting thriller — existing nicely on its own terms, but forever cursed by the "what might have been" stigma when one imagines Siodmak's original casting. For all of Ridges' richness of part, Karloff elegantly dominates the film; suave, imperious, dapper in his derby hat and black suit, smoking cigarettes, uttering lines like "Transplanted brain cells will live and function! What a triumph! *Think* of it!" He is excellent. Mad doctor though he might be, Karloff's Sovac is light-years away from the pathetic old misfits he was playing at Columbia in his "Mad Doctor" series; there's a pride and arrogance in his performance, in place of the Columbia pathos. In final analysis, Karloff gives his own Jekyll/Hyde portrayal in *Black Friday,* evolving from humanitarian surgeon to ruthless, money-lusting villain; it's a keen, razor-sharp performance.

Ridges is superb; he accomplishes the change of personality with a minimum of Jack P. Pierce makeup and a maximum of subtle vocal and facial mannerisms. *Black Friday,* however, becomes his duet with Karloff when it might have been Karloff's duet with Lugosi. Learning of the casting switch, a viewer of *Black Friday* can find himself fantasizing, envisioning Karloff switching from dreamy, poetry-spouting professor to rabid gangster, à la his role in *Scarface.* Was Karloff wise to forsake a part with so much mustard on it? And how easy to imagine Lugosi, tall and suave and smirking in the role of the ambitious, European refugee Sovac...

What we get, however, is Lugosi, in a sack suit, his ego and talent trapped in a third banana role, inexplicably looking in certain shots like Jerry Falwell. A mere change in "type" does not make an actor versatile; it's what he does with each role. In *Black Friday,* Karloff's shadings of Sovac are much more colorful and impressive (despite the "Mad Doctor" trappings of the part for Boris) than Lugosi's ultimate slumming as Marnay (despite the offbeat nature of the part for Bela).

So — who to blame for *Black Friday?* Karloff, for his characteristic humility in forsaking a tailor-designed showy role? Universal, for allowing him to do so? Lugosi, for not raising a riot and insisting he receive his rightful role or nothing? Stanley Ridges (who played a very similar role in Republic's 1945 *The Phantom Speaks*), for not realizing or caring that taking the richest part in a Karloff and Lugosi film could only be regarded by posterity as an intrusion?

Or, film scholarship — for rattling bones in the Universal closet, wondering what might have been, instead of being satisfied with what was fated to exist as *Black Friday?*

11
You'll Find Out, 1940

Ladies and Gentlemen of the Motion Picture Audience—We've had a lot of fun making our picture, and we certainly hope you've enjoyed it. But there's one thing I want to get clear in your minds. Remember Boris Karloff, Peter Lorre, and Bela Lugosi? Well, they aren't really murderers at all! In fact, they're nice fellas, and good friends of mine. You know, things like this don't actually happen. It's all fun!

—Kay Kyser, in the tag of *You'll Find Out*

Much has been written about the peculiar sensation of radio, the giant media of the 1930s and 1940s. Historians have frequently wondered, for instance, how Edgar Bergen—whose lips moved, anyway—could become a millionaire by plying ventriloquism on the radio?

Of course, Bergen's genius was creating the personality of Charlie McCarthy, the dummy in top hat and monocle, whom audiences could conjure up perfectly as he flirted with Dorothy Lamour or insulted W.C. Fields. The major radio stars of the day—Jack Benny, Burns and Allen, Bob Hope, Fred Allen—all possessed these vibrant personalities which served them fully as they traveled over the airwaves weekly into millions of homes. And most of them eventually invaded movie theatres.

Kay Kyser was no exception. It would be easy—too easy, really—to ridicule the late Kay Kyser: his shiny, wire-rim glasses, his tiny, dime-slot mouth, the skinny body; dressed in his mortarboard and academic gown as "the Old Perfessor," mugging and prancing as he conducted his Kollege of Musical Knowledge. The North Carolina born-and-bred Kyser had first hit the air in 1938; quickly he became a major Wednesday night star on NBC with his 60-minutes of comedy, music, and "kollege brainbuster question" worth $400 to the contestant who could answer it. Ginny Simms, Harry Babbitt, Sully Mason and Ish Kabibble were his regulars; later, his show also featured the King Sisters, a young crooner named Mike Douglas, and "gorgeous Georgia Carroll"—a famous cover-girl/singer whom Kyser wed in 1944.

Something about Kyser's energy, his blend of "zany" corn, comedy, music, and personality, clicked with his audiences. The man was no fool; Mike Douglas recalled that Kyser privately vowed that he'd quit show business as soon as he had become a millionaire—and by 1951, he had done just that. Just as soon as this shrewd showman established himself on the radio, he had moved into the movies.

It was RKO — producer of such classics as *King Kong,* Katharine Hepburn's early vehicles, and the Astaire-Rogers films — which made Kyser the winning bid. His debut: 1939's *That's Right, You're Wrong* (his trademark line on radio), featuring Lucille Ball and the Kyser regulars. And in 1940, this unusual show business figure made his second film — *You'll Find Out,* which not only boasted Peter Lorre, but became the seventh and worst feature film of Karloff and Lugosi.

* * *

> Sully Mason: Ish, why do you suppose the Prince wears that towel around his head?
> Ish Kabibble: Well, he probably just washed his hair and can't do a *thing* with it!

Since *Black Friday,* both Karloff and Lugosi had been busy. By the time *You'll Find Out* went into production in midsummer, 1940, eight 1940 releases had starred Boris Karloff, as he continued his *Mad Doctor* series at Columbia, *Mr. Wong* series at Monogram, and concluded his Warner pact with the melodrama *British Intelligence.* Lugosi's career, still rebuilding, was taking some unusual routes: he had toured with Ed Sullivan's *Stardust Cavalcade,* and had even modeled for the Demon King of Disney's *Fantasia.*

It was David Butler (1894–1979) who would produce, direct, and cowrite the story for *You'll Find Out.* He had begun his career at Fox with 1927's *High School Hero;* at 20th Century–Fox in the late '30s, he directed such stars as Shirley Temple in *Captain January,* Eddie Cantor in *Ali Baba Goes to Town,* and the Ritz Brothers in *Kentucky Moonshine.* He was directing Bing Crosby and Joan Blondell in *East Side of Heaven* at Universal about the time of *Son of Frankenstein,* and had directed Kyser's first film.

The old house formula seemed a perfect vehicle for Kyser to mug and carry on in, and RKO made overtures to Peter Lorre, Karloff, and Lugosi to be the bogeymen. The appeal of such a movie was obvious: Kyser's popular radio show would undoubtedly plug their names shamelessly as *You'll Find Out* went into release, and the publicity for all would be considerable.

RKO Studios expired in 1956. In 1983, the RKO Archives rested in a warehouse, in a Korean section of Hollywood. Deep in the file cabinets lurked the figures for *You'll Find Out:*

●On July 20, 1940, Boris Karloff signed a contract for *You'll Find Out.* His performance as Judge Mainwaring called for $4166.66 per week, with a three-week guarantee; the production also assured him of special billing.

●On July 23, Bela Lugosi signed for *You'll Find Out.* His portrayal of

Opposite: **Poster for You'll Find Out, 1940.**

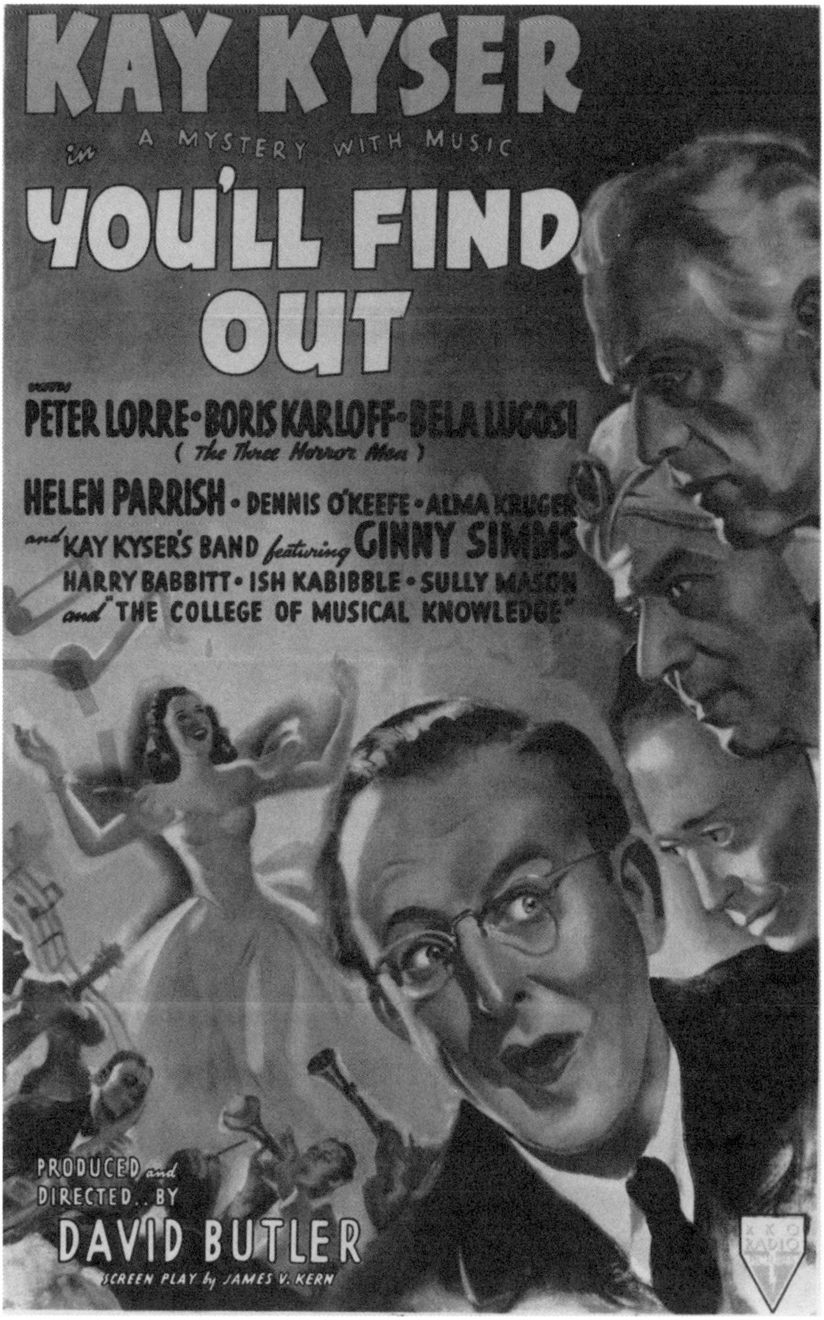
KAY KYSER
in A MYSTERY WITH MUSIC
YOU'LL FIND OUT
PETER LORRE • BORIS KARLOFF • BELA LUGOSI
(The Three Horror Men)
HELEN PARRISH • DENNIS O'KEEFE • ALMA KRUGER
and KAY KYSER'S BAND featuring GINNY SIMMS
HARRY BABBITT • ISH KABIBBLE • SULLY MASON
and "THE COLLEGE OF MUSICAL KNOWLEDGE"
PRODUCED and DIRECTED.. BY
DAVID BUTLER
SCREEN PLAY by JAMES V. KERN
RKO RADIO

Prince Saliano would pay $1250 per week, with a three-week guarantee. He was promised only "the best billing possible."

•Actually, Peter Lorre, then free of his 20th Century–Fox contract and a year away from *The Maltese Falcon,* secured the best deal of the three villains, winning the primary billing as Professor Fenninger and $3500 per week on a four-week guarantee. Of course, Kay Kyser had them all beat, receiving a $75,000 advance for himself "and his associates."

On August 8, 1940, *You'll Find Out* began shooting.

The plot, strung out over the space of 97 often-agonizing minutes, hardly rates academic dissection. However, as a curiosity of its era, the movie does rate some interest.

It's Wednesday night, and Kay Kyser and his Kollege of Musical Knowledge are on the air. "Students!" shouts Kyser in close-up—his trademark cry to the crowd when the contestants missed a correct answer. We see Kyser in mortarboard and professor gown, and meet his stars: brunette chanteuse Ginny Simms; the band "heartthrob," Harry Babbitt; comic singer Sully Mason; and the inimitable Ish Kabibble, bangs and all. The real show, however, is Kyser, who leads the band in "Like the Fella Once Said" (the first of several James McHugh/John Mercer songs in the film). Kyser minces, hikes up the leg of his gown, sticks out his tongue, and enjoys badinage with his band:

> KYSER: Hey, Ish—you know what the bug said to the windshield?
> KABIBBLE: Yeah! That's me all over!

The band responds to this mirth by standing up, twirling their instruments around, and kicking and lurching spasmodically. Then Kay brings it home, with a climactic, furious tap dance.

Meanwhile, ensconced in this time capsule on 1940 audience taste is dapper Dennis O'Keefe, playing Kyser's business manager Chuck Deems, and Helen Parrish, playing heiress Janis Bellacrest. Miss Parrish was already acquainted with both Karloff and Lugosi; she had played a communion girl in *Bride of Frankenstein,* and had just toured with Lugosi in Ed Sullivan's *Stardust Cavalcade.* Perhaps best remembered as Deanna Durbin's unspeakably bitchy cousin in Universal's 1939 *First Love,* Miss Parrish tragically died in 1959, a cancer victim at the age of only 36.

". . . Somebody's trying to get me out of the way," the pistol-packing heiress tells boyfriend O'Keefe. And as the plot would have it, Kay and friends are set to play for Janis's 21st birthday party at Bellacrest Manor, a spooky old domicile. The Manor is a natural backdrop for the three star villains—full of masks and weird objets d'art, presided over by Janis's superstitious Aunt Margo (Alma Kruger). Then playing the role of head nurse Molly Byrd in MGM's *Dr. Kildare* series, Miss Kruger was a radio celebrity herself, playing

Opposite: **Ginny Simms, Helen Parrish, Karloff, Lugosi, Peter Lorre and Kay Kyser, all of *You'll Find Out*, pose for the still photographer.**

"Aunt Emily" on *Those We Love,* then a popular Monday night radio show on CBS. First heavy on the scene is Karloff, as Judge Spencer Mainwaring, family legal counsel; he gets a nice introduction, with flashes of lightning. Boris is so white and woolly in this film that he looks, for all the world, like one of his Bedlington terriers.

Next comes Bela, as psychic Prince Saliano — appearing in a mirror (wouldn't Dracula have been surprised!) behind Kyser, receiving some nice close-ups from director Butler, looking proud and fierce (if a bit aged) in his turban and tuxedo.

Lastly, there comes Peter Lorre, as Professor Fenninger, supposedly an exposer of psychic trickery — first glimpsed spying in the window of Miss Parrish's boudoir. The scene revealed miniglimpses of both Miss Parrish and Miss Simms in their slips, which must have titillated 1940 audiences; it climaxes with Bela, peeking through a mask on the wall, blowing a poison dart at Miss Simms (he thinks she's the heiress) — and missing.

Of course, the plot is see-through: Karloff, Lorre and Lugosi are an unholy triumvirate, hell-bent on keeping Miss Parrish from inheriting her estate. They prefer to kill her, and continue to fleece the aunt with phony séances.

Meanwhile, to keep the picture lively and pleasing to the eye, *You'll Find Out* ushers in a bevy of Janis's 400 club society girlfriends, all here to celebrate with her. The honey of the bunch is Louise Currie, a lovely, shapely blonde with Katharine Hepburn cheekbones, a Sarah Lawrence College education, and dramatic training via Max Reinhardt. Well remembered as the heroine of Republic serials *The Adventures of Captain Marvel* (1941) and *The Masked Marvel* (1943), the actress also was fated to costar in two of Bela's most infamous Monograms: *The Ape Man* (1943) and *Voodoo Man* (1944). Miss Currie enters *You'll Find Out* with the cry, "Where are the men?" and charmingly animates every scene in which she appears.

Today, Louise Currie, who later operated her own interior decoration shop in Hollywood, lives luxuriously in Beverly Hills, and kindly reminisced for me about *You'll Find Out:*

> *You'll Find Out* really was fun; it was light-hearted, the whole idea was a spoof, and everybody was happy. I think that Kay Kyser was madly in love with Ginny Simms, and they were going together at the time. He didn't marry her (he later married Georgia Carroll); still, it was quite a romance. So they were *very* happy!
>
> I remember meeting all the girls (we were all supposed to be debutantes) — a nice group of girls. As for the horror men . . . Boris Karloff, interestingly enough, was very quiet. He didn't participate on the set too much — he was, I'd almost say, rather a recluse. I distinctly felt you just didn't run up and start chatting with him! Nor do I remember having too much contact with Peter Lorre, who, as I recall, was a strange little fellow — much the sort he portrayed on the screen! But Bela Lugosi was different. I remember long chats with Lugosi: he was a very educated, polished, interesting man. It was amazing, to me, that he got into the horror end of Hollywood; he could easily have been a serious actor, and have

gone in another direction. We had long conversations, which continued on the other films I did with him, *The Ape Man* and *Voodoo Man*...

Meanwhile, the bridge to the manor house explodes. The band, the girls, the heiress and the villains are trapped in the house. Being a 1940 movie, one of the girls goes to call her mother to say she won't be home that night, allowing Karloff to intone a line reminiscent of *The Black Cat:* "The telephone is probably dead. The storm, you know."

Of course, Kay and the gang entertain. Harry Babbitt sings, "You've Got Me This Way," as the society girls look hungry; then it's time for a Kyser novelty act: "The Bad-Humor Man." It must be seen to be believed: Ish Kabibble, riding an ice cream truck wagon, trimming his bangs; Kay, sporting a beanie hat and bouncing a ball, skipping about crying "School's out"; the band wearing funny hats singing in falsetto; while the sexy girls all looked tickled.

Actually, this outrageous musical episode rates a footnote. According to the trade papers, *You'll Find Out* originally envisioned "The Bad-Humor Man" *not* for Kyser and company—but for Karloff, Lugosi and Lorre, who were supposed to sing, "We're the Bad-Humored Men." One can only wonder if any rehearsals proceeded before sanity prevailed!

After Ginny Simms gets her chance to solo with "I'd Know You Anywhere," a pseudohorror vignette arrives—a séance. While not as frightening as the band's rendition of "The Bad-Humor Man," the séance has some atmosphere. Lugosi, officiating in turban and swami robes, reveals "the invisible ray" of electricity to detect evil spirits; he chants a bit, and then flowers float, a native mask chants, and the head of the late Elmer Bellacrest appears in the dark, whining in a bizarre voice. Climactically, a chandelier with a wicked spike falls from above Miss Parrish, whose fainting spell seconds before saves her from having her skull drilled by the villains.

Meanwhile, on the set, Boris, Bela and Peter all took advantage of the publicity bonanza promised by *You'll Find Out.* A UPI feature quoted Karloff on movie villainy:

> "It's nice work if you can get it, but very few can do it... In what other field can three men monopolize one branch of a profession? There is not another field like ours. The work is steady, the pay is good and we take a certain artistic delight in our portrayals. Isn't that so, gentlemen?"
>
> "Absolutely," chimed in Bela. "Our roles are always full of variety and we have virtually no competition."
>
> Lorre demurred slightly. "I'm tired of haunting houses," he purred. "I want to bite somebody."
>
> "That's my field, Peter," said Bela.

Karloff and Lorre became fast friends. Many years later, Boris contrasted the Hungarians Lorre and Lugosi as he reflected on the latter:

He didn't really learn the language in which he earned his bread and butter, and that made it difficult for him. He was in America much longer than Peter Lorre. I've worked with both . . . in fact we all worked together in a film with Kay Kyser. But there was no difficulty for Peter; he really got down to the language. Bela didn't, and I think that handicapped him enormously. It was a pity.

Incidentally, Lillian Lugosi (who spoke fluent Hungarian) was impatient with Karloff's remarks about Bela's English. "Bela knew the language very well," she once told me. "I venture to say that Bela's vocabulary was larger than Karloff's!"

Back to the movie: Kyser and O'Keefe share a bed; Ish Kabibble's dog Prince (outfitted with a toupee and bangs so he looks like his master) leads Kyser and O'Keefe through a secret passageway; a suit of armor nearly decapitates Kay with its sword ("Benny Goodman fan," conjectures O'Keefe); Kyser holds hands with a stuffed gorilla on a skateboard, which falls on top of him. At length, he discovers the phony apparatuses employed by Saliano, including the "Sonovox" — a gimmick which distorts the voice.

Another séance is held. Once again, the head of Elmer Bellacrest is floating in the darkness, whining, "Believe." However, Kyser, unusually heroic for a horror comic stooge, knocks out Bela in the secret passage, and shouts "This is Kay Kyser!" over the Sonovox. Karloff whips off the rubber mask of Bellacrest, and escapes at gunpoint, only to grapple with Kyser.

Then there's a scream — and the villains get their climactic moment. Boris and Peter have guns; Bela has a stick of dynamite.

"Put up your hands — all of you," orders Lorre.

"You're a very clever young man, Mr. Kyser," sneers Boris. "See how many clever things you can think of in the few minutes before this explosive blows you all to bits!"

"But you can't kill all these people like that!" protests O'Keefe. "It's crazy! It's mass murder! You'll never get away with it!"

"Identifying your bodies will be rather difficult," grins Lorre. "I daresay the police will assume that ours are among them. Light that fuse!"

"Goodbye, Mr. Kyser," says Karloff.

"I regret that our acquaintance should be — blown up — so soon!" says Bela, and he tosses the lit dynamite.

However, it's Ish Kabibble's dog, Prince, to the rescue. He picks up the dynamite, chases the villains outside — and blows them up, returning to the exulting crowd with Bela's turban in his mouth.

Come the denouement, it's Wednesday night again, Kay is in his "Old Perfessor" getup, the band is using the Sonovox as a new novelty act (Harry Babbit forming the words and the instruments singing them) and O'Keefe, Miss Parrish, Alma Kruger and the "400 Girls" are all enjoying the show. Kay Kyser absolves the horror stars of their guilt, gets caught between the electrodes of Bela's séance paraphernalia, and zaps away for THE END.

"The picture was one of the happiest I ever did," said the late David

You'll Find Out: **an on-set candid shot of Lugosi with Helen Parrish and Ginny Simms.**

Butler, who went on to direct such hit comedies as Paramount's Crosby-Lamour-Hope *The Road to Morocco* (1942). "Everybody simply had fun making it." *You'll Find Out* wrapped October 11, 1940, running 13 days over schedule, and coming in at a final cost of $367,689.90. This figure did not include the $75,000 advance Kyser and associates received; add it in, and *You'll Find Out* — roundly regarded as Boris and Bela's lowest tandem effort — becomes their highest budget movie!

As was to be expected, *You'll Find Out* delivered the publicity potential the stars had recognized. On Wednesday, September 25, 1940, Karloff, Lorre and Lugosi all guest-starred on Kay Kyser's NBC radio show. RKO was delighted with the film's preview — "There was a constant riot of laughter and hysteria," notes a report in the archives; indeed, the Kyser opus apparently received far more respect from the front office than any of Val Lewton's later work at that intriguing studio.

On November 14, 1940, *You'll Find Out* opened at New York's Roxy Theatre. There was plenty of competition on Broadway: MGM's *Strike Up the Band* with Judy Garland and Mickey Rooney, and *Escape* with Norma Shearer; 20th Century–Fox's *Down Argentine Way*, with Betty Grable, and *The*

Mark of Zorro, with Tyrone Power, Linda Darnell and Basil Rathbone; Paramount's Cecil B. DeMille saga *North West Mounted Police;* United Artists' *The
Great Dictator,* with Chaplin; and Universal's *Spring Parade,* with Deanna Durbin. The Roxy's *You'll Find Out* boasted a special attraction—Kay Kyser
himself, with all the gang, would appear on stage with the movie. "The Biggest Stage and Screen Show in Roxy History!" promised a *New York Times*
advertisement. "80 People in a Giant Jamboree including the Gae Foster
Girls." The Roxy opened its doors at 8:00 a.m., three hours earlier than
usual, for this engagement. RKO sold the film as "A Mystery with Music,"
and the film's poster hailed the three villains as "The Three Horror Men."

"The Messrs. Karloff, Lugosi, and Lorre go in for the heavy leers and
obvious melodramatics of the gaslit era," reported the *New York Journal-
American,* while the *Times* lamented:

> *You'll Find Out* is one of these silly shudder-comedies, in which Mr. Kyser
> and his hep-cats appear as the innocent bystanders who naturally become in-
> volved in an eerie attempt at murder... Apparently the script writers were
> scared out of their wits by their own ideas, for the dialogue and plot
> developments indicate that little was devoted to them. With three of the most
> calculating villains vis-à-vis Mr. Kyser in one film, you would think that
> something more original than shrieks in the night and sliding panels and hidden
> passageways could have been contrived to confound them...

You'll Find Out was a respectable, studio-backed, well-promoted picture
and, despite its silliness, was regarded at the time as a properly prestigious
vehicle for the horror stars. As for Mr. Kyser, he went on in movies:
humiliating John Barrymore in his last film, RKO's 1941 *Playmates* (in which
he did a swing version of Shakespeare) and working for MGM and Columbia. In 1951, he retired, returned with wife Georgia Carroll to North
Carolina, and was very active in Christian Science. In 1974, he moved to
Boston to supervise production of Christian Science films. He died in his
beloved North Carolina in 1985. His age was reported to be 79.

*   *   *

> ...Obvious and overlong (to say the least); a real disappointment to anyone
> anxious to savor the Karloff/Lugosi/Lorre team; more suited for fans of Ish
> Kabibble.
>
>   —Leonard Maltin on *You'll Find Out,*
>   *TV Movies and Video Guide,* 1988 edition

> I think Karloff and Lugosi are so popular today because their roles were so
> much more unusual. They weren't just playing straight character parts, but
> something so imaginative—and the way they portrayed these parts had so much
> imagination. Of course, they also were very fine actors, and they took their work
> seriously.
>
>   —Louise Currie

You'll Find Out is one of those movies which one finds hard to forgive in the light of posterity. The film opens with a shocker. We see "Kay Kyser in *You'll Find Out*," the bandleader's name dominating the title, followed by the supporting cast:

> Peter Lorre
> Dennis O'Keefe
> Helen Parrish
> Bela Lugosi
> Alma Kruger

Promised "the best billing possible," this was the best RKO would do for Bela; he's even more humbled when, a few title cards later, we read, on a special billing card all its own, "and BORIS KARLOFF." (This might have been a compromise; in the closing credits, Lorre, Karloff and Lugosi immediately follow Kyser, in that order, with O'Keefe and Miss Parrish taking the lower echelon in the cast list.)

Beyond the billing, of course, is the tone itself. *You'll Find Out* is the first big film to spoof horror, predating *Abbott and Costello Meet Frankenstein* by eight years. Like that much more popular film (but without any of its flair, atmosphere and excitement), *You'll Find Out* basically treats the horror stars with respect. However, it is too preoccupied with its inherent silliness (and too determined to showcase Kyser) to allow the heavies chance to do much more than skulk.

You'll Find Out clearly did no harm to the careers of the star villains. Lorre was about to begin his most popular era at Warner Bros., Karloff was on the eve of Broadway's *Arsenic and Old Lace,* and Lugosi faced the busy, lucrative World War II years. Nor did it harm the horror genre; Universal would introduce *The Wolf Man* in 1941, and RKO itself would be the site of the classic work of Val Lewton, beginning with 1942's *Cat People.* The real harm of *You'll Find Out* is the way it dates as a precursor to later comedy/horror films which truly made muck of the horror genre, the way it virtually wastes three major stars of Hollywood legend as comic foils for an entertainer whose style dates so badly.

All the villains apparently regarded *You'll Find Out* as a vacation from the usual screen mayhem. One wonders, however, if the antics of Kyser and the Kollege of Musical Knowledge ever wore on them. In the course of the film, Peter Lorre poses a question, one which might have entered the minds of his *You'll Find Out* costars, "Why do I have to waste my time outwitting morons?"

12
Arsenic and the War Years

> I was scared stiff about how they'd like me. After all, I was just a provincial actor. I'd never played in New York before, and I certainly wasn't going to use my screen reputation!
> — Boris Karloff on his Broadway debut in *Arsenic and Old Lace*

Friday, January 10, 1941, was one of the truly terrifying nights in Boris Karloff's life. The curtain had risen at Broadway's Fulton Theatre on *Arsenic and Old Lace,* a black comedy penned by Joseph Kesselring after pondering the most unlikely thing a sweet old lady might have done. As Act I wickedly rolled, Josephine Hull (as Aunt Abby), Jean Adair (Aunt Martha), Allyn Joslyn (Mortimer) and John Alexander (Teddy), all Broadway veterans, had been reaping huge laughs while Karloff haunted the wings, his lucky 1928 silver dollar in his pocket, awaiting his first entrance as Jonathan Brewster.

"Jonathan was the kind of boy who liked to cut worms in two," Joslyn informed the audience — "with his teeth." Laughter...

Boris might well have wished he was back at the old Lucey's Restaurant in Hollywood, where he had agreed timidly to his Broadway debut over lunch with Russell Crouse. The Horror King was the first and only choice of Crouse and Howard Lindsay (producers of Broadway's record-breaking *Life with Father*) for mad killer Jonathan, and Crouse was amazed when Boris modestly demurred:

> ... in the eyes of New York playgoers I was strictly a film player and I'd be darned if I'd take a chance by starring in my first big city play. If, I said, there were a couple of other parts better than mine, it would be okay with me. As it turned out, of course, the two old aunts were the stars of the show, its very backbone, and what a splendid job they did! My part was simply mustard on a plate of good roast beef.

Still, Karloff began rehearsals in a panic. He stuttered. He lost his voice. He walked the streets of Manhattan all night one evening, trying to conceive a gracious way to leave the play. But he had survived the 10-day tryout in Baltimore, and now, he was rapping at the set door, and hearing

Jean Adair say his entrance cue line: "We'll just have to pretend we're not at home."

Karloff stepped before the footlights as Jonathan Brewster, to the polite applause of the first-nighters. With his assistant, Dr. Einstein (Edgar Stehli), a plastic surgeon who had drunkenly refashioned Jonathan's face in most hideous fashion, he discussed his liquidation of one Mr. Spenalzo, whose cadaver supposedly reposed offstage in the rumble seat:

> EINSTEIN: . . . You shouldn't have killed him, Jonny. He's a nice fellow —
> he gives us a lift — and what happens?
> JONATHAN: He said I looked like Boris Karloff. . . !

It was the line that had sold Boris on the part — and the line that sold the audience on Karloff. The opening night house roared, and Karloff's fear soon turned to joy as he romped through "the happiest role of my life."

". . . What extraordinary luck!" laughed Karloff afterwards in his dressing room, cuddling a toy panda sent for luck by daughter Sara Jane. "A broken-down movie actor in a hit play!"

Arsenic and Old Lace became one of the great hits of the American Theatre, running 1444 Broadway performances. Karloff found the play "a great joy"; he loved playing before a live audience ("The most beautiful thing of all is the complete stillness of an audience so intent it scarcely breathes!"). He won a whole new "legitimate" following. And, he made a great deal of money. In addition to paying Boris $2000 weekly, Lindsay and Crouse had held out a $5000 investment in the play for the star (who had cautiously refused to invest) until after the hit reviews. The money would be returned many times over.

It was an exciting new life for Boris Karloff: signing autographs nightly at the Fulton stage door, enjoying many guest appearances on the premiere 1941 season of radio's *Inner Sanctum Mysteries,* playing Santa Claus at Christmas of 1941 for the children's wing of the Beekman Downtown Hospital. (The children were so anxious to get to Boris's "Santa" that they accidentally "upset" the wing's giant Christmas tree!) He also worked the "graveyard shift" as a Manhattan Air Raid Warden.

On June 27, 1942, Boris left the New York company of *Arsenic and Old Lace,* was replaced by a stage-fright suffering Erich von Stroheim (who had been playing Jonathan in the Chicago company), and returned to Hollywood to complete his Columbia contract. The vehicle: *The Boogie Man Will Get You,* a horror spoof clearly inspired by *Arsenic* and costarring Peter Lorre. Then Boris began a 66-week national tour as the nightmarish Jonathan (during which time he selected the horror tales for the anthology, *Tales of Terror*). It was, for Boris, a wonderful adventure, and he remembered the *Arsenic and Old Lace* years as, professionally, the happiest time of his life.

Incidentally, the Fulton Theatre, where *Arsenic and Old Lace** tallied its 1444 performances, later became the Helen Hayes Theatre. Over 13 years prior to *Arsenic's* opening night, it had been the sight of another famous hit: *Dracula,* starring Bela Lugosi.

Meanwhile, back in Hollywood, life was good for Bela Lugosi. Thanks to his Universal and Monogram contracts, Bela had bought a new home — his "Dracula House" at 10841 Whipple Street, on the "flats" of North Hollywood, just north of Universal City. It was a Gothic house, with a steeple, a huge latticed front window, and ornamental storks on the roof; banana trees loomed over the house, and the beautiful grounds included a pond. Inside was a Black Forest fireplace, a Wild West bar, and, as was the star's custom, a great staircase...

Once again, Bela could play the great host, the wine and rich Bavarian beer flowing as guests played the grand piano and Gypsy musicians serenaded until the dawn. The grounds of the "Dracula House" were great fun for Bela, Jr., and the little estate was Bela's favorite of all his movie colony abodes. Lillian Lugosi once showed me pictures in her album of the "Dracula House," and noted, sadly, how it no longer exists.

The word of *Arsenic and Old Lace's* historic success, and Karloff's triumph, taunted Bela Lugosi. So did Universal's casting him in roles like Eduardo, "keeper of the cats," in 1941's awful *The Black Cat.* And so did the rot he was doing at Monogram, such as 1941's *Spooks Run Wild,* with those perennial, nauseating pubescents, the Bowery Boys.

Still, there were consolations: he was making good money, and Karloff, his dominating "rival," was 2500 miles away. Bela trusted that, as soon as Hollywood realized this fact, he could reclaim the title of King of Hollywood Horror Films. And then, Hollywood history wickedly repeated itself.

> Even a man who is pure in heart,
> and says his prayers by night,
> may become a wolf when the wolfbane blooms,
> and the autumn moon is bright.

On December 9, 1941, ten years and three days after the release of *Frankenstein,* Universal released *The Wolf Man.* The title role went to a beefy,

---

* *Why wasn't Karloff in the Frank Capra Warner Bros. movie of* Arsenic and Old Lace, *shot in late 1941, released in 1944? Several accounts have been passed down. One claims that Karloff, understandably thinking himself indispensable to the movie, set a price Capra was loath to pay; the producer/director was willing to pay only one star salary, and opted for Cary Grant, who mugged as Mortimer. This might have been negotiable, but Lindsay and Crouse let it be known they would not allow Karloff the same two-month leave-of-absence they gave Hull, Adair and Alexander for the movie, fearing it might cause a box office slump. According to Cynthia Lindsay in* Dear Boris, *Karloff was "heartbroken" that he couldn't make the movie, but counted his blessings for the play itself. The costars loved him for allowing them a Hollywood excursion while he stayed with the play; "What a saintly thing to do for two old ladies!" chorused Miss Hull and Miss Adair.*

Lon Chaney, Jr. (left), poses with Bela's tired old monster, in *Frankenstein Meets the Wolf Man,* 1943.

prosaic, 35-year-old actor with a wart beside his nose, a tragic alcohol problem, and a name famous in the history of Universal: Chaney. And, cruelly enough, it was Bela, in a cameo appearance as Bela, the Gypsy werewolf, who got the job of gnawing Creighton Chaney (aka "Lon" Jr.). Chaney (1906–1973) had scored as moronic Lennie in United Artists' 1939 *Of Mice and Men,* after seven years of misadventures at various Hollywood lots; *The Wolf Man* now crowned him as one of Universal's most shamelessly tub-thumped talents of the war years. Forty-seven years later, MCA's packet for the videocassette of *The Wolf Man* still proclaims Lon Chaney, Jr., as "The new Master Character Creator."

The *Wolf Man* was Universal's million-dollar hit of the season, Curt Siodmak's screenplay presenting some of the studio's greatest folklore: the dynamics of the great Claude Rains, his incredible eyes never more emotional than when he looked upon the silver wolf's head cane and realized he had killed his lycanthropic son with it; the quavering "The way you walked was thorny" prayer, awesomely intoned by Maria Ouspenskaya, as Maleva, the old Gypsy seer; the presence of Ralph Bellamy, Warren William, Patric

Knowles; Bela's tragic Gypsy, the Frank Skinner/Hans J. Salter score; and of course, Universal's Queen of the Horrors, the beautiful Evelyn Ankers, keeping her chic pose even as she ran gracefully through the foggy forest in her high heels, her blonde hair bouncing, and her magnificently lush scream becoming one of the classic sensations of horror movie history.

Indeed, Universal had surrounded its young star with grand talent, presumably hoping it would rub off. And it did. The real triumph of *The Wolf Man* rightfully belonged to the star. He played Lawrence Talbot with a tragedy that made both character and actor a legend. Sadly, the legend would tarnish; Chaney was a limited actor, retrospectively regarded (by most fans) as a sadly inferior second-stringer as he made his way through such roles as Frankenstein's monster, Count Alucard, the Mummy (three times), a specially concocted *Inner Sanctum* series, and, ultimately, four great encores as the Wolf Man. As Ethan Mordden wrote in his acclaimed 1988 book, *The Hollywood Studios:*

> Chaney inherited the post by right of genes. But Chaney is no Chaney. With his toneless voice and Mr. Potato Head features, he prefigures the B-movie actors of the 1950s, those who played everything, and everything badly. There is simply no terror in this man: no evil, no Angst, no frisson. Poe would have looked right through him. Lugosi and Karloff, whatever their thespian talents, were genuine macabre personalities. . . .

Sadder than his acting was Chaney's personal life. A lifelong alcoholic, he was a truly tragic man, agonized by many nightmares. "He was a complex guy, always a little let down by the way his father had treated him," said Elisha Cook, Jr. Curt Siodmak tells how Chaney, Sr., would beat little Creighton with a strap, warping his psyche for life; he also feels Lon, Jr., had homosexual problems. Reginald Le Borg related how "The Man of a Thousand Faces" (Sr.) haunted "The Screen's Master Character Creator" (Jr.), taunting him into doomed attempts to top his "old man" as an actor. Indeed, perhaps Lon, Jr., was not to blame for the emotional burden he carried. But it all came out aggressively, and Lon, Jr., became Universal's bad boy of the war years.

It took its toll on his coworkers, as Lon was not often a gentleman. One lady who felt his wrath was poor Evelyn Ankers. Lon's leading lady of so many movies was a bit hefty, and Lon rapidly lamented that he wasn't about to pull muscles lifting her in horror films. He insisted Universal provide an apparatus which would tie his blonde costar to him, to take some of the weight off his arms. Hence, the creation of Universal's "Evelyn Ankers Strap"—a device which hardly could have delighted the female vanity of its lovely namesake.

Universal had its fill of wild, temperamental, colorful characters in the World War II years—Abbott and Costello, Maria Montez, and of course, the very powerful Deanna Durbin. Chaney, Jr.'s misadventures at Universal read like a Hollywood Canterbury Tales:

•On *The Wolf Man:* Creeping up behind Evelyn Ankers on the set of *The Wolf Man,* grabbing her and roaring in her face.

•On *The Ghost of Frankenstein:* Complaining that the forehead piece he wore as the monster was uncomfortable, insisting it be removed, and—when nobody would remove it—tearing it off himself, ripping open his forehead.

•On *Son of Dracula:* Creeping up behind director Robert Siodmak, taking aim, and smashing a vase over the director's bald head.

•On *The Mummy's Curse:* Walking up a crooked old staircase on the back lot, very intoxicated, carrying Virginia Christine, who was tied to Lon via the "Evelyn Ankers strap," and who was terrified at what might happen if the 220-pound mummy took a tumble down the steps with her tied to him. (Director Leslie Goodwins noted the danger and had a stunt man complete the shot.)

Of course, along with these crimes was the fact that Universal, strangely accommodating this behavior, allowed Chaney to overshadow Bela Lugosi. For Bela, Karloff had just gone away, and now Lon, Jr., was Universal's special attraction. Bela still had all his powers; he was magnificent as Ygor in 1942's *The Ghost of Frankenstein,* winning the acting honors in a cast of Sir Cedric Hardwicke, Ralph Bellamy, Lionel Atwill, Evelyn Ankers and Lon, Jr., as the monster. Who can forget the fervor with which Belá, wanting his own brain popped into the monster's skull, told the boisterous Chaney, with an incredible emotion, "Tonight, Ygor will die for you!" Yet Universal rewarded him by casting him as a red-herring butler in 1942's *Night Monster,* which, oddly, was the only Universal film of the forties to give him star-billing.

So, for top-billing and major roles, Bela had to slum at Monogram, giving his all for producer "Jungle Sam" Katzman in such atrocities as 1942's *Black Dragons* and *The Corpse Vanishes.* At last report, only two buildings remained at the old Monogram site, 4376 Sunset Drive, the only studio in the forties which really treated Bela Lugosi like a star—while sentencing him to horrid little movies which forever tarnished his reputation.

In the summer of 1942, Bela toured Eastern stock theatres, reprising scenes from *Dracula.* And then, in the fall, came the strangest engagement of all.

Universal had originally announced that *Frankenstein Meets the Wolf Man* would be a Lon Chaney, Jr., bonanza—the star would play both monster and Wolf Man, with the aid of doubles. However, as George Waggner (producer/director of *The Wolf Man*) blueprinted production, the idea of Chaney vs. Chaney became less and less practical. Waggner and director Roy William Neill needed a monster. . .

It was Universal history that Bela Lugosi had scorned the monster role in *Frankenstein* in 1931. But the studio needed an actor, preferably a horror name—and, as they knew, Bela no longer could be so selective. One of Bela Lugosi's great sources of pride was telling how he had turned down the monster role. Now—eleven years later—would he turn it down again?

On October 12, 1942, Universal began shooting *Frankenstein Meets the Wolf Man,* with Bela Lugosi as the monster.

There were two consolations for the aging, humbled Bela. First of all, the monster, in a cue from the finale of *The Ghost of Frankenstein,* would be blind — hence giving the role a bit more of the "meat" Bela desired. But, best of all (for Bela), the monster of Curt Siodmank's shooting script *spoke* — and Bela eyed the juicy dialogue of the monster:

> Die? Never! Dr. Frankenstein created this body to be immortal! His son gave me a new brain, a clever brain. . . . I will rule the world! I will live to witness the fruits of my wisdom for all eternity!

The shooting of *Frankenstein Meets the Wolf Man* was an agony for Bela: rising at 2:30 a.m. in his "Dracula House" to soak in a hot tub to prepare himelf for the makeup ordeal; Lillian driving Bela to the studio at 5:00 a.m. for the Jack P. Pierce costume and makeup; working all day under the hot lights in the hideous guise made famous by Karloff.

On October 20, 1942, in the midst of production, Bela turned 60 years old. "Bela Lugosi was a very nice man," recalled the late Ilona Massey, blonde opera diva top-billed in *Frankenstin Meets the Wolf Man,* "but by then he was getting old, and most of his stunts were done by a stuntman and not by him." The stuntman was Eddie Parker, and Lugosi would sit sadly on the sidelines, puffing his cigar, watching the stuntman do the demanding work.

The worst was yet to come. After shooting was completed, the Universal powers-that-be screened *Frankenstein Meets the Wolf Man,* and heard Bela fervently delivering the monster's dialogue.

"With Lugosi it sounded so Hungarian funny that they had to take it out!" laughed Curt Siodmak. "A monster with a Hungarian accent!"

Fearful that Bela's monster would be a farce, editor Edward Curtiss cut the dialogue scenes. In one episode, where the monster shows Chaney the portrait of Elsa Frankenstein in the ruins, the scene couldn't be cut — so Universal *erased* Bela's dialogue, leaving him with his lips moving but no words coming out. And also pruned were any references to the monster's blindness — hence making Bela's groping and staggering mannerisms senseless in the release print contest.

Frankenstein Meets the Wolf Man was released in March of 1943. Bela's monster, never very dimensional to begin with, was a mess in the postediting state; the performance, ˜ ̣ ̣J its total inferiority to the Karloff concept, haunted Bela Lugosi, causing buffs over the decades to "prove" Boris's acting superiority over Bela's.

While Karloff played to standing-room-only theatres in the national company of *Arsenic and Old Lace,* Frankenstein's monster was enjoying another laugh on Bela Lugosi.

Yet, in posterity, Bela's poor monster has become a legend in itself. When

MCA released *Frankenstein Meets the Wolf Man* on videocassette in the fall of 1986, New York City video stores sold every copy in stock on the very first day of the tape's release.

*   *   *

After the debacle of *Frankenstein Meets the Wolf Man*, Bela left Universal. At Monogram, he did perhaps his most notorious '40s film, *The Ape Man* (1943); as Dr. James Brewster, Bela has to slouch and growl like an ape in hirsute makeup, sharing a cage with a gorilla (actually Emil Van Horn, in suit). The movie does have its devotees, ranging from audiences with absolutely no taste, to sadists who enjoy the sight of the heroine, the lovely Louise Currie, climactically lashing poor, hairy Bela with a whip.

For some fans, there is something almost endearing about the Monogram output, and the films have won a growing following in recent years. One Monogram admirer is Miss Currie, whose memories of her adventures on the Sunset Drive lot with the Bowery Boys, Charlie Chan and Bela Lugosi are affectionate ones:

> As for Monogram — yes, I got kind of a kick out of it! For one thing, in everything I did at Monogram I had a leading role, which made it much more interesting for me. Monogram called me their Katharine Hepburn! I don't know if they referred to the "look" as much as I had gone to Sarah Lawrence College, and had studied acting with Max Reinhardt. . . .
>
> I enjoyed working "fast" — it was easier for me than sitting around, as we did on "big" productions, and more stimulating. I would feel we had really accomplished something. Of course, things were cheaper; in the Monogram pictures, for example, I wore my own clothes, because sometimes in the cheaper films, if you get it out of wardrobe, you don't do very well!

Most vividly, Louise Currie remembers the team spirit and working with professionals — like Bela Lugosi:

> It was amazing that I even got to know Lugosi, because we worked so fast, and constantly. But on *The Ape Man*, and later *Voodoo Man*, I found him a very intelligent, extremely interesting man. I remember long chats with Lugosi about his family life, and I enjoyed meeting his wife, who was on the set a few times.
>
> William Beaudine, who directed both these films, was a wonderful director, a wonderful man — quiet, kind, and not tempestuous, like some directors could be. He was very well-liked by all his cast. In *The Ape Man*, there was Wallace Ford, an awfully nice man and good actor; Emil Van Horn, the "ape," a very nice young chap; in *Voodoo Man*, there was John Carradine, so tall and lanky — and excellent! When you worked with people like that, a film became much more fun. And there was the benefit of a film made in a small studio — you worked together, you pulled together, you tried harder. A smaller studio, like Monogram, was more of a family, and you pulled to do a good film in a short amount of time — so it would be a standout.

Monogram at its most odious: Louise Currie takes a whip to hirsute Bela in *The Ape Man,* **1943.**

Indeed, it was the sincerity, and 100 percent commitment that Bela Lugosi gave films like *The Ape Man,* which contributed to his legacy today. What a shame that, at the time, his rewards for his pains were yet another touring company of *Dracula,* and a new Monogram opus with the Bowery Boys, *Ghosts on the Loose.*

*   *   *

Meanwhile, Bela Lugosi was not the only horror star having his problems. Lionel Atwill, whose billing topped Bela's in *The Ghost of Frankenstein,* and even *Frankenstein Meets the Wolf Man,* was adrift in one of Hollywood's great scandals. During the Christmas holidays of 1940, "Pinky," reportedly dressed up as Santa Claus, hosted a yuletide orgy at his Pacific Palisades hacienda, showing lewd movies, leading the guests in stripping and reprising the sex plays on a tiger skin rug, before his blazing fireplace, while a pianist played Viennese waltzes. Atwill, of course, had denied it all—but on October 15, 1942, three days after Universal began *Frankenstein Meets the Wolf Man,* with Atwill billed above Lugosi as the jolly Burgomeister of

Vasaria, the actor was convicted of perjury—and sentenced to five years' probation.

Atwill's lawyer, Isaac Pacht, managed to have the decision reversed in April of 1943. However, much damage had been done. The Atwill scandal largely reduced his rivalry to Bela Lugosi. Karloff continued touring in *Arsenic and Old Lace.*

Bald, bug-eyed George Zucco, marvelous British menace, was providing his share of diabolical leers, in films such as 20th Century-Fox's *Dr. Renault's Secret,* and Universal's *The Mad Ghoul* (marvelous as the evil professor lusting after Evelyn Ankers); he was also the top-rank heavy of lowly PRC Studios. For all the work, Zucco, Colin Clive's old costar from London's *Journey's End,* called himself "Hollywood's unhappiest actor—because I'm always cast as an evil, bloodletting old man."

John Carradine, great Hollywood character player of *The Prisoner of Shark Island, Captains Courageous, Jesse James, Stagecoach,* and *The Grapes of Wrath,* had created his own Shakespearean company, and was working madly in Hollywood studios to raise the money. He began his horror career in Universal's 1943 *Captive Wild Woman,* turning a gorilla into Acquanetta, who reverted when angered or sexually aroused. The almost-Nazi overtones of this outrageous film (Acquanetta turns black before she reverts to gorilla) make it truly a horror; still, it's worthwhile, just to see the great wild animal footage from a Clyde Beatty film, and the evil flicker on heroine Evelyn Ankers' face as, in chic bonnet, she climactically unleashes a gorilla on villainous Carradine. The Shakespearean player also patronized Monogram, starring in *Revenge of the Zombies,* before returning to Universal to play high priest Yousef Bey to Chaney, Jr.'s moldy old mummy in *The Mummy's Ghost.*

Saddest of all, however, was the fate of Dwight Frye. Lugosi's servant Renfield and Karloff's tormenting Fritz had fallen on very hard times; at Universal he was glimpsed as an angry villager in the opening of *The Ghost of Frankenstein,* and had played the sizable role of Rudi, the villager of *Frankenstein Meets the Wolf Man;* at PRC, he was Zolaar, the hunchback servant of Zucco in *Dead Men Walk* (1943), looking sadly aged. He was working at the Douglas Aircraft Factory by night, and haunting the casting offices by day, trying to salvage his dying career. Then came a great break: Frye won the role of Secretary of War Newton D. Baker in 20th Century-Fox's *Wilson.* It was a small role, but *Wilson* was to be Zanuck's extravaganza for 1944, and Frye was thrilled. In an interview with *Midnight Marquee* magazine, Dwight Frye, Jr., today active in stage production, remembered the "very, very high weekend" that followed, and the last Sunday night his father, mother and himself spent together:

> That Sunday I remember the three of us went to see a movie at the Pantages Theatre on Hollywood and Vine. . . . I do remember our having to wait in line

Karloff as mad Jonathan Brewster, in Broadway's *Arsenic and Old Lace*, 1941.

in this rather warm theatre for a long time. We got in to see the movie. It was crowded, came out of the movie and we ran to the corner to catch the bus to go home. As we got on the bus and it pulled away my father dropped in the middle of the aisle of the bus.... I was 12.

Dwight Frye died of a heart attack 11:15 p.m. that night, November 7, 1943, at the Hollywood Receiving Hospital. He was 44 years. old. Three days later, the actor was buried at Forest Lawn, Glendale.

Lugosi as Jonathan Brewster, in a 1943 National Company of *Arsenic and Old Lace*.

Frye, Jr., in the same interview, talked of his father's famous costars:

> I remember him talking about being closer probably to Karloff than
> anybody he ever worked with. When I was quite young, I can't remember
> whether it was just before or after my father died, Boris Karloff did a production
> of *Arsenic and Old Lace* on the stage in downtown Los Angeles. I went down and
> saw it then went backstage and gave my name. I must have been 11 or 12 at the
> time and Karloff welcomed me with open arms. That was Karloff. Now Lugosi

I never met or had any connection with and I have a feeling that my father knew him only when they worked but not at all otherwise. I have never heard that Lugosi had a great deal of charm or that he was even interesting as a person, but Karloff was quite a different story....

In talking with Lillian Lugosi, I got the impression that Bela perhaps regarded his "Renfield" of *Dracula* (Frye also appeared with him in a stage revival in the early '40s) with wary ego — and a sense again, of rivalry. Lillian hinted this when she once exclaimed, "Dwight Frye — he had to be the worst Renfield ever!"

*   *   *

On June 7, 1943, *The Hollywood Reporter* proclaimed two upcoming Karloff and Lugosi frightfests. The first was Universal's *Chamber of Horrors,* to be produced by George Waggner, and to star Karloff, Lugosi, Chaney, Lorre, Rains, Zucco, Atwill — even Henry Hull. *Chamber of Horrors* was to feature the Invisible Man, the Mad Ghoul, the Mummy, and "other assorted zombies." Also announced that day was RKO's *Star-Strangled Rhythm* — à la Paramount's 1942 *Star-Spangled Rhythm,* which had featured most of the Paramount lot. The farce would star Karloff, Lugosi and Lorre, with Boris and Bela as actors possessed by their screen horror creations. One wonders what really was behind these curiosities, other than publicity; neither project ever proceeded.

In the late summer of 1943, Bela Lugosi returned to the stage. With Karloff nearing the end of his national tour of *Arsenic and Old Lace,* Lugosi agreed to headline a different company — and to play Karloff's role of Jonathan Brewster.

It was not the first time he had been offered the role; Josephine Hull, "Aunt Abby" herself, had tried to interest Bela in replacing Erich von Stroheim in the Chicago company. Lillian recalled that Bela would have loved it, but he didn't want to inherit a role created on Broadway by Karloff.

Now, two and a half years after Karloff's opening night, after those awful Monogram movies, after *Frankenstein Meets the Wolf Man,* Bela Lugosi wasn't so choosy. On August 5, 1943, Bela opened at the Tivoli Theatre in San Francisco in *Arsenic and Old Lace,* visiting the Music Box Theatre in Los Angeles later in the month (when he began Columbia's *Return of the Vampire,* directed by Lew Landers, aka Louis Friedlander of *The Raven*).

There was, of course, a major alteration in the play script. When Einstein asked Jonathan Brewster why he had killed Mr. Spenalzo, Jonathan did *not* reply, "He said I looked like Boris Karloff!" The line now read, "He said I looked like Bela Lugosi!"

13
The Body Snatcher, 1945

"We medicals have a better way than that," said Fettes. "When we dislike a dead friend of ours, we dissect him."
—from Robert Louis Stevenson's *The Body-Snatcher* (1885)

No punches pulled... No details hidden... No facts sugar-coated in this startling and horrific expose of the methods used by surgeons years ago to get bodies for dissection!
—PR copy for RKO's *The Body Snatcher* (1945)

Three men, Mark Robson, Robert Wise and Val Lewton, have proved to be the very best working combination in my life. They're cultured and articulate, we thresh things out, go into reason, for-an-agin and I think the ultimate results bear every trace of it. I can't begin to tell you how happy such a setup makes me!
—Boris Karloff

In early 1944, lights burned again on Boris Karloff's farm, high in Coldwater Canyon. The star was back in Hollywood, following the year-and-a-half Broadway romp in *Arsenic and Old Lace,* and the 66-week national tour. Upon his triumphant return to the cinema colony, the king of Hollywood macabre discovered that the genre was experiencing a revolution.

At Universal City, of course, the usual fashion prevailed: Lon Chaney, Jr., was still sweating in his mummy costume, Jack P. Pierce was still sculpting in his makeup laboratory, and Evelyn Ankers was still screaming in her girdle.

"At Universal," said young RKO director Mark Robson, "the prevailing idea of horror was a werewolf chasing a girl in a nightgown up a tree."

It was at 780 Gower Street in Hollywood that Robson's boss, Vladimir Ivan Lewton, RKO's "Maharajah of Mayhem," was creating shadowy, suggestive nightmare tales such as 1942's *Cat People* and 1943's *I Walked with a Zombie* and *The Seventh Victim.* Karloff, for one, found Lewton's work to be "fabulous."

And in 1944, Boris Karloff and Val Lewton, novel producer of poetic, sinister shadows, would join forces to create one of the greatest horror films of the era—and the final tandem movie effort of Karloff and Bela Lugosi.

When I was a child, I lived in a world of my own, full of ghosts and monsters and scaly things. I would look up and see an army of the most frightful green snakes swimming in the sky. They were the branches of a tree, and I knew they would come down and swallow me, and that they were snakes, and that they were absolutely pitiless...

All this, I suppose, was useful when I began to make low budget horror films for RKO....

— Val Lewton

When Val Lewton was a two-year-old in his native Russia, his old peasant nurse would sit in his darkened room at night and tell fairy tales in the gory Russian tradition. The child listened raptly as the nurse lovingly detailed the climax of *Little Red Riding Hood,* in which the evil wolf was sliced down the middle by the heroic hunter, dying splattered by its own blood and innards.

It was an excess Lewton eschewed in his own horror films when, in 1942, at the age of 38, and after eight years as assistant to David O. Selznick, he became a "B" producer at RKO. In his pre–Hollywood days, this emotional, high-strung, hypersensitive man had an eclectic and unusual writing career; he had penned a book of verse (*Panther Skin and Grapes*), written nine novels (one of which, *No Bed of Her Own,* had become the Clark Gable/Carole Lombard 1933 *No Man of Her Own*), scripted a radio series (1933's *The Luck of Joan Christopher*), had worked in nonfiction, newspaper, and public relations, and even dabbled in pornography (a book entitled *Yasmine,* which Lewton proudly noted in his résumé is said to be "one of the most beautifully illustrated books ever published, and retails for $75.00 a copy"). He had a quick, decidedly irreverent humor, and enjoyed telling friends that his "associate producer" post at RKO was usually shortened in title to "ass. prod."

Lewton was a very complex man — loved by his friends, such as Alan Napier, who recalls him as "a darling," and disliked intensely by many Hollywoodites who resented his brilliance. A big, heavy, bearlike man, he lived on Corsica Drive in Brentwood with his wife, Ruth, his son and daughter, and an apparent Hemingway fixation. He was a fanatical yachtsman, although never at ease on his own boat, and had a hobby which amused his friends: hiding in his garage at night, awaiting raccoons or coyotes who would attack his garbage cans, and shooting them with his bow and arrow.

Val Lewton had two special phobias — being touched (dreading even handshakes) and cats. Ironically, his first film was *Cat People:* dark, shadowy, alive with subtle sexual undertones and Simone Simon's feline performance, this $134,000 movie darkly, perversely told the tale of a woman who feared she would turn into a bestial creature if her husband made love to her. The film grossed $4 million internationally; along with another studio "B," *Hitler's Children, Cat People* saved RKO (then in the wake of free-spending Orson

Welles' *Citizen Kane* and *The Magnificent Ambersons*) from bankruptcy. Lewton carried on with studio-tested titles like *I Walked with a Zombie, The Leopard Man, The Seventh Victim, The Ghost Ship, The Curse of the Cat People, Youth Runs Wild,* and *Mademoiselle Fifi* — all moneymakers, and all crafted by Lewton with a personal, passionate involvement that emotionally exhausted him.

"I think that few people in Hollywood show in their work that they know or care half as much about movies or human beings," wrote James Agee of Lewton's work. Yet there was little respect for the man. Certainly none came from his mother, sophisticate Nina Lewton (for years head of MGM's New York story department), or his famed actress aunt, Alla Nazimova. The late DeWitt Bodeen, author of the *Cat People* screenplay, told me:

> Nina Lewton was so shocked that she wouldn't go see *Cat People* even after it had become a box office hit. I offered to get a projection room in New York City and show it to her, but she only shook her head, with a shudder.

Nor was there much respect even at RKO. In 1944, the studio engaged a new executive producer to oversee Lewton's work — Jack J. Gross. He was formerly of Universal, where he had been associate producer of such films as the Technicolor 1943 *Phantom of the Opera.* Lewton considered his new supervisor "abysmally ignorant and stupid," for Gross had his own ideas as to producing horror films — and they clashed violently with Val Lewton's.

Lewton had two beloved protégés at RKO: Mark Robson (who died in 1978) and Robert Wise. Today, after Best Director Oscars for *West Side Story* and *The Sound of Music,* Wise remembers his RKO days (where he began as a film porter) with a great affection. He told me:

> Yes, there was controversy between Val Lewton and Jack Gross in really the overall concept of how horror films should be done. Lewton had made quite a reputation for himself in the early 1940s, creating what was known as the psychological horror film. In these, you didn't frighten people so much with the monsters such as the Frankensteins and other fiends, but by fear of the unknown: was something there, or was something not there? Lewton's whole belief was that you could frighten people more by being less specific, sometimes, if you were skillful...
>
> Mr. Gross came from the school that took the opposite side and held that a horror film should have the casting of obvious types of monsters and the use of overt scare tactics. It was Mr. Gross who urged and insisted on bringing Mr. Karloff to RKO for a horror film, or a series of them....

Initially, Lewton was crestfallen. For the producer who made audiences scream via a perversely timed screech of bus brakes in *Cat People,* the idea of hiring Karloff was akin to contracting the bogeyman. As Mr. Wise continued:

> Mr. Lewton, with nothing personal against Mr. Karloff, found this not really very much to his taste, but searched for story material that would have

quality, even though he was using the "scare" actor who had made his name as Frankenstein's monster.

Karloff, meanwhile, was back at Universal. His old studio had jumped to sign him as soon as he returned from his *Arsenic and Old Lace* tour. On February 1, 1944, Karloff began a specially-engineered Universal deal: the studio would boast his services for 13 weeks; Karloff would work 12 of those weeks, at $5000 weekly; and in that period of time, he would star in two pictures. The first eight weeks and $40,000, would be devoted to *The Climax,* a remake of the 1930 Universal chestnut, filmed in Technicolor largely on the "Phantom Stage" by *Phantom of the Opera's* music-loving producer, George Waggner. Waggner also directed this $750,000 melodrama, adapted by Curt Siodmak and boasting Susanna Foster, Turhan Bey, and Gale Sondergaard.

Then, on April 2, 1944, Karloff (then starring in his won Tuesday night radio show *Creeps by Night*) began working the final four weeks and earning the additional $20,000 for *The Devil's Brood,* fated to be released as *House of Frankenstein,* produced by western veteran Paul Malvern, directed by Universal workhorse Erle C. Kenton, and with a story by Curt Siodmak (who has little to say about the film; Edward T. Lowe wrote the actual screenplay). Karloff starred as mad Dr. Gustav Niemann, who escapes from Neustadt Prison for the Criminally Insane with a deranged, lovesick hunchback (J. Carrol Naish), hijacks the traveling Chamber of Horrors of Prof. Bruno Lampini (George Zucco), and wildly proceeds to resurrect and unleash Count Dracula (John Carradine), the Wolf Man (Chaney) and (of course) Frankenstein's monster (here galumphed by western heavy Glenn Strange). Elena Verdugo as a tragic gypsy girl, Anne Gwynne as a newlywed seduced by Dracula's powers, and Lionel Atwill as an inspector who pursues Dracula into the dawn helped fill the colorful cast of this $350,000 production.

It was the usual Universal. One can only wonder how Karloff felt in this "monster rally," seeing how madly Universal was bastardizing its once awesome goblins. One wonders, too, how he felt playing his death scene on the back lot at 3:00 a.m., Tuesday, April 25, a mob of torch-bearing villagers standing by, watching as Strange sank in a pool of studio-whipped "quicksand," pulling Karloff under the muck with him for the film's final close-up.

And one wonders what Bela Lugosi felt—receiving his second slap-in-the-face from Universal regarding the casting of Dracula. First, Chaney, Jr., had been given *Son of Dracula;* now, super character actor Carradine—then touring "John Carradine and His Shakespeare Players" up and down the West Coast, barnstorming as Hamlet, Shylock, and (alternately) Othello and Iago—had won the fabled role.

Early studio publicity had hinted that Lugosi was slated to recreate Dracula in *House of Frankenstein,* and he was available. However, Universal had preferred signing Carradine—despite his $3500 per week price tag—and

Advertisement for *Return of the Ape Man,* 1944. Monogram awarded Lugosi billing over John Carradine, yet when Universal produced *House of Frankenstein* it preferred the Shakespearean Carradine to Lugosi for Count Dracula.

the actor, nightmarishly sensual in his top hat and cape, gave a novelly perverse portrayal.

The curious fact is Lugosi had just worked with the rococo Carradine at Monogram. That lowly lot reverentially gave Lugosi superior roles and billing over his Shakespearean costar in both *Voodoo Man* (in which Carradine was Lugosi's bongo-playing geek of a henchman) and *Return of the Ape Man* (in which Bela transplanted Carradine's brain into Frank Moran, that unforgettably awful caveman in long drawers that the stars thawed out of the cellophane ice). Yet Universal, where Lugosi had won his immortality, preferred Carradine over Lugosi for Dracula.

Meanwhile, as Karloff starred at Universal, Val Lewton — under pressure from Jack Gross — arranged for Karloff to visit RKO to meet him and Robson and Wise. For Lewton and company, it was a very pleasant surprise. "When he turned those eyes on us," Wise told Cynthia Lindsay in *Dear Boris,* "and that velvet voice said, 'Good afternoon, gentlemen,' we were his, and never thought about anything else."

*   *   *

And as Fettes took the lamp his companion untied the fastenings of the sack and drew down the cover from the head. The light fell very clear upon the dark, well-moulded features and smooth-shaven cheeks of a too-familiar countenance, often beheld in dreams of both these young men. A wild yell rang up into the night; each leaped from his own side into the roadway; the lamp fell, broke, and was extinguished; and the horse terrified by this unusual commotion, bounded and went off toward Edinburgh at a gallop, bearing along with it, sole occupant of the gig, the body of the dead and long-dissected Gray.
— the final paragraph of Robert Louis Stevenson's *The Body-Snatcher*

The first meeting had done it. Lewton warmed to the Karloff idea. Not only did he personally like Boris, but there was in Lewton a severe desire to escape his "B" environs. While he loved the freedom of low-budget movie-making, this complex man felt acute pressure to move up the Hollywood rung to more prestigious work — and believed the star name of Karloff might aid the cause. So, while Karloff fulfilled his Universal deal, Lewton busily researched material to fit the horror star and hopefully appeal to Karloff so to cinch the RKO contract.

Karloff project #1 was *Isle of the Dead*, from the Boecklin painting. It had fascinated Lewton in his childhood, as it hung in "Who-Torok," Nazimova's country cottage in the "Sleepy Hollow" region of New York state. Lewton used to enjoy scaring himself, making up gruesome stories about the painting. Karloff project #2 came from literature: a forsaken Robert Louis Stevenson tale titled *The Body-Snatcher*.

Stevenson's *Dr. Jekyll and Mr. Hyde* (1886) evolved from a nightmare; *The Body-Snatcher* (1885; with the hyphen) came from history. It was in Edinburgh in 1827 that William Burke suggested to his landlord, William Hare, that they steal the body of an old lodger named Donald and sell it to Dr. Robert Knox, who operated a Surgeon's Square anatomy school. Burke and Hare stole the body from the coffin, filled the empty casket with tanner's bark and received £7 from the grateful Knox. When another dying lodger took his time in succumbing, Burke and Hare accelerated matters, and smothered him — making another sale to Knox. With the aid of Burke's mistress and Hare's wife, the duo managed to kill an additional 14 to 28 drunks, hags and whores, all of whom were plied with liquor and held down by Burke while Hare "Burked" them (i.e., held his hand over their nose and mouth until they smothered). All victims ultimately were delivered to Knox's cellar.

Burke and Hare's downfall finally began when they "Burked" Mary Paterson, a beautiful 18-year-old voluptuary instantly recognized by Knox's young anatomy students — several of whom had known her to have been very well, and alive, when they had recently enjoyed her favors. Later, authorities apprehended the pair concealing a female corpse, and a sensational trial became the talk of the British Isles.

Hare gave state's evidence and was freed. A mob encouraged him —

violently — to flee England. Burke, who refused to give evidence, was con-victed and doomed to the scaffold in the Grassmarket. On Wednesday, January 28, 1829, William Burke was hanged before a rapturous crowd of 30,000. As the hangman slipped the noose around Burke's neck, the mob became hysterical. "BURKE HIM!" they screamed. Ironically, he himself was dissected at Edinburgh University Medical School.

As for the patrician Dr. Knox? In a sign of the class-conscious times, he simply went into exile.

Stevenson's short tale is actually a "story within a story," beginning years after the Burke and Hare scandal. An "old drunken Scotsman" named Fettes, drinking with his cronies one night in a tavern, learns that Dr. Wolfe MacFarlane is treating a patient there. He angrily confronts the medico as "Toddy" MacFarlane, and ominously whispers: "Have you seen it again?" This sends MacFarlane crying out into the night, and as Fettes goes home, his drinking companions amuse themselves creating a background for the mysterious altercation.

In the men's imaginings, both Fettes and MacFarlane were young assis-tants in the Edinburgh anatomy school of Dr. Knox (mischievously referred to by Stevenson as "Mr. K_____"). MacFarlane was an arrogant dandy, who coolly informed the shocked Fettes that virtually all the bodies delivered to the school's cellar for dissection were murder victims. However, Mac-Farlane's hauteur withered at a tavern when he met Gray — a seedy scoundrel who enjoyed a mysterious blackmailing power over "Toddy" MacFarlane. Eventually MacFarlane killed Gray and dissected him. But, when Mac-Farlane and Fettes robbed the grave of an old farmer's wife on a black, stormy night, both men received a shock — a shock that would become the famous climax of Val Lewton's *The Body Snatcher.*

In an RKO interdepartment communication dated Wednesday, May 10, 1944, Lewton wrote:

Dear Mr. Gross:

Subject to your approval we have decided upon Robert Louis Stevenson's *The Body Snatcher* as the best possible subject for the second Karloff picture. The story needs development because as it is told now, the character we would like Karloff to play is a fragmentary one called "Gray." But if you will read the story you will see the possibility of developing Gray into a truly horrendous person.

You probably want to know the reasons for our selection of this story above the others. They are as follows:

1. The title seems good to us.

2. There is exploitation value in the use of a famous Robert Louis Stevenson classic.

3. There is a ninety percent chance that this is in the public domain. The legal department is now searching the title.

4. The characters are colorful. The background of London medical life in the 1830's is extremely interesting. The sets are limited in number but effective

in type. The costumes are readily procurable and no great difficulties of any sort so far as production is concerned are evident.

    5. There is also an excellent part for Bela Lugosi as a resurrection man.

So, with reason number 5, Lewton set the stage for the eighth and climactic feature teaming of the talking screen's greatest horror stars. Despite what has been written in several books, Lugosi did *not* have any picture deal at RKO at this time; Lewton tossed his name in here like spice in a stew, an almost spoofed concession to his "abysmally ignorant and stupid" executive producer.

And, at this time, as Karloff awaited RKO's official proposal, Lugosi was preparing to embark with Lillian on a summer stock tour, reprising scenes from *Dracula.* In May of 1944, as *The Body Snatcher* (without the hyphen) slowly took form, Lugosi—suffering from ulcers—visited a Hollywood doctor, appealing for medication to relieve his pain during the trip. The doctor responded unethically, supplying the aging actor with "medicine" which, in time, would spotlight Lugosi with the most garish and cataclysmic publicity of his life.

The doctor gave Bela Lugosi morphine.

*   *   *

    Gray, the cabman, although in point of footage subservient to MacFarlane...is the most important part and so far Boris Karloff, who is to play it (God willing) agrees on the value of the character....

    Josef, the janitor, is a sneak; servile and consumed with evil cunning. The character of Josef should present us with few difficulties so far as casting is concerned...

    —letter from Val Lewton to RKO's casting official Ben Piazza,
September 11, 1944

On Monday, May 8, 1944, Universal had "wrapped" *House of Frankenstein.* Ten days later, Thursday, May 18, 1944, Universal experienced its own horror as Karloff, having departed Universal and studied Lewton's proposals on *Isle of the Dead* and *The Body Snatcher,* happily signed a two-picture RKO star contract. The salary: $6000 a week for each picture.

Isle of the Dead began shooting Friday, July 14, 1944. Mark Robson directed, with a cast including Ellen Drew, Marc Cramer, and Alan Napier—one of Lewton's best friends, and fated to become a close friend of Karloff as well. As shooting began, Karloff was in agony—back trouble. He bravely carried on, even after the pain forced him into a wheelchair between scenes. Nevertheless, eight days into production, Karloff's condition became so severe that he entered the hospital and *Isle of the Dead* shut down. The cast dispersed, and shooting was suspended—not to resume until December 1, 1944.

As Karloff recuperated, *The Body Snatcher* evolved. From its inception, Lewton wanted his friend Robert Wise to direct. The 30-year-old Wise had risen through the RKO ranks, from film porter to editor of Welles' *Citizen Kane* to second unit director of *The Magnificent Ambersons* to director of Lewton's 1944 *The Curse of the Cat People* (replacing the "too-slow" original director, Gunther von Fritsch) Wise's first solo directorial effort had been *Mademoiselle Fifi*, a Lewton pet project based on de Maupassant stories. Lewton was immensely proud of him. The two men had great affection for each other.

To write the screenplay, Lewton was given Philip MacDonald.* He had provided the stories for such acclaimed films as RKO's 1934 *The Lost Patrol,* and Columbia's 1943 *Sahara,* as well as a number of 20th Century–Fox's *Mr. Moto* melodramas. In MacDonald's early drafts, Gray became the resurrection man who had shielded MacFarlane in the Burke and Hare scandal and who now reveled in his blackmailing power. MacDonald's conferences with Lewton created the new characters of Meg, Mrs. Marsh and Georgina, and Josef. Executive producer Gross had wanted gore, and Lewton had given it to him; in the original script, there was an episode in which the character of Mrs. MacBride, in Lewton's words, "passes through the horrors of attempting to identify her dead son among the flotsam and jetsam of human limbs and portions on the anatomy tables...."

Then RKO received a shock of its own. Lewton sent the September 8, 1944, "estimating script" for *The Body Snatcher* to the almighty Breen Office for its obligatory blessing. The Breen Office reply of September 27:

> We have read with close attention your estimating script of September 8, for your proposed picture *The Body Snatcher,* and regret to advise that this story is unacceptable under the provisions of the code, because of the repellant nature of such matter, which has to do with grave-robbing, dissecting bodies, and pickling bodies...the undue gruesomeness which would unavoidably be attached to the picturization of such scenes could in no wise be approved....

Lewton was in a quandry: Jack Gross demanded gore, and the Breen Office demanded the gore removed. Since Breen counseled that the film's only chance was "some new locales, away from dead bodies, and new dialogue situations," Lewton himself went back to work on the script. He developed further the romance between Fettes and the Widow Marsh, and eventually wrote all of the final screenplay himself. MacDonald scorned the producer's writing acumen. He demanded that Lewton share blame if the film flopped. Hence, Lewton took screenplay credit (under the nom de plume of "Carlos Keith") with MacDonald while appeasing the Breen Office.

Lewton wanted *The Body Snatcher* to be a "special," hoping for an impressive cast; his previous films had relied almost exclusively on low to moderate-priced RKO contract talent. Citing Universal's 1941 *The Wolf Man,* Lewton appealed to RKO for a high-priced cast. With a few notable exceptions, this wasn't to be.

For John Gray, the Body Snatcher, Karloff was the one and only choice. Also an actor's dream, however, was the part of Dr. "Toddy" MacFarlane, the proud, cold anatomy teacher haunted by Gray. Lewton and company

Gross had rejected Lewton's choice of writer Michael Hogan, as well as Lewton's secondary choices Dana Burnet, Byron Morgan, Eugene Vale, Lilie Hayward, and Fanya Lawrence.

came up with a variety of ideas for this key role: Albert Dekker, the tall, husky character actor best remembered as *Dr. Cyclops* (Paramount, 1940)*; John Emery, a John Barrymore look-alike who had played in Lewton's *Mademoiselle Fifi* and whose chief fame was as the only husband (from 1937 to 1941) of Tallulah Bankhead; George Coulouris, the snitty Walter Parks Thatcher who dragged little Charles Foster Kane away from his sled "Rosebud" in *Citizen Kane;* Philip Merivale, a distinguished character actor who had starred as Death in Broadway's 1929 *Death Takes a Holiday,* and was then playing supporting parts at RKO; and Alan Napier, Lewton's close friend, who had played in Lewton's *Cat People* and *Mademoiselle Fifi,* and had just scored in Paramount's 1943 *The Uninvited.*

In the end, all these gentlemen lost to Henry Daniell, the incisive Englishman whose sly, foxy Baron de Varville had so deliciously agonized Garbo's *Camille* (MGM, 1937). Daniell was one of the era's great unsung movie villains, be he dueling with Errol Flynn in *The Sea Hawk* (Warner Bros., 1940) or causing Charlie Chaplin to delete his best scene as the Nazi "Garbitsch" (Chaplin feared Daniell was funnier than he was!) in *The Great Dictator* (United Artists, 1940). Daniell was something of a mystery in Hollywood. Alan Napier told me:

> Henry Daniell was a nice man — we got on well — but he was a crazy man; believed in the devil, and that sort of thing. He had a belief in the powers of evil. He used to come up here to the Pacific Palisades and walk the beach at night... I can tell you one thing he lacked — warmth.

Ironically, these peculiar traits of fear and coldness made Daniell the perfect choice for the tragic MacFarlane. On October 24, 1944, Daniell signed a free-lance contract with RKO to play Dr. MacFarlane; the terms: $1500 a week with a two-week guarantee.

RKO's Russell Wade (who had a small part in Lewton's *The Leopard Man,* and had costarred with Richard Dix in Lewton's 1943 *The Ghost Ship*) was the sole choice for Donald Fettes, MacFarlane's conscience-plagued assistant. For Meg, MacFarlane's lusty, lower-class wife ("Mr. Wise always described her with the two words, 'raw sex,'" noted Lewton in his casting notes), who masquerades as a housekeeper to appease her husband's social vanity, Lewton signed Edith Atwater, one of his favorite actresses. For Fettes' romantic interest, the Widow Marsh, contractee Rita Corday won the part over contenders Gwen Crawford and Audrey Long; for her crippled daughter, Georgina, Lewton and Wise cast Sharyn Moffet, an appealing little girl who

---

And decades later for one of Hollywood's most bizarre deaths. On the night of May 5, 1968, the 62-year-old Dekker was found hanging from the shower pipe of his Hollywood apartment. He had hand-cuffed himself, written obscenities over his body in lipstick, garbed himself in silky lingerie and stuck a hypodermic needle in each arm. Los Angeles coroner Thomas Noguchi judged the death to be accidental, believing the actor was seeking gratification from a "near-death" experience; nevertheless, the case remains a mystery.

Ad art for *The Body Snatcher*, RKO, 1945.

surpassed first choice Ann Carter (who had played so memorably in *The Curse of the Cat People*).

The role of Josef (as it was originally spelt) wasn't even discussed in the casting brainstorm session; nor had it appeared in Stevenson's story. "The whole part of Joseph," says Robert Wise, "actually was created to accommodate the casting of Lugosi." Contrary to some rumors, Lugosi—whom Jack Gross very much wanted for *The Body Snatcher* because of the commercial value of linking Lugosi's name with Karloff's—was never considered for the costarring part of MacFarlane. As Mr. Wise stated:

> We never considered giving Lugosi the role of MacFarlane. He didn't have the right quality for it, and he certainly didn't have the acting talent to have provided the acting "duel" that Henry Daniell had with Boris Karloff. . . . [T]he small role of Joseph was created specifically so we could put Lugosi in it.

RKO didn't have to look far to find Bela. Hosting a short-lived radio series, *Mystery House,* he had visited the Gower Street lot to play a mad doctor in *Zombies on Broadway,* starring the studio's Abbott and Costello facsimiles, Wally Brown and Alan Carney; the film had "wrapped" at RKO October 5, 1944. These were unhappy days for the aging Bela Lugosi. His wife Lillian had separated from him (they soon reconciled), taking six-year-old Bela, Jr., and leaving her spouse alone in the "Dracula House" on Whipple Street. Bela was drinking heavily. And, since spring, he had been using drugs.

Desperate for money, Lugosi signed to play Joseph October 25, 1944. His contract was a simple, one-page, two-sided free-lance form, promising $3000 per week on a one-week guarantee—as opposed to Karloff's over 30-page, $6000 per week star pact. On the same Wednesday that Bela Lugosi signed his contract, *The Body Snatcher* officially began shooting.

*   *   *

> Val Lewton was a charming gentleman, a terrific talent, and Robert Wise was great to work with—very astute. Karloff and I got along well; he was typically British, very "clipped," and I enjoyed rehearsing with Karloff and Henry Daniell. It was remarkable what Lewton could do with so little time and so little money.
>
> —Russell Wade

> *The Body Snatcher* was only a small budget picture, but they call it a classic now! And no wonder—such talents. Val Lewton was a very nice man, and often on the set. Boris Karloff was a very nice, gentlemanly person—very gentle, very quiet, and soft-spoken. He was a fine actor; he could do anything. Henry Daniell was a marvelous actor—a very intense man, even offscreen. I admired those men—Bela Lugosi, too!
>
> Bobby Wise was a fine director, a very thorough sort of person, not excitable. I can see why he became a major director in Hollywood. And working with such talents bring out the best in you.
>
> —Rita Corday

The Body Snatcher: **Bela as Joseph, sporting a hat he does not wear in the film.**

"The shooting schedule on *The Body Snatcher* was someplace in the area of 18 to 20 days," says Robert Wise. "The budget was around $180,000 to $200,000 — I can't be exact — but very close to that dollar amount."

The Body Snatcher begins beautifully, hauntingly. The scene is 1831 Edinburgh; the title credits run against a backdrop of Edinburgh Castle, and the opening shots show shepherds moving a flock through Edinburgh as a street singer (Donna Lee, later described by *Life* as "RKO's corporate challenge to

Deanna Durbin") sweetly sings a Scottish ballad. Actually, the exteriors are from RKO's 1939 *The Hunchback of Notre Dame,* on the studio ranch, and Lewton had captured Stevenson's mood by showing Hogarth paintings to his director, stars and cameraman (Robert de Grasse, cinematographer of Lewton's *The Leopard Man*).

In Grayfriar's Kirkyard, a little dog named Robbie guards a grave as young medical student Fettes who has chosen to lunch in the cemetery, tries to feed him. Wade, handsome, ingenuous, once received one of the highest "likability" scores in an audience test; here, he is immediately sympathetic and likable as Fettes. Also in the cemetery is Mrs. MacBride, the mother of the dead man, whose grave the dog loyally guards.

"A fine lad he was — gentle with all little things — like Robbie here," says Mrs. MacBride — played by plump, white-haired Mary Gordon, who had been tossed into the incinerated windmill by Karloff's monster in *Bride of Frankenstein,* and, more recently, had tidied up after Basil Rathbone's Sherlock Holmes at Universal. "Now I canna get the dog to leave here. But it's probably for the best — for I havena' got the money to afford a grave watcher."

"Not much danger here, ma'am, I wouldn't think," says Fettes, "right here in the heart of Edinburgh."

"Oh, they're uncommon bold, the grave robbers," says Mrs. MacBride, "and the daft doctors who drive them on!"

Fettes himself was studying to be a doctor. That is, he was, until to-day... There is the clip-clop of horses' hoofs — and a coach rolls by the churchyard, with a driver hunched on his seat.

"Now you watch sharp, little miss, for my horse to give you a hello!" smiles cabman John Gray, as he carries little crippled girl Georgina (Sharyn Moffet) to the door of Dr. MacFarlane. In his top hat, sideburns and bright smile, Karloff is marvelously picaresque, a merry demon from a Hogarth nightmare; it is his most brilliant performance. Robert Wise recalls:

> Boris Karloff was an absolute joy... He was a very well-educated and well-read, cultured man, with fine manners — soft-spoken, and a gentleman in every sense. He was a delight to work with as an actor — very responsive, very professional. Boris was particularly keen about doing *The Body Snatcher.* He felt it was his first opportunity to show what he could do as an actor, a fine actor of great skill and great depth...

In high spirits over his plum role, Boris often displayed his offbeat sense of humor. One day, RKO treated a squad of soldiers to a studio tour, and ushered them onto the set of *The Body Snatcher.* The men were thrilled at the prospect of seeing the great Boris Karloff, and as Wise called "Action" Karloff made his entrance, in top hat and with a "body" over his shoulder, grinning wickedly at the camera. As soon as Wise called "Cut!" Karloff merrily plopped down the dummy, looked at the awestruck troops, and grinned, "Goddammit, this thing is heavy!"

At MacFarlane's house, Meg, his "housekeeper," answers the door. Edith Atwater, oddly sensual, exchanges a mysterious look with Karloff as the Widow Marsh and her little daughter enter the great house.

The cold interiors of the Victorian MacFarlane domain actually were a revamping of the set from 1944's *Experiment Perilous,* which had starred Hedy Lamarr and George Brent. Lewton's ever-resourceful art directors Albert S. D'Agostino (formerly of Universal, where he was set designer for *Werewolf of London, The Raven, The Invisible Ray* and *Dracula's Daughter*) and Walter Keller stylized the set, under the supervision of Lewton, who at one point rejected a candleholder because it was of the type common to miners—not medical students.

Enter Henry Daniell's Dr. "Toddy" MacFarlane—tall, striking, austere. "Daniell was a pro," said Karloff years later, "a real honest-to-goodness pro. There was no rubbish with him, no faking." He was one of the movies' finest actors, having trained under Gerald du Maurier, and regarded Hollywood (according to Alan Napier) with "withering contempt." The arrogance perfectly suits his MacFarlane.

"Born paralyzed?" he snaps at Miss Corday (lovely and charming as the widow) as he coldly scrutinizes little Georgina (played by Sharyn Moffet with scarcely a touch of saccharine). In Daniell's coldness, we immediately glimpse the tragedy of MacFarlane—a brilliant man of whom Fettes will say, "He taught me the mathematics of anatomy, but he couldn't teach me the poetry of medicine."

Georgina, sensing MacFarlane's coldness, will tell him nothing, but warms to Ward's Fettes when he enters. "It was very hard for me to keep up with Henry Daniell," says Ward, "a very fine actor, and on the cold side as a person." An examination reveals a traumatic tumor, caused by the accident of three years before which had killed her father and crippled Georgina. MacFarlane believes that a very delicate operation, never before performed, could cure the girl, but he refuses to do it himself—using his teaching commitments as an excuse. "And that's a great responsibility upon me, ma'am," he tells the heartbroken Mrs. Marsh. "A great responsibility."

After mother and daughter leave, Fettes enters to inform MacFarlane that the financial troubles of his father, a country vicar, dictate that he give up medicine. "You're too good a man, Fettes, I'll not let you quit," says MacFarlane, who offers him a paying post as an assistant. Meg overhears, and after Fettes leaves the room, she talks with her secret husband.

> "You're not having Fettes for your assistant?"
> "Why not? He's a good lad—bright and able."
> "Aye. He is a good lad. That's why I ask you, MacFarlane."
> "You think it'll spoil the boy. Wasn't I assistant to Knox?"
> "Aye."
> "Did it spoil me, Meg, my lass?"

Karloff as The Body Snatcher.

Miss Atwater doesn't answer; but her eloquent face speaks volumes. As the script described the tag of the scene: "He kisses her off-handedly. She wraps her arms around his neck and kisses him with fierce passion. He releases himself, goes into the next room."

MacFarlane and Fettes enter the anatomy room of the school. "At one of the tables," noted the script, in a revision made just two days before shooting started, "is the hunched, dark and evil figure of Joseph, the janitor of the school."

On October 20, 1944 — Bela Lugosi's 62nd birthday — Jack J. Gross had written this RKO memo to Lewton:

> I think that it is quite important that you give Bela Lugosi a definite characterization. In one of the Frankenstein pictures he played a hunch-back with a muff, which made him a terrifying looking character. This is merely a suggestion.
>
> —JG

To which Lewton replied:

> Okay. We'll hump him.
>
> —Val

Slightly humped, hair parted in the middle, Bela Lugosi had never looked so slimy or so old. Russell Wade remembers Bela as "kind of in another world," "not with it," "seeming very old," and "pretty far gone." In sad truth, the actor was ailing, drug-handicapped, and sometimes hung over. And most painfully for the proud Bela, here was old "rival" Karloff, chewing the scenery in a marvelous role, while he, Lugosi, was playing his stooge.

Joseph eavesdrops on the conversation, and Daniell snaps at Lugosi, "Joseph! What the devil are you doing, sneaking about like a Redskin? Make a little noise man. Let people know you're about."

"Yes, doctor, yes," says Joseph meekly, scubbing the anatomy table.

"Otherwise," says Daniell prophetically, "I might get the idea you are trying to spy on me."

MacFarlane discusses with Fettes the bodies they use for dissection. Fettes believes they are the bodies of paupers, delivered by the Municipal Council. "That's what the law stipulates," says MacFarlane — "but there aren't enough of them, Fettes — there aren't enough of them."

There follows the film's first real moment of horror — at night, in Grayfriar's Kirkyard, where little Robbie is still lying on his master's grave. We here the echoing clip-clop of horses' hoofs on the cobbled streets, and, as the script described the scene, in a revision of October 23, 1944:

> The great black shadow of a man in a caped overcoat and top hat with a spade over his shoulder is thrown into the wall of Grayfriar's Kirk by the street

lamp. The huge shadow looms high over the tiny dog. Robbie rises valiantly to his feet, snarling. As he does so, the actual figure of the man, as black and indistinct as his own shadow, comes past the camera, blacking out the little dog. There is a deeper growl from Robbie. The man swings his spade down. As the spade drives home there is a little weak sound from the dog.

ANOTHER ANGLE. With his foot, Gray pushes the dead body of the little dog to one side, strikes the spade into the ground and starts to dig.

With Roy Webb's moody music, and de Grasse's shadowy cinematography, it is a terrifying vignette.

Later that night, the horse and coach pull up to MacFarlane's house and Fettes answers the cellar door. "Hey, give me a hand, this is heavy!" says Karloff, sociably sinister.

"You'll find the specimen in good condition," says Gray. "He was as bright and lively as a thrush not a week long gone! A likely lad, I'm told."

"Mr. Gray?" queries Fettes, with just the right amount of fear and loathing.

"That's right!" smiles Karloff's Body Snatcher, hugely enjoying the student's fear — and his role. "Cabman Gray. I've had some dealings with MacFarlane in the past, you understand, and I've always gotten on with his assistants — providing, of course, they understand my humble position!"

It's a great scene — Wade nervously paying the resurrection man, Karloff hugely enjoying his nervousness. "My respects, Master Fettes," leers Karloff at the door, "and may this be the first of many profitable meetings!"

From the top of the stairs, Fettes hears laughter. Peering into the basement is MacFarlane. "Your first meeting with the redoubtable Gray," says MacFarlane. "You can count it a milestone in your medical career!"

The next morning. In the anatomy room, the students have gathered. Among the stock RKO players as the students are Bill Williams, and Robert Clarke — later the star of Edgar Ulmer's 1951 *The Man from Planet X*, and 1958's *The Hideous Sun Demon* (the "cult film" which he produced, directed and cowrote besides playing the title role). Clarke (today a public relations spokesman for a Los Angeles bank) graciously and keenly observed Karloff and Lugosi on *The Body Snatcher,* and told me:

> I just have the greatest, loving memory of Mr. Karloff. He was a thoughtful, kindly, friendly, helpful person who took an interest in the young people, and was willing to talk with you anytime, one-on-one. He was a great human being.
>
> I remember once he was talking to me about stage fright. Suffering from it myself, I was fascinated — a star who would admit to stagefright! But he told me that he had it so bad when he had gone to New York for *Arsenic and Old Lace* that he was once up all night, just walking the streets of New York. "Come the dress rehearsal, someone pushed me onto the stage," Karloff said in his wonderfully British, kindly way, "and I don't remember a thing — except that I had diarrhea for three weeks!"

Opposite: **Karloff, Lugosi and Henry Daniell in *The Body Snatcher.***

Mr. Clarke's memory of Bela Lugosi is different:

> Certainly at this point, Karloff was the star. He had a picture deal at RKO, and then they dragged poor Bela in to do this featured part — and not much of a part at that.
>
> Lugosi was quite ill — as I learned later, he had become very dependent on drugs due to an illness or injury — and he was not very communicative. He talked very little to anyone. He was off by himself, and he spent a lot of his time lying flat on his back in his dressing room. When the assistant director called him, he came out and did his stuff. But it was a time of illness for him — and he looked bad.

Joseph interrupts Fettes' work with the students to say there's a lady to see him — Widow Marsh, who pleads Fettes to use his influence to persuade MacFarlane to operate. And shortly afterwards, as he whistles through the Edinburgh streets, Fettes suffers a shock. A crowd has gathered at Grayfriar's Kirkyard — where a heartbroken Mrs. MacBride, having discovered her son's desecrated grave, leaves the cemetery, cradling the little dead dog.

"They killed his wee doggy, too," she tearfully tells Fettes. "Little Robbie."

It's a stomach-punching scene — for the audience, and Fettes, who returns to MacFarlane to give up medicine. For all the pathos of the preceding scene, Daniell presents a stirring defense, condemning the laws that have damned the progress of medical science. "If that dam will not break," he attests, "the men of medicine have to find other courses — understand?" He expresses sorrow for Mrs. MacBride — "but her son might be alive today if more doctors had been given the opportunity to work with more human specimens. As for me — I let no man stop me when I know I'm right . . . if you're a real man, and want to be a good doctor, you'll see it as I see it."

That evening, MacFarlane and Fettes go to Hobbs tavern. There is plenty of the atmosphere Lewton so loved in his movies: a boy is singing by the spit, where a prize "porker" roasts, and the "men of medicine" warm themselves by the great, roaring fire.

"A fine specimen, isn't he — Toddy MacFarlane?"

Karloff's Gray — in his top hat and biggest smile, hoisting a mug, jolly as the devil himself.

MacFarlane, high spirits dampened, sits at the cabman's table and agrees to buy him a drink. "I'm a pretty bad fella m'self," smiles Gray to the shocked Fettes, "but MacFarlane's the boy! Ho, ho, ho, Toddy MacFarlane. . .!"

"I will not have you call me by that name!" snaps MacFarlane.

"You will not have it?" mockingly sneers Gray.

Covering for MacFarlane, Fettes changes the subject. He brings up the Widow Marsh, and implores MacFarlane to operate. He refuses. But Gray is interested . . . he wants MacFarlane to operate. "I'd like to have you prove that a lot of things I know haven't hurt Toddy MacFarlane any... Maybe there are some private reasons between you and me that will make ya' ... some long lost friends, eh Toddy?"

MacFarlane, trying to cover up — "It might be an interesting case."

"That's a good boy, Toddy!" rejoices Gray.

Losing his composure, almost childish in his anger, MacFarlane wheels on Gray. "You only want me to do it because I don't want to. That's it, isn't it, Gray?"

"Toddy hates me!" Gray laughingly boasts to Fettes. "Did you ever see the lads play knife?" Gray grabs a table knife and viciously plunges it into a loaf of bread.

"Toddy," leers Karloff with a sick pride, "would like to do that all over my body!"

"We medicals have a better way than that," says Fettes. "When we dislike a friend, we dissect him."

"You'll never get rid of me that way, Toddy," says Gray. "You and I have two bodies — aye, two very different sorts of bodies — but we're closer than if we were in the same skin. For I saved that skin of yours once — and you'll not forget it."

Karloff had drowned, strangled, sacrificed, crushed and beheaded screen victims in his career — but nothing is quite as sinister as his gloating, perverse, wickedly jolly torment of Henry Daniell in this scene — much of the dialogue taken almost directly from the Stevenson story and, once again, added by Lewton to the script only two days before shooting started.

While Fettes joyfully tells Widow Marsh and the wheelchaired Georgina (who is listening for Gray's white horse) on the ramparts, MacFarlane, the morning after, sits at his fireplace in his dressing room, almost maniacally smashing a piece of coal with his poker. "Gray's head — is that it, Toddy?" teasingly laughs Meg, her hair braided, and in her nightgown. The scene suggests strong passion between them, and they almost appear to be ready to bed when Fettes interrupts. Meg leaves the room, Fettes tells MacFarlane of his meeting with Mrs. Marsh, and MacFarlane erupts — he claims his promise was only "given in drink" and blames the lack of a spinal column in the dissecting room for the inability to perform the operation. Fettes' mind runs to finding a spinal column...

In the original script, the scene now focused on Joseph in the anatomy room:

> Joseph at the desk. He has the account book open before him and with index finger moving from letter to letter, he is laboriously but silently spelling out the words. Suddenly he hears footsteps behind him on the stairs and quickly slams the book and begins dusting the desk.

The scene called for Fettes to ask Joseph where Gray the cabman lived, and Joseph to insinuate a bribe. "I'd gladly run with a message, sir, for a florin," Lugosi was to say. "It's not much, considering it's Sunday." Fettes finds Joseph distasteful, and goes himself. Judging from a surviving production still, the brief scene apparently was shot; one of Bela's few scenes, it ended up on the cutting room floor.

JOHN GRAY—CABMAN reads the lettering on Gray's dwelling and Fettes ventures into what Lewton's script calls "almost Stygian darkness." There follows one of *The Body Snatcher's* most ingeniously frightening moments: "Suddenly from the darkness looms a tremendous white figure," noted the script. "It is the cabman's horse." The sudden appearance of the horse, and its snort, superbly timed and under Webb's moody music, was a Lewton "bus"—a sublime shock trademark of the producer, named after the famous sudden appearance of the bus and the release of its pneumatic brakes in *Cat People*. The innocuous horse caused screams wherever *The Body Snatcher* played.

Gray is his usually patronizing self—"I'm honored—honored!" he says to Fettes, who asks of Gray's chances to get him a subject. Gray isn't encouraging—"There was a dog that bothered me during the last job. People are so concerned about dogs—all in all it raised the very father and mother of a row. They say the kirkyards are to be guarded!" Yet he doesn't dismiss the idea: "You may tell Toddy that I will do what I can, when I can—as he knows I will. But he must wait and see—like the children do." Fettes leaves. And outside, Gray hears the ballad of the street singer.

Lewton and Wise made something very strange of Donna Lee's street singer, described by Fettes as "a wild lassie from the Highlands"; Lewton described her in his character notes as "a girl of wild, untutored loveliness" and she seems unusually pathetic, haunting. She is also fated to be the victim of an unforgettably filmic murder. As Lewton detailed the scene in *The Body Snatcher* script:

> It is a long deserted street. At the near end a lantern on a house wall casts a sphere of dim radiance.... From behind the camera comes the street singer, walking slowly, singing and rattling her begging bowl. She walks on. Just before her figure is lost in the darkness, from behind the camera can be heard the clop-clop of hoofs, the creak of carriage springs, and the rolling wheels of Gray's cab. As the singer disappears completely into the darkness, the cab goes past the camera. It, too, disappears into the darkness. The CAMERA HOLDS. The sound of the carriage ceases. A moment later, the song of the street singer comes to an abrupt, choked end.
> LONG DISSOLVE OUT

It is episodes like this one, meticulously crafted by the producer and faithfully delivered by his protégé directors, that make Val Lewton the highest profile producer of horror films.

"A stroke of luck, you might say!" smiles Gray when he delivers the street singer's corpse to Fettes in the cellar. Fettes, shocked at seeing the girl dead, accuses Gray of murder—but Gray curtly informs him he's mistaken, collects his £10 and bids Fettes goodnight. The next morning, Fettes relates his suspicions to MacFarlane; in a superbly effective scene, as Lugosi's clay pipe–smoking Joseph eavesdrops, and the spectral voice of the street singer wails on the soundtrack, Fettes announces his plan to report the crime—"It's like Burke and Hare all over again!" But MacFarlane coolly dissuades him; after all, Fettes ordered the specimen and paid for it—making him a party to murder. "I should advise complete dissection," says MacFarlane, who wants the whole centrum system himself for spinal work. "You know why," he tells Fettes.

*   *   *

The operation on Georgina is performed—with no anesthesia in 1831. Even the medical students look effectively squeamish as MacFarlane operates. Robert Clarke recalls the scene vividly;

> This incident speaks so well of Mr. Wise, who tried to make you feel at ease. It was the scene where Henry Daniell is operating on the little girl. The scene really belonged to Daniell, a polished, very accomplished actor, and not too interested in the "anatomy student" young actors who were really window-dressing for his scene. Still, in the midst of all his lines, I had a line or two to say....
>
> Well, I arrived on the set about 10 minutes late—I got caught in traffic, or something. "This is not good, Bobby, being late," said Wise, who placed me into the scene they were setting up. Well, I had such stage fright, and was so nervous about being late, that when the cue came for my line, I was too scared to say it! Henry Daniell walked right over me and kept delivering his lines.
>
> So Bob Wise stopped him. He said to Daniell, "Wait a minute. Let Bobby say his line." Daniell was very courteous, and I always felt a warmth and appreciation that Wise made sure I got in my line!

The operation is performed. Optimistic, MacFarlane tells Gray (escorted in by Joseph, in Karloff and Lugosi's first scene together) he plans to lecture more and dissect less—hence, he'll be needing no more bodies. Gray takes it sportingly: "I'll be stopping by, once in a while, to see you and Meg, for auld lang syne." At the door, Gray turns—with a terrible smile.

"And do ya' think you're getting rid of me, Toddy?" laughs Gray, his laughter rising hellishly as he exits...

Outside, Boris and Bela have a brief scene. Joseph approaches the laughing Gray, intending blackmail; Fettes' arrival interrupts.

Georgina, meanwhile, has recovered from the operation—but will not walk. "Child, I say to you, get up out of that chair and *walk!*" demands MacFarlane. Once again, we see the coldness of MacFarlane in contrast to the sympathy of Fettes, who combats MacFarlane's bullying.

"But she must *want* to stand!" says Fettes. "She must *want* to walk!"

"Confound me, the child's a cripple," shouts MacFarlane; "of course she wants to walk!"

But Georgina only cries. "Then all my surgery is no good," says MacFarlane, who heads for Hobbs, where he drinks into the night — "getting stiffer than the bodies he demonstrates," says a waiter to Gray, who joins Toddy at his table.

In a scene revamped on the first day of shooting, Karloff and Daniell go at each other with dramatic fury:

"Gray, you know something about the human body."

"I've had some experience!"

MacFarlane drunkenly stacks glasses to show how he reassembled Georgina's spine. Gray violently knocks them asunder.

"You're a fool, Toddy, and no doctor. It's only the dead ones you know!"

"I am a doctor! I teach medicine!"

"Like Knox taught you? Like I taught you? In cellars, in graveyards. . .? Look, look at yourself!"

Daniell looks into a mirror behind him; he stares at his vain, pampered face, while Gray — his own face a gargoyle — taunts him.

"Could you be a doctor, a healing man, with the things those eyes have seen? There's a lot of knowledge in those eyes, but no understanding. You'll not get that from me."

MacFarlane lashes back. "Why should I be afraid of you? What are you holding over me?"

"I'll tell ya' what. I stood up in the witness box and took what should a' been coming to you. I ran through the streets with the mud and the stones around my ears and the mob yelling for my blood because you were afraid to face it, yes, and you're *still* afraid!"

"Shout it from the housetops!" snaps MacFarlane. But, as he reminds the commoner, Gray: "They hanged Burke. They mobbed Hare. But Dr. Knox is living like a gentleman in London. . . If you have any regard for your neck you'll leave now. And stay away from my house, my school, and from me!"

"Well, I've no wish for a rope cravat. I never liked the smell of hemp. So I'll bid ya' good night — Dr. MacFarlane."

Gray returns home. He has a visitor — the blackmailing Joseph.

Robert Wise had discovered that his problems on *The Body Snatcher* weren't just the $200,000 budget, the leftover sets, the rapid shooting schedule. He also had to extract a character performance from an aging, ailing, drug-and-alcohol handicapped Bela Lugosi. Wise recalls:

> At that time, Lugosi was not in particularly good health, so it was a case of having to work very carefully with him. He certainly was willing, but I found getting my thoughts and ideas over to him took more time. He was a little slower grasping what the director wanted than Karloff. Karloff was very quick and very keen. . . . Lugosi was slower of movement, slower in thought processes and slower to grasp everything that was wanted. . . .

It must have been poignant—and sad—for both men as they worked together on *The Body Snatcher* at Halloween time of 1944. Here was Karloff, enjoying a deluxe contract and perhaps the best role of his career; here was Lugosi, trapped in a creepy cameo, serving as Karloff's stooge. To make matters worse, Bela was lethargic on the set, and kept forgetting his lines.

Now, on *The Body Snatcher* set, Bela's old dislike of Boris only aggravated his professional shortcomings. Playing opposite Karloff, Bela would lose his character and blow his lines so often that the young, genial Wise was, as he recalls, "embarrassed" asking for so many retakes. Had Karloff seriously pursued this "rivalry" over the years, he might have enjoyed seeing his sadly humbled colleague forgetting simple lines and requiring take after take, but such was not his style; "He was too much of a gentleman," says Wise. Instead, as the director remembers, Boris did all he could to be friendly to Bela—even though he had always sensed the bitterness that his costar harbored for him.

The stars had to work intimately together in the famous scene where Gray "Burkes" Joseph. In his usual jolly way, Gray invites the blackmailer to take a seat by the fire; Gray himself takes a seat, his cat, Brother, curled up in his lap.

"I know you kill people, to sell bodies… Give me money, or I tell the police you murder the subjects," says Joseph, nervously.

Gray (after asking if Joseph came on his own accord) merrily gives him money, £16. In fact, he fills his glass with brandy, and plays the happy host.

"Drink, Joseph, drink!" smiles Karloff. "You and I should work together!"

"You mean, we would sell the bodies to the doctors together?" replies dimwit Joseph. "To dig 'em up?"

"No, … the kirkyards are too well-guarded. We will, so to speak— 'Burke' them."

As Bela's Joseph sits in a chair with dense expression and limited dialogue, Boris's Gray dances around him, singing a ditty, plying his victim with liquor, mesmerizing Joseph—and the audience:

> GRAY: The ruffian dogs, the Hellish pair,
>   The villain Burke, the meagre Hare,
> JOSEPH: Never heard of the song. What did they do?
> GRAY: Eighteen people they killed and sold the bodies to Dr. Knox. Ten pounds for a large, eight for a small. That's good business, Joseph!
> JOSEPH: Uh—but where did they get the people?
> GRAY: That was Hare's end. Ah, you should have seen him on the streets. When he saw some old beldam deep in drink, how he cozened her! "A good-day to you, Madame Tosspot, and would you like a little glass of something before you take your rest? Come with me to my house and you shall be my guest. You shall have quarts to drink if you like!" Ha, ha! How he cozened them!

JOSEPH: We can do that! But when we get them there—then what?
GRAY: Nor did they handle axe or knife
    To take away their victim's life—
    No sooner done than in the chest
    They crammed their lately welcome guest—
JOSEPH: I don't understand the song. Tell me plain how they did it.
   GRAY: I'll show ya' how they did it, Joseph—I'll show ya' how they
    "Burked" them. No, put your hand down. How can I show ya', man! This
    is how they did it, Joseph. . .

After a wild struggle, Joseph is dead. As a final indignity, Gray, merrily humming his Burke and Hare ditty, carries Joseph's carcass into Mac-Farlane's cellar and tosses it into a brine vat. Long after midnight, Mac-Farlane returns home, drunk, to find Gray sitting with an unwilling Meg, and drinking. "You grudge me a glass with me old crony Meg?" asks Karloff. "Crony indeed!" snaps Miss Atwater. MacFarlane starts to throw Gray out by physical force, but Gray warns, "I wouldn't do it, Toddy, I wouldn't be heavy-handed. It might become known that, when the great Dr. MacFarlane finds his anatomy school without subjects, he provides them himself from the midst of his own household. . . . Take a look down the stairs, Toddy. . ."

In a particularly ghoulish scene for 1945, MacFarlane, assisted by Fettes, discovers Bela's body, in the brine vat; he pulls the head out of the vat and into a camera close-up. It couldn't be done with a double, and "poor Bela" had to submerge his aging self under the brine. As Robert Wise remembers:

> Lugosi did have to immerse himself into the brine vat, and he did it willingly as any good professional would do. We had no problem—I think I had to make it only once or twice—but it is Lugosi who did that particular bit in the picture.

MacFarlane is incensed—he leaves to confront Gray, and Meg confronts Fettes with the true story of MacFarlane's past: how he was to the infamous Knox what Fettes is to him; how MacFarlane took the last of Meg's savings to hire Gray to shield him in the sensational trial of Burke and Hare and Knox; how MacFarlane, who will not publicly acknowledge his own wife because of her "common" background, has always been chained by the shame of the old life. With her "second sight" of the Highlands, Meg says, "I see MacFarlane and Gray—the pit yawns for them. I would have you away from them and safe out of the torment!"

By the time Gray arrives home, MacFarlane is there. "Gray, I must be rid of you. You've become a cancer—a malignant, evil cancer, rotting my mind." The doctor offers his persecutor riches if he'll go away.

"That wouldn't be half so much fun for me as to have you come here and beg," answers Gray.

"Beg! Beg of you, you crawling graveyard rat?"

"Aye! That is my pleasure."

"Very well then. I beg of you! I beseech you!"

"I would lose the fun of having you come back and beg again!" In a superbly bitter speech, laced with chilling self-contempt and sick evil pride, Karloff says, "I am a small man, a humble man, and being poor I have had to do much that I did not want to do. But so long as the great Dr. MacFarlane jumps to my whistle, that long am I a man. And if I have not that, I have nothing. Then I am only a cabman and a grave robber.

"You'll never get rid of me, Toddy!"

As Gray's cat, Brother, watches, the two men fight wildly; at length, MacFarlane rises, grabs a chair and smashes Gray's skull. The Body Snatcher is dead.

The next day, MacFarlane dissects Gray. The following day he takes the cabman's horse and carriage to a country town and sells it. While he's in the tavern there, Fettes arrives with wondrous news — Georgina has walked — she thought she heard Gray's white horse, and stood to see the animal (a sequence sensitively handled by Wise). "The doctors from my school will perform miracles!" cries the exhilarated MacFarlane, convinced that Gray's death has turned the tide. Then a gaggle of mourners enters the inn; they have just buried an old woman in a country cemetery . . .

That night, as a terrible storm brews, MacFarlane and Fettes plunder the fresh grave and bundle the old woman's body into the coach. As they drive back to Edinburgh through the horrific storm and the desolate countryside, the wind seems to be shrieking, taunting . . .

"Toddy . . . Toddy . . ."

The body keeps jostling, bumping into MacFarlane. He stops the coach. Daniell, his face magnificently fearful, looks at the shrouded corpse. "It's changed!" he cries, almost childishly terrified. The doctor unwraps the shroud and sees . . .

"GRAY!"

In flashes of lightning, it is the naked, luminous cadaver of Gray; as Fettes watches in horror from the road, the horse bolts and the coach with MacFarlane and Gray's haunting cadaver careens madly away. Here, Lewton and Wise bring the ancient but potent fear of a dead body to gloriously macabre life, as Karloff's skeletal arms bounce and wave, perversely trying to embrace the hysterical doctor. It's a classic scene, one which filled theatres with cacaphonies of screaming and was hailed by James Agee in *Time* as "all out hair-raising a climax to a horror film as you are ever likely to see."

Finally, the coach rolls over a cliff, the shrill scream of MacFarlane rising above the crash of the storm. Fettes reaches the scene of the accident. There is the corpse of the old woman. Nearby lies the body of MacFarlane — a victim of his past, his shame, guilt, fear — and Gray. As Roy Webb's music stirringly rises, Fettes begins walking back to Edinburgh, and Lewton ends the film with words of Hippocrates:

It is through error that man tries and rises. It is through tragedy he learns. All the roads of learning begin in darkness and go out into the light.

The rainy shock climax of *The Body Snatcher* thoroughly drenched Karloff, Daniell and Wade—the last playing the scene despite being very ill with a high fever. RKO was so grateful to Wade for not holding up production (he recalls that Karloff would have received a bonus if the film went too far over schedule) that the studio sent him to recuperate in Palm Springs— where, today, he's a very successful real estate agent. Years later, Karloff was asked what the makeup department had sprayed on him to make his body so horribly luminous in the climax.

"I really can't recall," said Karloff. "But you can be sure that it was something *foul!*"

The Body Snatcher completed shooting Friday, November 17, 1944. Robert Clarke remembers:

> At the end of the picture, I went to the set to the "Wrap Party." Karloff was there, and he was graciously signing, for anyone who wanted one, an 8 × 10 photograph of himself. I still have the picture he signed for me, and it gives you an idea of the man's modesty. It reads, "To Bob Clarke—Be as lucky as I am."

*   *   *

GRAVES ROBBED!   CORPSES CARVED!
THE DEAD DESPOILED!

—RKO publicity for *The Body Snatcher,* 1945

Exactly two weeks after *The Body Snatcher* completed shooting, Lewton, Mark Robson and Karloff resumed filming *Isle of the Dead* (December 1–12). This atmospheric, frightening but poorly constructed shocker, featuring Karloff as a Greek general and Katherine Emery as a cataleptic woman buried alive, concluded Karloff's two-picture pact.

Meanwhile, both Lewton and Karloff were punch-drunk over *The Body Sntcher.* Lewton loved the film's "Stevensonian mood," and anticipated a wonderful box office. So delighted was Karloff with his RKO friends (and vice versa) that, on January 17, 1945, he signed a new RKO three-picture contract worth $100,000.

Roy Webb, who had scored all of Lewton's horror films, added a beautifully moody score to *The Body Snatcher,* and on Tuesday, February 13, 1945, RKO previewed *The Body Snatcher* at the studio for the trade press. *The Hollywood Reporter* gave a "rave":

> ...an unqualified lulu, certain to satisfy the most ardent chill-and-thrill craver, for this is about as grisly an affair as the screen has ever ventured to

Poster for *The Body Snatcher*.

offer. . .a veritable orgy of killing and grave-robbing. . . . Karloff plays the title
role with a sardonic humor which makes his performance doubly effective. . . .
Henry Daniell gives an excellent portrayal which carries conviction. . . . Bela
Lugosi appears briefly as a sinister servant who falls victim to his own cupid-
ity. . . . Robert Wise gives the picture distinctive direction . . . [and] for Val
Lewton, this is another top production credit. . .

Karloff, meanwhile, had taken off to the South Pacific, where he was
playing in a G.I. version of *Arsenic and Old Lace.* "I should be the envy of all
beholders for I am having the time of my young life!" Boris wrote to RKO
Feb. 21, 1945 — requesting that the studio send him two 16mm prints of *The
Body Snatcher* to entertain the men.

Lugosi also returned to the stage; on February 26, 1945, he opened at
San Francisco's Curran Theatre as Bharat Singh in *No Traveler Returns,* which
apparently promptly folded.

Delighted by *The Body Snatcher's* trade reviews, RKO set a May release
date and mounted a deluxe promotional campaign. Although *Variety* had
warned that the movie was "a bit too much on the ghoulish side . . . for the
weaker-stomached among patrons," RKO's advertising department enjoyed
a horrific field day. "Foul Fingers Crimson with Dead Men's Blood!" shrieked
one poster; "Midnight Murder! Body Blackmail! Stalking Ghouls!" promised

another. Most posters featured a morbidly tantalizing episode not even in *The Body Snatcher:* a sketch of Karloff, dragging a ghastly white but very well-endowed female cadaver from its grave!

Karloff alone received top-billing, above the title, on the credits of *The Body Snatcher* and all promotional materials. Lugosi, despite the fact his own role was virtually a cameo and despite Henry Daniell's superb performance, topped the supporting cast list. His contract had promised:

> . . . second (2nd) male billing of the entire cast on all positive prints of said photoplay and in all lithographs known as twelve (12) sheet and twenty-four (24) sheet advertising issued by the Producer. . .

Robert Wise resented this inequity:

> This was another of Jack Gross' ideas and his kind of thinking about horror films — that it would be a great idea to "team" Karloff and Lugosi, even though the part that Henry Daniell had was really the co-starring part with Karloff. . . . Lugosi was put up there with second billing purely for commercial reasons.

Of course, the Karloff and Lugosi box office potential was enormous, and RKO milked it for all it was worth in the trailer. "The Hero of Horror, BORIS KARLOFF, joins forces with The Master of Menace, BELA LUGOSI, in the UNHOLIEST PARTNERSHIP This Side of the Grave!"

For all the hooplah, *The Body Snatcher* would surpass RKO's highest hopes.

On Thursday, May 10, 1945, RKO premiered *The Body Snatcher* at Hollywood's Hawaii Theatre. Not only did the film enjoy the support of a second feature (RKO's *The Brighton Strangler*); there was also a special grave-robbing display in the lobby, and a live prologue on the Hawaii stage, where a ghoul (actor Eric Jason) sought a live patron to pop into his coffin! The result was a sensation. *The Body Snatcher* smashed all first week records at the 956-seat Hawaii. "It was a real 'audience picture,'" remembers Russell Wade. "Some of those scenes, as directed by Robert Wise — such as the sudden snort of the horse, and Karloff's murder of the street singer — got tremendous audience reaction."

The terrifying climax, of course, always inspired wild screaming in the audience such as movie exhibitors hadn't heard since the original release of *Frankenstein.*

Audiences also enjoyed the film's mordant dashes of humor. For example, there's the scene in the tavern, where a drunken MacFarlane says to Gray, "You know something about the human body," and the Body Snatcher slyly smiles, "I've had some experience." "That," reported *The Hollywood Citizen-News,* "brought down the house!"

Then, as RKO rejoiced, a problem suddenly loomed: Censorship. On May 15, 1945, Sid Kramer reported to RKO that *The Body Snatcher* had been

> condemned in its entirety by the city of Chicago and the state of Ohio, but with certain eliminations to be made, an adult permit at least will be forthcoming for Chicago. As for Ohio, a cut version of the picture has to be submitted for further consideration. . . .

Another broadside came from the Roman Catholic National Legion of Decency. The august group slapped *The Body Snatcher* with a class B rating: Objectionable in Part, due to "excessive gruesomeness." As Kramer reported, "I feel that there is too much unanimity of opinion on the part of the people in the legion about this picture to secure any better classification than the present one." The most outrageous censorship misadventure would come in Britain — where the Censor cut Gray's climactic apparition, hence emasculating the film of its climax and message!

Of course, such travails only gave the movie more notoriety, and *The Body Snatcher* became Val Lewton's greatest critical and popular success since *Cat People*. The film opened at New York's Rialto on Friday, May 25, 1945, and its Broadway movie neighbors included MGM's *The Valley of Decision*, with Greer Garson, *Thrill of a Romance*, with Van Johnson and Esther Williams, and *The Picture of Dorian Gray*, with George Sanders and Hurd Hatfield; Warners' Bette Davis vehicle, *The Corn Is Green;* 20th Century–Fox's *Thunderhead, Son of Flicka;* Paramount's Bing Crosby musical, *Here Come the Waves;* and RKO's own *Murder My Sweet* and *The Enchanted Cottage.* John McManus reported in his influential *PM* reviews:

> *The Body Snatcher* inherits class from its Robert Louis Stevenson parentage; it has the distinction, like many an ancient and honorable British ballad, of being a shocker with an edifying background of fact; and it has the advantage of production by Val Lewton, the *Cat People* originator. . . . Boris Karloff . . . makes an evildoer's holiday of his part. . . . *The Body Snatcher,* if you are one for well-told legends, for balladry or just for shockers by preference, is something you won't want to miss. Dracula, in all his gory, was never arrayed like this.

Bela Lugosi would have disagreed. Certainly the film did little for him, although *Variety* rewarded him a deserved "excellent" for his creepy cameo. Lillian Lugosi Donlevy once referred to *The Body Snatcher* with one word: "Lousy."

All in all, *The Body Snatcher* was a bonanza for Boris Karloff, whose performance both climaxed his horror portrayals and established him as a major Hollywood character star. It was also a triumph for Val Lewton. James Agee, then film critic for *Time* and *The Nation,* selected *The Body Snatcher* (as well as

Isle of the Dead) as among the best films of 1945, writing that they showed "some of the most sensitive movie intelligence in Hollywood."

There was also a lovely testimonial from Boris Karloff. He praised Val Lewton as "the man who rescued me from the living dead and restored my soul." It was, however, simply too late for Lewton to restore the soul of the horror genre.

* * *

> Poor Val was a lovely man and too good to fight with the front office people at RKO. But the hucksters prevailed. Fighting for what he wanted wore Val out, and failure to get it broke his heart. He should have been an independent producer, but he needed the protection of a big studio.
> —Alan Napier

The Body Snatcher reigns today as a beloved film; besides being the final Karloff and Lugosi movie, it survives as the richest, most dramatic of Lewton's RKO horrors, and, indeed, bids powerfully to be the greatest horror film of the 1940s. It has the power of a haunting ballad, and the literacy, taste and atmosphere of Lewton at his best. Yet it also scores dramatically, with Karloff's evil Gray and Daniell's tragic MacFarlane—while the sad but effective casting of Lugosi gives the film a depth of emotional power.

In his top hat, scraggly sideburns, and wicked 'smile, Karloff's Gray is the stuff great nightmares are made of as he makes his "crawling graveyard rat" one of the most mesmerizing villains in screen history. Who can forget Gray's sick pride as he viciously jabs a knife into a loaf of bread and leers, "Toddy'd like to do that all over my body!" Yet there's also a superb gallow's humor, and a fascinating element of self-hatred in Karloff's Body Snatcher, which boils in his final taunt to MacFarlane. To garnish the character, Karloff provides Gray with an aura of deep, unholy, almost Lovecraftian evil that makes his classic, climactic apparition all the more horrific.

Henry Daniell makes a proud, virile, clever and cold MacFarlane, with a palpable hatred for Gray that makes his "Toddy" striking, sympathetic, and thoroughly tragic. It is an exceptional star performance from an underrated character player.

And as for Lugosi—his Joseph is a genuinely effective portrayal, vile, creepy, far more creatively played than the mad doctors he was then doing for Monogram. One suspects that *The Body Snatcher* was one of the few times in the '40s that Lugosi ran up against a director who actually directed him, and didn't just prop him up in front of the camera and told him to "play Lugosi." While the final result might disappoint those Lugosiphiles who revere the actor for his "personality," and certainly upset the actor himself because of its humble proportions and nuances, Bela's pathetically tragic Joseph is one of his best screen performances. His final scene with Karloff is one of the most haunting in the career of both actors.

In a true rarity for a horror film, the entire cast is very good: Edith Atwater sensual and moving as Mcg; Russell Wade and Rita Corday totally convincing and appealing as Fettes and the Widow Marsh; little Sharyn Moffet a touching Georgina, playing with scarcely a touch of the cutes.

Robert Wise remembers *The Body Snatcher* as "one of my seven or eight favorite films," of the 40 he has now made, and indeed he directed with élan and an obvious savoring of the possibilities. He masterfully blended the Lewton standard of scenic beauty with moody atmosphere, potently delivered the repertoire of now-classic shock moments (the chilling graveyard raid, in which Karloff slays the little dog, the Lewton "bus" with Gray's horse, the murder of the street singer, the two wild fights, the shot of Joseph's head pulled up out of the brine vat, and, of course, the great climactic apparition scene), and smoothly refereed the excellent performances.

In final analysis, *The Body Snatcher* is not so much about bodies as it is about souls — about one man's imperfect soul agonized by another's wholly evil one. In a line of dialogue in the original script, not in the release version, Fettes gestures to MacFarlane's anatomy room and says, "I suppose one must pass through this purgatory to the heaven of being a good doctor." Lewton's *The Body Snatcher* becomes MacFarlane's purgatory, hellishly ruled by Gray. That this marvelously dramatic vision joined with the poignancy of Karloff and Lugosi's final film makes *The Body Snatcher* one of the most moving of all horror films.

In the wake of *The Body Snatcher,* the paths of Karloff and Lugosi and Lewton nearly intersected at RKO. In July, 1945, Karloff began Lewton's *Bedlam,* the first of his three new RKO films, and directed by Mark Robson. Of course, Karloff received top billing, a salary of $32,500 and a beautifully sketched role of Master Sims, the evil "Apothecary General" of tragic, terrible Bedlam.

RKO "wrapped" *Bedlam* August 17, 1945. On August 18, the studio began *The Master Minds,* a "B" vehicle for RKO's Wally Brown and Alan Carney and fated to be released in August, 1946, as *Genius at Work.* RKO offered the top villain role of "The Cobra" to Lionel Atwill, who — still rebuilding his career after the cataclysmic "orgy trial" — agreed to terms of $1250 per week with a three-week guarantee. For "The Cobra's" stooge and servant, RKO sought Lugosi. While Bela's terms — $2500 per week with a two-week guarantee — surpassed Atwill's compensation, a note in the RKO Archives illustrates Lugosi's sad fortune at this time:

> He has agreed that his name may come after those of Anne Jeffreys and Lionel Atwill. However, his name must appear in the same size type as that used to display the names of Anne Jeffreys and Lionel Atwill.

Shortly afterwards, Universal began a new monster rally, *House of Dracula.* Once again, Lugosi read that Universal had signed John Carradine to play the Count with Chaney's Wolf Man and Strange's monster.

Tragically, however, it was Lewton who faced the real immediate tragedy; he was fated to predecease his costars of *The Body Snatcher.* Departing RKO, Lewton signed a very promising contract with Paramount. It was a nightmare, as the sensitive producer sunk in a morass of studio politics; in all, he would produce only three more films: *My Own True Love* (Paramount, 1948), *Please Believe Me* (MGM, 1950), and *Apache Drums* (Universal, 1951). He became bitter and paranoid; plans to work independently with Robert Wise and Mark Robson ended traumatically; his secretary would hear him weeping alone in his office. "I never knew anybody who was so desperately unhappy," said DeWitt Bodeen, "who lost all faith in himself." On March 14, 1951, a heart attack killed the 46-year-old producer. At the funeral, his friend Alan Napier gave the eulogy, indicting the film industry for Lewton's early death. Napier remembered sadly:

> My agent, who was present, told me, "There wasn't a dry eye in the house, Alan" — which would have made Val laugh. He had always been trying to find me a good part in one of his pictures, and here I was having a triumph at his funeral.

Robert Wise, of course, has gone on to a very celebrated career as a director of films of every genre, including five special ventures into the realm of supernatural/science fiction: *The Day the Earth Stood Still* (Fox, 1951), *The Haunting* (MGM, 1963), *The Andromeda Strain* (Universal, 1971), *Audrey Rose* (MGM, 1977), and *Star Trek* (Paramount, 1980). To this day, he salutes Val Lewton as the one "tremendous influence on my career."

Henry Daniell continued a busy career in films, on Broadway, in television (including several visits to Karloff's *Thriller* series in the early 1960s). Following a day's work as the Prince of Transylvania in *My Fair Lady,* Daniell died of a heart attack at his Santa Monica home on Halloween night, 1963. He was 69. Ironically, Alan Napier, his old competitor for the role of Mac-Farlane, replaced him in the remaining scenes.

And, as for Karloff and Lugosi, *The Body Snatcher* would be their final screen union as the horror genre's own Burke and Hare. They would never work together again. Yet, in the following decade, their legends would take on a truly melodramatic aspect as they began the final, moving, and ultimately tragic act of their historic relationship.

14
The Decline, 1945 to 1955

Twenty years ago, I was banned from my homeland, parted from my wife
and son, never to see them again.... I was classed as a madman, a charlatan,
outlawed in the world of science which previously honored me as a genius. Now
here in this forsaken jungle hell I have proven that I am all right!
— Bela Lugosi in 1955's *Bride of the Monster*

On January 14, 1946, Universal City began shooting the 143rd of its 144
serials, *Lost City of the Jungle.* It was engineered to delight any postwar liberal,
as well as cliff-hanger fans. The hero was Russell Hayden, promoted from
playing Hopalong Cassidy's sidekick "Lucky," to heroic agent of the "World
Peace Foundation." The heroine was Jane Adams, upgraded from hunchbacked nurse of *House of Dracula.* Hayden's sidekick was Keye Luke.
However, for the villain, Universal went traditionally gothic, and signed
Lionel Atwill. In panama hat, spats, and his ever-shiny monocle, "Pinky" Atwill played Sir Eric Hazarias, the serial's maniacal warmonger.

The natty costume disguised a dying actor. Atwill, fighting bronchial
cancer, would never finish the serial; his fatal illness forced Universal to add
an entirely new villain (John Mylong) and double Atwill with actor George
Sorel in the last week of shooting. After a long siege of illness, Atwill died,
age 61, on April 22, 1946, at his Pacific Palisades house, leaving his young
wife Paula and their six-month-old baby Lionel.

Ironically, the last scene Lionel Atwill played before leaving *Lost City of
the Jungle* on the night of February 4, 1946, was Sir Eric's death scene. This
time, however, the scene was not a castle laboratory, as it had been a few
months before in *House of Dracula,* but a getaway airplane. And the cause of
death was not being hurled into a monster-reviving electrical monolith, but
perishing in an apocalyptic atomic explosion, à la Hiroshima.

It was the end—and the beginning—of an era. The first atomic bomb
had devastated Hiroshima while Karloff was at work on *Bedlam,* while Lugosi
was about to begin *Genius at Work,* and while Universal was blueprinting
House of Dracula, its one last straight monster rally. In the true horrors of
atomic mutants, flag-shrouded coffins, the boy-next-door back home from the
war without arms or legs or a face, the midnight shows of a monster stitched
together from the dead or a vampire lusting after maiden's blood were neither

279

appetizing — nor frightening. There was no need for make-believe horror; and, in the exultation of a country free from war, there seemed to be no need for escapism. The Academy Award for Best Picture of 1946 went to Goldwyn's *The Best Years of Our Lives,* and that said it all. In its story and its sophistication there was a new world, and a new Hollywood.

Horror films, once again, were on their deathbeds. On January 19, 1946, Monogram let loose the last of its horrors, *The Face of Marble,* graced by John Carradine.

On February 20, 1946, PRC unleashed *The Flying Serpent,* George Zucco's saddest 59 minutes, shared with the title creature, Quetzalcoatl. Later that year, PRC would market *The Brute Man,* the posthumous swan song of Universal's "Monster Without Makeup," acromegalic Rondo Hatton. Universal, which had produced the movie, considered it such an embarrassment that it sold the film to the lowliest of Poverty Row's lots.

On March 22, Universal released *The Spider Woman Strikes Back,* which mixed Academy Award winner Gale Sondergaard with the unfortunate Mr. Hatton (who died a month before the film's release); one week later, the studio released *House of Horrors,* Hatton's sad "masterwork."

On April 15, *Film Daily* reviewed three horrors on the same day: Universal's *She-Wolf of London* and *The Cat Creeps,* both lowly "B's"; and PRC's *The Devil Bat's Daughter,* in which Miss America of 1941 Rosemary La Planche nonsensically vindicated a very guilty Bela Lugosi for his crimes of 1941's *The Devil Bat.*

On April 19, RKO's *Bedlam,* last of the Val Lewton horrors, opened at New York's Rialto. This last hurrah of Lewton terror won a spread in *Life* magazine. Karloff, as Master Sims, curator of the horrid St. Mary's of Bethlehem, vainly hiding his gray hair under a dark wig, sadistically committing heroine Anna Lee to Bedlam for crusading against its atrocities, won praise from the *New York Daily News* as "the personification of evil genius."

On April 20, Republic released its entry in the moribund horror sweepstakes, *The Cat Man of Paris.*

On August 5, 1946, *Film Daily* reviewed RKO's *Genius at Work,* the Brown and Carney comedy featuring Lugosi and Atwill; RKO had finally previewed it, almost a year after its completion and over three months after Atwill's death.

On August 23, Universal released Britain's *Dead of Night,* the offbeat and acclaimed thriller about dreams and reality.

And then, as if to symbolize the new Hollywood, there was — once again — a new Universal. On October 1, 1946, Universal officially mated with International Pictures, becoming Universal-International, under the aegis of William Goetz — Louis B. Mayer's erudite, art-collecting son-in-law. The new pledge was for "prestige" pictures, a promise legitimized by the studio's contracting to release Britain's classy J. Arthur Rank product. Evelyn Ankers and her war years repertory group had long deserted their bungalows, with only Deanna Durbin and Abbott and Costello the headliner hangovers from the old regime. The studio had a whole new face—and a new man to make up the faces; Jack P. Pierce was "let go" in the new studio's purge, and was replaced by younger, faster Bud Westmore.

On December 20, 1946, *Film Daily* reviewed Warners' *The Beast with Five Fingers,* directed by Robert Florey, scripted by Curt Siodmak, starring Peter Lorre, with Max Steiner's music flowing as the dismembered hand raced over the piano keys. "The maker of *Frankenstein* would be jealous of this film!" crowed Jack Warner to Florey—unwittingly reminding him of a very painful memory. However, the film flopped. Horror movies, presumably, were dead.

Lon Chaney contracted with Paramount to do a Lennie takeoff in Bob Hope's *My Favorite Brunette.* John Carradine moved to New York to devote himself to Broadway. George Zucco took roles like the French fishing village priest in MGM's Greer Garson homage, *Desire Me.*

*   *   *

Old, Gothic Horror films were withering, but Boris Karloff's life was flourishing—personally and professionally. In April, 1946, Boris wed his fifth (sixth?) wife, Evelyn Hope Helmore (former wife of actor Tom Helmore) in Reno, immediately after his divorce from Dorothy. In his new, very happy and lasting marriage, Boris also found a new career—as his laurels from *The Body Snatcher* launched him as a major Hollywood star character actor.

There were movie extravaganzas for Boris, such as Samuel Goldwyn's 1947 *The Secret Life of Walter Mitty,* with Danny Kaye, Virginia Mayo and the Goldwyn Girls; Cecil B. DeMille's 1947 *Unconquered,* with Gary Cooper and Paulete Goddard; Universal-International's 1948 *Tap Roots,* with Susan Hayward, Van Heflin, and Boris—all three movies in lush Technicolor. He acted on the Hollywood stage in 1946 in *On Borrowed Time,* and stormed Broadway in two new plays: *The Linden Tree* (Music Box Theatre, March 2, 1948, seven performances) and *The Shop at Sly Corner* (Booth Theatre, January 18, 1949, seven performances)—each a flop, but both winning the actor excellent reviews. He guest starred on radio, and toplined an early television/radio anthology for ABC, *Starring Boris Karloff,* playing a new show each week and winning the undying admiration of Alex Segal, who began his distinguished career on this pioneering television effort. Boris still spoofed his image here and there, as he did completing his RKO pact with Morgan Conway and *Black Friday* costar Anne Gwynne in *Dick Tracy Meets Gruesome.*

"If I didn't know better," says Pat (Lyle Latell), Tracy's sidekick, in this potboiler, "I'd swear we were doing business with Boris Karloff!"

The climax of this happy time for Boris Karloff came April 24, 1950, playing Mr. Darling/Captain Hook in the Broadway musical *Peter Pan,* with Jean Arthur. Critics hailed Karloff's performance(s) as "wonderful," "captivating," "a sheer delight" and "pure story book." The play was a smash, and Boris romped through a New York run of 321 performances before embarking on a national tour. A trademark of Boris's engagement came after each show, as the pirate king opened his dressing room to the children from the audience, sitting each on his lap and asking each the same question:

"Would you like to try on my hook?"

What of Bela Lugosi in these postwar days? Once again, offers shriveled. As Karloff associated with people like Goldwyn, DeMille, Danny Kaye, Gary Cooper and Jean Arthur, Bela slummed in Screen Guild's *Scared to Death* — directed by Christy Cabanne, and featuring Douglas Fowley, George Zucco, Molly Lamont, dwarf Angelo Rossitto, and a cheap process called Cinecolor, which allowed Lugosi fans to see that Bela's eyes were blue. Shot in 1946, it eked into theatres in 1947, a year that Bela tried to stay solvent in yet another summer tour of *Dracula.*

In 1948, Universal-International released the year's Oscar-winning Best Picture: Olivier's *Hamlet,* from the British Rank Organization. Although the studio only released the film, the company crowed, enjoying its first Best Picture win since 1930's *All Quiet on the Western Front.* But making much more money at the box office that year was U-I's *Abbott and Costello Meet Frankenstein.* Considered a sacrilegious travesty by some, this handsome, exciting, now-classic entertainment gave Dracula, the Wolf Man, and the monster an affectionate, respectful final curtain, terrifying Abbott and Costello and the audience one last time, Bela's Dracula in his cape, Chaney's Wolf Man and Glenn Strange's Frankenstein's monster in their Westmore sponge rubber makeups, all to the crashing of Frank Skinner's wonderful musical score.

It was Bela Lugosi's last great performance in a major movie.

Over the years, a former agent of Bela's (a man who later made money selling copies of the actor's letters and funeral announcement) got considerable mileage out of a story about how he won Bela the role of Dracula, in *Abbott and Costello Meet Frankenstein,* when U-I wanted Ian Keith (who had competed with Bela for the part in 1930). According to this gentleman, he stormed into Goetz's office on the eve of production, waving telegrams from exhibitors noting the money they had made showing *Dracula,* shaming the President into giving Bela the part — at $1500 per week on a ten-week guarantee.

The studio records tell a different story. According to Universal-International's "Outside Talent Sheet" for production #1572, then titled *Brain of Frankenstein,* Bela Lugosi is set for the role of Dracula, at $2000 per week and a pay period of four weeks and one day. Lon Chaney, who so dominated Bela during the war years, now received the same terms — $2000 weekly (although his pay period originally was for a full five weeks). Glenn Strange, in his third go-around as the monster, got $750 per week, as did Lenore Aubert, the amazonian brunette who played Dracula's sexy partner-in-evil, Dr. Sandra Mornay.

Bela, Lillian and Bela, Jr., were now living on the shore of Lake Elsinore, south of Los Angeles, where Bela, Jr., attended military school. Bela moved back in with friends in Los Angeles during the shooting. Once again, the 65-year-old, drug-addicted Bela was Dracula, magnificent, commanding — despite age, Westmore face powder, dark hair dye, and addiction. As director Charles T. Barton (who died in 1981) told me:

> Bela Lugosi? He was a hell of a good actor. He was very helpful to Lon, and to me, and to everybody. Particularly that wonderful, beautiful girl, Lenore Aubert. I remember in the scene where Lugosi told her, "Look into my eyes," how he tried to help her look as if she were really hypnotized. It was a hard scene to do, and damn, he worked with her like a real pro. He was a lovely, lovely guy.

Bud Abbott went home early several days without warning, Lou Costello indulged in on-the-set pie fights and the shooting was wild and raucous. Bela was in great spirits, proudly bringing Lillian and Bela, Jr., on the set, and enjoying himself hugely — most of the time. Outtakes from *Abbott and Costello Meet Frankenstein* have been making the rounds over the past several years. One shows Bela, resplendent in his lounging robe, descending the castle staircase to intone, "You should be more careful." Unknown to Bela, a little figure in cloak and hat is skulking behind him on the staircase — presumably Bobby Barber, whom Universal tolerated on the payroll to keep the comics happy and amused. Bud, Lou and the rest of the cast and crew break up at the interloper, Bela suspiciously turns around — and does *not* look amused as he lambasts the intruder!

Released in the summer of 1948, *Abbott and Costello Meet Frankenstein* became one of the biggest hits in Universal's history, and one of the top-grossing films of 1947/1948. Also on the big money list that season were the Karloff films *The Secret Life of Walter Mitty, Unconquered,* and U-I's own 1948 *Tap Roots,* which featured Boris as an Indian. While no available records prove that U-I desperately offered Boris Karloff the part of Frankenstein's monster in *Abbott and Costello Meet Frankenstein,* it's always been presumed that Boris rejected the offer, out of respect for his dear old role. Still, the studio was so hell-bent to associate Boris with the film that it offered to pay his hotel bill if he would pose for publicity pictures outside New York's Criterion Theatre when *Abbott and Costello Meet Frankenstein* opened July 28, 1948.

Boris had accepted the deal — "as long as I don't have to see the movie!"

It's curious that, the following year, Boris did accept U-I's offer to star in 1949's *Abbott and Costello Meet the Killer, Boris Karloff,* also directed by Barton and also featuring the charming Lenore Aubert. Boris wouldn't spoof the monster — but he had no reluctance to spoof himself. "Karloff was great — one hell of a guy," said Charlie Barton. "Bud and Lou loved him." Boris, incidentally, picked up $20,000 for his red herring role of a swami in this film — double what Bela had received for *Abbott and Costello Meet Frankenstein.*

*   *   *

Bela Lugosi took all of this in—bitterly. His career was again in cataclysmic trouble. Now in New York, hoping for a "comeback," he was surviving primarily via a horror act, touring the East Coast, following cheaply-rented Monogram movies in a stage show with a gorilla. Atomic age teenagers hooted at him. During yet another summer tour of *Arsenic and Old Lace,* the Lugosis met Richard and Alex Gordon, the British film producers, kind gentlemen with respect for Bela's career and a deep desire to help him revitalize it. Recently, Richard Gordon spoke with me from his New York office:

Alex and I were interviewing personalities in New York for British film magazines, and we met Karloff first—he was appearing in Broadway in *The Linden Tree,* and later *The Shop at Sly Corner.* He was marvelous on the stage, an absolutely first-rate actor with a tremendous stage presence. Then, later, we met Lugosi when he did *Arsenic and Old Lace* at a summer stock theatre on Long Island. Afterwards, he and Lillian very kindly took us out to dinner. He realized he was being interviewed for a British fan magazine, so naturally he didn't get too much into personal things, or anything detrimental to the interview.

Shortly afterwards, however, Bela asked my brother and me if we wanted to manage his business affairs, to try to get him some additional jobs. Then we came to know him better. We were exposed to his famous generosity. We helped to arrange the deal he had to do *The Cask of Amontillado* with Romney Brent, which was done as a live television play. After the telecast, Bela got his check, took everyone to his favorite Hungarian restaurant on the East Side, and spent the whole check on the party!

We also came to know his bitterness about Boris Karloff. He felt that Karloff had made a much more successful career in Hollywood than he did, felt he should have had the same opportunities that Karloff did. And, of course, he always made reference to the fact that he was offered the part of the Frankenstein monster first, and that if he had accepted it, as he put it, "Karloff might still have been a bit player on the back lot at Universal." What he never made reference to, in talking with us, was that he turned down the role down because he felt that, after *Dracula,* it was a bad thing for him, since there was no dialogue and his face would be covered by makeup.

I had an office in the old General Motors Building on Broadway, and I had pictures on the wall of a number of actors that I knew, or had interviewed, or was working with on my films. Naturally, I had a picture of Karloff and also a picture of Lugosi, and it seemed perfectly natural that they would be hanging side by side. But when I started working with Lugosi, and he started coming to my office, I noticed that he looked very unhappy when he saw the pictures of himself and Karloff side by side! By that time, I was aware of his feelings toward Karloff, so when I knew Lugosi was coming up to see me, I would take Karloff's picture down and put something else up there. Then after he left, I would put Karloff's picture back up!

Of course, in the late 1950s, after Lugosi's death, I worked with Karloff on the films *The Haunted Strangler* and *Corridors of Blood.* He was a gentleman, he was a friend, and no matter what he did—and he, too, made some very poor pictures—he went about it with the same dedication as if it were Shakespeare. I must tell you that, in all the years I knew Karloff, whenever the subject of Bela

Lugosi came up, Karloff never said anything really detrimental about Lugosi. He felt sorry for him, he regretted that Lugosi had this bitterness, he regretted that Lugosi's career never went further than it did, but blamed it partly on Lugosi's inability to soften his accent and make his general casting more easy, and his whole attitude. But he never expressed any resentment towards Bela whatsoever.

* * *

Bela Lugosi had landed a guest spot on the phenomenally popular *Milton Berle* television show. In the summer of 1950, Bela joined a play, *The Devil Also Dreams,* which played Toronto, Canada, but never made it to Broadway.

Bela was desperate. In the 1980s a story has been making the rounds, reportedly "hushed" during the time, which gives a new dimension to the Karloff versus Lugosi rivalry. Buddy Barnett, manager of the popular Cinema Collector's Bookstore in Hollywood and a great Lugosi fan, told me this story, passed down by a former Lugosi agent:

> Around 1950, while Karloff was on Broadway in *Peter Pan,* a Las Vegas producer was interested in doing a horror act with Karloff and Lugosi. They came to Lugosi's agent, with an offer of $10,000 a week. "$10,000 per week!" exclaimed Lugosi. "That's pretty good." "Yeah, but here's the bad news, Bela," said his agent. "They'll give Karloff $9000 of it, and you $1000." Well, Bela got mad, and was screaming! Still, Lugosi wasn't at all in demand, so he thought about it, and agreed to it. But when they proposed the offer to Karloff, he wasn't interested. The agent came back and gave Lugosi the news. "Karloff doesn't want to do it . . . but maybe if *you* go and ask him . . ."
>
> "Oh no!" said Lugosi, "I *won't* do that!"
>
> But Lugosi wanted the money, so supposedly he went to Karloff in New York. "No, sorry" said Karloff—it was about the time of *Peter Pan,* and he was busy with other things. "But you get $9000 a week, Boris!" shouted Lugosi. "Why would you want to turn it down?!"

Could this have happened? Possibly. Lugosi later did play Las Vegas in 1954. Karloff probably was too gentlemanly to talk about it, and Lugosi too humiliated.

In 1951, the Gordons managed to get Bela to England to revive *Dracula* on the stage—a tour set for the provinces before premiering in London. Richard Gordon regretfully recalls what happened:

> The principal shortcoming was that the whole cast was amateurish, with the exception of Bela Lugosi, because the management spent absolutely no money on getting competent actors, or enough rehearsal time getting the show into shape. They figured it was enough to sell it on Lugosi's name. He carried on to the best of his ability, but it was extremely difficult for him; he was already a little bit hard of hearing, and with the kind of actors he was playing with, he sometimes didn't hear the cues. In a way, it didn't matter, because he knew the play by heart; but if one of the actors fluffed a line, or didn't come in with a line, Lugosi would come in too soon—or respond to something that hadn't been said!

It was very embarrassing, sometimes producing laughter in the wrong places, and it became very discouraging and very disheartening for him.

Unfortunately, the *Dracula* revival was no success at all. It never made it to London, left a lot of debts behind; Bela wasn't paid the money that was owed to him, and it was a total disaster.

During Bela's misadventures in England, Boris Karloff was wrapping up his smash Broadway engagement and tour in *Peter Pan*. Meanwhile, Bela, with Lillian at his side, gave a British press conference to promote his doomed *Dracula*. In the midst of it, he offered this observation: "The horror business is certainly not what it used to be. Boris Karloff, a great horror specialist — look what he is driven to. Comedy stuff in New York!"

*   *   *

The horror of science fiction was ablaze in Hollywood, with movies like RKO's 1951 *The Thing,* and 20th Century–Fox's *The Day the Earth Stood Still.* The early 1950s would be populated with such space horrors, but Universal-International was still making money re-releasing the old classics like *Dracula, Frankenstein,* and even *The Black Cat* (released with the new title of *The Vanishing Body*). Universal-International decided to entice Boris Karloff back, for three old-school horror films. First 1951's *The Strange Door,* with Charles Laughton, featured a notorious dining scene, a climax à la *The Raven* with walls coming together, and Boris as a servant. Then 1952's *The Black Castle,* a fine thriller, was stocked with gothic flourishes such as Stephen McNally's one-eyed Count Bruno, Lon Chaney, Jr.'s mute bodyguard Gargon, and a castle pool of crocodiles; Boris was an old castle alchemist, à la Friar Laurence of *Romeo and Juliet.* And 1953's *Abbott and Costello Meet Dr. Jekyll and Mr. Hyde* featured a pretty heroine (Helen Westcott), the cinematography of George Robinson, and Boris in the Robert Louis Stevenson dual roles.* This last feature engaged Boris for three weeks' work and a fee of $15,000.

Here is where an admirer of Karloff and Lugosi become totally frustrated. Why didn't Universal extend any offer to Bela Lugosi? With work offered to Boris and to Lon Chaney, Jr., why wasn't Bela engaged? At any rate, it soon was too late. In 1954, Universal abandoned the gothic horrors for *The Creature from the Black Lagoon,* which dynamically plunged into science fiction while retaining, in its Gill Man, the loneliness, pathos and sexuality of the studio's nightmares of old.

The failure of *Dracula* in England had left Bela stranded, without the money to come home. The Gordons arranged for Bela to play in Britain's *Old Mother Riley Meets the Vampire,* which paid him a reported $5000 and got him home. Meanwhile, Boris was about to visit his beloved England to star in his

---

Eddie Parker, who doubled Bela in Frankenstein Meets the Wolf Man, *was recruited to double Boris (in a Westmore rubber mask) here—so extensively that the studio engaged Parker for two weeks and five days, at $300 per week.*

new teleseries, *Colonel March of Scotland Yard,* chewing the scenery as the title sleuth with the black eyepatch.

"He tells me he loves me every single day," Lillian Lugosi had told the British reporters about her husband of almost twenty years. "I think that's very nice. Don't you?" However, the years of living with this emotional, extremely jealous, dominating, drug-addicted man were taking a terrible toll on Lillian. Arriving home from England, the Lugosi family took an apartment in the Baldwin Hills, a very modest area southeast of Los Angeles, while Bela took the only work offered, 1952's *Bela Lugosi Meets a Brooklyn Gorilla.* Duke Mitchell and Sammy Petrillo imitated Dean Martin and Jerry Lewis so flagrantly that their Paramount producer, Hal Wallis, threatened a lawsuit when this curiosity played the Rialto Theatre in New York.

With Bela out of work, sitting home, brooding, jealous, growing increasingly deaf, calling to make sure Lillian had gone to the dentist and not to a rendezvous with a lover, Lillian Lugosi told her husband she was going to divorce him. She went looking for work, and found a job as a bookkeeper on the *Dangerous Assignment* television/radio series, starring Brian Donlevy. The dapper Donlevy, a veteran Broadway/Hollywood actor, had won an Academy nomination as the nightmarish Sergeant Markoff of 1939's *Beau Geste,* and stardom in the title role of Preston Sturges' 1940 *The Great McGinty;* in 1966, he would marry Lillian Lugosi. He was a shy, gentle man, a loner who loved writing poetry; in later years, his own career would capsize in a lifelong battle with alcohol. However, in the early 1950s, he was a major leading man, with a mansion at Malibu Beach, a retreat in Palm Desert and his own radio/ television show.

Bela's jealousy flamed. Lillian once told me:

> One day, Bela called the *Dangerous Assignment* office, and Brian picked up the phone. Bela wasn't aware of whom he was talking to. "I want to speak to Mr. Donlevy," demanded Bela. "That man is destroying my marriage!"

Of course, it was Bela's own jealousy which had truly destroyed the marriage. In the summer of 1953, Lillian went to divorce court, but only after doing a very courageous thing: she weaned Bela of his drug addiction. By the time Lillian divorced Bela in 1953, winning custody of Bela, Jr., demanding no alimony or child support, Bela appeared to be a cured man.

"She gave me the shots," Bela later revealed. "And she weaned me. Finally, I got only the bare needle. A fake shot, that's all. I was done with it. Then she left me. She took our son. He was my flesh. I went back on the drugs. My heart was broken."

"The divorce was catastrophic to my father's spirit," wrote Bela Lugosi, Jr., in his introduction to Robert Cremer's "authorized" *Lugosi: The Man Behind the Cape,* "and he never recovered from that trauma."

Shortly afterwards, about the time of the separation, a Los Angeles

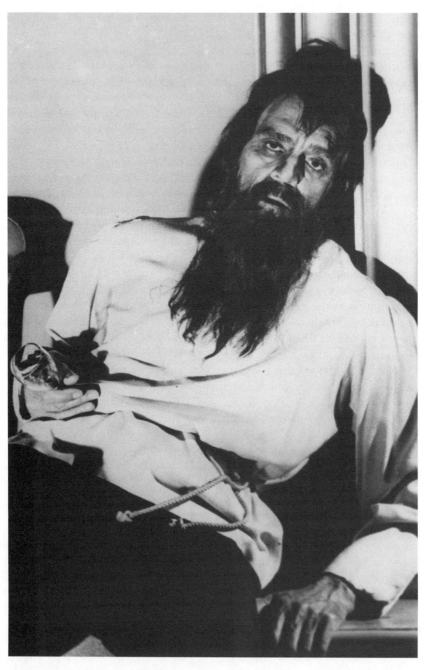

Above: **Boris Karloff as Rasputin in "The Black Prophet" episode of television's** *Suspense!* (March 17, 1953). *Opposite:* A 125-lb. Bela Lugosi tragically poses for the press after committing himself for treatment as a drug addict in 1955.

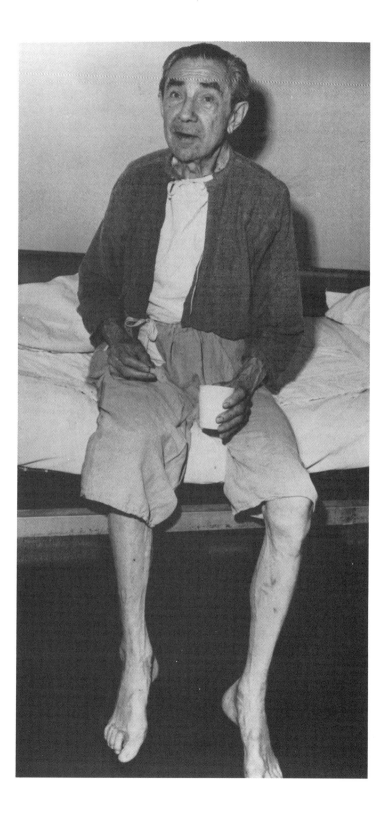

newspaper had reported that Lugosi had attempted suicide. He vehemently denied the report. Now divorced, he moved back into Hollywood, into a tiny apartment on Carlton Way. He was hurt by the loss of Lillian and Bela, Jr., drinking catastrophically, relying on friends for food — and back on drugs.

And, as Bela faced the nightmares of divorce, drug addiction, and Hollywood apathy, only one true professional hope loomed ahead: a possible reunion picture with Boris Karloff.

Since Bela's return to Hollywood, Alex Gordon had tried desperately to find work for him. It was through Mr. Gordon that Bela did *Bela Lugosi Meets a Brooklyn Gorilla* (1952) for Jack Broder Productions; it was also through the British producer that Bela met the notorious Edward D. Wood, Jr., whose infamous union with Bela Lugosi began with 1953's *Glen or Glenda?* — the classic camp transvestite saga, produced, directed, written by (and starring) transvestite Wood himself.

All the while, Alex Gordon wanted to provide a worthy vehicle for Bela. Today an executive with Gene Autry's production company, the genial Gordon recalls:

> While working for Walter Reade Theatres in New York, as a booker, I wrote a script called *The Atomic Monster,* about a giant octopus. This was about 1948. I was hoping it eventually would be made into a picture. After coming out to Hollywood, and having become friends with Lugosi, the idea was to make a picture with Lugosi from that script (which later became *Bride of the Monster*). I tried to make a deal with Jack Broder, and Hal Roach, Sr., but it never panned out. . . .

Eventually, Gordon found himself at Allied Artists — based on the old Monogram lot, 4376 Sunset Drive, where both Bela and Boris had made their most infamous potboilers. Steve Broidy, head of Allied, was interested in *The Atomic Monster* — but not for Bela Lugosi. "Broidy wanted a double bill," recalls Gordon. "*The Atomic Monster,* for Boris Karloff, and a vampire picture (for which we had a script as well) for Lugosi. 'If you can get Lugosi to do that one,' said Broidy, 'and get Karloff for *The Atomic Monster,* it's a deal.'"

> So I had to go to Lugosi. . . . I was very apprehensive, because we were so friendly, and he wanted to do *The Atomic Monster* very badly — not because it was great shakes as a script, but because he hadn't worked in a while. I told him the only way I could get this off the ground was for Karloff to do *The Atomic Monster,* and Bela to do the vampire script. So Bela agreed.

During this era, Karloff was in Hollywood, guest-starring on television shows like the March 17, 1953, *Suspense!* episode, "The Black Prophet," in which Boris was a magnificent, black-bearded Rasputin. Gordon realized the deal now balanced on Karloff's attraction to *The Atomic Monster.*

Bela, in his disastrous personal appearance at the Hollywood premiere of *House of Wax*, 1953.

So I went to see Karloff, at the Chateau Marmont, where he would stay in Hollywood. He was very, very pleasant, and I left the script with him. He called me a couple of days later and said he would do it. I was absolutely jubilant, although, in retrospect, I'm horrified to think he felt he had to do a script like that!

Gordon's triumph was short-lived: a tortuous series of studio deals evolved, including engaging Ford Beebe (Lugosi's old Universal director of the 1939 serial *The Phantom Creeps* and the 1942 feature *Night Monster*) to direct the films and write two new scripts. Then Lon Chaney, Jr., was added to the Lugosi film. And then, ultimately everything collapsed — Beebe was out (he was given westerns instead), as Allied Artists decreed it wanted only *one* film, which would star all *three* horror names. Gordon pondered the sensitivity of Lugosi working with Karloff again — and vice versa:

> Bela didn't talk much about Karloff. However, when the subject did come up, he would always tell us about the fact that he was a star when Karloff was a bit player, how he had been offered *Frankenstein* — and then he would do a terrific imitation of the Frankenstein monster, with grunts — "AAAGH! AAAGH!" He, being a Shakespearean actor and a movie star since 1920, tried to justify his turning the monster down. Of course, he realized, he had made a big mistake there, and that Karloff had become bigger than he was.
>
> Karloff always felt sorry for Lugosi; whenever his name came up, Boris would say, "poor Bela." He felt very sorry that Lugosi had been reduced to taking almost anything.... He thought Lugosi was certainly a very good actor in his own way, but that he would rather not make another picture with Lugosi — however, if he had to, he certainly would. There was no enmity on Karloff's part; it's just that he felt self-conscious. After all, Karloff had made it so much bigger than Lugosi; he was still getting quite a bit of work, while Lugosi was struggling — and getting very little.... Karloff realized that if they worked together in this Allied Artists picture, both men would realize deep down this very real personal sensitivity.

Indeed, Karloff sadly recalled the trauma on *The Body Snatcher;* now, almost a decade later, he feared what he might find on the set of *House of Terror,* which became the new script for Karloff, Lugosi and Chaney, Jr. As the new project formulated, Alex Gordon sought ways for Bela to get some publicity, to ballyhoo this production....

In 1953, *House of Wax,* in Technicolor and 3-D, crowned Vincent Price as Hollywood's new horror star. Sadly, Bela was fated to play court jester at the gala Hollywood premiere; as Alex Gordon recalls:

> I thought that might stimulate interest in the Karloff/Lugosi/Chaney movie.... I called the people at Warner Bros., and they thought it would be a great idea if he showed up in his Dracula cape. Well, they also thought it would be a good idea if he showed up with a gorilla on a leash! I had tremendous problems getting him to do this, with the man in the gorilla suit on the leash, but I pleaded with him (as an old "yellow journalism" publicist!), realizing this would get into the papers, and thinking it would help him...
>
> Well ... he was to be interviewed there by Shirley Thomas, then sort of the Jane Pauley of the Hollywood interview set. Bela was a bit hard of hearing, so he asked for a set of questions ahead of time so that, in all the hustle and bustle of the crowd, he would know what to answer. She asked the questions in a different order — and he was answering them the way he had memorized them. It was a

Bela relaxing on the set of *Bride of the Monster*, 1955.

terrible mess! Meanwhile, he had this gorilla figure on the leash, jumping all over the place. . . . After the questions, he was in such a disturbed state, and the press wanted to photograph him drinking milk (instead of blood) with the girls in the milk bank. He staggered through the tumultuous crowd, confused, trying to hear what was being shouted at him; he grabbed the milk girl, in order to pose like Dracula, to bite her neck. And she was so surprised at that that her hands went up, and she threw milk all over him! We finally got inside—but Bela did not want to stay for the movie. . . .

Alex Gordon also managed to line up Bela to join Lon Chaney, Jr., and Peter Lorre on the Halloween, 1953, *Red Skelton Show.* "It was a terrible experience," says Mr. Gordon.

> Red Skelton ad-libbed in rehearsals, and Bela pleaded with him not to do that. Skelton promised time and again to give Bela his actual cues, and stick to the script. But on the live show, Skelton ad-libbed, time and again. I stood in the wings, holding Bela's cigar, watching; Lugosi was almost in tears, because he didn't know when to come in with his lines. Somehow, Lorre and Chaney managed, but Lugosi was in a terrible state. . . . Bela came off the stage in a state of complete collapse.

Sadly, all of these publicity ploys were for nothing. Allied Artists— "really a miserable outfit," says Alex Gordon—dropped *House of Terror,* and the whole idea of Karloff, Lugosi and Chaney. At this time, Bela took to the Las Vegas stage, headlining *The Bela Lugosi Revue* at the Silver Slipper for six weeks, before the age, addiction, and strain of working seven nights a week in a showroom exhausted him.

The last chance for Boris Karloff and Bela Lugosi to work together again had expired.

*   *   *

On January 5, 1955, the *Best of Broadway* presented *Arsenic and Old Lace,* with Boris Karloff reprising Jonathan Brewster, Peter Lorre as Einstein, Helen Hayes and Billie Burke as the old aunts and John Alexander in his Broadway/movie role of Teddy. At this time, Bela Lugosi was playing in Edward D. Wood's *Bride of the Monster,* his final starring role. For many, this is Bela's finest hour; gaunt, almost frighteningly thin and drawn, he mixes his familiar flamboyance with a very real bitterness which is almost heartbreaking to watch. The film is one of the darlings of the "Worst Films" crowd, with its rubber octopus whose limp tentacles the victims must pull around themselves, its feeble supporting cast and the hulking presence of the "Super Swedish Angel," ex-wrestler Tor Johnson, who would costar with Bela in the star's final three films.

"I was classed a madman, a charlatan, outlawed in the world of science which previously had honored me as a genius," says Bela in this film, tears

Going in for a marriage license, Bela and wife number five, Hope Lininger, 1955.

welling in his eyes, feverishly performing this emotional speech without the prearranged cue cards and all in one classic take. "Now here in this forsaken, jungle hell, I have proven that I am all right!"

During the shooting, Bela had excused himself at least once to go home and take his "medicine." After *Bride of the Monster,* he admitted himself to the Motion Picture Country House, but because he had not worked in a "Union" project for too long a period, the Country House refused him free treatment. Outraged, bitter, vindictive toward Hollywood and his ex-wife, Bela now decided to play his most horrifying role of all: Bela Lugosi, dope addict.

On April 21, 1955 — Lillian Lugosi's 44th birthday — Bela Lugosi publicly committed himself as a drug addict. The man's brutal, deliberate timing would haunt Lillian all her life. Committed to Metropolitan State Hospital in Norwalk, California, for a minimum of three months or maximum of two years, Bela threw himself into his role of addicted Hollywood freak with chilling abandon: exaggerating that he had been taking drugs since 1935; posing and smiling for those horrible, shocking photos of him at a wasted 125 pounds, Lugosi was so grateful for some attention from the press that he posed in his hospital sackcloth, revealing the needle marks on his skeletal legs; filling the *Inquirer* with juicy quotes about his withdrawal:

> I cannot describe the tortures I underwent. My body grew hot, then cold. I tried to eat the bedsheets, my pajamas. My heart beat madly. Then it seemed to stop. . . .

The Hollywood reaction to the Lugosi scandal was odd. Letters poured into the Metropolitan State Hospital from all over the world, as well as donations from fellow Hungarians such as Paul Lukas. However, when Ed Wood and company arranged a May 11, 1955, Hollywood premiere of *Bride of the Monster* (then known as *Bride of the Atom*), as a benefit for Lugosi, ticket sales were pathetically poor. Wood, Vampira, Paul "Kelton the Kop" Marco, Tor Johnson, and Bela, Jr., all appeared onstage at the benefit, but ticket sales were very poor.

"Sales were very, very bad," Paul Marco told Tom Weaver in his book, *Interviews with B Science Fiction and Horror Movie Makers,* "and we were all disappointed that more money wasn't raised, because Bela really did need it. Ed tried very hard selling blocks of seats, and Universal didn't even buy any. You'd think, after all the money Lugosi's pictures had made for them, they'd buy a block. We raised very little money, and that was very, very disheartening."

Once again, Hollywood legend has tried to cast Boris Karloff as one of Bela's salvations during this cataclysmic episode. However, there's no evidence that Bela heard from him. "The only star I heard from was Sinatra," said Bela, who received $1000 from his crooner fan. Why didn't Boris help?

One might guess it was British propriety; one might also believe that Boris believed his aid would have humiliated the fallen Bela ever more painfully.

In the minimum amount of time—three months—Bela Lugosi left Metropolitan Hospital, claiming he was cured for good, vowing to refrain from drugs and alcohol, clutching the script for a new Ed Wood film, *The Ghoul Goes West,* which was to star him with Gene Autry. Lillian and his nephew drove him to his Hollywood apartment, where he instantly called Wood, to learn when he started work. Wood's hemming and hawing made Bela realize his new project was going to fall through. Instantly, the recovered star took off for the neighboring liquor store.

Actually, Bela was about to begin a new melodrama, of sorts—his last marriage.

"What I could tell you about that woman goes back years!" Lillian Lugosi once exclaimed to me about Hope Lugosi. "Every Father's Day, a card from Hope Lininger. Every holiday, a card from Hope Lininger. So, who does he end up marrying? Hope Lininger!"

During his stay at Metropolitan Hospital, Bela had received daily letters from a fan who signed her missives, "A Dash of Hope." She was, indeed, Hope Lininger, a blonde Pennsylvania-raised 39-year-old fan who had lived her life in awe of Bela Lugosi. She had taken jobs to move her to Hollywood, and near him; there, working as a studio clerk, she paid people to spy on Bela, and bring her reports. Bela quickly tracked her down; 20 days after his release from Metropolitan State Hospital, August 25, 1955, Bela Lugosi married for the fifth and last time.

The marriage ceremony, performed by none other than Dr. Manley Hall, who had "hypnotized" Bela on the set of *Black Friday,* almost never happened. One evening, Lillian Lugosi, in a mood to remember, told me:

> He called me the day he married her. He was drunk—oh yes, he was. He said, "Oh, I wish I was marrying you, Lillian." I made it clear we weren't going to be married, and he said, "Well, will you come to the ceremony?" I said, "No! I don't want to come!" Bela Jr. was there, and was his father's Best Man.

The words had sounded a bit scornful, but Lillian's voice grew sad. "Maybe I shouldn't have done that to him," she said, very sadly. "He just couldn't stand being by himself."

The lonely Bela Lugosi arrived hours late at his wedding, fortified by many drinks and willing to take the vows. Bela toasted the press, thanking them "for giving an old man a chance for a comeback."

"I've been a fan of Bela's ever since I was a kid," said the new Mrs. Lugosi.

15
The Year 1956 and Lugosi's Death

> One thing is sure. I'm not going to go in the role (of Dracula) forever . . .
> and end like Lugosi, a morphine addict playing in tasteless parodies. . . .
> — Christopher Lee

On November 17, 1955, Boris Karloff opened at Broadway's Longacre Theatre as Cauchon, Bishop of Beauvais, in Lillian Hellman's play, *The Lark*, starring Julie Harris. It was the triumph of his acting career. The *New York Times* reported that Karloff "brings the play most of its humanity," and the play was a critical and popular hit, running 229 performances.

"And what a distinguished company!" said Karloff of his cast, including Christopher Plummer, Joseph Wiseman, and Theodore Bikel. "All of them — especially Julie Harris. She plays Joan with the hand of God." Miss Harris, in reply, wrote a letter to "Dearest Boris" after the play: "I have never been so happy acting with someone as I have been with you. I love you. . . ." (Miss Harris and Boris would costar on the February 10, 1957, *Hallmark Hall of Fame* special of *The Lark*, which added Basil Rathbone to the cast and attracted a viewing audience of 26 million.)

After a performance of *The Lark*, Karloff went home to wife Evie at their apartment, high in the eaves of the Dakota on 72nd Street, overlooking Central Park. It was, in many ways, the high point of Boris Karloff's life.

Meanwhile, at 5620 Harold Way in Hollywood, the shadows were closing broodingly on Bela Lugosi. Although released from Metropolitan Hospital, he was a very sick old man, physically and emotionally — his mental state growing as sadly fragile as his body.

Hope Lininger's marriage to her dream Dracula had become a warped reality. Her Vampire was now a bitter, brittle old man who kept Scotch sequestered in every nook and cranny of the Harold Way apartment. As Hope dressed daily and went off to work, her ever-jealous spouse sat alone, suspicious of his fifth wife, weeping over his lost Lillian and Bela, Jr., drinking, and — sadly — harboring a dread fear of dying.

And the fifth marriage apparently did little to ease Bela's deep fears.

"Afraid of *him*? He was afraid of *me*!" crowed Hope Lugosi when the *National Enquirer* showed up for an interview in 1957, a year after Bela's death.

Karloff and Julie Harris in their Broadway roles in *The Lark*.

"He never stopped acting. Like all actors, he was a big ham. . . . I had to show him who was boss." Hope clearly had no understanding of or sympathy for her one-time dream man ("I got what I wanted, but I did lose a year of my life, let's face it"):

> He dramatized everything. If it were lamb stew cooking, he would dramatize it. If I never see lamb stew again it'll be too soon! When the meal was

done he would invariably kiss my hand and say, "That was a truly marvelous dinner." He was always impressing himself. . .

Lillian Lugosi deeply loved Bela, and had indulged his ego. Hope delighted in puncturing it.

> Bela was very jealous. . . . He wanted to be center of attention. . . . Sometimes in an evil mood he would laugh like Dracula. He had a morbid sense of humor. The pictures on our wall proved it. I had five cemeteries adorning the wall and a life-sized painting of him. I'll use that for a dart board someday. I told him that once and he almost blew up the house.

Worse than the insults to the ego, however, were Hope's refusals to assuage Bela's bitter fear of death. He kept a glass of his drinking water, imported from Europe, next to his bed at night — "to ward off evil spirits." Hope sometimes taunted her 73-year-old husband that, while he was asleep, she would take away the drinking water — a threat that terrified him. But saddest of all was Hope's response to Bela's desperate need to be comforted about an afterlife:

> I made a very unfortunate remark one time. I got so sick of his eternal religious arguments that I said, "You know, Bela, I don't think I even believe in God." He was furious. He had a memory like an elephant, you know, and he would always throw it up to me. "You don't even believe in God."

Bela never forgot his fame. One night, he announced that Hope was to drive him and fan Richard Sheffield to see his long-lost Hollywood houses.

"I am Bela Lugosi. I used to live here and I have come to see my house!" the actor would announce to the startled owners.

They visited the house above Beachwood Drive; the mansion on Outpost Drive, which he had lost during the horror blackout of the late 1930s; and his favorite, "the Dracula House," on North Whipple Street above Universal City — all of which he had shared with Lillian. As Hope Lugosi told *Filmfax:*

> . . . Late one night we went to visit his old house in North Hollywood. It had huge groves of tall foreboding trees and other spooky things enshrouding it. Even though we woke up the people who were living there at the time, they were delighted to see us and show us around. The furniture was mostly Spanish, very heavy wood. It was quite spectacular.

In February, 1956, Howard W. Koch offered Bela a part in *The Black Sleep,* an "all-star" horror show starring Basil Rathbone as a pioneering brain surgeon, hell-bent on curing his young wife's coma, and harboring his human guinea pigs in his castle cellars. Akim Tamiroff, as Rathbone's gypsy henchman, Lon Chaney, as "Mungo," a once-brilliant professor-turned-zombie courtesy of Rathbone's scalpel, and John Carradine, a madman in long white beard chanting "Kill the infidel!" had small but juicy roles.

The role offered Bela was Casmir, Rathbone's servant — and a mute. It seemed a cruel and bitter joke, perpetuated by Frankenstein's monster. However, Bela took the part.

The cast warmly greeted Bela, presenting him with a bound copy of the script, but the actor behaved strangely during the shooting. "There is Basil playing my part," he told a reporter. "I used to be the big cheese. Now I'm playing just a dumb part." Perhaps Rathbone, a very sensitive man, sensed this resentment, and he sent Bela a note:

Dear Bela,
I found this in reading last night. "That which is past is irrevocable; and wise men have enough to do with things present and to come. Therefore they do not trifle themselves that labour in the past matters."

"He hadn't been too happy with his part," recalled Richard Sheffield, who played hookey two days so as to accept Bela's invitation to the set, "and was drinking on the set but when rehearsing or on a take he was fine and completely in character. Lon Chaney, Jr., joked a lot with him and once lifted him over his head playfully. Bela just wasn't in the mood for that kind of game but took it gracefully."

The director of *The Black Sleep* was the gifted Reginald Le Borg, who had directed *The Mummy's Ghost, Weird Woman* and other Universal shockers of the World War II years. Mr. Le Borg, who died in March of 1989, offered perhaps the sharpest cameo portrait of the devastated Bela Lugosi at this time. He told me:

On *The Black Sleep*, Lugosi was in very bad shape. He had a man with him, continuously, who helped him, and walked with him, because Lugosi was bound to "burst out." He was cooperative, but "whiny," you know. He was coming to me and saying, "Herr Director! I'm a star, I'm a star! Give me some lines!"
I said, "I can't give you any lines, because you're playing a mute. Your character's tongue was cut out!"
He said, "But, I'm a STAR! Give me CLOSE-UPS!"
So, to pacify him, I put him in a scene, behind Rathbone. But during Rathbone's speech, Lugosi made grimaces — which of course took away from the scene. I knew I couldn't use that, and told him.
"But I'm the star!" Lugosi argued. "I'm the STAR! I've got to do SOMETHING!"
So I said, "Well, I'll give you a separate close-up" — figuring it would end up anyway on the cutting room floor. But that satisfied him. He said, "Thank you, Herr Director," and went back to his dressing room, and had a smoke.

Le Borg would also direct 1957's *Voodoo Island*, which starred Boris Karloff. He contrasted the two actors:

Lugosi had been a silent star . . . . He was Hungarian, he had prided himself on his beautiful looks he had when he was very young and a Matinee Idol. He had been "a lover," and was "the external," "the face"—he was not very schooled.

Karloff was an intelligent guy—schooled, British, college. He was a gentleman, talked like a gentleman, and behaved like a gentleman. The other one, Lugosi, was Hungarian—hot-blooded, fighting, and what not. So, from the exterior alone, you could see that Karloff and Lugosi were opposites.

No film offers followed Bela's humble cameo in *The Black Sleep*. On June 8 and 9, 1956, Bela appeared at the Troupers-Green Room in Hollywood as the "International Drug Smuggler" in the amateur play, *Devil's Paradise*. It ran three performances, and offered the lure, "After the performance meet Mr. Bela Lugosi, the man who won a 25-year battle with dope."

Meanwhile, *The Black Sleep* was set for summer 1956 release. Forrest J Ackerman has told the story frequently of accompanying Bela to the Hollywood premiere, where the ailing star rose magnificently to the occasion when reporters met him in the lobby. The story is all the more impressive when one learns about the West Coast personal appearance tour Bela joined to promote *The Black Sleep*.

The tour, boasting Bela, Lon Chaney, John Carradine, Tor Johnson and Vampira, was set for San Francisco (one of Bela's favorite cities), Portland, and Seattle. Bela had so deteriorated, was so suicidal, and was drinking so heavily that he terrified his roommate, the gentle Tor Johnson. Chuck Moses, who was handling Howard W. Koch's Bel-Air Productions, met the company at San Francisco's St. Francis Hotel, where the stars had quartered the night before. Moses (who later became a noted psychical investigator whose activities included the Amityville house) told me of the chilling situation he found there:

Tor Johnson, known in Wrestling as the "Super Swedish Angel," met me in the lobby. The "Angel" had been Lugosi's nursemaid on the shooting of *The Black Sleep,* and I got the impression he was his nursemaid off the picture as well, with the job of taking care of him. Well, the Angel was extremely nervous, and told me, "It's really very difficult—Lugosi's drinking has reached the point where he was just running around the walls of the hotel room last night! He does it often!" Lugosi was drinking boilermakers—he'd mix beer and whiskey. So I went up to see him—he was in bad shape, and I ordered no alcohol be sent to his room, because I didn't want him to be out of it. Now I have a degree in Clinical Psychology, and realize I was depriving his system . . .

Well, we got up to Portland, and it was impossible for Lugosi to go on. The Angel took me into his room, and Lugosi was shaking—he looked like a man who was dying. I okayed that he have a shot of alcohol. Meanwhile, the press was waiting in a restaurant across the street! So we came up with a very dramatic act. I told Bela, he wasn't really well, he had to go home, and the best way to do this was to put on a little show for the press, in which he would not be subject to questions—he couldn't answer them. So, he came into the room for the press, and—as planned—he collapsed. In actuality, Lugosi really collapsed—but it

Bela Lugosi on stage as Dracula.

was planned that way, and Lon Chaney, his good friend and a prince of a guy, carried him out. Then we sent him home. The man could just not operate; he was just too addicted and too shot to do anything. . . .

Later I worked with Boris Karloff; in fact I wrote one of his pictures, *Frankenstein — 1970* (which was later rewritten so that I forced the producer to put his name on it), as well as putting together a supernatural series, with Karloff as host (it didn't sell). He was fun and easy to work with — a prankster who loved practical jokes. I don't recall him ever mentioning Bela Lugosi. They weren't in the same league.

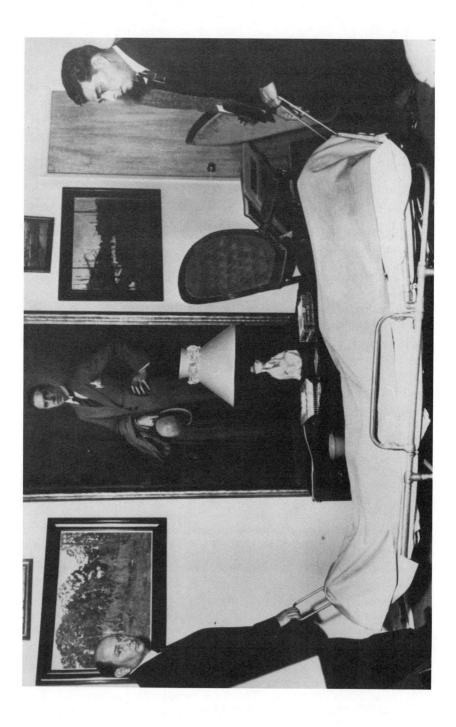

Before the tour was over, even long-suffering "nursemaid" Tor Johnson had apparently lost patience with Bela. In *Fangoria #22,* Johnny Legend recorded a memory Johnson (who died in 1971) had regarding his roommate:

> ...Tor recalls that Bela was at his lowest spiritual ebb, deeply depressed and suicidal, continuously muttering that he "just wanted to die." Growing weary of Bela's constant whining, Tor snatched him roughly by the collar and held him dangling from their hotel room several stories above street level. "Is this what you want, you miserable Hunkie?" Tor demanded. Lugosi finally came to his senses and admitted he wanted to live, at which time Tor hauled him back into safety....

Bela Lugosi returned home from *The Black Sleep* tour. A very short time later, he would be dead.

* * *

In the midsummer of 1956, the infamous Edward D. Wood, Jr., got his hands on $800 worth of "front money," and began work on *The Vampire's Tomb.* Naturally, he called Bela, who needed the money and agreed to lend his presence, even though his role offered no dialogue. Wood claimed Bela was too ill to speak it.

Of course, this brief footage was sadly fated to become a part of Wood's legendary *Plan 9 from Outer Space,* which would costar the provocative Vampira (who recalls Bela calling her once, crying pitifully that Bela, Jr., hadn't called him on Mother's Day) and the hulking Tor Johnson (never more grotesque than in his pre-ghoul footage, playing a cop in a snap-brimmed hat, and announcing his intention to "Knock around a little"). The film was destined to be hailed as perhaps the worst movie ever made, which has given this execrable thing not only a warped prestige, but a perennial audience. If ever a film should have been "lost," this is it. Like some celluloid parasite, *Plan 9* gobbled up the brief Lugosi footage from *The Vampire's Tomb;* the scenes of Bela Lugosi, filmed only days before his death, are painfully sad. As he stands, small, gnarled, shrunken in his Dracula cape, in grainy footage taken in a forsaken Spanish cemetery in the San Fernando Valley, there is something almost frighteningly unhappy about the humiliated actor. Lovers of "camp" hoot at the vignette in which Bela, in his cape and a black homburg, leaves a Hollywood house (reportedly Tor Johnson's), looking like a trapped Dracula under the merciless California sun, gently picking a flower as Criswell's smarmy voice lisps Wood's awful narration ("The ever-beautiful flowers she had planted with her own hands, became nothing more than the lost roses of her cheeks..."). However, the pain and sorrow and dread in Bela's face in this episode are all too real—and surely more chilling than anything in all his horror movies.

Opposite: **August 16, 1956.**

Wood had run out of money on *The Vampire's Tomb*. Work shut down, temporarily. Bela Lugosi went home to await his next call.

Only a few nights before his death, Bela Lugosi awoke in the middle of the night. When Hope asked him what was wrong, Bela said Karloff was in the living room — and that he had to get dressed to go in and see him.

Thursday, August 16, 1956. Hope Lugosi went to work. When a bottle of Bela's imported water arrived, he called his young fan Richard Sheffield to ask him to lift it up onto the dispenser. When Sheffield arrived, Bela answered the door in his underclothes; a neighbor had already lifted the bottle. Bela told Sheffield he felt "really bad." The fan helped his idol back to bed and left the apartment.

That evening, Hope Lugosi returned to 5620 Harold Way with groceries. The fifth Mrs. Lugosi called to her husband, who was in bed. There was no answer. Bela Lugosi had died, approximately 6:45 p.m., of a coronary occlusion. Hope Lugosi said:

> He was just terrified of death. Toward the end he was very weary, but he was still afraid of death. Three nights before he died he was sitting on the edge of the bed. I asked him if he were still afraid to die. He told me that he was. I did my best to comfort him, but you might as well save your breath with people like that. They're still going to be afraid of death.

Word spread so quickly that a photographer managed to snap a picture of the undertakers wheeling Bela's covered body past his giant portrait that graced the small apartment. The next morning, Hope Lugosi began giving away his clothing and memorabilia. Eventually, she even gave away her Bela Lugosi scrapbook (in which she had pasted his death certificate) to Forrest J Ackerman, who went on to edit *Famous Monsters of Filmland*. In 1987, the scrapbook would be listed among Ackerman's memorabilia at the "Auction of the Century" in New York; a writer in attendance told me the pages had been ripped out and scattered about a table when he attended the auction.

The heartbroken Lillian Lugosi (who never gave away her scrapbook) and Bela, Jr., joined in the funeral plans.

At 2:30 p.m., Saturday, August 18, 1956, the corpse of Bela Lugosi, poetically wrapped (as he wished) in his Dracula cape, lay inside the Strother Chapel of the Utter-McKinley Mortuary, 6240 Hollywood Boulevard. For decades, Utter-McKinley had been a macabre landmark in Hollywood, right across the street from the Pantages Theatre, and over the years, a number of film colony luminaries had rested there: Wallace Reid, the movie hero whose death from drug addiction shocked the world in 1923; June Mathis, Valentino's "discoverer," in 1927; Peg Entwhistle, the actress who won morbid immortality by jumping off the HOLLYWOODLAND sign in 1932.

Opposite: **A proud Bela Lugosi with his son Bela, Jr., on the set of *Abbott and Costello Meet Frankenstein*, 1948. The star signed this photo "in character."**

The faithful, about 100 in number, filed past the casket. There were few celebrities present: Carroll Borland, "Luna" of *Mark of the Vampire;* a very emotional Tor Johnson; and Edward Wood, Jr. (who would later use his wife's chiropractor, Dr. Tom Mason, to double Bela's *The Vampire's Tomb* footage in *Plan 9 from Outer Space*).

"I couldn't believe it," Carroll Borland told me, emotionally. "He looked so small in his coffin. He was a big man, but he seemed small — as though he had been shrunken by life. And he may have been — it was such a bad ending."

Of course, Hope Lininger Lugosi, the actor's 40-year-old widow, exactly one week short of her first anniversary as Mrs. Bela Lugosi, was on hand. As she later said:

> Death is no stranger to me. Everybody I ever had has died. My mother, my father, my brother, my friends. I dug my own grandfather's grave in the hills of Pennsylvania. So death doesn't hold the curse for me it did for him. When I saw him lying there in the coffin I realized he looked entirely too peaceful. Sure couldn't have been bad.

Also, of course, there was Lillian — whose guilt about Bela's final miserable years would haunt her the rest of her life. Comforted by 18-year-old Bela, Jr., Lillian had won a major battle with her successor (whose passionate fan mail to her husband Lillian well-remembered). Hope had wanted Bela simply and economically cremated at Hollywood Cemetery. Lillian emotionally protested, demanding her ex-husband have a memorial. Lillian paid for the funeral, as well as a plot in the lovely Grotto section of Holy Cross Cemetery, right next to the Crosby family plot. Hope paid for the coffin.

Sadly enough, Lillian would stand bereaved in the same mortuary (Hungarian friends managed it) in 1972, as the widow of actor Brian Donlevy, for whom she was working in 1956 as a secretary.

A countryman of Bela's played a moody violin tribute. And then, Hollywood legend states, a hush fell over the mourners. Into the mortuary whisked Boris Karloff. The "monster" Bela had created in 1931 approached the casket, bent over the cloaked corpse of his old costar, and stage-whispered a line that would win infamy:

"Come now, Bela. Are you putting us on?"

But Boris Karloff didn't say this. He wasn't at the funeral.

*   *   *

The flat headstone in Holy Cross Cemetery reads:

BELA LUGOSI
Beloved Father
1882–1956

Also nearby in the Grotto section of the Catholic cemetery are Charles Boyer (who committed suicide after the death of his beloved wife) and Sharon Tate, victim of the Manson murders.

Many admirers have visited the grave site over the years. George Hamilton even visited Bela's grave as a publicity stunt when he promoted *Love at First Bite.*

The estate of an actor destined posthumously to become one of Hollywood's most legendary names amounted to about $1900 in the bank, and a building lot worth about $1000. Although Bela was buried in one of his Dracula capes, there was at least one other. Fortunately, after probate, Bela, Jr., got the cherished cape before Hope Lugosi could fulfill her plan to make a dress out of it.

Hope Lugosi, who has told a number of Lugosi fans over the years that she truly is a witch, eventually left Hollywood. Richard F. Sheffield, Jr., in his feature "Lugosi's Last Years" for *Famous Monsters of Filmland,* wrote, "Hope Lugosi was and is a fascinating person . . . great with us kids" (who visited Bela at his apartment evenings of his final year). Paul Marco, who played "Kelton the Cop" in *Bride of the Monster* and *Plan 9 from Outer Space,* told Tom Weaver in his book *Interviews with B Science Fiction and Horror Movie Makers* that Hope was "a very lovely lady . . . a wonderful girl."

At last report, Hope Lugosi was working in the hospital on the leper colony of Molokai.

Three nights before Bela Lugosi died, Boris Karloff had guest-starred on NBC's *The Ernie Kovacs Show;* 19 days after Lugosi's funeral, September 6, 1956, Boris Karloff guest-starred on CBS's *Climax,* with Angela Lansbury. The ironic title: "Bury Me Later." On October 25, 1956, Karloff guested on *Playhouse 90* for CBS, in "Rendezvous in Black"; on November 27, 1956, he was the guest star on CBS's *The Red Skelton Show,* cavorting with the comic who had so traumatized Bela on the air several years before. Karloff finished out the year in which Bela Lugosi died guesting on the December 11, December 18 and Christmas, 1956 airings of CBS's *The $64,000 Question,* selecting children's stories as his specialty—and taking home $16,000.

It's amazing how myth grows and blossoms in Hollywood. The association of Karloff with Lugosi in the mind's eye of the public caused stories to circulate how Boris, ever-sympathic, had taken Bela out on the town in Hollywood after the latter's drug cure for a warm evening of festive reminiscing. Another rumor, and one that appalled Lillian (who died in 1981), was that Karloff secretly paid for Bela's funeral. And, quickly, the mythology of Hollywood created that black comedy tale of Karloff visiting the funeral parlor. Karloff, then living in New York, probably wasn't even in Hollywood at the time. Yet how sadly significant it was: Hollywood casting Lugosi, even in death, in Karloff's dominating shadow.

*   *   *

Today, Bela G. Lugosi, Jr., a very successful Los Angeles lawyer, lives with his family in Flintridge, California. Tall and handsome, he resembles his famous father, but has inherited apparently very little of his rather tempestuous (and tragic) personality.

Mr. Lugosi recently spoke with me about the phenomenon of Bela Lugosi:

> You're not quite as conscious of distinction when you're young, and live in the same house with somebody. But I still noticed that my father received a lot of attention. When he walked into a room, people noticed him. . . .
>
> I first saw him on the screen when I was small. My mother would take me and my little friends to the movies to see my father. I was more interested in the reactions of my friends, who were hiding under the seats in terror. To me, that man on the screen was just "Dad"!
>
> My early memories go back to Dad's "Dracula House" on Whipple Street. It was a great house, with high walls around it, so it was like a whole little island in the middle of the North Hollywood neighborhood. Everything was custom-built; every window in the house had colored, lead glass. Inside was a Steinway concert piano, and a great circular staircase; outside were stork nests on the roof, and there was a pond on the grounds. I remember the Hungarian musicians, and how Dad loved a good party! Of course, the house was demolished long ago, and there are condominiums there now. . . .
>
> I would visit the sets of Dad's films, like *Abbott and Costello Meet Frankenstein*. I remember that he was highly respected. He was famous for getting a scene on the first take, and he was very nice to everybody, the cast, and grips, and all.
>
> My favorite of Dad's films? I like *Dracula* — and the movies in which he played non-horror roles. As for his work with Karloff, there was no friendship there that I knew; I think Dad thought he was overrated.
>
> Today, I have one of Dad's Dracula capes. And a day doesn't go by that somebody doesn't comment on the name Bela Lugosi, and remember him.

16
Karloff's Last Act

> In one sense, Boris Karloff could be judged a failure. A lifetime of roles in-
> tended to create horror and loathing only succeeded in making him one of the
> most loved of actors....
> The inarticulate pathos of Karloff's portrayal of the Monster, innocent and
> bewildered, staggering beneath the burden of emotions it can neither express nor
> control, lent the film dignity and depth, creating a lasting classic. Lugosi had re-
> jected the role; had he not, his histrionic style could hardly have inspired the icon
> of the popular mythology originated by Karloff....
> — Philip Kemp, *The International Dictionary of Films and Filmmakers*

After the death of Bela Lugosi, Boris Karloff would spend 12 years as one of the world's busiest actors and one of Hollywood's greatest legends. It was a recognition that Lugosi had never lived to enjoy—and a recognition that compelled Karloff to play one of the most moving final acts of any star's career.

In the fall of 1957, Screen Gems released the *Shock Theatre* package, televised Friday and Saturday nights. Already a character star, Boris Karloff now found himself a legend as well, as his "dear old monster" won a whole new generation of admirers. With his caring (and slightly domineering, but he liked it that way) wife, Evelyn, Boris happily traveled the world, always the epitome of professionalism, a "quick study" filled with energy, humor, and dedication to his craft.

There were two dozen movies, ranging from bombs like 1958's *Frankenstein–1970* to the fun American-International spoofs, 1963's *The Raven* (with Price and Lorre) and *The Comedy of Terrors* (with Price, Lorre, and "Wolf von Frankenstein," Basil Rathbone). There were over 100 television shows, everything from singing and dancing on variety shows to hosting NBC's *Thriller* (1960–1962; he also acted in several episodes) and the BBC's *Out of This World* (1962), to reprising Jonathan Brewster one more time in the *Hallmark Hall of Fame* special of *Arsenic and Old Lace* (February 5, 1962), to masquerad-ing as his monster on the "Lizard's Leg and Owlet's Wing" episode of *Route 66* (October 26, 1962, with Lorre in cape and top hat and Chaney appearing as Quasimodo, the Mummy and the Wolf Man), to singing "The Monster Mash" on the Halloween, 1965, *Shindig*. He returned to the stage in 1960 in

A snapshot (circa mid-1960s) of Karloff, his wife Evelyn (left), daughter Sara Jane, and grandsons.

On Borrowed Time, narrated recordings, spent over ten years recording daily excerpts for *Reader's Digest.* . . .*

Karloff was the monarch of horror; as its elder spokesman, he gently censored the new bloodletting style of cinema horror, while defending the classic horror tales:

Karloff endured a peripheral and scandalous tragedy late in life. On the night of December 18, 1958, two grandnephews of Karloff, 13-year-old Martin Bromley and his 10-year-old brother Stephen Bromley, were found dead in their country home near Haslemere, England, their throats slashed by a razor. Thomas Bromley, of the British Ministry of Defense, found the bodies of his sons (who had come home from school for the Christmas holidays), as well as his 39-year-old wife, Diana (daughter of Boris's brother Sir John Thomas Pratt), unconscious with her throat cut. Two days later, after Mrs. Bromley was released from the hospital, police arrested Karloff's niece on the charge of murdering her two sons (after which she presumably had turned the razor on herself).

Boris camping it up as "Mother" in "The Mother Muffin Affair" on NBC's *The Girl from U.N.C.L.E.*, 1966, with Stefanie Powers and Robert Vaughn.

> There is more horror and violence in nursery rhymes than in TV or films. Forget *Frankenstein.* Take *A Frog He Would A-Wooing Go.* By golly, a cat kills a mouse, and a frog is eaten by a duck. Awfully cruel and savage. As for Grimm's Fairy Tales . . . well, for heaven's sake!
> We were all brought up on fairy tales, and none of us have turned out to be monsters—except maybe me!

To many, Karloff seemed as indestructible as his monster: starring in 1965's *Die, Monster, Die!;* going drag, in red wig and frilly blouse and Victorian bonnet, as the awesomely kinky Mother of "The Mother Muffin Affair" on *The Girl from U.N.C.L.E.,* with Stefanie Powers and Robert Vaughn (1966); narrating the 1966 special, *How the Grinch Stole Christmas,* the Dr. Seuss fable that has become a Yuletide tradition, and in which Boris also was the voice of the Grinch (has anyone ever noticed how much the Grinch, in voice and leers, resembles Karloff's evil Count Gregor of 1935's *The Black Room...?*).

Yet, to many, there was true concern—by the late 1960s, Karloff was not a well man. "Of course, he's nearly doubled over now, the poor dear man, but he'll never say die!" said Basil Rathbone—who, as fate had it, died suddenly of a heart attack in 1967, over a year-and-a-half before Karloff. Boris's history of back trouble now truly deformed him; and his leg was in a steel brace; an operation had left him with only half a lung. He walked with a cane; increasingly, he got about in a wheelchair.

Why did he do it? By all accounts a very wealthy man, why did he leave his lovely English cottage, near the sea in Bramshoot, and his London apartment? Why didn't he (as reporters constantly asked him) retire?

"If I did," Karloff would say, with emotion, "I'd be dead within a few months. I intend to die with my boots, and my greasepaint, on."

In the spring of 1967, Boris Karloff began work on a project destined to be titled *Targets.* The director was Peter Bogdanovich; Karloff's role was Byron Orlok, old horror movie star, who confronts and conquers the real-life horror of the 1960s in the form of a sniper at a drive-in movie. "Karloff's epitaph and apotheosis," wrote Denis Gifford of *Targets* in *Karloff: The Man, the Monster, the Movies:* "we should regard this as his ultimate triumph."

In one scene of *Targets,* Karloff, in shirtsleeves and suspenders, sits in his hotel room, preparing for a personal appearance at a drive-in showing his new movie (American-International's *The Terror*). He regards the bee-bop sixties deejay with wonderful comic disdain:

> D.J.: When I was a kid, Mr. O, I must have digged your flicks four zillion times! You blew my mind.
> KARLOFF: Obviously!

The old Horror Star vetoes the D.J.'s idea of asking questions like "Is Byron Orlok your real name?" and suggests he tell the drive-in audience a story, the one used by John O'Hara in *Appointment in Samarra.*

"King" Karloff with Hazel Court in American-International's *The Raven,* **1963.**

The scene was shot, after midnight, following a long, hard day — and Karloff delivered the two-page monologue in one take. Bogdanovich got Laszlo Kovacs' camera on Karloff as he told this fable, beautifully, powerfully, with all of his magic. The crew burst into applause, which deeply moved the actor. "I can't tell you the deference I felt for that man," said Bogdanovich.

It would have been the perfect farewell film — but Karloff would have none of it. In April, 1967, at Hollywood's Magic Castle, Karloff had a press party, to proclaim the release of Decca's record, *An Evening with Boris Karloff and His Friends,* which he narrated. Characteristically, Boris made light of his failing health:

> My leg in a steel brace . . . operating with only half a lung . . . why, it's a public scandal that I'm still around! But, as long as people want me, I feel an obligation to go on performing. After all, everytime I act I provide employment for a fleet of doubles!

*   *   *

In February, 1968, Boris Karloff became very ill with bronchitis while starring with Christoper Lee in Britain's *The Curse of the Crimson Altar.* A cold, rainy night of location shooting had aggravated the critical illness.

On March 15, 1968, the 80-year-old Boris Karloff appeared on the cover of *Life* magazine — blowing out birthday candles for the 150th anniversary of Mary Shelley's *Frankenstein.*

And then, in the spring of 1968, a strange, sad, ultimately gallant thing happened. Boris Karloff came to Hollywood, to star in four films in four weeks — a "deal" brewed by Columbia Pictures and Mexico's Azteca Films. The four pictures — *The Fear Chamber, Isle of the Snake People, House of Evil,* and *The Incredible Invasion* — were hardly worthy of a legend, and fated to be spliced together with pornography footage. Karloff was seriously ill — sitting on the mercilessly hot soundstage on Santa Monica Boulevard, in his wheelchair, reaching now and then for his oxygen mask; writer Bill Warren, who was on the set, recalled that it was a physical strain for the star to sign an autograph (although he always graciously did so). Yet, when it was time to act, he rose from the wheelchair, straightened up, and gave a dynamic performance. It was a lucrative offer; reportedly, there was approximately $350,000 on deposit for Karloff in a Mexican bank at the time of his death. But money, apparently, was not his motivation.

On September 24, 1968, Boris Karloff and Vincent Price were the guest stars on *The Red Skelton Show.* The skit, "He Who Steals My Robot Steals Trash," pitted Boris and Price against Skelton's Clem Kadiddlehopper. In *Dear Boris,* Vincent Price remembered the show:

> . . . as I look back at my association with Boris, two things stick — his humor and his bravery. I knew his suffering . . . and almost at the end of his life had a really amazing experience of his bravery on a *Red Skelton Show.* Boris, with braced legs, etc., was wheeled into the scene by a midget in Frankenstein makeup. In the audienced dress rehearsal he came off and asked if I had the same feeling he did that the humor of the scene was deadened by the audience sympathy for a man in a wheelchair. I had to admit that I did — whereupon Boris, with infinite courage, played the rest of the rehearsal on his feet and the show went well. . . .

The 80-year-old Karloff, with a cane, played the 22-minute skit on his feet. He also did a walk-on (on his feet) and joined Price, seated in a motor-car, singing "The Two of Us" with lyrics spoofing horror movies.

Karloff also was guest star on the October 30, 1968, *The Jonathan Winters Show,* playing in a horror skit with Winters and Agnes Moorehead. Also on the show, he sang—very movingly—"It Was a Very Good Year." The November 29, 1968, episode of *The Name of the Game,* which Karloff did play in a wheelchair, would be his final telecast.

Why did this very wealthy, very famous, very beloved man feel so deep a need to work? Bela Lugosi, after all, had desperately needed money—what could Boris Karloff have needed so badly that he'd leave his English cottage, visit the decaying, ugly, "pop" Hollywood of the late sixties, and push his octogenarian body through such agony? His best friends in Hollywood—C. Aubrey Smith, Edmund Gwenn, James Gleason—all were dead; the drug culture must have appalled a man who once said that manners were the most important thing in life; and one recalls a line he said in *Targets,* looking at the "new" Los Angeles of the sixties: "God, what an ugly town this has become!"

Perhaps he enjoyed adding to his fortune. Perhaps he, like Lugosi, had a fear of dying—or (more likely in Karloff's case) a fear of waiting to die, a dread of realizing he would never enjoy his beloved craft again. However, in the December, 1969, edition of Leonard Maltin's late and lamented *Film Fan Monthly,* critic Jack Edmund Nolan posed the same question—and arrived at the same answer as so many Karloff fans:

> The roar of the crowd is no answer; a player has little rapport with a studio audience or even with hanger-onlookers surrounded as he is these days by a minimum 16-man crew. The need to continue in the limelight might be an answer, yet, to me at least, it seems he was as famous the world over as anyone might expect to be (and a few more TV shows wouldn't help). I'd like to believe that William Henry Pratt's movitation was his sense of responsibility to his fans—to keep them remembering that Karloff lived.

*   *   *

The end finally came, peacefully and mercifully, at Edward VII Hospital in Midhurst, England. Karloff was 81 years old; the date was Sunday, February 2, 1969. The worldwide press eulogized him, while only four people reportedly attended the very private funeral at the Guildford Crematorium. Evelyn Karloff erected a memorial plaque at England's "Actor's Church," St. Paul's, in Covent Garden. The words are from Andrew Marvell's *Upon Cromwell's Return from Ireland:*

> He Nothing Common Did or Mean
> Upon That Memorable Scene

Karloff's ashes are buried at the Garden of Remembrance. At last report, his widow still maintains her apartment in London.

Karloff and the "dear old monster."

Boris Karloff's daughter, Sara Jane, is a tall, dark-haired, beautiful woman, with the striking eyes of her father. She is the mother of two grown sons (one of whom looks very much like Sara's famous father), and now is delighted to have a granddaughter. Living near Palm Springs, she graciously shared these memories for this book:

When my father was doing *Peter Pan* on Broadway, I was living with my mother in San Francisco. It was decided that it would be a grand idea for me to visit him and my stepmother in New York to see my father play "on Broadway." The day before I was to leave I broke my ankle doing tomboyish things and the trip was canceled and rescheduled when the show was playing in Chicago. I arrived for a week long visit with preparations made for me to watch the show from the wings each night as well as from the audience. Unfortunately, at that point in my young life I fell madly in love with Nana the St. Bernard dog in the show and paid far more attention to her than to my father's performances as both Mr. Darling and Captain Hook. My father soon realized that his only child certainly did not have the "fire in her belly" necessary for an actor. I had a wonderful time, my father certainly overcame his momentary disappointment, and I got "to fly" across the stage just like Peter Pan and Wendy. Unfortunately I never did see my father on Broadway.

I used to visit my father and stepmother in Los Angeles when they were on the coast. I lived in San Francisco. There were those times when my poor father was not quite sure what to do with a 10- or 11-year-old girl, so he proceeded to teach me how to play gin rummy. He beat the pants off me continually, and to this day I can remember our games, hour after hour and my great delight if ever I would win a hand. He taught me not to give up or give in, but also not to expect to be given in to. A most valuable lesson.

My favorites of my father's films? *Targets* — it was superb — and the remake of *The Raven*.... He was extremely grateful for the part of the monster.... The world is filled with hungry superb actors. Frankenstein enabled my father to be a well-fed superb actor....

I do remember that when I was little he told me stories. His favorite was about Groundhog Day. Something about it always appealed to him: the little thing emerging from its hole, seeing its shadow, and scurrying back into its hole. He died on Groundhog Day...

*   *   *

Bela Lugosi was always haunted by the ghost of Karloff's Frankenstein monster. One wonders if Karloff was ever haunted by the ghost of Bela Lugosi; not the famous Count Dracula figure, but the forlorn, drug-addicted, alcoholic Lugosi, forsaken, out of work, a skeleton heartbreakingly desperate for attention.

Just as forlorn as Lugosi was in his final days, so was Karloff celebrated; surely Boris, aware of the horror of Bela's last days, how truly miserable he was, counted his own blessings. It must have influenced his vow to work, even with his braced leg, his half a lung, his wheelchair, assuring his fans that "Karloff lived," in boots and greasepaint, almost to the very end.

Always independent of Lugosi, Karloff nevertheless realized, in his last years, how legendary they had become — and, yet, what a tragedy that presented. Karloff had been blessed to live long enough to realize that he truly had found immortality via his legendary monster and screen portrayals. Lugosi had not; he had only his ego and wracked pride to promise him the legacy that Karloff was assured of every day of his late life. No wonder Karloff felt such gratitude. No wonder he was willing to endure such agony, because "people still want me...."

In those final years, Boris Karloff rarely met an interviewer who didn't ask about Bela Lugosi. There were memories of the rivalry, the resentment, the tragedy that colored his classic association with the "charming man" who was "a fool to himself." However, Karloff kept most of it to himself. He had lived long enough to feel the true impact of their legend, to realize the romanticism and escapism their films gave so many people. And Karloff always offered a tribute to the complex and tragic man with whom he created some of the most wonderful episodes of cinema terror:

> Bela was a great technician—he was worth a lot more than he got. Poor Bela, he had a very tragic life you know. A very sad life. . . . But Bela was a kind and lovable man, and I remember our work together with affection.

17

The Myth and the Rivalry

Frankenstein [4 stars]: . . . "restored" version of Boris Karloff's timeless classic. . . . Karloff's performance retains its power (his is great acting, not great *camp* acting à la Lugosi). . . .
— video review in *USA Today,* October 23, 1987

. . .Technically, Lugosi might not have been as good an actor as Karloff, but he had a superior screen personality and as a personification of dark evil had no peer in Hollywood or elsewhere. . . .
— Ephraim Katz, *The Film Encyclopedia*

Comparisons are odorous.
— Mrs. Malaprop

Gable and Harlow and stars like that were, after all, ordinary human beings. Very fascinatingly handsome, and every eyelash in place — but they were people. Lugosi and Karloff were not quite human. They have survived, because they are the demon lovers. . . .
— Carroll Borland

The HOLLYWOOD sign still stands, gallantly and defiantly, atop Mount Lee. However, as many film historians know, a trip to Hollywood of the eighties can be a traumatic experience; it's like paying a call on a once ravishing beauty, only to find her now bald and blotched from syphilis. It's hard to believe that the gods and goddesses of the cinema's Golden Age ever promenaded up and down Hollywood Boulevard, today an ugly traffic of hookers and pushers, where the most alluring tourist attraction of the time is the new Brassiere Museum of Frederick's of Hollywood.

Yet somehow, in a town where even the palm trees look perverted, the dream is still there. So are the dreamers: people touched deeply by the magic of movies, living and working in Hollywood just to be near the ruins, like Schliemann at Troy, or Carter at Egypt. A few stars have the lasting power to entice these disciples: Marilyn Monroe; Rudolph Valentino; Jean Harlow; and Boris Karloff and Bela Lugosi.

Visit the popular Collectors Book Store, 1708 North Vine Street in Hollywood, and talk with Malcolm Willits, the manager. He deals every day with these explorers, seeking tangible bits of the old Hollywood magic:

There are certain things that have entered the national consciousness, like that picture of Marilyn Monroe, with her dress going up over the subway grate, or King Kong on top of the Empire State Building. So have the four great 1930s horror movies: *Frankenstein, Dracula, The Mummy,* and *King Kong.* And so have the two great 1930s horror stars. There is so little of the stuff around today, in mint condition; it's becoming as rare (or rarer) as a Shakespeare first folio, or a manuscript by Sinclair Lewis or Ernest Hemingway. . . .

Talk to the followers themselves: people who have adopted Karloff or Lugosi as a way of life; who know all the dialogue from the masters' films; who take the Universal Studios Tour in the spirit of a holy pilgrimage; who drive up Coldwater Canyon to peek at Karloff's haunted farmhouse, or trek up Outpost Drive to gaze at Lugosi's earthquake-proof mansion; who pour their money into stills and posters and memorabilia; who live for the horror/fantasy conventions; who reverently visit the Hollywood Walk of Fame Stars for Karloff (who has two "stars"—one at 1734 North Vine Street, and one near the Larry Edmunds Bookshop on Hollywood Boulevard) or Lugosi (whose star is at Hollywood Boulevard and Ivar Street); who tour Forrest J Ackerman's Museum of Horror, Fantasy and Science Fiction, who reverently pay respects at Lugosi's grave at Holy Cross Cemetery. . .

The magic survives. And so does the rivalry.

In 1983, the editors of *Consumer Guide* published (with tongue at least partially in cheek) a book called *Rating the Movie Stars* (Beekman House Publishers). The book rated over 400 actors and actresses, awarding them anywhere from one (least) to four (most) stars, along with a film credit listing, and a little write-up.

Boris Karloff rated an impressive 3.17 stars, placing him above such luminaries as Henry Fonda, Katharine Hepburn, Clark Gable, Peter O'Toole, Bette Davis, and Meryl Streep.

Bela Lugosi scored a lowly 1.90, putting him in the bottom 10. The only stars to rate lower (in descending order): Pat Boone, Frankie Avalon, Ali MacGraw, Elvis Presley, Jayne Mansfield, Annette Funicello, and—at the dead bottom—Universal's Queen of Kitsch, Maria Montez.

Actually, both stars were dominated by genre rivals: Laughton (3.66), Lorre (3.62), Rathbone (3.40), and even Colin Clive, who, at 3.22 (and tied with Jean Harlow), was praised as "cinema's greatest sadomasochist."

But how much trust can be put into a book that gives four stars to James Dean, Ben Kingsley and Eddie Murphy? And also, a Lugosiphile might argue, if Karloff still reigns supreme, why is there a Bela Lugosi Fan Club—with members in the United States, England, Canada, Mexico, Australia, Austria, and elsewhere—while (apparently) no Karloff fan club still exists?

Truce. First of all, let it be recognized that Karloff and Lugosi each survive today as super legends. Collectors Book Store manager Willits said:

Bela strikes a Dracula pose at Boris, at their first official encounter at Universal Studios, 1932.

In [a recent] auction, we had a mint lobby card from *The Mummy;* the suggested starting bid was $2000. The winning bid: $8,784! About a year or two before that, we had a Bela Lugosi scrapbook, that he had compiled, covering his New York years, 1921 to 1929. It was signed by Lugosi, had newspaper notices, and other personal things too — photographs, and such, with over half of it devoted to the stage *Dracula*. It was a wonderful one-of-a-kind Lugosi item, and a very wealthy man in Orange County (who collects on *Dracula*) bought it for $1210.

When Lugosi went to Hawaii for 1931's *The Black Camel,* the company stayed at the Royal Hawaiian Hotel, and Lugosi gave the manager a beautiful 11 × 14 autographed portrait of himself taken in gardens of the Royal Hawaiian. That framed picture (along with a framed shot of the movie being filmed, signed by a Fox business manager) sold for $495. A 1947 three-sheet reissue poster for *Dracula* sold for $4,121. We've never had an original *Frankenstein* poster — but it would easily go today for $10,000 to $15,000!

The $8784 lobby card from *The Mummy,* incidentally, went in the same auction that brought $5696 for a Marilyn Monroe signed check, and $5354 for the original art of a daily Mickey Mouse comic strip of April, 1935, featuring Mickey, Peg-Leg Pete, and (in his comic strip debut) Donald Duck. Karloff and Lugosi material usually rate the top price tags.

Meanwhile, with the passionate interest in the two horror stars, the rivalry of Karloff and Lugosi goes on and on, apparently destined never to be resolved. Karloff disciples have adopted a confident serenity over the years, but the Lugosi buffs insist that the rivalry is still unsettled.

Of course, Karloff always dominated Lugosi ever since the Yuletide 1931 release of *Frankenstein.* His billing was always superior, his salary always at least double that of his costar, his box office power much more potent. In the more that twelve years that Boris outlived Bela, the dominance naturally snowballed; Boris became "King," while Lugosi became regarded, more and more, as "Poor Bela."

Then, in the years following Karloff's death, a strange thing happened. There was a slow but steady uprising of Lugosiphiles, arguing for Bela's superiority as king of the horror genre. They went about this attempted insurrection by simply reversing the prevailing standards of critical judgment: Karloff's touted versatility made him "just an actor"; Lugosi's characteristically one-note screen persona made him a "personality." To summarize, as fairly as possible, the debates that followed:

The popular claims of the Lugosi disciples noted that Bela Lugosi was blessed with a demonic glamour, a mad flamboyance, a radiant personality — something Karloff, supposedly, lacked. When the films were worthy, such as *Dracula, Murders in the Rue Morgue, The Black Cat,* and *The Raven,* this personality was wonderful to behold; and, when a role offered Bela a special challenge, like old Ygor of *Son of Frankenstein,* he could throw off the mannerisms and rise brilliantly to the occasion. However, when the films were abominations, such as the Monogram bombs and 1955's *Bride of the Monster,* Lugosi fell back on that great personality, fleshing out the flyweight scripts and becoming a show in himself. As such, the ravings and posturings of Bela's mad scientists in the forties potboilers are far more apt to keep a viewer awake when televised at the usual unholy hours than the sincerity and intelligence of Karloff's mad doctors in his Columbia series of 1939 to 1942. Lugosi champions also argue that Karloff often depended on makeup to achieve his special distinction, while Lugosi rarely employed it. Instead, the

Hungarian traded on his aristocratic, cruelly handsome face, famous accent, and rich style.

Karloff disciples believe there most certainly was a "personality" in Boris's gaunt face, deep, strange eyes and melodic, lisping voice — along with a sad, melancholy aura in his acting, especially in his most creative era of the early 1930s. It was, of course, this "queer, penetrating personality" which inspired James Whale to cast Karloff as the monster in *Frankenstein,* and it was this same personality around which several later horror films were constructed — e.g., Warner Bros.' 1936 *The Walking Dead.* Versatility, say the Karloff fans, is not to be mistaken for lack of personality. At its best, Karloff's acting had poetry *(The Mummy),* theatricality *(Five Star Final),* chilling, sinister flair *(The Black Cat),* ingenious brilliance *(The Black Room),* and startling depth *(The Body Snatcher);* and, if "ham" is a gauge by which to measure actors, Lugosi never neared the mad, cackling, barnstorming hysteria which Boris spewed as the religious fanatic of John Ford's 1934 *The Lost Patrol.* As for Boris's famous makeups, the star used them, but never relied on them; to illustrate, no actor who followed Karloff as the monster (least of all Bela in 1943's *Frankenstein Meets the Wolf Man*) ever displayed the moving repertoire of emotions that Karloff did. Karloff forces argue that Lugosi's "personality" is a polite synonym for his "playing himself," and that a garden-variety movie watcher who tunes into the middle of a Lugosi film usually thinks he's watching a Dracula movie. And, while such actors as Christopher Lee and Frank Langella have been triumphant as Dracula, no one has ever contested Karloff's masterpiece performance as the hapless monster.

As these debates clashed in film circles, the video age dawned. A new entertainment phenomenon entered the lifestyles of the 1980s; a film fan could now carry a videocassette of *Dracula* and *Frankenstein* in each pocket, and the Karloff versus Lugosi debate became wide open — and very topical. The lion's share of attention, naturally, went to the top horror films releases. *Frankenstein, The Mummy, Bride of Frankenstein, The Black Room, The Body Snatcher,* all beautifully transferred to tape, freshly impressed the journalists who reviewed them, and proved triumphs for Karloff all over again. Bela's *Dracula* was his one great solo video bequest, while MCA's release of the "KARLOFF and Bela LUGOSI" trio *(The Black Cat, The Raven* and *The Invisible Ray),* and *Son of Frankenstein,* all did at least as much for Boris (showcasing his versatility) as it did for Bela (showcasing his personality). Various public domain companies rushed out prints of wildly varying quality of *White Zombie,* and Lugosiphiles loudly cheered MCA's release of *Frankenstein Meets the Wolf Man* and *Abbott and Costello Meet Frankenstein.*

Yet the consensus was again clear. The video age had reanointed Karloff as the supreme star of horror.

So much for the major video market, and critics. What do the *buffs* think? The days when the covers of magazines like *Famous Monsters of Filmland* and *Castle of Frankenstein* leered on newsstand racks are long gone. Yet hard-core horror film fans publish their own journals, often with insight and iconoclasm lacking in their big-gun predecessors.

Gary J. Svehla is editor/publisher/writer for *Midnight Marquee*, the oldest current magazine devoted to the serious study of horror, science fiction and fantasy films. In 1988, Gary published a special 208-page twenty-fifth anniversary issue (featuring a striking color portrait of Karloff and an *Evil Dead II* goblin on the front cover) of the magazine he originated in 1963 at age 13, under the more graphic title of *Gore Creatures*. Svehla, who has organized several conventions of East Coast fans, and who tries to strike a happy mixture of "Gothic" and "gore" in his magazine, in a recent issue authored *"Midnight Marquee's* Best and Worst in Horror and Science Fiction Cinema." He made this choice for "Best Fantasy Film Genre Actor":

> Without doubt, Boris Karloff has turned in more superior and varied performances than any other genre actor. Consider his stellar performances: the Frankenstein monster, the grave robber from *The Body Snatcher,* the decaying Im-Ho-Tep from *The Mummy,* or his Oriental villain from *The Mask of Fu Manchu.* And even when Karloff slummed, his performances were always interesting and refreshing to behold.

Svehla graciously augmented his ideas for this book:

> Karloff's chief resource was the obvious fact that he was a multitalented character actor, able to transform himself into a menagerie of classic screen villains.... Karloff was a character actor whose thespian talents relied on the whole package: voice, physical stature, makeup, mime, and body language.... Even during the twilight years, Karloff would shine, whether he was making a string of Mexican horror movies or singing "The Monster Mash" on *Shindig.*
>
> While one could argue that Lugosi never mastered the range of Karloff (Lugosi always managed to portray Lugosi no matter what the role!), his chief downfall resulted from his personal self-delusion. Karloff obviously knew the difference between a wise career move and a poor one: he was always the pragmatist who was dealt the "heavy aces" cards. Lugosi, to his credit, treated every performance as though it were the performance of his life — be it a Universal film or a Monogram production. Lugosi's integrity and talent shine through almost always.... Yet this blindness, this inability to differentiate between the diamonds and the glass, is both Lugosi's greatest strength and weakness.... However, even though audiences realized more about Lugosi's limitations than Lugosi himself ever did, his integrity and spirit [elevated] sleazemania such as *Bride of the Monster* to greater heights than it ever deserved.
>
> Karloff can be viewed as the over-achiever, the performer who accomplished so much more than audiences could ever predict. Lugosi, on the other hand, is the performer of missed opportunities and bad business judgment. Fortunately for Karloff, he held all the aces in his hand while Lugosi blindly played his deuces as aces. How fortunate for movie audiences everywhere that in the cinematic game of poker, even the loser wins.

Tom Weaver, of Tarrytown, N.Y., an editor at two genre magazines, author of *Interviews with B Science Fiction and Horror Movie Makers* (McFarland, 1988) and coauthor of *Universal Horrors* (McFarland, 1990) is an adventurous researcher with an encyclopedic memory. He has interviewed dozens of horror directors, actors and writers, with a special preference for the genre films of the 1950s. Tom maintains his own maverick opinions on movie history and offered these views on the Karloff/Lugosi phenomenon:

> It really goes without saying that Karloff at his best was, by far, the better actor and that Lugosi would appear to have the larger and more vociferous fan-following. The (seemingly) larger Lugosi crowd can be easily explained: noisy cults usually don't grow up around respectable people or pictures that have already gotten their fair due. (As James Stewart says in *Mr. Smith Goes to Washington*, "The only cause worth fighting for is a lost cause.") So naturally, given a choice between Boris and Bela, the Hertz and Avis of horror film stars, many fans rally around the underdog, the Number Two man who (like Avis) always seemed to be trying harder. But (let's stay with the car motif) there's no denying that many of Karloff's films are the Rolls-Royces of horror movies while Lugosi's film vehicles often turned out to be jalopies, Edsels and flat-out lemons.
>
> Is there really anybody out there that doesn't think Karloff is a better actor? Anyone who holds the untenable opinion that Lugosi outshines Karloff (at his best) should sit down to a screening of Karloff's *The Black Room*. Karloff plays twin brothers Anton and Gregor De Berghman; Anton is the soul of kindness and Gregor is the embodiment of evil, and Karloff is excellent in both roles. When the picture reaches the point where Gregor impersonates Anton, Karloff is now essentially playing yet another role (Gregor-as-Anton) appreciably different from the other two, and turns in a third remarkable performance within the space of a 67-minute B movie. Lugosi could never have done justice to these three roles; in pictures like *The Mysterious Mr. Wong* and *Black Dragons* he doesn't do justice to dual roles; and (let's be honest) there are plenty of pictures in which he doesn't quite do justice to one role....
>
> Now that Bela Lugosi fans have probably already skipped away in disgust, let's wipe the smiles off the faces of Karloff fans. Karloff was guilty of something that Lugosi never stooped to: feeling superior to his material and letting his audience know it. Karloff was the toast of Broadway in the forties, and it seems like this went to his head a little bit: in the last twenty or so years of his movie career there were very few outstanding performances, and quite a few bad ones. In pictures like *Voodoo Island* and *Frankenstein 1970,* he's so smug, condescending and just plain irritating that the pictures are completely spoiled. Lugosi gave his all right up to the end; fat-cat Karloff clearly could not be bothered.... And the Karloff fans who get a kick out of Lugosi's decline and films like *Bride of the Monster* and *Plan 9 from Outer Space* should also be reminded that Karloff sank far lower than Lugosi ever did when he appeared in those Mexican science fiction semiporn films in the late sixties — films that make Ed Wood's misguided efforts look like high art by comparison.
>
> Common sense insists that our preferences should run toward Karloff, whose best work leaves Lugosi eating dust, but for all his many faults it's the mixed-up Hungarian with the heavy accent and the stuck-up attitudes that I've always had the softer spot for. Sure, he did a lousy job in a number of pictures, but it was never for lack of trying; most of the time it was from trying too *hard.* To my mind that always commands respect, no matter what the results.

Karloff in the glory days after 1931's *Frankenstein*.

Philadelphia's John E. Parnum, formerly the editor of *Cinemacabre,* a slick horror/fantasy/science fiction magazine that covers films, books, television, and video, is a lifelong aficionado of the horror genre. He has 67 scrapbooks on the classic films, and is an eloquent and vociferous spokesman for the Gothic. Parnum wrote these thoughts on Karloff and Lugosi:

> For my first attendance at a fright flick, a dear aunt from New York, in order to quiet the annoying pleadings of her young nephew, took me to see *House of Frankenstein.* I still remember the awesome thunderstorm that opened the film, with the guard at Neustadt Prison descending the dank stone steps to the dungeon catacombs below, opening the small window of the cell door, and being throttled by the hand of Boris Karloff as Dr. Niemann. "Now will you give me my chalk?" the wild-eyed, bearded prisoner demanded. After a brief vitriolic exchange of curses between the guard and Niemann, Karloff, chalk in hand, turned to the hunchback in the adjacent cell and gently intoned, "Now, friend Daniel, we can get on with our lesson." It was, I believe, this unusual ability to act cruel one minute and then show kindness the next that was Karloff's forte in many of his horror movies. It was especially evident the next year in one of his finest films, *The Body Snatcher.* But, of course, we know that it all began with that

Opposite: **Lugosi with canine friend at his home in Hollywood in the 1930s.**

memorable portrayal of Frankenstein's monster when his snarl could chill the most hardened audience and then only a few minutes later elicit sympathy with a groan of pain as a sadistic Fritz thrust a burning torch in his face.

It was not long after *House of Frankenstein* that I saw my first Bela Lugosi flick, a reissue of *The Devil Bat.* I remember being terribly disappointed; no monsters except for a rather worn looking bat that a tired Lugosi carried around on a coat hanger. In the middle of the movie, the film broke and I thought to myself that this would never happen during a Karloff film. . . .

What I do remember about Bela Lugosi were his eyes. Those incredible orbs were his most striking feature – all compelling and sinister, filling the screen and usually highlighted by a pinpoint of light, topped off with bushy eyebrows. They were commanding in *Dracula, White Zombie* and even *Abbott and Costello Meet Frankenstein* when they should have been dimmed by the actor's addiction at the time to drugs, which says a great deal for Lugosi's dedication to his craft. . . .

Karloff's salient feature, on the other hand, was his mouth – the sinister snarl of the monster as he wrestles with Frankenstein on the mountain top, the trembling lower lip when he is rejected by his mate in *Bride of Frankenstein,* the smile of anticipation when offered a glass of wine by Dr. Pretorius. Or as Gray, the cabman in *The Body Snatcher,* with a cruel line of mouth giving way to a genuine smile of compassion for the little crippled girl petting his horse.

Both actors were masters of gesticulation – in command of superb hand movements that expressed so well the characters they were playing. Lugosi hypnotically waving his hand like the maestro of some phantom orchestra to capture his victim in a spell. Karloff reaching for a shaft of sunlight or pleading for companionship from an unsympathetic shepherdess and then angrily thrashing out to silence her screams. But while Karloff's gestures could be wild and frenzied, Lugosi's were slower and more controlled, cultivated from years of training on the stage. Lugosi was definitely conservative in his acting and his sometimes stilted unfamiliarity with the English language (from scripts that were an insult to the English language) caused me to prefer Karloff as the mixer in my horror tonic.

. . . Both actors have thrilled us all with diversified roles in so many memorable movies. I fondly recall when that same aunt of mine took me to see the play *The Linden Tree,* an English drawing-room comedy drama by J.B. Priestley. Boris Karloff portrayed the kindly old Professor Linden in an atypical performance dealing with postwar Europe and the professor's philosophical attitude toward retirement and the resolution of family problems. Much to my delight, this wonderful aunt somehow got me backstage to see Mr. Karloff. After some perfunctory pleasantries, I announced to the horror king that I had seen all his movies. Karloff, garbed in a plain dressing robe, gently but solemnly instructed me, "Well, my boy, you just forget about all those movies and concentrate more on what you've learned here in the play today."

Forget about those movies? Impossible!

Lugosi does dominate the world of ascetic free-spending collectors. "Bela Lugosi is *definitely* more collectible," says Malcolm Willits, "and always outsells Karloff in our store, and I imagine in any movie memorabilia store. Lugosi was always the more pure horror, so sinister; almost anything on Lugosi will go, while Karloff did things like *House of Rothschild* – which nobody wants." Willits thinks part of the Lugosi appeal has to do with the timeless vampire theme:

I was a high school teacher for seven years, and my students were not exactly Rhodes scholars.... I despaired of ever being able to teach them anything,
but one thing I did note: every member of every class I ever had knew exactly
how to kill a vampire. They were quite familiar with the most minute details of
a vampire's lifestyle, and knew what corrective actions to adopt if confronted
with one.... I do know one thing: if Russia ever sends an army of vampires
against us, we will know how to deal with them.

Buddy Barnett, manager of the Cinema Collectors Shop of Hollywood
(1507 Wilcox Avenue), has carefully noted the appeal of each actor with his
patrons. He told me:

I have to admit that I prefer Lugosi to Karloff by a wide margin....
However, that doesn't change the facts as to which one is more popular in today's
market as far as sales and requests go. The truth of the matter is that Lugosi
outsells Karloff by a margin of about ten to one. It is kind of sad that he is not
around to see it.

There is *The Bela Lugosi Society,* headed by Garydon Rhodes (330 G
S.W., Ardmore, Oklahoma 73401). It issues a journal which includes interviews, reviews of Lugosi videos, records, and memorabilia, and stills and art-
work (in late 1989 it was feared that the fan club would collapse due to lack
of sustained interest).

On January 18, 1988, the Academy of Motion Picture Arts and Sciences
and the Academy Foundation presented a special Hollywood bouquet to the
Karloff legend—*Boris Karloff: A Centenary Tribute.* George Schaefer hosted the
celebration, and the guests included Vincent Price, Mae Clarke, and Anna
Lee, directors Robert Wise and Peter Bogdanovich, and screenwriter Richard
Matheson. The tribute featured excerpts from *The Nicklehopper, The Bells, Scarface, Frankenstein, The Mummy, The Mask of Fu Manchu, The Lost Patrol, The Black
Cat, Bride of Frankenstein, The Raven* (1935), *The Invisible Ray, The Body Snatcher,
Bedlam, The Raven* (1963), and *Targets.* It was an excellent program, presenting
a composite portrait not only of a versatile actor, but of a very well-loved per-
sonality. Karloff's widow was present and delighted at the packed house.

The MCA Home Video company has offered its own tribute to both
Karloff and Lugosi by "restoring" *Frankenstein* and *Dracula.* Working with bits
and pieces of film and soundtrack gathered from a variety of sources (including the American Film Institute and the British Film Institute), MCA
gave *Frankenstein* a new lease on life by adding most of Colin Clive's "In the
name of God!" hysteria in the creation scene, a longer scuffle with Clive,
Karloff, Frye and Edward Van Sloan in the laboratory, new close-ups of
Karloff and Frye in the dungeon torture scene, the shot of Van Sloan injecting
a hypodermic needle into the monster, the complete lake episode with Little
Maria, and even the exit music after the closing credits. The restored
Frankenstein was released on laser disc in December, 1986, and on video in
October, 1987. *Dracula,* with restored "censored sound cuts," including

Lugosi's groans as he is impaled by Van Sloan, was released in October, 1988 — so far appearing only on laser disc.

*   *   *

The great Vincent Price, Hollywood's happiest heavy, was asked many years ago on *The Mike Douglas Show* who he believed to be the greatest of horror stars. "The greatest horror star," he said, "always has been, always will be, Boris Karloff." Price, who of course, acted with Boris in Universal's 1939 *Tower of London,* AIP's *The Raven* and *The Comedy of Terrors,* and in the famous 1968 *Red Skelton Show,* remembers him warmly — one of his favorites in a long Hollywood career. In the January, 1989, *Cinefantastique,* featuring a comprehensive Price cover story (compiled by Steve Biodrowski, David Del Valle and Lawrence French), Price spoke of Karloff — and the horror "image" they both shared:

> ... I felt an enormous closeness as a friend, and a coworker. He had this marvelous sort of warmth as a human being. We used to go out to dinner in London, which was wonderful fun. The two of us would walk into a restaurant, and we would clear the place. We never had to make reservations. We had our choice of any table!

Then there's Christopher Lee, Hammer's *Dracula* (and an increasingly controversial personality among the horror buffs). In 1970, Lee wrote an afterword (Vincent Price wrote the introduction) for *The Ghouls,* a book of tales which inspired great horror films, edited by Peter Haining. Lee stated that his purpose was to give his estimation of "the actors who have played ghouls," and wrote: "Let me say right away that I consider Lon Chaney the greatest of them all, a genius in fact, with Boris Karloff running a close second." His elaboration on Boris:

> Boris Karloff, with whom I had the pleasure of working on several occasions (including one of his last films, *Curse of the Crimson Altar*), was also a brilliant actor and greatly underrated. His *Frankenstein* is the most famous of all horror films and his performance probably the finest piece of individual acting we have ever seen on the screen. I think we shall not see his like again.

Lee opined that "these two are head and shoulders above all others," but added, "I must also accord mention to several others: Basil Rathbone, Bela Lugosi, Peter Lorre, and my contemporaries, Vincent Price and Peter Cushing. . . ."

The Karloff and Lugosi personas have loomed so large that they have become dream roles for actors, inspiring rumors of Hollywood biopics. For a time, Edward D. Wood, Jr., notorious "director"/purveyor of Lugosi's *Glen or Glenda?, Bride of the Monster,* and *Plan 9 from Outer Space,* was planning a film based on the life of Bela Lugosi, which surely would have been a cruel irony. To play Bela, Wood had set his friend Peter Coe (who had acted in such Universal's as 1944's *House of Frankenstein* and *The Mummy's Curse*). The impoverished Wood died in 1978 and this project passed with him. There also were rumors that a biopic of Lugosi was in the works—with rock star Alice Cooper set for the lead! Meanwhile, there has been in the late eighties vague talk of a Karloff biopic, with Willem Dafoe considered for the starring spot.

Of course, talk of the ghosts of Karloff and Lugosi haunting Hollywood surprises few people in the cinema colony. In his book, *I Used to Be an Animal, but I'm All Right Now,* rock singer Eric Burdon (formerly of the Animals) wrote of renting Karloff's Bowmont Drive farmhouse in 1969. His girlfriend, "rummaging in an old cupboard," found a safe under a floorboard. Burdon's attempts to open the safe failed, and he finally called movie explosives man Eddie "Boom Boom" Taylor to assist. Burdon and "Boom Boom" drove the Karloff safe out to the Mojave Desert, fitted it with plastic explosives, and blasted the safe ten feet into the air. It crashed back to the desert—still locked. According to Burdon:

> After we tried to blow up the safe, I got a strange feeling that Karloff was trying to get a message to me: "Don't do it." I just had this sense that I was intruding into another man's world, and it really wasn't any of my business. His presence after death was uncanny. You could almost reach out and touch him. I gave up, took the safe back to the house and put it back under the floorboards. As far as I know, it's still there—and hasn't given up any of its secrets.

A reader might recall that, when Karloff moved into the Bowmont Drive house in the early 1930s, Katharine Hepburn already had moved out—fearing the hacienda's ghost. Could Karloff's ghost have joined it?

As for Lugosi's "ghost," Hollywoodites have spied his spectre in the halls of his Outpost Drive house, at the surviving buildings of Monogram Studios, and near the site of the old Utter-McKinley Mortuary on Hollywood Boulevard, where he lay in state in 1956.

*   *   *

At any rate—when I was six years old, *Shock Theatre* came to Baltimore. The coming attractions of *Frankenstein* played constantly on television's Channel 11, the name "Boris Karloff" proclaimed like some legendary villain of mythology. I pleaded with my parents to let me stay up to see it. They finally agreed. However, when Edward Van Sloan appeared, and presented his "friendly warning," my courage deserted me and I fled to my bedcovers.

Yet the lure was still there—and, not long afterwards, my dad sat up with me to watch *Frankenstein Meets the Wolf Man.* I was fortunate to see the whole film; at Chaney, Jr.'s first transformation into Lycanthrope, I impulsively grabbed a *Life* magazine from the coffee table and covered my face—just as my mother walked into the room, naturally presumed the movie was horrifying her little boy, and suggested we turn it off. But I begged to see more—after all, we hadn't seen the monster yet. When we did, it was, of course, "Poor Bela," humbled into playing this monster so cataclysmic in his own life, coping with emotions under his makeup which I wouldn't learn about for many years. It was not a very impressive performance, even to a six-year-old, and the fact that my dad chuckled at Lugosi's emoting, and told me, "Boris Karloff is the *real* monster," must have prejudiced me as a Karloff disciple at that very early stage.

Shortly afterwards, however, came the special night. My parents were out at a dance, and I sat up with a babysitter to see *Son of Frankenstein*. As the camera retreated, and I saw the giant, magnificent figure of Karloff's monster on the bier in the Frankenstein catacombs, I was awestruck. Lugosi's wonderful Ygor fascinated me, as well. And near the climax of this epic fairy tale, as Karloff's monster knelt over his friend Ygor, realized he was dead and let out that great cry of sorrow, I cried too. Part of it, of course, was sympathy; but I suspect that I was moved by the epic excitement of the whole thing, its very special, imaginative, Gothic beauty.

At the age of six, in Karloff's monster and Lugosi's Ygor, I had found playmates for my "maturing" imagination — and for this, on that night, I loved them both.

Perhaps, too, what made this so very exciting was that these men were *real.* Bela Lugosi had been dead for only a year; learning that he had suffered as a drug addict, and had been buried in his Dracula cape, made him all the more fascinating. Boris Karloff was very alive and well, very busy acting all over the world. The fact that Karloff was still working, that I had seen his monster in comparison to Bela's, and that (later) he answered my fan letter by sending an autographed portrait and a shot of himself as the monster, all undoubtedly sustained my early preference for him. However, Lugosi's passion and flamboyance and touching sincerity caused him to grow steadily over the years in my estimation, and the two men became more than movie stars to me. They became, as they have become to so many others, loyal friends, fulfilling our needs for escapism, for pretending and make-believe, to cope with the complexities of life...

Researching their lives, I found Karloff saying, "These stories are bogey tales, fairy stories...," and Lugosi exclaiming, "Why, they even wanted me to play the Big Bad Wolf in *The Three Little Pigs!*"

The Bela Lugosi Career

Born Bela Ferenc Dezso Blasko, October 20, 1882, Lugos, Hungary. Son of baker (and later banker) Istvan Blasko and his wife Paula; two brothers, one sister. Educated, Hungarian State Superior Gymnasium, Lugos; Academy of Performing Arts, Budapest. Original vocation: mine laborer. Military experience: second lieutenant and captain, 43rd Infantry Regiment, Hungary, during World War I.

Marriages: (1) 1917, actress Ilona Szmik, divorced 1920; (2) 1921, actress Ilona von Montagh, divorced 1924; (3) 1929, Beatrice Woodruff Weeks, divorced 1929; (4) 1933, Lillian Arch, son, Bela Jr. (b. 1938), divorced 1953; (5) 1956, Hope Lininger.

Died August 16, 1956, at his home, 5620 Harold Way, Hollywood, California; interred Holy Cross Cemetery, Culver City, California, August 18, 1956.

Theatre

Made stage debut at age nine, writing, producing and starring in plays he presented, free, in an empty Lugos warehouse.

Lugosi's first documented appearance, with the National Actors Company, Deva, Transylvania, was as Count Konigsegg in *Ocskay Brigaderos* (*Brigadier General Ocskay,* 8/24/02); followed by Potykai in *Hazasodjunk* (*We're Married,* 8/25/02); master tailor Vendl Csik in *Felho Klari* (*Claire Felho,* 9/18/02); Antonio Caraffa in *Kurucz Feja David* (*Stubborn King David,* 2/10/03); Aubespine in *Maria Stuart* (2/26/03); Orias in *Ezeregy Ejszaka* (*The Arabian Nights,* 3/1/03); Frosh in *A Denever* (*The Bat,* 3/3/03); Marco the father in *Monna Vanna* (3/4/03); Dr. Lorrck in *Fedora* (3/5/03).

With the Franz Josef Repertory Theatre of Temesvar, Lugosi played Gecko in *Trilby* (12/29/03); Oszkar in *Tartalekos Ferj* (*Husband in Reserve,* 1/8/04); Fr. Gyorgy Feher in *Himfy Dalai* (*Himfy's Song,* 1/11/04); Boros, the assessor in *Az Aranykakas* (*Ye Golden Rooster,* 1/14/04); Melos, the messenger in *A Kereszt Jeleben* (*In the Sign of the Cross,* 1/15/04); Baron Oszkar Eltey in *Rang Es Mod* (*Rank and Style,* 2/17/04); Lord Brockelhurst in *Egyenloseg* (*The Admirable Crichton,* 2/19/04); Dr. Servan in *A Vasgyaros* (*The Iron Manufacturer,* 4/6/04); a financier in *A Bajusz* (*The Mustache,* 4/10/04).

With the Szeged Repertory Theatre, Lugosi played Romeo in *Romeo and Juliet* (9//2/10); Major Kadisa in *Aranyember* (*Golden Man*, 9/4/10); Pista Balogh in *Az Ingyenelok* (*The Parasites*, 9/4/10); Joska in *Az Obsitos* (*The Operetta*, 9/5/10); Armand Duval in *Kamelias Holgy* (*The Lady of the Camellias*, 9/7/10); Lt. Lorand in *A Dolovai Nabob Leanya* (*The Daughter of the Nabob of Dalovai*, 9/8/10); Janos in *Az Ordog* (*The Devil*, 9/9/10); writer Otto Lindner in *Taifun* (*Typhoon*, 9/10/10); Sinom in *Bilincsek* (*Fetters*, 9/16/10); Dr. Emil Csipkes in *A Postas Fiu Es Huga* (*The Mail Boy and His Sister*, 9/18/10); John Shand in *Amihez Minden Asszony Ert* (*What Every Woman Knows*, 9/20/10); Prince Bligny in *A Vasgyaros* (*The Iron Manufacturer* 10/10/10); landowner Erno Rozgonyi in *A Kard Becsulets* (*Honor of the Sword*, 10/19/10); Asztolf Ormodi in *A Csikos* (*The Cowboy*, 10/23/10); Confidant Szelim in *Szigetvari Vertanuk* (*The Martyrs of Szigetvar*, 11/1/10); Assemblyman Viznemissza in *A Kormanybiztos* (*The Government Commissioner*, 11/11/10); a lieutenant in *Bank Ban* (*The Ban Bank*, 11/12/10); Frigyes Gentz in *A Sasfiok* (*The Eaglet*, 11/23/10); Max Heim in *A Balkani Hercegno* (*The Balkan Princess*, 11/25/10); Gaston in *A Balga Szuz* (*The Foolish Virgin*, 11/30/10); Ferko Selyem in *A Gyerekasszony* (*The Child-Woman*, 12/6/10); Bevallan in *Egy Szegeney Ifju Tortenete* (*The Story of a Poor Lad*, 12/13/10); Count Vronski in *Anna Karenina* (12/17/10); George, Prince of Clarence in *Richard III* (12/20/10); Lebourg Amedee in *Baccarat* (1/8/11); composer Sidney Clark in *Narancvirag* (*Orange Blossom*, 1/8/11); appeared in *Meguntam Margitot* (*I Tired of Margaret*, 1/14/11); Count Zakonskine in *A Szent Liget* (*The Sacred Grove*, 1/20/11); the archduke in *Saraga Liliom* (*Yellow Lily*, 2/14/11); Janos, the medico in *A Medikus* (*The Medico*, 2/25/11); Ramajanah in *Lotti Ezredesei* (*Lotti's Colonels*, 3/7/11); Cassio in *Othello* (3/9/11); Sam Bandheim in *A Jomadarak* (*The Scoundrels*, 3/11/11); law student and Stanislav Lubomirzki in *Az Aranylakodalom* (*The Golden Wedding*, 3/15/11); Arthur Malam in *Robin Orvos* (*Doctor Robin*, 3/16/11); Fernande Legardes in *A Tolvaj* (*The Thief*, 3/23/11); Count Dabilio Danilovics in *A Vig Ozvegy* (*The Merry Widow*, 3/30/11); Laertes in *Hamlet* (3/31/11); Lucentio in *A Makrancos Holgy* (*The Taming of the Shrew*, 4/2/11); Don Enrique de Palacios in *A Boszorkany* (*The Witch*, 4/5/11); Akos in *Viola — Az Alfoldi Haramia* (*Viola, Outlaw of the Lowlands*, 4/10/11); Lazlo Kapolnay in *A Becstelen* (*The Ignominious*, 4/11/11); journalist Bela Pomandy in *Delibab* (*Fata Morgana*, 4/21/11); Baron Szentgrothy in *A Kilvandorlo* (*The Emmigrant*, 4/27/11); Presbyterian minister Pal Simandy in *Elnemult Harangok* (*Silent Bells*, 4/30/11); Artanezzo in *Botrany* (*Scandal*, 5/2/11); Marquis Roger de Monclars in *Babjatek* (*Puppet Show*, 5/3/11); Peti in *A Sarga Csiko* (*The Yellow Colt*, 5/7/11); Prince Rochermartel in *Trilby* (5/8/11); the judge in *A Tanitono* (*The Teacher*, 5/9/11); Lambertin in *Az Allamtitkam Ur* (*The Secretary of State*, 5/11/11); Rudolf in *A Zseni* (*The Genius*, 5/14/11); Dr. Bela Szilvassy in *A Sabin Nok Elrablasa* (*The Rape of the Sabine Women*, 5/17/11); Max in *Anatol* (5/20/11).

With the Hungarian Theatre of Budapest, Lugosi played Count Vronsky in *Anna Karenina* (9/3/11); lawyer Asztalos Kalman in *Sarga Liliom* (*Yellow Lily*, 9/18/11); Max, the young officer in *Az Elet Szava* (*The Call of Life*, 10/7/11); the archduke in *Sarga Liliom* (*Yellow Lilly*, 11/9/11); Navy Lieutenant Reginald Fairfax in *A Gesak* (*The Geisha*, 4/11/12); Count Vronski in *Anna Karenina* (8/22/12); and the archduke in *Sarga Liliom* (*Yellow Lily*, 9/5/12).

With the National Theatre of Buda, Lugosi played Pontac in *A Vasgyaros* (1/5/13); Catalus and the Marquis in *Az Ember Tragediaja* (*The Tragedy of Man*,

1/6/13); journalist O'Gorman in *Mary Ann* (2/1/13); Second Marquis in *Cyrano De Bergerac* (2/3/13); Count Bellievre in *Maria Stuart* (2/7/13); Sir Walter Herbert in *Richard III* (2/10/13); Egyptian Commander Achilles in *Caesar and Cleopatra* (2/21/13); Major Kadisa in *Aranyember* (*Golden Man*, 3/3/13); Cardinal Pandolf in *King John* (3/4/13); Demetrius in *A Midsummer Night's Dream* (3/4/13); Plato in *The Tragedy of Man* (3/5/13); Mariann's sweetheart Valere in *Tartuffe* (3/10/13); Commander Solari in *The Captivity of Rakoczi II* (3/15/13); Eugenio Fray in *The Witch* (3/16/13); Rosenkranz in *Hamlet* (3/17/13); the taxidermist Herve in *A Faklyak* (*The Torches*, 3/28/13; appeared in *Bizanc* (*Byzantium*, 4/8/13); Farkas Weer in *Draghy Eva Eskuje* (*The Oath of Eva Draghy*, 4/14/13); Gilbert Rivels in *A Fogadott Apa* (*The Adopted Father*, 5/2/13); Courtier Don Sanebo in *Hernani* (5/8/13); Senator Marcus in *Kegyenc* (*The Confidant*, 5/16/13); Michael and first student in *Faust* (5/22/13); Melazzo in *Endre and Johanna* (5/28/13); Varville in *Lady of the Camellias* (6/3/13); a bodyguard in *Visla* (9/13/13); Malakov, the revolutionary in *Bolondok Tanca* (*Dance of the Fools*, 9/19/13); a knight in *King Lear* (9/29/13); La Spagna, the painter in *Az Utolso Nap* (*The Last Day*, 10/3/13); Lucein de Mere in *Az Attache* (*The Attache*, 10/23/13); lieutenant in the national militia in *A Konventbiztos* (*The Convention Commisar*, 10/24/13); Count Southampton in *Essex Grof* (*Count Essex*, 11/8/13); Saint Priest and Breteuille in *Marie Antoinette* (11/21/13); cowboy in *Az Egyszeri Kiralyfi* (*The One-Time Prince*, 12/19/13); Vedio in *Monna Vanna* (12/22/13); first actor in *Karacsony* (*Christmas Dream*, 12/23/13); Enzio in *Eva Boszorkany* (*Eva, the Witch*, 1/1/14); Pesta, the best man in *Matyo Lakodalom* (*The Matyo Wedding*, 1/16/14); Angus in *Macbeth* (1/30/14); Clausevitz in *A Kolcsonkert Kastely* (*The Borrowed Castle*, 2/6/14); Dorsus in *Aesop* (2/20/14); De Montegre in *A Nok Baratja* (*The Woman's Friend*, 2/24/14); Baron Varkovy in *Fenn Az Ernyo* (*The Umbrella Is Up*, 3/7/14); a dandy in *Liliomfi* (3/9/14); teacher Jack Strahan in *Az Igazgato Ur* (*The Principal*, 3/20/14); department counselor in *Egy Karrier Tortenete* (*The Story of a Career*, 4/3/14); Baron Prefont in *A Vasgyaros* (*The Iron Manufacturer*, 4/13/14); Prince Limoges in *King John* (4/17/14); Cinna in *Julius Caesar* (5/4/14); vassal Pal Flida in *A Tronkovetelok* (*Contenders for the Throne*, 5/15/14); Othello in *A Peleskei Notarius* (*The Notary Public of Peleske*, 6/4/14); Count Bellievre in *Maria Stuart* (4/10/16); Jesus Christ in *The Passion* (4/15/16); Fortinbras, Prince of Norway in *Hamlet* (4/30/16); Lenox in *Macbeth* (5/2/16); Lodovico in *Othello* (5/6/16); Escalus in *Romeo and Juliet* (5/10/16); Tengeri in *Szokott Katona* (*The Deserter*, 9/17/16); Laertes in *Hamlet* (9/23/16); Lord Mowbray in *Henry IV* (10/11/16); Diodor in *Aesop* (10/14/16); a lad in *Zsuzsi* (*Susie*, 10/27/16); Prince Feria in *Don Carlos* (11/10/16); Gaston in *Egy Szegeny Ifju Tortenete* (*The Story of a Poor Lad*, 11/22/16); journalist Czernay in *A Harom Testor* (*The Three Bodyguards*, 12/9/16); Lucentio in *The Taming of the Shrew* (12/19/16); the poet in *Unnepi Jatek* (*Festive Play*, 12/30/16); first mason in *Komitives Kelemen* (*Kelmen, the Mason*, 1/12/17); first worker in *The Tragedy of Man* (1/19/17); Prince Henri Talmont in *A Hadifogoly* (*The POW*, 2/9/17); Lt. Elusdi in *A Partutok* (*The Dissenters*, 2/12/17); Louis, the Dauphin in *King John* (3/15/17); Demetrius in *A Midsummer Night's Dream* (3/16/17); Leonard in *Maria Magdalena* (5/19/17); Kalman in *Nagymama* (*Grandmother*, 5/26/17); Jacques in *As You Like It* (1/18/18); Pal Csefalvi in *Charlote Kisasszony* (*Mademoiselle Charlotte*, 2/22/18); Laszlo Hunyadi in *Arva Laszlo Kiraly* (*Lone King Laszlo*, 3/3/18); Count Hatzfeld in *Emperor Joseph II* (4/5/18); Armand Duval in *A Kamelias Holgy* (*Lady of the Camellias*,

Bela Lugosi

4/7/18); Imre Adorjan in *Gorogtuz* (*Greek Fire*, 5/3/18); Tybalt in *Romeo and Juliet*
(6/7/18); Turkish Ambassador Ahmed Khan in *Byzantium* (11/9/18); Henry,
Count of Richmond in *Richard III* (11/15/18); Suffolk in *Henry VIII* (11/24/18);
Marsy in *Bagatelle* (12/29/18); the prince in *Sancho Panza Kiralysaga* (*The Kingdom
of Sancho Panza*, 1/10/19);

Following revolution and political exile, Lugosi came to the United States,
1921; created own Hungarian repertory company in New York, producing and
starring in such plays as *Fata Morgana*, *The Tragedy of Man*, and *Yellow Lily;* made
English-speaking New York debut as Fernando, the Apache in *The Red Poppy*
(Greenwich Village Theatre, 12/20/22, 14 performances); played Don Eliphas
Leone in *The Werewolf* (Blackstone Theatre, Chicago, 7/15/24); returned to
Broadway as Shiek of Hamman in *Arabesque* (National Theatre, 10/20/25, 23 performances); Sergius Chernoff in *Open House* (Daly's Sixty-Third Street Theatre,
12/14/25, 73 performances); Father Petros and Kardos, the Greek bandit in *The
Devil in the Cheese* (Charles Hopkins Theatre, 12/29/26, 165 performances); and
played Count Dracula in *Dracula* (Fulton Theatre, 10/5/27, 265 performances).

Starred in touring companies of *Dracula* (1928–1930); played mad scientist Lukar in *Murdered Alive* (Carthay Circle Theatre, Los Angeles, 4/2/32); returned to Broadway as Siebenkase in *Murder at the Vanities* (New Amsterdam Theatre, 9/12/33, 298 performances); toured vaudeville houses, late 1933, in scenes from *Dracula;* played Commissar Gorotchenko in *Tovarich* (Curran Theatre, San Francisco, 3/22/37); toured with Ed Sullivan's *Stardust Cavalcade Revue* (Spring, 1940); made several summer tours, 1942–1946, reprising scenes from *Dracula.*

Toured in *Dracula* (commencing 5/3/43, Plymouth Theatre, Boston); played Jonathan Brewster in a national company of *Arsenic and Old Lace* commencing Tivoli Theatre, San Francisco, 8/5/43); Bharat Singh in *No Traveler Returns* (Curran Theatre, San Francisco, 2/26/45); starred in try-out of *Three Indelicate Ladies* (New Haven, CT, '46/'47 season); toured 1947 summer stock as *Dracula;* toured 1948 summer stock as Jonathan in *Arsenic and Old Lace;* made horror show personal appearance tours, East Coast, 1949–1950; played the Hungarian butler in *The Devil Also Dreams* (His Majesty's Theatre, Montreal, Canada, 8/22/50); toured London provinces, Spring, 1951, in *Dracula;* starred in *The Bela Lugosi Review* at the Silver Slipper Saloon, Las Vegas, 1954; and played the international drug smuggler in *Devil's Paradise* (Troupers-Green Room, Hollywood, 6/8/56).

Films

Lugosi made his movie debut under the name of Arisztid Olt, as a red herring in *Alarcosbal* (*Masked Ball,* Star Film Budapest, 1917); as Dorian Gray's butler in *Az Elet Kiralya* (*The Royal Life,* aka *The Picture of Dorian Gray,* Star Film, 1917); an aristocrat in *A Lepoard* (*the Leopard,* Star Film, 1917); Bertram, the famed violinist in *A Naszdal* (*The Wedding Song,* Star Film, 1917); a discarded suitor in *Tavaszi Vihar* (*Spring Tempest,* Star Film, 1917); under name of Bela Lugosi, played a crook in *Az Ezredes* (*The Colonel,* Phoenix Film, Budapest, 1917); suitor to a rich man's daughter in *Casanova* (Star Film, 1918); the romantic lead in *Lulu* (Phoenix Film, 1918); and played in *Kilencvenkilenc* (Phoenix Film, 1918).

In Germany, Lugosi played a hypnotist in *Sklaven Fremdes Willens* (*Slave of a Foreign Will,* Eichbert Film, Berlin, 1919); a gang leader in *Nat Pinkerton* (Dua Film, Berlin, 1920); a "reckless saboteur" in *Der Fluch Der Menschheit* (*The Curse of Man,* Eichberg Film, 1920); Dr. Jekyll's butler in *Der Januskopf* (*The Head of Janus,* based on Stevenson's *Dr. Jekyll and Mr. Hyde,* Lipow Film, Berlin, 1920); played in *Die Frau Im Delphin* (*The Woman in the Dolphin,* Gaci Film, Berlin, 1920); "lecherous Arab Sheik" in *Die Todeskarawane* (*The Caravan of Death,* Ustad Film, Droop & Co., Berlin, 1920); the Indian Chingachgook in *Lederstrumpf* (*Leatherstocking,* Luna Film, Berlin, 1920); played in *Die Teufelsanbeter* (*The Devil Worshippers,* Ustad Film, Droop & Co., 1920); played a western heavy in *Johann Hopkins III* (*John Hopkins the Third,* Dua Films, 1920); and played a Parisian aristocrat in *Der Tanz Auf Dem Vulkan* (*The Dance on the Volcano,* Eichberg Film, 1921).

Lugosi's first documented U.S. film role was Hisston, evil foreign agent in *The Silent Command* (Fox, 1923); followed by Jean Gagnon in *The Rejected Woman* (Distinctive Pictures, 1924); Nicholas Harmon, patron of the arts in *The Midnight*

Girl (Chadwick Pictures, 1925); villainous Communist agent Serge Oumansky in *Daughters Who Pay* (Banner Productions, 1925); Harlequin in the 20-minute short subject, *Punchinello* (Famous Lovers Production, 1926); a bit in *How to Handle Women* (Universal, 1928); an ill-fated suitor in *The Veiled Woman* (Fox, 1928); dubbed Conrad Veidt's role for Hungarian distribution in *The Last Performance* (Universal, 1928).

Lugosi made his official "sound" debut as Brottos in *Prisoners* (First National, 1929); followed by Inspector Delzante in *The Thirteenth Chair* (MGM, 1929); plastic surgeon Dr. Erdmann in *Such Men Are Dangerous* (Fox, 1930); hosted Hungarian version of *King of Jazz* (Universal, 1930); Felix Brown in *Wild Company* (Fox, 1930); the Marabout in *Renegades* (Fox, 1930); Frascatti, the singing teacher in *Oh, for a Man!* (Fox, 1930); and an ambassador in *Viennese Nights* (Warner Bros., 1930).

Lugosi recreated his stage role as *Dracula* (Universal, 1931); followed by a magician in *Fifty Million Frenchmen* (Warner Bros., 1931); Prince Hassan in *Women of All Nations* (Fox, 1931); Tarnevarro, the fortune teller in *The Black Camel* (Fox, 1931); jealous Pancho in *Broadminded* (First National, 1931); mad Dr. Mirakle in *Murders in the Rue Morgue* (Universal, 1932); zombie master Murder Legendre in *White Zombie* (United Artists, 1932); Roxor in *Chandu the Magician* (Fox, 1932); the Sayer of the Law in *Island of Lost Souls* (Paramount, 1932); red herring Joseph Steiner in *The Death Kiss* (World-Wide, 1933); red herring Prof. Adam Strang in the 12-chapter serial *The Whispering Shadow* (Mascot, 1933); as comic heavy Gen. Nicholas Branovsky Petronovich in *International House* (Paramount, 1933); mystic Degar in *Night of Terror* (Columbia, 1933); the military prosecutor in *The Devil's in Love* (Fox, 1933).

Lugosi joined Karloff, playing Dr. Vitus Werdgast in *The Black Cat* (Universal, 1934); played an Apache (à la Fernando of the play *The Red Poppy*) in a guest bit in *Gift of Gab* (Universal, 1934), also with Karloff; heroic Chandu in the 12-chapter serial *The Return of Chandu* (Principal Pictures, 1934); villainous Dr. Boehm in *Best Man Wins* (Columbia, 1935); maniacal Mr. Wong in *The Mysterious Mr. Wong* (Monogram, 1935); pseudo-vampire Count Mora in *Mark of the Vampire* (MGM, 1935); rejoined Karloff, playing Poe-worshipping Dr. Richard Vollin in *The Raven* (Universal, 1935); played the Perry twins in *Murder by Television* (Imperial-Cameo Pictures, 1935); visited England to play the one-armed Lorenzen in *Mystery of the Marie Celeste* (Hammer, 1935); returned to Hollywood to join Karloff as Dr. Felix Benet in *The Invisible Ray* (Universal, 1936); as villain Benez in *Postal Inspector* (Universal, 1936); mad scientist Victor Poten in the 15-chapter serial *Shadow of Chinatown* (Victory, 1936); and wicked inventor Boroff in the 12-chapter serial SOS Coastguard (Republic, 1937).

After a spell of unemployment, Lugosi came back as broken-necked Ygor, friend to Karloff's monster in *Son of Frankenstein* (Universal, 1939); played Peters the butler in *The Gorilla* (20th Century–Fox, 1939); Dr. Alex Zorka in the 12-chapter serial *The Phantom Creeps* (Universal, 1939); Commissar Razinin in Garbo's *Ninotchka* (MGM, 1939); vile Dr. Orloff in Britain's *Dark Eyes of London* (aka *The Human Monster,* Pathe Films Ltd., 1939); the smuggler's accomplice in *Saint's Double Trouble* (RKO, 1940); reteamed with Karloff as gangster Eric Marnay in *Black Friday* (Universal, 1940); joining with Karloff again (and with Peter

Lorre) as Prince Saliano in *You'll Find Out* (RKO, 1940); played mad Dr. Paul Carruthers in *The Devil Bat* (PRC, 1941); Eduardo, the keeper of the cats, in *The Black Cat* (Universal, 1941); dual personality Dr. Charles Kessler in *The Invisible Ghost* (Monogram, 1941); "the monster" in *Spooks Run Wild* (Monogram, 1941); Bela, the Gypsy fortune teller in *The Wolf Man* (Universal, 1941); reprised Ygor in *The Ghost of Frankenstein* (Universal, 1942); Nazi Dr. Melcher in *Black Dragons* (Monogram, 1942); mad Dr. Lorenz in *The Corpse Vanishes* (Monogram, 1942); Prof. Brenner in *Bowery at Midnight* (Monogram, 1942); and Rolf the Butler in *Night Monster* (Universal, 1942).

Lugosi played Karloff's role of the monster, which he had originally tested for in 1931, in *Frankenstein Meets the Wolf Man* (Universal, 1943); hirsute Dr. James Brewster in *The Ape Man* (Monogram, 1943); Nazi Emil in *Ghosts on the Loose* (Monogram, 1943); vampire Armand Tesla in *Return of the Vampire* (Columbia, 1943); zombie-keeping Dr. Marlowe in *Voodoo Man* (Monogram, 1944); ruthless Prof. Dexter in *Return of the Ape Man* (Monogram, 1944); Larchmont the butler in *One Body Too Many* (Paramount, 1944); joined Karloff for the final time as Joseph, the blackmailing servant of *The Body Snatcher* (RKO, 1945); played zombie researcher Prof. Renault in *Zombies on Broadway* (RKO, 1945); Stone, servant to Lionel Atwill in *Genius at Work* (RKO, 1946); magician Leonide in *Scared to Death* (Screen Guild, 1947); a magnificent Count Dracula in *Abbott and Costello Meet Frankenstein* (Universal-International, 1948); mad Dr. Von Housen in Britain's *Old Mother Riley Meets the Vampire* (Renown Pictures, 1952); Dr. Zabor in *Bela Lugosi Meets a Brooklyn Gorilla* (Jack Broder Productions, 1952); the spirit/mystic of *Glen or Glenda?* (Screen Classic Productions, 1953, aka *I Led Two Lives* and *He or She*); Dr. Eric Vornoff in *Bride of the Monster* (Rolling M Productions, 1955).

Following his drug cure, Lugosi returned for two final film roles: mute Casmir of *The Black Sleep* (United Artists, 1956); and the ghoul man in *Plan 9 from Outer Space* (Reynolds Pictures, released 1959).

Short Subjects

Lugosi played a "gag" bit as Dracula in the short *Hollywood on Parade* (Paramount, 1933); was interviewed by Dorothy West in the short, *Intimate Interviews* (1933); played chess with Karloff in *Screen Snapshots #11* (Columbia, 1934); gave blood for the war effort in *Screen Snapshots* (Columbia, early '40s); was interviewed in an entry of *Ship's Reporter* (1952).

Radio

Among Lugosi's radio credits: a speech about *Dracula,* broadcast over Los Angeles' station KFI (3/27/31); joined Karloff, "duetting" with *Ozzie and Harriet* (late 1930s?); joining Karloff and Peter Lorre on *Kay Kyser's Kollege of Musical Knowledge* (9/25/40); guest-starring in "The Doctor Prescribed Death" episode of *Suspense!* (CBS, 2/2/43); guest-starring on *Mail Call* (1943); hosting his own syndicated show, *Mystery House* (1944); appearing on Allen Funt's *The Candid Microphone* show, posing as proprietor of a ghoulish curio shop (ABC, 1947);

guest-starring on *The Abbott and Costello Show* (ABC, 5/5/48); and guest-starring on the "Gasoline Cocktail" episode of *Crime Does Not Pay* (syndicated by MGM, late '40s or early '50s).

Television

Lugosi guest-starred on *The Milton Berle Show* (late 1940s); appeared in a dramatization of Poe's *The Cask of Amontillado* (on *Suspense!* (CBS, 10/11/49); guest-starred on *Starlit Time* (Dumont, 1950); guest-starred with Lon Chaney, Jr., and Peter Lorre on *The Red Skelton Show* (CBS, October 1953); performed his "Vampire Illusion" on *You Asked for It* (1953).

Addenda

Clips of Lugosi appear in: *Dracula* (Universal's Spanish version, 1931; footage from his own *Dracula*); *Revolt of the Zombies* (Academy, 1936; footage from *White Zombie*); *Lock Up Your Daughters* (New Realm, 1956; footage from various films); *The World of Abbott and Costello* (Universal, 1965; footage from *Abbott and Costello Meet Frankenstein*); *Games* (Universal, 1967; footage from *Dracula*); *Head* (Columbia, 1968; footage from *The Black Cat*); *The Love Machine* (Columbia, 1971; footage from *The Return of the Vampire*); *It Came from Hollywood* (Paramount, 1982; footage from Ed Wood films).

Various Lugosi clips and film footage appear in the documentary, *Lugosi, the Forgotten King* (Operator 13 Productions, 1985).

Lugosi appeared in three Universal Newsreels: in 1934 (publicizing *The Black Cat* with Karloff); in 1935 (making a personal appearance at the San Diego Exposition); and 1940 (being hypnotized for his death scene in *Black Friday*).

The Boris Karloff Career

Born William Henry Pratt, November 23, 1887, Dulwich, England. Son of Edward John Pratt (British Civil Servant) and his wife, Eliza Sarah Millard Pratt; seven older brothers, one older sister. Education: Merchant Taylors' School, Uppingham School, King's College of the University of London. Original vocation: farmer, lumberjack.

Marriages: (1) c. 1912, actress Olive de Wilton, divorced; (2) 1920, musician Montana Laurena Williams, divorced; (3) 1924, actress/artist/dancer Helen Vivian Soule, divorced 1928; (4) 1930, Dorothy Stine, daughter Sara Jane (b. 1938), divorced 1946; (5) 1946, story editor Evelyn Hope Helmore.

Died February 2, 1969, King Edward VII Hospital, Midhurst, England; cremated, Guildford Crematorium, England.

Theatre

Karloff made his stage debut at age nine, as the demon king of *Cinderella* (Enfield parish Christmas play, 1896); after diplomatic training at King's College, was "exiled" by family (due to love of the theatre) to Canada, arriving 5/17/09; made professional debut with the Ray Brandon/Jean Russell Players, Kamloops, British Columbia, as Hoffman, the old banker of *The Devil* (1910); toured western Canada with the troupe for over a year, winning acclaim as the blackest villain ever to foreclose a mortgage on a hapless widow; joined the Harry St. Clair Players, Prince Albert, Canada, 1912, touring Canada and the northern United States in such plays as *Paid in Full, Charley's Aunt, East Lynne, Way Down East, Bought and Paid for, Baby Mine, What Happened to Jones, Why Smith Left Home,* and many melodramas, playing in 106 plays in 53 weeks; joined the Billie Bennett company of *The Virginian,* touring through Minnesota, Iowa, Kansas, Colorado, Nevada, arriving in Los Angeles, December, 1917; toured southern California with the San Pedro stock company; ultimately played everything in stock from Shakespeare to one of the ugly sisters in *Cinderella.*

Karloff acted on the Los Angeles and San Francisco stages in the late 1920s in such plays as *The Idiot, Hotel Imperial, Kongo, Window Panes,* and as Galloway in *The Criminal Code* (1930); toured Vaudeville houses, 1938, delivering Poe's *The Tell-Tale Heart.*

Karloff made his Broadway debut on January 10, 1941, at the Fulton Theatre as evil Jonathan Brewster in *Arsenic and Old Lace;* after a year-and-a-half on Broadway, starred in a 66-week national tour (1942–1943), and a G.I. version on the Pacific Islands (1945); appeared on the Los Angeles stage, 1946, as Gramps in *On Borrowed Time;* returned to Broadway as Professor Robert Linden in *The Linden Tree* (Music Box Theatre, 3/2/48, seven performances); as the Devil's Island escapee/antique shop owner Descius Heiss in *The Shop at Sly Corner* (Booth Theatre, 1/18/49, seven performances); reprised Gramps in *On Borrowed Time* in Atlanta (January, 1950); enjoyed a Broadway triumph as Mr. Darling and Captain Hook in the musical *Peter Pan* (Imperial Theatre, 4/24/50, 321 performances), also touring in his role(s); climaxed Broadway career as Bishop Cauchon in *The Lark* (Longacre Theatre, 11/17/55, 229 performances); played 1960 summer stock as Gramps in *On Borrowed Time.*

Films

Karloff denied the rumor he had made his debut in Anna Pavlova's *The Dumb Girl of Portici* (Universal, 1916); was a "guinea extra" in *His Majesty the American* (United Artists, 1919); appeared in the 15-chapter serial *The Masked Raider* (Arrow, 1919), and the 15-chapter serial *The Lightning Raider* (Pathé, 1919); played a bit in *The Prince and the Betty* (Pathé, 1920); as French-Canadian trapper villain Jules Borney, "crazed with the lust of blood upon him," in *The Deadlier Sex* (Pathé, 1920); Tavish, baby-kidnapper of *The Courage of Marge O'Doone* (Vitagraph, 1920); an Indian in *The Last of the Mohicans* (Associated Producers, 1920); the priest of Kama-Sita in the 15-chapter serial *The Hope Diamond Mystery* (Kosmik, 1921); Ahmed Khan in *Without Benefit of Clergy* (Brunton, 1921); Baptiste, sinister half-breed in *The Cave Girl* (Inspiration, 1921); Nei Hamid in *Cheated Hearts* (Universal, 1921); crook Dell Monckton (disguised as Maharajah Jehan) in *The Man from Downing Street* (Vitagraph, 1922); Nabob of Menang in *The Infidel* (Preferred, 1922); Raoul Maris in *The Woman Conquers* (Preferred, 1922); holy teacher Iman Mowaffak in *Omar the Tentmaker* (Associated First National, 1922); Hugo in *The Altar Stairs* (Universal, 1922); a bit on the Hoot Gibson western, *The Gentleman from America* (Universal, 1923); Prince Kapolski in *The Prisoner* (Universal, 1923).

Following a dry spell as an actor, during which time he worked as a truck driver, Karloff played in the 15-chapter serial *Riders of the Plains* (Arrow, 1924); an outlaw in *The Hellion* (Sunset, 1924); Tony Garcia in *Dynamite Dan* (Sunset, 1924); Pierre, French Apache in *Parisian Nights* (R.C. Pictures/Gothic, 1924); Diego in *The Prairie Wife* (Eastern, 1925); Pietro Castillano in *Forbidden Cargo* (R.C. Pictures/Gothic, 1925); wicked Spaniard Cabraza in *Lady Robin Hood* (R.C. Pictures, 1925); played in the 15-chapter serial *Perils of the Wind* (Universal, 1925); a bit in *Never the Twain Shall Meet* (Cosmopolitan, 1925); a scissors grinder in *The Greater Glory* (First National, 1926); railroad bandit Blackie Blanchette in *Flames* (Associated Exhibitors, 1926); blackmailer Dave Sinclair in *The Golden Web* (Greater Gotham-Lumas, 1926); evil cocaine addict Snipe Collins in *Her Honor the Governor* (R.C. Pictures, 1926); the mesmerist in *The Bells* (Chadwick, 1926); a "half-naked cutthroat" in *The Eagle of the Sea* (Paramount, 1926); a lecher who tries to "pick up" Mabel Normand in the three-reeler, *The Nickel Hopper* (Pathé/Hal Roach, 1926); villainous half-breed Gaspard in *Flaming Fury* (R.C. Pictures, 1926), starring Ranger the dog; a bit in *Valencia* (MGM, 1926); a bit in *The Man in the Saddle* (Universal, 1926); Saracen pirate in *Old Ironsides* (Paramount, 1926); Owaza in *Tarzan and the Golden Lion* (R.C. Picures, 1927); "Y" the crook in *Let It Rain* (Paramount, 1926); Frenchman Pavel in *The Princess from Hoboken* (Tiffany, 1927); Al Meggs in *The Meddlin' Stranger* (Action, 1927); Mexican border smuggler Ramon in *The Phantom Buster* (Action, 1927); chief conspirator in *Soft Cushions* (Paramount, 1927); ship's purser in *Two Arabian Knights* (Caddo, 1927); Fleming in *The Love Mart* (First National, 1927); Pug Doran in Hoot Gibson's *Burning the Wind* (Universal, 1928); played in the 10-chapter serial *Vultures of the Sea* (Mascot, 1928); Maurice Kent in *The Little Wild Girl* (Hercules/Trinity, 1928); Mullins in the 10-chapter serial *The Fatal Warning* (Mascot, 1928); played in the 10-chapter serial *Vanishing Rider* (Universal, 1928); Boris in *The Devil's Chaplain* (Rayart/Rich-mont, 1929); played in *Anne Against the World* (Rayart, 1929); Cecil in *Two Sisters* (Rayart, 1929); French-Canadian fur-stealing murderer Jules Gregg in *The Phantom of the North* (Biltmore/All Star, 1929).

Karloff made his "talkie" debut as the Soudanese servant in *Behind That Curtain* (Fox, 1929); gang leader Macklin in the 10-chapter serial *King of the Kongo* (Mascot, 1929); Abdoul in *The Unholy Night* (MGM, 1929); a guard in *The Bad One* (United Artists, 1930); Corsican in *The Sea Bat* (MGM, 1930); Baxter in *The Utah Kid* (Tiffany, 1930); Mustapha in the 12-episode serial, *King of the Wild* (Mascot, 1930); a murder victim in *Mother's Cry* (First National, 1930).

Karloff recreated his Los Angeles/San Francisco stage role of vengeful jailbird Ned Galloway in *The Criminal Code* (Columbia, 1931); followed by a prison warden in *The Last Parade* (Columbia, 1931); a revolutionist in Wheeler and Woolsey's *Cracked Nuts* (RKO, 1931); a doomed expedition member of the *Dirigible* (Columbia, 1931); dope-pusher Cokey Joe in *Young Donovan's Kid* (RKO, 1931); gambler Sport Williams in *Smart Money* (Warner Bros., 1931), with Edward G. Robinson and James Cagney; the professor in *The Public Defender* (RKO, 1931); a menacing jail prisoner in the French version of Laurel and Hardy's *Pardon Us* (Roach/MGM, 1931); Luigi in *I Like Your Nerve* (First National, 1931); T. Vernon Isopod, pervert posing as preacher, in *Five Star Final* (First National, 1931); Fedor's father in *The Mad Genius* (Warner Bros., 1931); gangster Joe Terry in *Graft* (Universal, 1931); lecherous, drunken orderly in *The Yellow Ticket* (Fox, 1931); gangster Tony Ricca in *The Guilty Generation* (Columbia, 1931).

Karloff won immortality as Frankenstein's monster in *Frankenstein* (Universal, 1931); followed by such roles as a comic waiter in *Tonight or Never* (Feature Productions, Goldwyn, 1931); Sheikh in *Business and Pleasure* (Fox, 1932); autopsy surgeon in *Alias the Doctor* (First National, 1932); Gaffney the gangster in *Scarface* (Caddo, 1932); and hoodlum Jim Henderson in *Behind the Mask* (Columbia, 1932) as Karloff signed a Universal Star Contract; guest-starred as himself in *The Cohens and the Kellys in Hollywood* (Universal, 1932); played crook Nikko in *The Miracle Man* (Paramount, 1932); nightclub host Happy MacDonald in *Night World* (Universal, 1932); consolidated his stardom as drunken butler Morgan in *The Old Dark House* (Universal, 1932); Fu Manchu in *The Mask of Fu Manchu* (MGM, 1932); and Im-Ho-Tep in *The Mummy* (Universal, 1932); visited England to star as

Boris Karloff

Professor Morlant, *The Ghoul* (Gaumont-British, 1933); returned to Hollywood, scoring as religious lunatic Sanders in *The Lost Patrol* (RKO, 1934); and Jew-hating Count Ledrantz in *The House of Rothschild* (Twentieth Century, 1934).

Billed only as Karloff, he played Hjalmar Poelzig, satanic high priest in *The Black Cat* (Universal, 1934), his first screen union with Bela Lugosi; guest-starred in *Gift of Gab* (Universal, 1934), again with Lugosi; magnificently reprised the monster in *Bride of Frankenstein* (Universal, 1935); played gangster Edmond Bateman in *The Raven* (Universal, 1935), costarring Lugosi; evil Count Gregor and good Count Anton, cursed twins of *The Black Room* (Columbia, 1935); and radium-poisoned scientist Janos Rukh in *The Invisible Ray* (Universal, 1936), again with Lugosi.

Starred in five melodramas for Warner Bros., commencing as John Elman, electrocuted musician resurrected by science in *The Walking Dead* (1936); visited England for two films, *The Man Who Changed His Mind* (aka *The Man Who Lived Again* (Gainsborough, 1936) and *Juggernaut* (JH Productions, 1936); played lisping opera star Gravelle in *Charlie Chan at the Opera* (20th Century–Fox, 1936); old inventor Dave Mallory in *Night Key* (Universal, 1937); Chinese war lord Gen. Wu Yen Fang in *West of Shanghai* (Warner/First National, 1937); red herring Jevries in *The Invisible Menace* (Warner, 1938); the title role in *Mr. Wong, Detective* (Monogram, 1938); and played the monster, for the third and final time, in *Son of Frankenstein* (Universal, 1939), tended by Lugosi's Ygor.

Karloff reprised Wong in *The Mystery of Mr. Wong* (Monogram, 1939); Wong again in *Mr Wong in Chinatown* (Monogram, 1939); began Columbia's "Mad Doctor" series as Dr. Henryk Savaard in *The Man They Could Not Hang* (1939); played Mord, bald, club-footed executioner in *Tower of London* (Universal, 1939); German spy Franz Strendler in *British Intelligence* (Warner, 1940); Wong yet again in *The Fatal Hour* (Monogram, 1940); Dr. Ernest Sovac in *Black Friday* (Universal, 1940), costarring Lugosi; Dr. Leon Kravaal in *The Man with Nine Lives* (Columbia, 1940); Dr. Charles Gaudet in *Devil's Island* (Warner, 1940); Wong for the fifth and final time in *Doomed to Die* (Monogram, 1940); Dr. John Garth in *Before I Hang* (Columbia, 1940); Dr. Bernard Adrian in *The Ape* (Monogram, 1940); Judge Spencer Mainwaring in *You'll Find Out* (RKO, 1940), with Lugosi and Peter Lorre; and Dr. Julian Blair in *The Devil Commands* (Columbia, 1941).

After Broadway smash in *Arsenic and Old Lace,* Karloff played Prof. Nathaniel Billings in *The Boogie Man Will Get You* (Columbia, 1942), with Lorre, before embarking on an *Arsenic* national tour; returned in triumph to Hollywood, and starred in two Universals, as Dr. Hohner in *The Climax* (his first in Technicolor) and Dr. Gustav Niemann, reviving Chaney Jr.'s Wolf Man, Carradine's Dracula and Glenn Strange's monster in *House of Frankenstein* (both 1944); signed with RKO, playing John Gray, *The Body Snatcher* (1945), his final movie with Lugosi.

Karloff starred in two more Val Lewton horrors at RKO, as Gen. Nikolas Pherides in *Isle of the Dead* (1945) and Master George Sims in *Bedlam* (1946); was villainous Dr. Hollingshead in *The Secret Life of Walter Mitty* (RKO/Goldwyn, 1947); screwball artist Charles Van Druten in *Lured* (United Artists, 1947); Gruesome in *Dick Tracy Meets Gruesome* (RKO, 1947); Indian Chief Guyasuta in DeMille's *Unconquered* (Paramount, 1947); Indian Tishomingo in *Tap Roots* (Universal/International, 1948); Swami Tapur in *Abbott and Costello Meet the Killer, Boris Karloff* (Universal/International, 1949).

Following Broadway run as Mr. Darling/Captain Hook in *Peter Pan,* Karloff played servant Voltan in *The Strange Door* (Universal/International, 1951); narrated *The Emperor's Nightingale* (Czech State, 1951); played Dr. Meissen in *The Strange Door* (Universal/International, 1952); General Pollegar in *The Hindu* (Frank Ferrin Productions, 1953); the famed dual role in *Abbott and Costello Meet Dr. Jekyll and Mr. Hyde* (Universal/International, 1953); starred in Il Mostro dell'Isola (*The Monster of the Island,* Romano Italian Productions, 1953); supernatural debunker Phillip Knight in *Voodoo Island* (United Artists, 1957); Baron Victor von Frankenstein in *Frankenstein 1970* (Allied Artists, 1958); James Rankin in *The Haunted Strangler* (MLC/Producers Associates, 1958); Dr. Thomas Bolton in *Corridors of Blood* (Producers Associates, 1958).

Joining Vincent Price and Peter Lorre, Karloff played Dr. Scarabus in *The Raven* (American/International, 1963); played Baron von Leppe in *The Terror* (American/International, 1963); Gorca in *Black Sabbath* (Emmepi/Galatea/Lyre, Italian, 1963); joined Price, Lorre and Basil Rathbone as Amos Hinchley in *The Comedy of Terrors* (American/International, 1964); a cameo as himself in *Bikini Beach* (American/International, 1964); as Nahum Witley in *Die Monster Die!* (American/International, 1965); Hiram Stokely in *Ghost in the Invisible Bikini* (American/International, 1966); the voice of the rat in the animated/live action in *The Daydreamer* (Videocraft International, 1966); Dr. Pierre Vaugiroud in *The Venetian Affair* (MGM, 1966); narrated *Mondo Balordo* (Cine Produzioni, Italian, 1967); Professor Monserrat in *The Sorcerers* (Tigon/Curtwell/Global/British, 1967); voice of Baron von Frankenstein in the "Animagic" *Mad Monster Party* (Videocraft International, 1967); Charles Badulescu in *Blind Man's Bluff* (aka *Cauldron of Blood,* Hispamer/Weinbach, 1967); and horror star Byron Orlok in *Targets* (Saticoy/Paramount, 1967).

Karloff starred as Professor Marshe in *The Crimson Cult* (aka *Curse of the Crimson Altar,* Tigon/American-International, 1968); and ended his film career in four Mexican/U.S. horrors for Azteca-Columbia, shot in Hollywood in Spring, 1968: Dr. Carl Van Boulder in *Isle of the Snake People,* and starring roles in *The Incredible Invasion, The Fear Chamber,* and *House of Evil.*

Short Subjects

Karloff appeared in *Screen Snapshots #11* (Columbia, 1934), challenging Lugosi to a game of chess; was a panelist in a series of *Information Please* short subjects (RKO/Pathé, 1941); narrated *The Juggler of Our Lady* (Terrytoons, 1957); narrated *Today's Teens* (Movietone, 1963).

Radio

Karloff guest-starred on many radio shows of the 1930s and 1940s, including *Hollywood on the Air* (1/27/34); *Shell Chateau* (NBC, 8/31/35); *The Charlie McCarthy Show* (NBC, January, 1938); paid five special visits to *Lights Out!* (NBC, March/April, 1938); guested with Lugosi on *The Ozzie and Harriet Show* (late 1930s?); joined Lugosi and Lorre on *Kay Kyser's Kollege of Musical Knowledge* (NBC, September 25, 1940); made many guest appearances on the first season of *Inner Sanctum* (Blue Network, 1941–1942); guested on *Information Please* (NBC, 1/24/41, 2/20/42); hosted *Creeps by Night* (Blue Network, Spring, 1944); guested on *Hildegarde's Radio Room* (10/23/45); *Inner Sanctum* (10/23/45 and 11/16/45); *The Fred Allen Show* (NBC, 11/18/45); played Jonathan Brewster in "Arsenic and Old Lace" on *Screen Guild Theatre* (CBS, 11/25/46); guested on *The Jack Benny Show* (NBC, 1/19/47); hosted a short-lived revival of *Lights Out!* (Mutual Network, 1947); guested on Bing Crosby's *Philco Radio Time* (ABC, 10/29/47); *The Jimmy*

Durante Show (NBC, 12/10/47); Al Jolson's *The Kraft Music Hall* (NBC, 12/25/47); *Truth or Consequences* (NBC, 10/30/48); *Bill Stern Sports Newsreel* (1/13/50); *Inner Sanctum* (CBS, 6/22/52 and 7/13/52); *Recollections at 30* (9/26/56); many more. Hosted *Starring Boris Karloff* (ABC, 1949); was disc jockey of a children's radio show, *Boris Karloff's Treasure Chest* (New York, 1950); and, for last decade of his life, taped daily spots for the *Reader's Digest* syndicated show.

Television

Karloff's television appearances include: *Chevrolet on Broadway* (NBC, 1949); as Jonathan Brewster in "Arsenic and Old Lace" on *Ford Theatre* (CBS, 4/11/49); guest-starred on *Suspense!* (CBS) in "A Night at an Inn" (4/26/49), "The Monkey's Paw" (5/17/49) and "The Yellow Scarf" (6/7/49); hosted *Mystery Playhouse* (1949); guested on *Celebrity Time* (ABC, 9/4/49); his own series *Starring Boris Karloff* (ABC, September to December, 1949); "Uncle Vanya" on *Masterpiece Playhouse* (NBC, 9/3/50); "The Leopard Lady" on *Lights Out* (NBC, 9/18/50); a haunted house skit on *Paul Whiteman Revue* (ABC, 10/29/50); *The Don McNeil TV Club* (ABC, 4/11/51); Milton Berle's *Texaco Star Theatre* (NBC, 10/9/51); *The Fred Waring General Electric Show* (CBS, 10/21/51); "The Kimballs" on *Robert Montgomery Presents* (NBC, 11/19/51); *Celebrity Time* (CBS, 11/25/51); "Mutiny on the Nicolette" on *Studio One* (CBS, 12/3/51); "The Lonely Place" on *Suspense!* (CBS, 12/25/51); "The Jest of Hahalaba" on *Lux Video Theatre* (CBS, 12/31/51); as "Don Quixote" on *Columbia Workshop* (CBS, 1/13/52); *The Stork Club* (CBS, 1/30/52); "Memento" on *Tales of Tomorrow* (ABC, 2/22/52); Milton Berle's *Texaco Star Theatre* (NBC, 4/29/52); *Celebrity Time* (CBS, 5/25/52); "Soul of the Great Bell" on *Curtain Call* (NBC, 6/27/52); "Death House" on *Schlitz Playhouse of the Stars* (CBS, 7/4/52); Milton Berle's *Texaco Star Theatre* (NBC, 12/16/52); "The Invited Seven" on *Hollywood Opening Night* (NBC, 3/2/53); as Rasputin in "The Black Prophet" on *Suspense!* (CBS, 3/17/53); "Burden of Proof" on *Robert Montgomery Presents* (NBC, 3/30/53); "The Chase" on *Plymouth Playhouse* (ABC, 5/24/53); "The Signal Man" on *Suspense!* (CBS, 6/23/53); Charles Branden in "House of Death" on *Rheingold Theatre;* guest spot on *I've Got a Secret* (CBS, 10/13/54); Dr. Nestri in "White Carnation" on *Climax!* (CBS, 12/16/54); a panelist on the game show *Down You Go* (Dumont Network, 12/17/54); his own syndicated series, *Col. March of Scotland Yard* (26 episodes, produced by ITV Productions, England, 1954*); Jonathan Brewster in "Arsenic and Old Lace" on *Best of Broadway* (CBS, 1/5/55); *Down You Go* (Dumont, 1/55); sang English music hall songs "Human Thing to Do" and "'Arry and 'Erbert" on *The Donald O'Connor Show* (NBC, 2/19/55); Mr. Mycroft in "The Sting of Death" on *Elgin Hour* (ABC, 2/22/55); a singing King Arthur in "A Connecticut Yankee in King Arthur's Court" on *Max Liebman Presents* (NBC, 3/12/55); game show *Who Said That?* (Dumont, 4/30/55); title role in "Mr. Blue Ocean" on *General Electric Theatre* (CBS, 5/1/55); *I've Got a Secret* (CBS, 8/24/55); as George Redford in "Counterfeit" on *U.S. Steel Hour* (CBS, 8/31/55); as Doc Dixon in "Even the Weariest River" on *Alcoa Hour* (NBC, 4/15/56); a guest spot with the mentalist

*Originally produced in 1952, syndicated first in U.S. in 1954; first three episodes incorporated into a feature, Colonel March Investigates, *released by Britain's Eros Films in 1953.*

Dunninger (NBC, 7/18/56); guest on *Frankie Laine* (CBS, 8/8/56); guest on *Ernie Kovacs* (NBC, 8/13/56); the Vicar in "Bury Me Later" on *Climax!* (CBS, 9/6/56); as Ward Allen in "Rendezvous in Black" on *Playhouse 90* (CBS, 10/25/56); guest on *The Red Skelton Show* (CBS, 11/27/56); won $16,000 in the area of children's stories on *The $64,000 Question* (CBS, 12/11, 12/18, 12/25, 1956); guest-starred as the "Wolf-Grandmother" in a Red Riding Hood skit, singing "You'd Be Surprised" on *The Rosemary Clooney Show* (NBC, 1/9/57); reprised Broadway role as Bishop Cauchon in "The Lark" on *Hallmark Hall of Fame* (NBC, 2/10/57); as Montgomery Royle in "The Man Who Played God" on *Lux Video Theatre* (NBC, 4/25/57); sang "The September Song" on *The Kate Smith Special* (ABC, 4/28/57); sang "Mama Look a' Boo Boo" on *The Dinah Shore Show* (NBC, 5/17/57); returned to *The Dinah Shore Show* (10/27/57), singing and performing Halloween skit; guested on *The Rosemary Clooney Show* (NBC, 10/31/57); Judge Winthrop Gelsey in "The Deadly Game" on *Suspicion* (NBC, 12/9/57); was the surprised guest on *This Is Your Life* (NBC, 1957); joined Buster Keaton on *The Betty White Show* (ABC, 2/12/58); Dr. Pierre in "Vestris" on *Telephone Time* (ABC, 2/25/58); narrator/Father Knickerbocker of "The Legend of Sleepy Hollow" on *Shirley Temple's Storybook* (NBC, 3/5/58); Prof. Theodore Koenig in "Shadow of a Genius" on *Studio One* (CBS, 3/31/58); guested on *The Jack Paar Show* (NBC, 4/22/58); as Kurtz in "Heart of Darkness" (by his favorite author, Joseph Conrad) on *Playhouse 90* (CBS, 11/6/58); starred in the pilot for an unsold series, *The Veil* (1958); guested in "It's Murder, My Dear" on *The Gale Storm Show* (CBS, 1/31/59); as Henry Church in "Indian Giver" on *G.E. Theatre* (CBS, 5/17/59).

Karloff played Guibert in "To the Sound of Trumpets" on *Playhouse 90* (CBS, 2/9/60); as Billy Bones in "Treasure Island" on *The Dupont Show of the Month* (CBS, 3/5/60); joined Tammy Grimes and Eddie Albert as hosts of *Hollywood Sings* (NBC, 4/3/60); hosted his own show, *Thriller* (premiere, NBC, 9/13/60), hosting 66 one-hour shows and guest-starring in five episodes: as Clayton Mace in "The Prediction" (11/22/60); Dr. Thorne in Poe's "The Premature Burial" (10/2/61); Dr. Farnham in "The Last of the Sommerviles" (11/6/61); Pop Jenkins in "Friend of the Dead" and Col. Jackson in "Welcome Home," the two one-act dramas of "Dialogues with Death" (12/4/61); and Dr. Konrad Markesan in "The Incredible Dr. Markesan" (2/26/62); hosted own science fiction show, *Out of This World* (ABC/BBC-TV, England, 1962); Jonathan Brewster in "Arsenic and Old Lace" on *Hallmark Hall of Fame* (NBC, 2/5/62); guested on tribute to George Schaefer on *PM* (syndicated, 2/12/62); as Sir Simon Flaquer in "The Paradine Case" on *Theatre '62* (NBC, 3/11/62); as himself, masquerading as the monster in "Lizard's Leg and Owlet's Wing" on *Route 66* (CBS, 10/26/62); was interviewed, along with Peter Lorre, on *The Hy Gardner Show* (WOR TV, 3/3/63); narrated "A Danish Fairy Tale" based on Hans Christian Andersen, on *Chronicle* (CBS, 12/25/63); guested on *The Garry Moore Show* (CBS, 4/21/64); visited the *Tonight Show* (NBC 6/64); did a pet shop skit on *The Entertainers* (CBS, 1/16/65); sang "The Monster Mash" on *Shindig* (ABC, 10/30/65); as Singh in "Night of the Golden Cobra" on *The Wild Wild West* (CBS, 9/23/66); as Mother Muffin in "The Mother Muffin Affair" on *The Girl from U.N.C.L.E.* (NBC, 9/27/66); narrated and was the voice of the Grinch in *How the Grinch Stole Christmas* (CBS, 12/18/66); as Don Ernesto Silvando in *I Spy* (NBC, 2/22/67); played with Vincent Price in the skit "He Who

Steals My Robot Steals Trash" and joined Price singing "The Two of Us" on *The Red Skelton Show* (CBS, 9/24/68); played a Halloween skit with Agnes Moorehead and sang "It Was a Very Good Year" on *The Jonathan Winters Show* (CBS, 10/30/68); and played Orlov in "The White Birch" on *the Name of the Game* (NBC, 11/29/68).

Karloff also performed in television commercials for Butternut Coffee (1966), Schaeffer Pens (1966), Volkswagen (1967), and A-1 Steak Sauce (1968).

Recordings

In the late 1950s/early 1960s, Karloff made many recordings, narrating the works of Kipling, *Peter and the Wolf, The Reluctant Dragon, The Three Little Pigs, The Ugly Duckling,* and many more. Narrated *An Evening with Boris Karloff and His Friends* (Decca, 1967).

Writings

Karloff edited *Tales of Terror* (World Publishing, 1943); wrote the introduction to *And the Darkness Falls* (World, 1946); and wrote the introduction to *The Boris Karloff Horror Anthology* (Souvenir Press, 1965).

Addenda

Clips of Karloff appear in: *The Phantom Creeps* (Universal serial, 1939; footage from *The Invisible Ray*); *The Mummy's Hand* (Universal, 1940; footage from *The Mummy*); *House of Dracula* (Universal, 1945; footage from *Bride of Frankenstein*); *Days of Thrills and Laughter* (20th Century–Fox, 1961; footage from a Karloff silent film); *Ensign Pulver* (Warner Bros., 1964; footage from *The Walking Dead*); *Head* (Columbia, 1968; footage from *The Black Cat*); *Hatchet for the Honeymoon* (AVCO Embassy, 1969; footage from *Black Sabbath*).

Karloff appeared in a Universal Newsreel of 1934, officiating with Lugosi at Universal's "Black Cats Parade" publicity stunt for *The Black Cat*.

Filmography
of Their Films Together

The Black Cat

Studio: Universal
Producer: Carl Laemmle, Jr.
Director: Edgar G. Ulmer
Screenplay: Peter Ruric (from a story
  by Ulmer and Ruric, suggested
  by the 1843 tale by Edgar Allan
  Poe)
Supervisor: E.M. Asher
Art Director: Charles D. Hall
Camera: John J. Mescall

Musical Director: Heinz Roemheld
Film Editor: Ray Curtiss
Special Effects: John P. Fulton
Makeup Artist: Jack P. Pierce
Asst. Directors: W.J. Reiter, Sam
  Weisenthal
2nd Cameraman: King Gray
Asst. Cameraman: John Martin
Script Clerk: Moree Herring
Supervisor's Secretary: Peggy Vaughn

Running time: 65 minutes

Produced at Universal City, California, February 28–March 17, 1934; additional scenes and retakes filmed March 25-27, 1934.

Original budget, $91,125; budget for retakes, $6500; final cost, $95,745.31.

New York premiere: Roxy Theatre, May 18, 1934.

The Players

Hjalmar Poelzig	KARLOFF
Dr. Vitus Werdegast	Bela LUGOSI
Peter Alison	David Manners
Joan Alison	Jacqueline Wells[1]
Karen	Lucille Lund
Thamal	Harry Cording
The Sergeant	Henry Armetta
The Lieutenant	Albert Conti
The Maid	Anna Duncan
Car Steward	Herman Bing[2]
Train Conductor	Andre Cheron
Train Steward	Luis Alberni
Bus Driver	George Davis

353

A Porter	Alphonse Martell
A Patrolman	Tony Marlow
Stationmaster	Paul Weigel
A Waiter	Albert Polet
A Brakeman	Rodney Hildebrand
Devil Worshippers	Virginia Ainsworth, King
	Baggot, Symona
	Boniface, Lois
	January, Michael
	Mark, Paul Panzer,
	John Peter Richmond,[3]
	Peggy Terry

Other versions: Germany's 1932 Unheimliche Geschichten; Universal's 1941 *The Black Cat,* directed by Albert S. Rogell, starring Basil Rathbone, Broderick Crawford, Anne Gwynne, Bela Lugosi, Gladys Cooper, Alan Ladd, and Claire Dodd, and bearing no relationship whatsoever to Poe's story or the 1934 film; Braverman's 1960 short subject, *The Black Cat,* directed by Frank Marvel and narrated by Basil Rathbone; American-International's 1962 *Tales of Terror,* directed by Roger Corman, which included *The Black Cat* as the second part of its Poe trilogy, and starred Peter Lorre, Vincent Price, and Joyce Jameson.

Footage from *The Black Cat* appeared in 1968's *Head.*

[1]AKA Julie Bishop.   [2]Footage deleted.   [3]AKA John Carradine.

*   *   *

Gift of Gab

Studio: Universal	*Adaptation:* Lou Breslow
Producer: Carl Laemmle, Jr.	*Music:* Albert Von Tilzer, Con
Director: Karl Freund	Conrad, and Charles Tobias
Screenplay: Rian James (based on a	*Photography:* George Robinson and
story by Jerry Wald and Philip	Harold Wenstrom
G. Epstein)	*Editor:* Raymond Curtiss

Running time: 70 minutes

Filmed at Universal City, California, July 2–24, 1934.
Budget: $230,000. Final cost: $251,433.79.
New York premiere: Rialto Theatre, September 25, 1934.

The Players

Philip Gabney	Edmund Lowe
Barbara Kelton	Gloria Stuart
Ruth	Ruth Etting
Absent-Minded Doctor	Phil Baker
Ethel	Ethel Waters
Margot	Alice White
Alexander Woollcott	Alexander Woollcott
Colonel Trivers	Victor Moore
Patsy	Hugh O'Connell

Nurse . . . . Helen Vinson
Crooner . . . . Gene Austin
Radio Announcer . . . . Thomas Hanlon
Janitor . . . . Henry Armetta
McDougal . . . . Andy Devine
Cabaret Singer . . . . Winnie Shaw
Telephone Girl . . . . Marion Byron
Sound Effects Man . . . . Sterling Holloway
Norton . . . . Edwin Maxwell
Orchestra Leader . . . . Leighton Noble
Room Owner . . . . Maurice Black
Mug . . . . Tammany Young
Alumni President . . . . James Flavin
Baby . . . . Billy Barty
Mother . . . . Florence Enright
Father . . . . Richard Elliott
Cop . . . . Warner Richmond
Dance Floor Extras . . . . Dennis O'Keefe, Dave
O'Brien
Guest Stars . . . . Paul Lukas, KARLOFF,
Roger Pryor, Bela
LUGOSI, June
Knight, Chester
Morris, Binnie Barnes,
Douglass Montgomery,
Graham McNamee,
the Beale Street Boys,
Candy and Coco, the
Downey Sisters,
Douglas V. Fowley,
Sidney Skolsky, Radie
Harris
and Gus Arnheim and his Orchestra

Songs: "Gift of Gab," "Talking to Myself," "I Ain't Gonna Sin No More," "Somebody Looks Good," "Don't Let This Waltz Mean Goodbye," "Walkin' on Air," "What a Wonderful Day," "Tomorrow, Who Cares?" and "Blue Sky Avenue."

* * *

The Raven

Studio: Universal
Producer: David Diamond
Director: Louis Friedlander (aka Lew Landers)
Screenplay: David Boehm (suggested by the poem *The Raven,* and the tale *The Pit and the Pendulum,* both

by Edgar Allan Poe)
Camera: Charles Stumar
Art Director: Albert S. D'Agostino
Music: Clifford Vaughan
Choreography (for "The Spirit of Poe" dance): Theodore Kosloff
Dialogue Director: Florence Enright

Editor: Alfred Akst
Makeup Artist: Jack P. Pierce, Otto Lederer
Asst. Directors: Scott Beal, Vic Noerdlinger

Script Clerk: Moree Herring
Hairdresser: Hazel Rogers
Secretary to Mr. Diamond: E.M. Haskett

Running time: 61 minutes

Filmed at Universal City, California, March 20–April 5, 1935.
Budget: $109,750. Final cost: $115,209.91.
New York premiere: Roxy Theatre, July 4, 1935.

The Players

Edmond Bateman . . . . KARLOFF
Dr. Richard Vollin . . . . Bela LUGOSI
Jean Thatcher . . . . Irene Ware
Dr. Jerry Holden . . . . Lester Matthews
Judge Thatcher . . . . Samuel S. Hinds
Mary Burns . . . . Inez Courtney
Geoffrey (Pinky) . . . . Ian Wolfe
Col. Bertram Grant . . . . Spencer Charters
Harriet Grant . . . . Maidel Turner
Mr. Chapman . . . . Arthur Hoyt

Other versions: American-International's 1963 spoof *The Raven,* directed by Roger Corman, starring Vincent Price, Peter Lorre, Boris Karloff, Hazel Court, and Jack Nicholson.

* * *

The Invisible Ray

Studio: Universal
Producer: Edmund Grainger
Director: Lambert Hillyer
Screenplay: John Colton (from a story by Howard Higgin and Douglas Hodges)
Camera: George Robinson
Special Effects: John P. Fulton, Ray Lindsay
Art Director: Albert S. D'Agostino
Music: Franz Waxman
Editor: Bernard Burton

Makeup Artist: Jack P. Pierce, Otto Lederer
Gowns: Brymer
Asst. Directors: Sergei Petschnikoff, Fred Frank
Sound Supervisor: Gilbert Kurland
Script Clerk: Myrtle Gibsone
Secretary to Producer: Camille Collins
Secretary to Director: June Blumenthal
Technical Advisor: Ted Behr

Running time: 80 minutes

Filmed at Universal City, California, September 17–October 25, 1935.
Budget: $166,875. Final cost: $234,875.74.
New York premiere: Roxy Theatre, January 10, 1936.

The Players

Dr. Janos Rukh	KARLOFF
Dr. Felix Benet	Bela LUGOSI
Diane Rukh	Frances Drake
Ronald Drake	Frank Lawton
Sir Francis Stevens	Walter Kingsford
Lady Arabella Stevens	Beulah Bondi
Mother Rukh	Violet Kemble Cooper
Briggs	Nydia Westman
Chief of Surete	Georges Renavent
Professor Meiklejohn	Frank Reicher
Professor Noyer	Paul Weigel
Madame Noyer	Adele St. Maur
Number One Boy	Lawrence Stewart
Zulu	Etta McDaniel
Headman	Daniel Haines
Celeste	Inez Seabury
Minister	Winter Hall
Frightened Native	Snowflake
Clinic Attendant	Hans Schumn

*   *   *

Son of Frankenstein

Studio: Universal
Producer and Director: Rowland V. Lee
Screenplay: Willis Cooper (suggested by the story written in 1816 by Mary Wollstonecraft Shelley)
Cinematography: George Robinson
Art Director: Jack Otterson
Associate: Richard H. Riedel
Musical Director: Charles Previn
Musical Score: Frank Skinner

Assistant Director: Fred Frank
Sound Supervisor: Bernard B. Brown
Technician: William Hedgcock
Set Decorations: R.A. Gausman
Gowns: Vera West
Film Editor: Ted Kent
Makeup: Jack P. Pierce
Special Effects: John P. Fulton
Music Arrangements: Hans J. Salter
Special Electrical Equipment: Kenneth Strickfaden

Running time: 99 minutes

Filmed at Universal City, California, November 9, 1938–January 5, 1939.
Budget (estimated): $300,000. Final cost: $420,000.
New York premiere: Rivoli Theatre, January 28, 1939

The Players

Wolf von Frankenstein	Basil Rathbone
The Monster	Boris KARLOFF
Ygor	Bela LUGOSI
Inspector Krogh	Lionel Atwill

Elsa von Frankenstein .... Josephine Hutchinson
                Peter .... Donnie Dunagan
              Amelia .... Emma Dunn
              Benson .... Edgar Norton
                Fritz .... Perry Ivins
   The Burgomeister .... Lawrence Grant
          Emil Lang .... Lionel Belmore
    Ewald Neumuller .... Michael Mark
     Frau Neumuller .... Caroline Cooke
             Burgers .... Gustav von Seyffertitz,
                                          Lorimer Johnson, Tom
                                          Ricketts
          Dr. Berger .... Edward Cassidy
  Guard at the Gates .... Ward Bond
Villager (footage deleted) .... Dwight Frye
   Double for Karloff .... Bud Wolfe

This is the third of the eight movies in Universal's famous Frankenstein saga.

*   *   *

Black Friday

Studio: Universal   *Editor:* Philip Cahn
Associate Producer: Burt Kelly   *Musical Director:* Hans J. Slater
Director: Arthur Lubin   *Makeup:* Jack P. Pierce
Story/Screenplay: Kurt Siodmak and   *Gowns:* Vera West
  Eric Taylor   *Set Decorations:* R.A. Gausman
Photography: Elwood Bredell   *Sound Supervisor:* Bernard B. Brown
Art Director: Jack Otterson   *Technician:* Charles Carroll
Associate Art Director: Harold Mac- *Makeup:* Jack P. Pierce
  Arthur   *Special Effects:* John P. Fulton
                   Running time: 69 minutes

Filmed at Universal City, California, December 28, 1939–January 18, 1940.
Budget: $130,750. Final cost: $126,000.
New York premiere: Rialto Theatre, March 21, 1940.

The Players

      Dr. Ernest Sovac .... Boris KARLOFF
          Eric Marnay .... Bela LUGOSI
  Prof. George Kingsley
          /Red Cannon .... Stanley Ridges
          Sunny Rogers .... Anne Nagel
            Jean Sovac .... Anne Gwynne
     Margaret Kingsley .... Virginia Brissac
          Frank Miller .... Edmund MacDonald

Kane	Paul Fix
Bellhop	Murray Alper
Bartender	Jack Mulhall
Police Chief	Joe King
Taxi Driver	John Kelly
Reporter	James Craig
Clerk	Jerry Marlowe
Newspaper File Attendant .	Edward McWade
Detective Farnow	Eddie Dunn
Detective Carpenter ..	Emmett Vogan
Detectives	Edward Earle, Kernan Cripps
Dr. Warner	Edwin Stanley
Chaplain	Frank Sheridan
Prison Doctor	Harry Hayden
Cab Drivers	Dave Oliver, Harry Tenbrook
Louis Devore	Raymond Bailey
Maid	Ellen Lowe
Headwaiter	Franco Corsaro
Fat Man at Bar	Frank Jaquet
Students	Dave Willock, Tommy Conlon, Wallace Reid, Jr.
Man	William Ruhl
G-Man	Victor Zimmerman
Nurses	Jessie Arnold, Doris Borodin

* * *

You'll Find Out

Studio: RKO Radio
Producer and Director: David Butler
Screenplay: James V. Kern (based on a story by David Butler and James V. Kern)
Special Material: Monte Brice, Andrew Bennison and R.T.M. Scott
Musical Director: Roy Webb
Musical Arrangements: George Duning
Music: James McHugh
Lyrics: John Mercer

Director of Photography: Frank Redman
Special Effects: Vernon L. Walker
Art Director: Van Nest Polglase
Associate Art Director: Carroll Clark
Gowns: Edward Stevenson
Set Decorations: Darrell Silvera
Recorder: Earl A. Wolcott
Editor: Irene Morra
Assistant Director: Fred A. Fleck
Special Sound/Musical Effects: Sonovox

Running time: 97 minutes

Filmed at RKO Radio Studios, Hollywood, California, August 8–October 11, 1940.
Final cost: $442,689.90.
New York premiere: Roxy Theatre, November 14, 1940.

The Players

Kay Kyser . . . . Kay Kyser
Professor Fenninger . . . . Peter Lorre
Janis Bellacrest . . . . Helen Parrish
Chuck Deems . . . . Dennis O'Keefe
Prince Saliano . . . . Bela LUGOSI
Aunt Margo . . . . Alma Kruger

and Kay Kyser's Band
featuring Ginny Sims
Harry Babbitt   Ish Kabibble   Sully Mason
and The College of Musical Knowledge
and

Judge Mainwaring . . . . Boris KARLOFF
with

Jurgen . . . . Joseph Eggenton
The *"Real" Professor*
Fenninger . . . . Leonard Mudie
And . . . . Louise Currie, Mary
Martha Wood, Joan
Warner, Mary
Bovard, Jane Patten,
Joe North, Frank
Miller, Bess Flowers,
Larry McGrath, Jeff
Corey, Eleanor Lawson

Songs: "Like the Fella Once Said," "I'd Know You Anywhere," "The Bad Humor Man," "You've Got Me This Way," "I've Got a One Track Mind."

*   *   *

The Body Snatcher

Studio: RKO-Radio
Producer: Val Lewton
Director: Robert Wise
Executive Producer: Jack J. Gross
Screenplay: Philip MacDonald and
Carlos Keith (aka Val Lewton),
based on the 1885 short story by
Robert Louis Stevenson
Director of Photography: Robert de
Grasse
Art Directors: Albert S. D'Agostino
and Walter E. Keller
Set Decorations: Darrell Silvera and
John Sturtevant

Sound Recorder: Bailey Fesler
Music: Roy Webb
Musical Director: C. Bakaleinikoff
Editor: J.R. Whittredge
Costumes: Renie
First Assistant Director: Harry Scott
Second Assistant Director: Nate Levinson
Re-recording: Terry Kellum
Script Clerk: Pat Betz
Camera Operator: Charles Burke
Assistant Cameraman: Tex Wheaton
Men's Wardrobe: Hans Bohnstedt
Ladies' Wardrobe: Mary Tate

Makeup Man: Frank LaRue
Hairdresser: Fay Smith
Gaffer: Leo Green
Best Boy: Frank Healy
1st Grip: Marvin Wilson
2nd Grip: Harry Dagleish

1st Propman: Milt James
2nd Propman: Dean Morgan
Boom Man: D. Dent
Laborers: Joe Farquhar, Fred Kenny
Painter: Joe Haecker
Dialogue Director: Mrs. Charlot

Running time: 78 minutes

Filmed at RKO Studios, Hollywood, and the RKO Studio Ranch, October 25–November 17, 1944.

Final cost (estimate): $200,000.

New York premiere: Rialto Theatre, May 25, 1945.

The Players

Gray	Boris KARLOFF
Joseph	Bela LUGOSI
Dr. MacFarlane	Henry Daniell
Meg	Edith Atwater
Fettes	Russell Wade
Mrs. Marsh	Rita Corday
Georgina	Sharyn Moffett
Street Singer	Donna Lee
Mrs. MacBride	Mary Gordon
Richardson	Robert Clarke
Gilchrist	Carl Kent
Bit	Bill Williams
Bit Boy	Jack Welch
Salesman on Street	Larry Wheat
Horse Trader	Jim Moran
Maid Servant	Aina Constant

Other versions: 1960's *The Flesh and the Fiends,* directed by John Gilling, with Peter Cushing as Dr. Knox, George Rose as Burke and Donald Pleasance as Hare: 1961's *The Anatomist,* based on the play by James Bridie, starring Alastair Sim; 1971's *Burke and Hare,* with Harry Andrews as Knox, Derren Nesbitt as Burke and Glynn Edwards as Hare; 1971's *Dr. Jekyll and Sister Hyde,* which mixed together both Stevenson tales; and, most notably, 1985's *The Doctor and the Devils,* produced by Mel Brooks, directed by Freddie Francis, released by 20th Century–Fox, this film was adapted by Ronald Harwood from a script originally penned by Dylan Thomas in 1953. Timothy Dalton starred as "Dr. Thomas Rock," with Jonathan Pryce and Stephen Rea as his graverobbers.

Index